Antifeminism in America

A Collection of Readings from the Literature of the Opponents to U.S. Feminism, 1848 to the Present

Series Editors

Angela Howard and **Sasha Ranaé Adams Tarrant**
University of Houston Clear Lake

A GARLAND SERIES

Contents of the Series

Redefining the New Woman, 1920–1963

Edited with introductions by

Angela Howard and **Sasha Ranaé Adams Tarrant**
University of Houston Clear Lake

GARLAND PUBLISHING, INC.
A MEMBER OF THE TAYLOR & FRANCIS GROUP
New York & London
1997

Library of Congress Cataloging-in-Publication Data

Redefining the new woman, 1920–1963 / edited with introductions by
  Angela Howard and Sasha Ranaé Adams Tarrant.
        p.   cm. — (Antifeminism in America ; 2)
      Includes bibliographical references.
      ISBN 0-8153-2714-5 (vol. 2 : alk. paper). — ISBN 0-8153-2712-9
  (3 vol set : alk. paper)
        1. Anti-feminism—United States. 2. Feminism—United States.
  3. Women—United States—Social conditions. I. Howard, Angela.
  II. Tarrant, Sasha Ranaé Adams. III. Series.
  HQ1426.R417 1997
  305.42'0973—dc21   97-38206
                                                        CIP

Printed on acid-free, 250-year-life paper
Manufactured in the United States of America

Contents

Series Introduction

Understanding the Opposition to U.S. Feminism

The purpose of this three-volume collection of primary sources is to generate a more complete understanding and appreciation of the social and political context in which the advocates of women's rights have labored and labor from 1848 to the present. The editors have selected original documents from mainstream literature to allow the reader immediate access to this continuing public discourse that accompanies the prospective and the real changes in women's role and status in the United States. Those opposed to the feminist goal of women's equality have addressed to the public, directly through contemporary popular books and magazines, their concerns regarding the particular nineteenth-century issues of the woman's rights movement. These include woman suffrage and dress reform, as well as topics relating to the discerning and enforcing the proper role and status of women. Public discourse over such topics has extended into the twentieth century, as opponents raised arguments against increased opportunities in women's employment and education, denied the propriety and practice of family planning, and admonished against women's involvement in political issues and activities. In these three volumes, the opponents of feminism speak directly to the reader who is free to evaluate the merits of each author's arguments.

Diversity of opinion and perspective has persisted among those who oppose the assertion of women's rights as reform movement, which challenges the concepts and institutions of patriarchy as well as the gender system that supports and perpetuates a gender-defined, limited, and segregated existence for women. The constellation of conservative definitions of proper womanhood has varied widely in approach, intent, and intensity. Over the past two-hundred years the critics of feminism, of advances in women's rights, and of the increased opportunity in education and employment for women have had to absorb changes in the status of middle-class women. These critics therefore have co-opted and redefined some of the fait accompli changes to maintain that contemporary practices uphold the primary limitation for women in any century, that for women "biology is destiny." All these opponents to sexual equality ultimately assert that an inescapable maternal duty grounds every woman's identity in her relationships to others and especially to men: each woman's usefulness to society through filial, uxorial, maternal, professional, and civic responsibilities define and limit her identity as an individual.

Some opponents merely dismissed or ridiculed advocates for changes in women's status, and eschewed the need to specify particular flaws in the feminist position on any particular issue. Others relied on interpretations of divine ordination, appeals to natural law, and manipulations of public fears of familial and social disintegration. Often opponents sought to discredit the propriety or to challenge the necessity of any change in the gender system proposed by advocates of women's rights. They utilized divisive tactics to separate women by race or ethnic group, religion, or economic class. Frequently, these critics resorted to ad hominum charges of lesbianism, communism, and socialism, or disgruntled spinsterhood against the advocates of women's rights and against the movement itself. Opponents defined the effort to promote the women's movement out of the domestic sphere and into the public arena of political, economic, and social reform as inherently destructive of social order. By focusing on maintaining a limited role for women, adversaries of the women's movement, both women and men, expressed their common fear that has been created by ongoing social, economic, and political changes beyond their control.

Therefore, much of the value in reading these sources is to experience the variety of perspectives that provide the historical and intellectual context for these documents from the distant and near past. The editors offer this varied selection of sources to allow the reader to assess the merit and validity of the arguments presented by these representative opponents of women's rights and equality. Not all opponents of specific feminist reforms would define themselves as antifeminist; most would deny that they are anti-woman, although opposed to expanding women's rights. For the student of women's history, the temptation to look for patterns of opposition will become irresistible. To facilitate an evaluation of the texts in their own historical context, the editors have grouped the documents within three major historical periods. Because the sources of mainstream opponents were more readily available, we elected to focus on the debate among writers who represented the middle class and who exerted a presence in the popular press. Especially for students of American women's history, this collection provides the opportunity to encounter directly the opinions of those who resisted and criticized the goals as well as the tactics of feminism in all its forms.

The documents in volume one, *Opposition to the Women's Movement in the United States, 1848–1929,* cover the initial era of the woman's movement, which began in the antebellum period and produced the *Declaration of Sentiments* of the Seneca Falls Woman's Rights Convention in 1848 as well as the Cult of True Womanhood (1820–1860). The sources in volume one extend through the culmination of the ratification of the Nineteenth Amendment to the U.S. Constitution that enfranchised women. The nineteenth-century critics of the emerging women's movement launched the conservative defense of a delineated woman's sphere and redefined the cult of domesticity with appeals to scripture and history, as well as to contemporary scientific theories that emphasized the physical-gender differences. By the twentieth century, the opponents of women's rights and equality faced formidable challenges to the validity of these translations of scripture, interpretations of historical development, and questionable "scientific" evidence and conclusions.

The sources provided in volume two, *Redefining the New Woman, 1920–1963,* offer reflections of the twentieth-century era from the "Roaring Twenties" through the

World War II period to the rise of the Civil Rights Movement. Both the 1920s and the 1950s were decades characterized by post-war antifeminism and a trend toward intellectually stifling social conformity for women and men; the maintenance of patriarchal values justified this repression. Those opposed to feminism added applications of Freudian psychology to the arguments based on biological and physiological "facts," firmly established before World War I. This psycho-biological approach reaffirmed that "biology is destiny" for women of the twentieth century as well as for the nineteenth. But developments in the postindustrial economy of the mid-twentieth century U.S. fostered changes in the middle class that redounded to increased women's opportunity in employment and education; the consequences of these changes seemed to threaten to lessen women's economic dependence upon men.

In volume three, *Reaction to the Modern Women's Movement, 1963 to the Present*, the readings span an era contemporary to the publication of Betty Friedan's *The Feminine Mystique* (1963), the so-called sexual revolution (in which women were more prisoners of war than combatants), and the rise of the modern women's movement. The impact of the Civil Rights Act of 1964, Title VII especially, no less than the rise of the women's liberation movement (1968–1972) and the development of women's studies within the standard curriculum of higher education created a climate for change that continues to occur throughout the last decade in the twentieth century. The 1980s ushered in the Reagan era with a backlash against the women's movement that capitalized on the insecurities of middle-class women, especially homemakers, that they would be discarded, abandoned, and stranded as single heads of households and the sole support of their children; middle-class men were told to fear the added economic competition of women and men of color. Conservatives reacted to the legacy of the 1970s—the questioning of authority—and bristled at the challenge of the women's liberation movement to patriarchal institutions and values. This generation of defenders of the gender system articulated the threat feminism posed to organized religion, "traditional" family values, the nation's future, and the free-enterprise economy.

This collection of readings developed from a shared experience and exasperation of a professor and her graduate student in a course on U.S. feminism. Dissatisfied with the limited sources available for studying contemporary criticism of the women's movement and feminism in U.S. history, the editors collaborated to find, edit, and present to the reader the kinds of sources that often appear in women's history courses as handouts—assorted items gathered over time and informally assembled. Our division of labor reflected our individual strengths: the professor brought the expertise gained from decades of teaching women's history as well as editorial experience; the graduate student (now well on her way to completing her Ph.D.) contributed impressive state-of-the-art researching skills and determination to locate, screen, and recommend documents most likely to represent the trends and standard arguments of the critics of the women's movement and feminism. From experience, the former knew that good intentions notwithstanding, "no good deed goes unpunished" and therefore anticipated that the best efforts would still garner candid criticism of purpose and selections; the latter maintained a conviction that this "good deed" needed doing regardless of the time and effort demanded. The idealism of youth won out. We drew into our quixotic vision other graduate students who provided crucial research as assistants to the editors:

Pamela F. Wille, Rae Fuller Wilson, and Susanne Grooms. All of us relied on the kindness and expertise of the professional librarians at U.H.C.L., including Susan Steele, and the professional staff of other libraries. The editors therefore accept any compliments on the results of the collaboration as only proportionally ours while we assert our sole claim of accountability for the inevitable errors (which we trust our readers will bring to our attention and that will be corrected in future editions).

Volume Introduction

After 1920, the woman vote failed to produced the catastrophic consequences predicted by opponents to women's rights before World War I. However, during the period between 1920 and 1963, opponents to women's rights and equality adjusted initial criticism to reflect quickly entrenched changes in twentieth-century women's status and role without conceding credit for those improvements to the activities of the women's movement. Historians of the eras after World War I and World War II still debate whether feminism died, went underground, or became so scattered into single issue movements that the presence of a coherent women's movement eluded the attention of postwar political fundamentalism and antifeminism. Publications of entrepreneur Henry Ford, as well as renown authors such as D.H. Lawrence and Norman Mailer, and presidential candidate Adlai Stevenson represented male-biased literary criticism and mainstream opposition to the feminist movement that lingered in varying degrees throughout the mid-twentieth century. Opponents hoped that the resurgence of conservatism after World War II would finally and completely extinguish the women's movement. Advances in science, still tainted by patriarchal assumptions, and collusion with well-respected social scientists seemed to confirm claims of an insurmountable biological impediment to fundamental changes in woman's role and to support admonitions of the grave hazards such unnatural changes would create in women, future generations, and the nation as a whole. One hundred years after Seneca Falls, in the middle of the twentieth century, the opponents of the women's movement were still arguing that "biology is destiny" for women.

Selections in part one of this volume concentrate on sources that were published during the interwar years, between 1920 and 1941, and indicate that the legacy of progressive social feminism exacerbated reactionary attitudes toward women in the context of postwar political fundamentalism, the Great Depression, and the New Deal. Opponents persisted in contesting the propriety and purpose of women's higher education and renewed their arguments for a limited role for women in general and a domestic role for married women.

The readings in part two contain material that appeared between 1941 and 1963 and that reflect the ambivalence and backlash toward the wives and mothers in the workforce and the public sphere, especially in the context of the social, political, and economic conservatism of the Cold War era. Two post-World War II trends alerted and alarmed the opponents of women's rights and feminism: the steadily increasing number of married women in the paid labor force and the rise in women's enrollment in postsecondary institutions. The expansion of public universities and community colleges facilitated the education of "nontraditional" middle-class women as well as working-class women who were graduating from high school during this period.

Redefining the New Woman, 1920–1963

all special provisions of differentiating men from women." Working women are ready for equality. It is the welfare worker who holds up to them the inferiority complex.

What Is Equality?

By CLARA MORTENSON BEYER

THOSE who subscribe to the program of absolute equality between the sexes could derive small comfort from the national industrial conference recently held by the Women's Bureau of the United States Department of Labor. Of the 360 delegates from 41 States representing all national women's organizations with the exception of the Woman's Party, only a handful were ready to support the program of industrial equality for men and women. Unfortunately, the Woman's Party refused to send delegates to the conference solely because the chairman refused to make a special exception in its case and give it, as an organization, a place on the program. Speakers were selected not because they belonged to a certain organization but because of their knowledge of women in industry.

Whether the Woman's Party was officially represented or not, its point of view on industrial legislation was expressed by two of the speakers: Miss Merica Hoagland, of the Diamond Chain and Manufacturing Company of Indianapolis, and Mr. Charles Cheney, of Cheney Brothers, silk manufacturers of Connecticut. These speakers opposed industrial legislation, for women as an interference with their property rights and their freedom of contract and an unnecessary discrimination against them in the labor market. There is nothing new nor startling in this position. Ever since the first labor legislation was enacted, employers have valiantly defended before the courts the freedom of contract and property rights of their workers. And, upon occasion, the judges take them seriously. Witness the recent decision of the District Court of Appeals on the minimum-wage law in the District of Columbia, in which the majority of the Court held that "no greater calamity could befall the wage-earners of this country than to have the legislative power to fix wages upheld. It would deprive them of the most sacred safeguard which the Constitution affords. Take from the citizen the right to freely contract and sell his labor for the highest wage which his individual skill and efficiency will command, and the laborer would be reduced to an automaton."

The Woman's Party takes the position that industrial legislation for women is discrimination against them in the field of industry. At present, it does not consider it feasible to wipe out such legislation for women. Therefore, in order to remove existing inequalities between the sexes, it proposes to extend industrial legislation for women to men. For all practical purposes, it might better work directly for the removal of such legislation for women. The effect, in all probability, would be the same in either case— women would be left without the safeguards which are peculiarly necessary to their well-being and men would be in exactly the same position as before. In the words of Dean Roscoe Pound, of the Harvard Law School, "there is no surer method of repealing all legal protection for women than to substitute for the laws now in force general statutes covering all persons." Therefore, when the advocates of equality in industry accuse their opponents of being selfish and unwilling to share with men the advantages to be derived from protective legislation, the answer is that

their opponents are advised by competent jurists that it is the part of foolishness to be generous in this respect, at least for years to come. Working women have the world to lose and nothing to gain but their chains. They have lost these chains all too recently to be willing to be shackled again merely for the sake of a theoretical equality.

The Woman's Party, as a result of a recent questionnaire, is rapidly proving, to its own satisfaction at least, that working women do not want protective legislation. When convinced of that, how can it hope to prove that working men want for themselves the legislation scorned by working women and, if the Woman's Party so proves, would it, as an organization, in the name of equality attempt to force the unwilling working women to accept legal standards satisfactory only to their brothers? Does "equality" deny women the right to differ from men?

Women cannot be made men by act of legislature or even by an amendment to the United States Constitution. That does not mean women are inferior or superior to men. Refusal to recognize the biological differences between men and women does not make for equality. Until the earth is populated with Mr. Shaw's Ancients, women will continue to bear children and certain physiological corollaries to this fact will continue to exist. Exposure to strain and over-fatigue in the child-bearing period, and wage-earning women are almost all in this period of life, is reflected in higher morbidity of working women than of working men, and in the excessive sickness and death-rate of children of working mothers. That long hours of constant standing or sitting are more injurious to women than to men is another well-established fact. These actualities may not be pleasant to our feminist friends, but they will not be removed by playing ostrich. Students of industry recognize that women are an unstable factor in industry, that the majority enter industry to fill the gap between school and marriage. They are, on the whole, unskilled workers. Because of their instability, their lack of skill, and their extreme youth, trade-union organization among women has been of slow growth, far slower than among men. Working conditions among women reflect this inability to organize. It was said at the women's industrial conference that 1,000 men were working the eight-hour day to every one woman. Over one-half of the wage-earning women of the country are earning less than enough to live on. Trade-union organizers familiar with these facts are advocating industrial legislation for women on the ground that unionism among them is too slow and has not reached the vast rank and file. They have further found that industrial legislation for women is a help rather than a hindrance to organization. We cannot expect overworked, under-nourished women to have the energy or enthusiasm for joining a union and attempting to better their conditions. While the masses of women workers are so far down the industrial scale, it is ludicrous to talk of their freedom to choose their occupations, to bargain freely for their wages and hours of work. It would be more to the point to talk of the freedom of employers to exploit their workers.

By legislation an effort is being made to bring women up to the point where industrial equality with men is more nearly possible. The time undoubtedly will come when women will need less special legislation than they do now, but until that time it is little short of criminal to deny them the opportunity for reasonable leisure and a living wage, which legislation alone can obtain for them.

2

Are Women's Clubs "Used" by Bolshevists?

Interlocking Directorates Used Effectively to Disseminate Propaganda.

By An American Citizen

GRAVE danger threatens the progress of organized womanhood in the world today. Leadership of women's organizations has fallen into the hands of radicals to an alarming extent. There is a conspicuous turning away from public work on the part of many able women who have formerly been active. Radical leadership may cost all that sane, progressive women have achieved through the centuries. It is inevitable that if a choice is compelled between the extreme feminist program under its present radical leadership and anti-feminist programs, the anti-feminists will win, since this is obviously the lesser of two evils.

One reason for many of our best women refusing to be candidates for office in women's organizations is that the advent of suffrage makes every organized unit a potential political factor.

To understand this it is necessary to examine the radical program for the control of leadership Tracing the personnel through the network of interlocking directorates which control women's organizations, national and international, we see how the radical works It is never the policy of the leaders to permit the rank and file of the members to know what the ultimate objective is. Women are drawn in through all sorts of camouflage interests—their dislike of war, their sympathies for prisoners, most of all by the frothy eloquence which depicts a woman's crusade against all evil, while at the same time their leaders are using the rawest form of political bludgeoning on politicians in the capitals, and are often in communication with the fountains of "red propaganda" in this and other countries. Of course, the good women who make up the rank and file are not supposed to know this.

Used for Red Purposes?

ON AUGUST 1, 1922, the Central Executive of the Communist International (Communist leaders who rule Soviet Russia) issued a signed proclamation "To the Central Committee of all Communist Parties," through the Communist "International Press Correspondence" service, in part, as follows:

"It is self-evident that the Proletarian United Front is not complete unless women are conscious and active co-militants . . . . It is the duty of the Communist parties of all countries to make full use of the existing possibilities to convert women into conscious militants .
See to it that the necessary measures be taken for carrying on Communist propaganda among the broad masses of women . . . . that steps be taken for the awakening and mobilization of the working women to take their places consciously and confidently in the United Proletarian Front . . . . This applies not merely to political work . . . . but more particularly . . . . in the trade unions and co-operatives. The Proletarian women . . . constitute deep and potent sources of vigorous fighting power and fighting energy . . . . To unlock these sources will be the duty and honor of the Communist parties of all countries and will serve as another guaranty for the success of the United Proletarian Front in the struggle against the bourgeoisie."

This order from Moscow illustrates the true objective of the Communists regarding work in women's organizations. Some intelligent women are now convinced that the legislative program being sponsored by women's organizations is a menace and that the women of America are being used for a purpose that is concealed from them.

The National Council of Women which held its biennial convention in November, 1923 at Decatur, Illinois, is the clearing house for national organizations. The constituent organizations are as follows:

National American Woman Suffrage Association, now National League of Women Voters.
National Women's Relief Society.
Young Ladies' National Mutual Improvement Society.
National Women's Relief Corps.
National Council Jewish Women
National Florence Crittenton Mission
Ladies of the Maccabees.
National Federation of Colored Women
Ladies of the Grand Army of the Republic.
Association of Collegiate Alumnae, now
American Association of University Women.
National Congress of Mothers and Parent-Teacher Association.
National Federation of College Women.
National Federation of Musical Clubs.
Needlework Guild of America.
General Federation of Women's Clubs.
Women's International League for Peace and Freedom, U. S. A. Section.
Women's Christian Temperance Union.
Young Women's Christian Association.
Woodmen Circle.
National Women's Republican Association.
Children of American Loyalty League.
Kansas State Council.
Rhode Island State Council.
Indianapolis Local Council.
Medical Women's National Association.
International Sunshine Society.
National American War Mothers.
National Kindergarten Association.
Sons of Veterans' Auxiliary.
National Auxiliary United Spanish War Veterans.
Association of Women in Public Health.
May Wright Sewell State Association.
American Legion Auxiliary.
Osteopathic Women's National Association.
Southern Women's Educational Alliance.
American Lovers of Music.

The combined membership of these organizations is more than eleven million. The National Council of Women of the United States is affiliated with the International Council of Women of which the Marchioness of Aberdeen and Temair is president. The International Council federates all national organizations in Europe and the Orient. The combined membership of the International Council is approximately thirty-six million. These astounding figures by no means represent the total number of women who are being reached through the affiliated organizations which contact. Many women in the organizations not affiliated with the National and International Council of Women are members of the International Suffrage Alliance, the Trade Union Organizations and the National Women's Party, all of which are more or less infected with the radical communist or milder virus.

At the convention of the International Suffrage Alliance, held in Rome, May 23 of last year, the attempt was again made to amalgamate the International Suffrage Alliance and the International Council of Women. So far, this plan has failed of accomplishment, but its sponsors are by no means discouraged.

Through teamwork on interlocking directorates, a few key women dominate the legislative program in most of the women's organizations. This is the central fact which explains what is accomplished by any of these conventions.

The tendency to federate all organizations nationally and internationally makes it comparatively easy to control great numbers by small minorities. Take the

National Council of Women as an example. There are fourteen committees, the membership of which is composed of the chairmen of like committees in the constituent organization. The representation of affiliated organizations in the National Council of Women is restricted to the president and five delegates. Members are welcome as visitors, but comparatively few attend the board meetings, as it takes both time and money to travel from one convention to another. The present officers in the National Council of Women have served through many years and there have been few changes in the chairmen of committees during the administration of Mrs. Philip North Moore, who was re-elected president for the fourth time at Decatur. Through means of these fairly continuous chairmanships the well-financed propaganda organizations are instructed to penetrate and control the women's organizations.

The two most conspicuous propaganda organizations affiliated with the National Council of Women are the National League of Women Voters and the Women's International League of Peace and Freedom. Mrs. Maud Wood Park, president of the National League of Women Voters, is a vice-president of the National Council of Women. Mrs. Park is said to have great influence over Mrs. Thomas G. Winter, president of the General Federation of Women's Clubs, herself a vice-president of the National Council of Women. The chairmen of the majority of committees in the National Council of Women are also members of either one or both of the above-mentioned organizations.

How Women's Bloc Works

ALL of the principal women's organizations maintain legislative representatives in Washington and the astute Mrs. Park some time ago organized what is known as the "Congressional Committee," of which she is chairman and of which Mrs. A. C. Watkins is secretary.

This "Women's Bloc," as it is called, can in co-operation with the radicals in Congress practically dictate our legislation, and our women, comprising the vast membership of these organizations, women who would quickly resent being called Socialists or Bolsheviki, are blithely passing resolutions and voting for a program that was inaugurated by Madam Alexandria Kollontay in her Soviet "Department of Child Welfare" in Russia.

The influence of many women is appreciable in the National Council of Women who do not personally attend these conventions. This comes because of their teamwork with the women who do attend. For example, Mrs. Raymond Robbins, formerly president of the National Women's Trade Union League, an organization which the Lusk Committee reports "adopted resolutions in favor of the Soviet government," and a contributor to the Rand School of Social Science where socialist leaders are trained, is one of the socialist women promoting pacifist and welfare propaganda. Miss Mary Anderson, chief of the United States Women's Bureau and chairman of the Industrial Relations Committee in the National Council, issued a call for a WORLD CONGRESS OF WORKING WOMEN, which met at Washington, November 6, 1919, and adopted the name International Federation of Working Women, of which Mrs. Robbins was made president. This congress gave special attention to "legislative reforms for the purpose of protecting maternity." The *Woman Citizen* magazine, the official organ of Mrs. Carrie Chapman Catt, reports that plans were recommended to secure state grants to mothers for each child born and to secure free medical, nursing and surgical care during maternity and, in addition, an allowance for the support of the mother and child during the maternity period." At the World Congress of Working Women they also advocated that there be organized an INTERNATIONAL LABOR OFFICE OF THE LEAGUE OF NATIONS BUREAU to collect information on best methods of maternity care.

The heart of everyone is touched by an appeal to care for mothers and babies. *The radicals find it easy to build their bureaucracy by selecting such obvious heart appeals* because by such means they sweep the uninformed to unknowingly to vote away individual freedom and Constitutional Government. All students of political economy know that bureau management is costly and inefficient. Under the Sheppard-Towner bill each community must raise part of the funds for the care of its own mothers and babies. The Federal Government contributes a similar amount and assumes direction of the work. *Some day the community will awake to the fact that it would cost less to pay for the care of its maternity cases without Federal aid and under community direction. The great danger, however, is not the increased taxes due to the upbuilding of this undemocratic machine, but the centralized political control thus established.*

It was Mrs. Raymond Robbins who brought forth the idea of a department of public welfare in America. As a "republican" in co-operation with Mrs. Harriet Taylor Upton, of the National Republican Committee, she organized a welfare demonstration at Marion, Ohio, October 1, 1920, at which Mrs. Robbins was the first speaker and at which President Harding, then candidate, was persuaded to come out for a welfare department and a new cabinet officer. As chairman of the WOMEN AND INDUSTRY COMMITTEE OF THE NATIONAL LEAGUE OF WOMEN VOTERS, Mrs. Robbins wrote the "Women and Industry" and the "Education Plank" of the Democratic National Platform which is identical in wording with that of the League of Women Voters *long before their convention met.* It gives us food for thought when the leading women in both the Democratic and Republican parties are members of the League of Women Voters which organization is admittedly working for pacifism and internationalism and is sworn to uphold the non-partisan movement among women.

Tap Party Treasuries

RATHER clever of the women! They tap the treasuries of both the Democratic and Republican parties for funds with which to break down party machinery. Not long ago Mrs. Harriet Taylor Upton, of the Republican National Committee and Mrs. Emily Newell Blair, of the Democratic National Committee, made a lecture tour for the League of Women Voters, almost, if not quite, together. And a story of this trip was printed in a Sunday Washington paper with authenticated interviews from each, together with their photographs.

When we realize that this same program is being carried out by women in European countries as well, and that the program in our country is backed by these women who manipulate all of the committees from the great national political parties to the humblest church societies, and that they are lobbying for a program identical with that promulgated by Madam Alexandria Kollontay, the director of welfare in Soviet Russia, what are we to think? Madam Kollontay is so radical that even Radak himself objects to her, yet Miss Mary Anderson, head of the Women's Bureau in our Department of Labor, and chairman of Industrial Relations in the National Council of Women, has succeeded in having printed *by the Government of the United States* this program of Women and Children's Work minus only its Soviet label! Think of the network of club machinery represented by the National Council of Women and realize that this program, through Miss Anderson's chairmanship, permeates the committee work of all the clubs in the United States with this Bolshevik doctrine. Then remember that through interlocking directorates practically the same program percolates through many organizations *not* affiliated with the National Council of Women, such as the National Women's Party, the National Women's Trade Union League, the International Suffrage Alliance, and others.

Note the important affiliation consummated through the appointment of Miss Charl Williams of the National Education Association as chairman of Elementary Education in the National Council of Women. Since Miss Whitney, the chairman of education, recommended her appointment, it is evident that she is expected to be sympathetic with the present politics of the organization. Certain it is the N. E. A. is strongly impregnated with Pacifist-Socialist propaganda, as its recent convention work proves.

4

Resolutions passed by small delegated bodies representing great organizations endorse the legislative program of Soviet Russia in the name of reform, of peace, and of child welfare, and the great majority of the membership of these organizations are unaware that a revolution in the United States is being set on foot through this work of women. The most valuable work being done to destroy Constitutional Government is being done by those who deny that they are radicals. Most of them believe their own statements. Radicalism is a wordy system with many aspects. Few people recognize it unlabeled. It is time that we examine beneath the label.

Few people understand the program of deceit which is essential to put across that portion of the radical program which they term "The Bloodless Revolution," or revolution by the ballot.

Let us now examine some of the most illuminating statements from the official records of the Communists. The Third Congress in conjunction with the International Women's Congress at Moscow, July 8, 1921, adopted the following resolution: "The interest of the working class, especially at the present moment, imperatively demands the recruiting of women into the organized ranks of the proletariat fighting for Communism in all places where the Communist parties exist illegally or semi-legally; the party should organize an illegal apparatus for work among women. In all legal bodies there must be at least one party member to organize the women for illegal work."

Sara Bard Field, one of the foremost leaders of the National Women's Party, was chosen with Jane Addams to make the presentation speech of the three suffrage statutes introduced in 1921.

Miss Field addressed the Speaker of the House of Representatives thus: "Mr. Speaker, I give you revolution!" On February 12, 1922, Miss Field, in a letter to Brigadier General Ames A. Fries, says, "I have no confidence in anything short of revolution. Peaceful by all means, if possible; bloody, if necessary, in every land, resulting in the establishment of the Communist idea in some form to do away with war. Women should stop short at nothing but the full abolition of war, pull the support from under it and go about the building of a new world as Russia is painfully trying to do."

Mrs. Gifford Pinchot was mentioned for a chairman of an important committee in the council. Mrs. Pinchot was not elected for the place, but she is one of the inner circle in the National League of Women Voters and her dominance in that organization has a vicarious reflection in practically everything done in the National Council of Women, because most of its chairmen are members of the League of Women Voters.

Recently the Boston *Transcript* published a series of articles by R. M. Whitney on the "Reds in America." In one of these articles, Mr. Whitney published the "Sucker List" meaning the list of names of those who contribute money to the Communist cause. Mr. Gifford Pinchot's name appears upon this list and in view of the fact that Gifford Pinchot is governor of one of our greatest states and a Presidential aspirant, this connection with radical propaganda should be pondered. Mrs. Pinchot is prominent in the International Women's organizations and Mr. Pinchot's election as governor is very largely attributed to the work which the "nonpartisan" League of Women Voters did in his campaign. Governor Pinchot is the father of paternalism or state socialism in the United States and if Count von Bernstorff, formerly German Ambassador to the United States, knows what he is talking about, these theories sponsored by Governor Pinchot were "made in Germany."

We have enumerated only a few of the women who are working to organize a bureaucracy that will control women and children, education and industry. The big idea is to centralize the control of all things possible in the Federal Government. And this *is* the destruction of Constitutional Government. This *is* Empire and it is of small consequence whether we call our ruler President or Kaiser.

The activities of the key women in the various organizations make possible an understanding of the methods by which these matters are to be accomplished. As these activities appeared at the Decatur convention, a glance at its program may be instructive.

Mrs. Maud Wood Park, president of the National League of Women Voters and vice-president of the council, gave an address upon the subject of "Women's Aims in Legislation." Mrs. Park has been ably assisted by Mrs. Florence Kelley, the Socialist translator of German Socialist works, who is herself president of the Inter-Collegiate Socialist Leagues, later called "League for Industrial Democracy." Mrs. Kelley is mentioned in the Lusk report as being connected with more than one Socialistic organization. The League of Women Voters proposes to conduct a school of politics. It has already held sessions in several of our important colleges and universities. Naturally, it is necessary for them to mis-label their work to secure entry.

The membership of this League of Women Voters is the preponderant influence today in the National Council of Women. Almost equally powerful within the council is the Women's International League of Peace and Freedom, *whose delegates refused to salute the flag at the Decatur biennial.*

Among the resolutions introduced by the International League of Peace and Freedom at the convention in Decatur of the National Council of Women was one calling for the evacuation of the Ruhr, another for the cancellation of war debts and still another for the recognition of Soviet Russia.

To comprehend the full significance of the reappointment of Mrs. Lucia Ames Mead as Chairman of Permanent Peace in the National Council of Women, one should know the proceedings of the Annual Conference of the Women's International League for Peace and Freedom held in Washington, D. C., March 13-16, 1923. Mrs. Lucia Ames Mead is lecturer and organizer in this organization.

Over the headquarters of the International League of Peace and Freedom at Washington no American flag floats.

At this convention the spirit of the Russian Communism prevailed. The recognition of Soviet Russia was urged and it was agreed to deluge the members of Congress with letters to that end. Helen Hoy Greeley advised our government to follow the example of Mr. Otto Kahn, of Kuhn, Loeb & Company, international bankers, who advocate full and immediate recognition of Russia.

Each item of work advised by this convention is to be found outlined in the Third International Documentary Instructions sent from Moscow to the Communists of the United States and now in the files of the government at Washington. It was specifically stated in this document that the suggestions made are for the purpose of weakening the government.

One of their principal points is the abolition of the Army and Navy, especially of the Chemical Warfare Department, since gas may be used to quell riots, and they plan the beginning of the revolution in the United States with riots. Disarmament is to come about gradually through the discouragement of military training in the schools and summer camps, and the eventual abolition of the National Guard.

Mrs. Harriet Conner Brown, wife of Herbert D. Brown, chief of the Efficiency Bureau of the Federal Government, said, among other things, "We women are going to repeal the Army Reorganization act . . . . Act as mugwumps ladies, vote the Democratic, the Republican or the Socialist ticket to gain our ends, and do away with the Army and Navy, the National Guard and every other form of militarism . . . ." She also said that there are three ways to accomplish this. They are "the ballot, passive resistance, and education of public opinion through our propaganda. There is much for us pacifists to do. We must get into all sorts of clubs, women's clubs, farmers' granges, welfare associations. We must get into religious organizations whenever and wherever possible—Chautauquas, schools—ev-

5

erything, and we must send our propaganda everywhere."
Mrs. Brown must be vastly pleased with the influence
exercised by Mrs. Mead and other members of the
International League of Peace and Freedom within the
National Council of Women.

THE UNFEMALE FEMININE

By Anthony Bertram

IT is a commonplace of contemporary criticism to talk of Marie Laurencin as the essentially feminine painter. I did it myself three weeks ago in these pages. Her exhibition at the Leicester Galleries, her first in London, is an occasion to examine this too easy commonplace. Certainly Marie Laurencin's work expresses femininity, but not all of it. Woman is not complete without man any more than man is complete without woman. Marie Laurencin has chosen to express unrelated woman—or rather, woman related only to herself. Mr. Jan Gordon in his ' Modern French Painters ' committed himself to the statement that her paintings " make one think of those impromptu tales which mothers invent for their children upon a winter's evening." With the most respectful deference to so distinguished a critic, I should say that they contain no hint of motherhood or the domestic atmosphere, but make one think rather of those impromptu tales which one imagines women invent for one another in that world where man never comes. In the presence of her pictures a man experiences something of that discomfort which he knows when women talk across him.

Her art is so interesting just because it is the first artistic revelation of that part of her mystery which woman has ever vouchsafed us. We glimpse *la belle dame sans merci* " in her shirt sleeves," ignoring man. We see woman, not as our opposite who attracts us, but as our equal, living her own separate life. It is interesting, but not entirely pleasing, an unfinished symphony, lacking the last complexity and fullest splendour of natural life, the interplay of sex. I am not piqued at being omitted from Marie Laurencin's world, but disconcerted at this cleavage of nature's harmony. I imagine that most women must feel the same. There are moods when all of us, men and women, wish to pursue our own lives apart, bachelor moods; they are moods of immaturity, of disappointment, of perversity, of religious, political or artistic exaltation. They pass—or should. They are not all of us, or we are incomplete and unreal. Marie Laurencin has captured such a mood and expressed it solely. She has invented a very beautiful method of expression, and in its directness and intensity she is a very considerable artist; but she is one-sided and cannot be called great.

Mr. Wilenski writes, in his introduction to the catalogue of this exhibition, that he is reminded in Marie Laurencin's work of a " twentieth-century Venusberg to which no blundering Tannhäuser has ever found his way." The natural transition of thought is to Beardsley's forbidden, repulsive, exquisite ' Story of Venus and Tannhäuser ' that, in its limited private edition in vellum and gold, so delights those who have little stomach for Rabelais. If there were men in Marie Laurencin's world, we feel that they would be like Spiridion, " that soft incomparable alto." "His eyes were full and black, with puffy blue rimmed hemispheres beneath them, the cheeks, inclining to fatness, were powdered and dimpled, the mouth was purple and curved painfully, the chin tiny and exquisitely modelled, the expression cruel and womanish."

The first impression that Marie Laurencin's exhibition produces is of very gracious, consummate design, shapely forms in delicate pinks and greys, blues and greens, with intensely emphasized blacks. The eyes, black significant lozenges, glint disturbingly out of the general harmony. We are pleased and intrigued by the beautiful novelty. Slowly the pictures gather body and differentiate themselves. We become conscious of the pathetic *gamines*, such as the ' Femme au Balcon,' ' Femme au Chapeau Gris,' ' Femme au Chien '; of the others, less pathetic, taking their intimate ease in open-air boudoirs and an atmosphere of *crême de menthe frappée*. We come away stirred by the masterly artistic expression of femininity broken off from woman as we know and love her, and, while we fully grant the right of art to deal with what it wishes, we must, in our non-æsthetic human selves, be conscious of some little repulsion from this unfemale femininity.

8

FEMINISM AND THE ECONOMIC INDEPENDENCE OF WOMAN

GUION GRIFFIS JOHNSON

SELF-EXPRESSION has been forced upon woman. There came the revolt of the American Colonies, setting up the theory that all men are born free and equal. Closely following was the French Revolution invading the civilized world with strange and alarming notions concerning liberty, equality, and human brotherhood. Nothing was more natural than that some woman, given an opportunity of education, should ponder these new theories in her mind and decide that a premise true for her brother might also hold good for herself. So it was that Mary Wollstonecraft came forth in 1792 with her *Vindication of the Rights of Woman.* She says scornfully:

This desire of being always women is the very consciousness that degrades the sex. . . . She (woman) must not be dependent on her husband's bounty for her subsistence during his life or support after his death; for how can a being be generous who has nothing of its own? or virtuous, who is not free? . . . How many women . . . waste life away, the prey of discontent, who might have practised as physicians, regulated a farm, managed a shop, and stood erect, supported by their own industry, instead of hanging their heads surcharged with the dew of sensibility. . . . How much more respectable is the woman who earns her own bread by fulfilling any duty, than the most accomplished beauty!!![1]

This new declaration of independence scarcely made an impression. Mary Wollstonecraft's sex that she so bitterly denounced was too busily engaged in "shaping itself to man's image of woman" to be concerned with unlady-like pursuits.

Then came the industrial revolution, upsetting the home, forcing woman outside to help in the struggle for food. But the industrial revolution alone would not have raised up disciples to the woman movement had it not been for the World War. The war, stripping young men from salaried positions as it did, gave to many women a taste of independence which otherwise would have come many years later, and thus were aggravated conditions going on before the war. The woman movement is, therefore, like all other movements which have brought about social change; an outgrowth of existing conditions. The feminist belief that woman of herself has risen from the mire of intellectual sloth to the fresh, clean air of free thought and action is as foolish as to maintain that the Russian serfs could have freed themselves without the aid of Russia's industrial revolution. Nevertheless, women would have been even more inferior than some students of biology and psychology have judged them had they not aroused themselves from their age-long lethargy.

Once being aroused, they have worked themselves into a fine frenzy. And the object of their rage is the male. Man who has kept woman in leash so long shall now be bound; and woman, once slave, shall rule. Students of the feminist school have set busily about establishing justification for their determination. C. Gasquine Hartley has come forth with the statement that "the male developed after, and, as it were, from the female. The female led, and the male followed her in the evolution of life."[2]

If one needs further proof, the contribution of Mrs. Charlotte Perkins Gillman might be considered: "Biological facts point to the very gradual introduction and development of the male organism solely as a reproductive necessity."[3]

Blanche Shoemaker Wagstaff goes even further. She will not only dethrone man, but she will banish him from existence. Man has strutted across the world, bringing misery and grief, and the price of his strutting shall be his annihilation.

The modern Woman's Movement may be called the manifestation of an *organic desire* to revert to a compound sex. . . . Hundreds of years from now nature may attain to its supreme end by evolving an ascendant form of human life possessing colossal reproductive energies. Man, as he is known to day, will almost cease to exist, occurring only at rarer and rarer intervals; he will be reduced to a mere functioning servility like the male bee, who is a stingless drudge. The superior force of the female will combine infinite generative power.[4]

---

[1] *Vindication of the Rights of Woman in The Humboldt Library of Popular Science Literature,* Vol. XV, pp. 76; 153; 156.

[2] *Truth About Women,* 1913, p. 44. See also Lester F. Ward, *Pure Sociology,* pp. 313-19. New York: Macmillan, 1916.
[3] *Woman and Economics,* 1908, 6th edition, p. 172.
[4] "Elimination of the Male," *International,* Nov., 1913, pp. 319-21.

It was a man, however, who gave the cornerstone to the feminist movement, Otto Weiniger who in his book *Sex and Character* tries to establish the theory that the "male principle is to be found in woman and the female principle in man." If there are "no men and no women, but merely sexual majorities,"[5] then woman's subservience to man is indeed on the same level as that of master and slave. The slave, possessing the same inherent qualities in the same quantities as the master, will when the opportunity arises free herself from servitude. Woman needs only the opportunity of education and an enlarged social environment to achieve as man has achieved.

Operating upon this assumption, the progressive feminists in the United States have organized themselves into the National Woman's Party, which at present is concentrating its energies on the passage of the Lucretia Mott Amendment to the National Constitution. By their effort they hope to bring about such changes that "woman shall no longer be in any form of subjection to man in law or in custom, but shall in every way be on an equal plane in rights, as she has always been and will continue to be, in responsibilities and obligations."[6]

A smaller group of progressive feminists is to be found in the Lucy Stone League, an organization for the purpose of creating sentiment in favor of woman's retaining her name after marriage. Thus the president, Miss Ruth Hale, does not permit herself to be called Mrs. Haywood Broun, even when accompanied by her young son.

The less radical advocates of woman's rights are represented in the ranks of the General Federation of Women's Clubs, an organization which boasts a membership of two million women. It cannot be said that the General Federation of Women's Clubs belongs to the feminist school, for it claims simply to be, "a group of organized women in every community who can be depended upon to promote movements looking toward the betterment of life." It deserves consideration, however, as belonging to the woman's movement which represents a gradual awakening of that stagnant and conservative civilization of which women have aways been the larger portion. Yet there are few officers of the General Federation

who would not maintain that women's clubs are "so powerful" that "men's organizations are amusingly afraid of them."

One of the important facts to be considered in a discussion of any phase of feminism is the apparent lack of organization of forces. There are innumerable women's clubs, all seeking in one way or another the right of woman to be recognized as a thinking individual, yet failing to realize the strength which a united effort would bring. It is too much to expect that in a group of many millions all should agree upon the method of achieving anything so abstract as the right to be considered capable of intelligence or even that all should be concerned about this right. There has come into existence, therefore, the National League of Women Voters, the National Council of Women of the United States, the American Home Economics Association, the Woman's Party, and many others, each, consciously or unconsciously, seeking to gain prestige for woman as an individual.

The two chief doctrines of the radical feminists, around which all others revolve, are economic independence for women and birth control. The latter doctrine at least is one which has met with favor by many students of reform and is considered by them not only as a means of relieving woman from the bondage of incessant child-bearing, but, more important, as one solution of the world's population problem.[7] But the feminist doctrine of economic independence for all women is frequently attacked with vigor. Accordingly the feminists are all the more vigorous in their clamor for the right to work outside the home—a right which of necessity fell upon the poor woman as upon the poor man when the industrial revolution came bringing with it new and monotonous occupations, a fact seldom considered by some advocates of woman's rights as they sit cozily in their comfortable studios.

"We claim all labor for our province," cries Olive Schreiner, "Give us labor and the training which fits for labor! We demand this not for ourselves, but for the race."[8]

It is not to be wondered at that the intellectuals in the feminist movement should, on pondering over the reasons for woman's inequality with man, decide that it is due to her economic dependence

[5] W. L. George "Feminist Intentions," *Atlantic Monthly*, Dec., 1913, p. 721.

[6] See Declaration of Principles, National Woman's Party.

[7] See Reuter, *Population Problems.* Philadelphia: J. B. Lippincott, 1923.

[8] *Woman and Labor*, p. 33. London: T. Fisher Unwin, 1911.

and thus determine to wrest all womankind from bondage. If woman no longer need "sell her body for the sustenance of her soul," can she not gain in a great way all the fine things her soul in slavery has yearned for?

But let the young feminist speak for herself:

I cannot remember when I first knew that I wanted always to earn my own living all my life, and belong completely to myself. The first step was the realization that I never wanted to be dependent on any one else for my living. Then, when people told me I couldn't do it, it became a principle to fight for, almost a religion which I must rigidly follow. I encountered much opposition to the idea during my university life, and on account of that opposition, I set about to study all the factors which enter into a woman's economic independence after marriage. I found nothing to convince me that it was either impossible or impracticable, and much to confirm me in my opinion that it is the only way to freedom for both the husband and wife, and the best way for people to be happy. Of course, some ideas of principle, justice, fairness, and all that sort of thing enter into my conviction, but my criterion for the usefulness of any institution is its contribution to individual human happiness.[9]

She is not the first woman who has perceived the dignity and independence which will accrue to women from opening to them the field of labor and permitting them to earn their own living. It is not surprising, then, that the feminist's mind is filled with scorn for the woman who permits herself to be supported by her husband.

Nor is their srorn wholly without cause. The middle class woman, free from the necessity of doing her own laundry and preparing the food for her family, able to employ one or more servants, finds herself with hours of leisure which she may spend as she chooses. Unless she is a woman of more than ordinary ability and energy she will elect to do what all her neighbors are doing: bridge, tea, gossip. In an attempt to busy themselves, such women have built a complicated system of social rank to which they have become slaves. Trivialities are glorified: calling cards, tea wafers, and *la modiste* are supreme.

Social waste is the term which Dr. Lorine Pruette has applied to the comparatively recent phenomenon of the idle house-wife. The industrial revolution, the putting of many of the old-time home tasks into the factories, she says, has made home-making "a part-time job." "From the individual standpoint they (married women) form a pathetic picture, often most poignant

when they have reconciled themselves to their comparative uselessness, but from the social standpoint, they form an actual menace. By the thousands they wander up and down the city streets looking for something to fill the idle, lonely hours."[10]

A practical consideration of this problem, however, must weigh the advisability of demanding that the mode be a lucrative job for every woman. It must also determine the kinds of work open to women, the conditions under which they must labor, and the resultant effect upon health. Obviously, industry itself places a limit on the number of jobs available. The continual unrest due to unemployment which has in part existed ever since the industrial revolution makes it absurd to insist that every woman abandon home and set to work seeking a job as long as the present condition of industry and society shall exist, for no matter how diligently she sought it every woman could not find a job. Likewise, however much a part-time job to supplement the part-time job of home-making, as suggested by Doctor Pruette, would opreate to make a more satisfied wife, it is hardly possible that all women, or even a half of all women, could find such a job.

Already women are in industry in large numbers. The national census for 1920 shows more than eight and a half million women employed in gainful occupations. And as fast as they can be absorbed they are being taken into new trades. The Bureau of the Census shows further that almost a half of this number, or 4,115,278, are engaged in domestic service and mechanical industries, labor which is listed lowest on the wage scale and yet requires the greatest physical and nervous strain. Only one million, or less than one-eighth of all women gainfully employed, are engaged in professional work, labor listed high on the wage scale.

What is more important, says Miss Alice Henry in her book *Women and the Labor Movement,* not only do women suffer from overwork and underpay, but working under conditions often inhuman, they necessarily become underbidders to men.

Society must realize how disgraceful, how dangerous it is that so many thousands of women should spend the promise of their youth in earning five or six dollars a

---

[9] Quoted from a letter by permission.

[10] See Lorine Pruette, *Women and Leisure.* New York: Dutton & Co., 1924.

week, that they should toil chilled by cold or exhausted by heat, subjected to the perils of unguarded machinery, to poisonous fumes or to the moral risks that so often attend unlimited overtime or work at night. . . . We have no lack of evidence that overwork of women, and the underpay both men and women themselves, and of men who have families to support, is the direct cause both of the loss of little babies, and of the death of mothers in the very act of giving life.[11]

Do the feminists see in the tired and haggard faces of young waitresses, who spend seventy hours a week of hard work in exchange for a few dollars to pay for room and clothing, a deceptive mask of the noble spirit within? C. Gasquine Hartley, feminist and author of *The Truth About Woman* has seen "a beautiful woman porter carry heavy luggage, running with it on bare feet, without sign of effort." She was the mother of four children," continues the feminist. "I saw in this Gallegan woman a strength and beauty that has become rare among women today."

The woman laborer herself sees nothing beautiful or exhilerating in the making of paper boxes or the constant tending of a machine. She is there because she must live. If given the alternative of marriage or a job, she is willing to gamble on marriage with the hope that it will bring less labor and more leisure. Too often she gets both marriage and labor.

Surely it is not an increasing army of jaded girls and spent women that pours every day from factory and shop that the leaders of the feminist movement seek. But the call for women to make all labor their province can mean nothing more. They would free women from the rule of men only to make them greater slaves to the machines of industry.

Ethnologists have commented on the early senescence of the hard-working savage women. Spencer and Gillen says:

As is usual in the case of savage tribes, the drudgery of food-collecting and child-bearing tells upon them (women) at an early age, and between 20 and 25 they begin to lose their graceful carriage; the face wrinkles, the breasts hang pendulous, and, as a general rule, the whole body begins to shrivel up, until at the age of 30 all traces of an earlier well-formed figure and graceful carriage are lost, and the woman develops into what can only be called an old and wrinkled hag.[12]

Nor is this condition restricted to savage women. Professor E. A. Ross, in his *Changing America,* in speaking of the condition which will arise if women are permitted to continue in industry as they are now, says:

In three or four generations we would have in this country all through the lower stratum that coarse type replacing the high-strung, high-bred, feminine type which is our pride and which extends up and down through all layers of society in this country. Do we want to have a reversion down in the stratum that has to work with its hands, of the feminine form to the masculine peasant type, to that Flemish-mare type that has lost the charm and grace of woman?[13]

Undoubtedly the intellectuals in the feminist movement are thinking in terms of the intellectual, and their cry for economic independence will be answered by women who are able to earn a livelihood by intellectual means. They alone can work under conditions sufficiently mild to enable them to couple motherhood and labor, and they alone have aspirations, ideals, illusions.[14] To the professional woman who has once experienced the exhileration of doing creative work, housekeeping with its annoying details of burning fat and dust behind the door is as loathsome as manual labor would be to the professional man. Nor should the professional woman be required to spend her days in the endless round of cooking, dusting, sweeping any more than should the professional man be committed to the ditch throughout his life.

If the trained woman of ability marries and elects to follow her profession after marriage, what will she do when the children begin to come? Many have been the solutions offered to solve the perplexing matter of motherhood and labor. Perhaps those set forth by Ellen Key on the one hand and Charlotte Perkins Gilman on the other are typical. Ellen Key believes that in return for one's service as a mother and teacher the state should guarantee women economic independence:

Even happy marriages suffer through the wife's subordinate position, economically as well as judicially.

It is, therefore, of great importance both in happy and unhappy marriages that the wife should retain control over her property and her earnings; that she should be self-supporting in so far as she can combine this with

---

[11] Alice Henry, *Women and the Labor Movement,* p. xi-xii. New York: George H. Doran, 1923.
[12] *Native Tribes of Australia,* p. 46. London: Macmillan, 1899.

[13] *Changing America; Studies in Contemporary Society,* pp. 74-75. New York: Century, 1912.
[14] See Avrom Barnett, *Foundations of Feminism,* p. 83. New York: Robert M. McBride Company, 1921.

her duties as a mother, and that she should be maintained by the community during the first year of each child's life.[15]

To other feminists this picture of motherhood and economic independence is no more than a compromise with the old order of things and will eventually lead to as much dominance by the male as woman has already suffered. Mrs. Gilman's solution is that women will labor and study beside men; their children will be reared and trained by specialists and the reward of their labor will be their economic independence. Nor is it strange that this is the status of motherhood and labor most often advocated by the younger generation of feminists.

One young woman who is not yet thirty years old but who has won some distinction as a newspaper woman of ability has decided the question for herself in the following manner:

Those of us who do not own our own business or engage in a profession that depends solely on our own initiative, but have to depend on the whims and prejudices of city editors or managing editors cannot be quite sure just what we shall do when we take time off for children. The ideal arrangement, as I see it, is to take off just what time is physically necessary—say two months, though certainly one could do some writing during those two months. Then, one should have experts care for the child while one went on with the profession or business or art in which she is an expert. When more women practice this than now do, there will be day nurseries and nursery schools just as accepted and as accessible as the public schools now are. In the meanwhile, the pioneers will have to bear heavy expense and heavy burdens of care.[16]

She was married two and a half years ago to a newspaper man, and since that time has left two good positions to go with him when he was transferred from one city to another. The last move was made recently. She says further:

But, suppose that I, in a new city, in a new job within the next year decide to have a baby. What will my city editor say when at the end of the third or fourth month of pregnancy I tell him my intentions? Unless I have made myself particularly indispensable, and he can think of some work where my distorted appearance won't

embarrass some tender-minded and delicate men associates, he will tell me in a rage that I deceived him, and that I can quit. So I shall have to find something to do that is harder for me—some kind of free-lancing. A regular job is always easier on me mentally and physically than free-lancing, because the things that interest me, unfortunately, are not the things that managing editors think interest the millions whom they want to buy their papers.[17]

Thus it will be perceived that the chief consideration of this feminist when thinking of labor and motherhood is, How can I find a position which will afford me work during the most trying period of pregnancy? Obviously, need for the money enters not so much as does the desire to overcome the tradition of woman's incapacity for labor as the time for confinement approaches. On the other hand, the wife of a day laborer, herself a wage earner, as she approaches childbirth wearily mutters to herself, "It seems I can't go on—but we gotta live." How do the feminists square this with their doctrine of all labor for woman's province?[18]

It, therefore, follows that, until childbearing is less strenuous and less weakening than it now is and perhaps has always been, the economic position of the average mother will seldom rise as high as that of the average father and will in few cases excell it. If the professional woman is to succeed, her efficiency and intellectual ability will necessarily have to exceed that of the man with whom she is competing to offset the disadvantages which childbirth brings.

Since the ideal of a salaried job for every woman seems impossible of realization and the dream of intellectual labor as a means to economic independence is even further removed, it would appear that the feminists have not followed to a logical conclusion some of the theories they advocate.

---

[15] Ellen Key, *Love and Marriage*, p. 637. New York: G. P. Putnam's Sons, 1911.

[16] Quoted from a letter by permission.

[17] Quoted from a letter by permission.

[18] The feminist might object that her birth-control program will alleviate such a condition as this. But birth control itself cannot create intellectual work for all women or fit all women for intellectual work. There will still be thousands of women whose work will be confined to mechanical labor. A woman engaged in intellectual pursuits might during the last months of pregnancy continue her work at home. Not so with the day laborer. Therefore, for the foregoing condition to be relieved, the wage of the mechanical laborer would have to be relatively higher than that of the intellectual woman, a condition not likely to arise.

The Collapse of Feminism

By Reginald F. Rynd

PERHAPS one of the most remarkable products of the modern spirit of revolt is the Woman's Movement and the immensely extended area of female enterprise that has resulted from it. For years the forces of rebellious feminism had worked silently, waiting, no doubt, for some indication that the leaven had produced a sufficient ferment in the body politic to make open warfare against the reactionaries inevitable.

When war did come, it was with a blast that swept an innocent and unsuspecting country off its feet.

The chief exponents of revolt flung themselves into the fray with a fury that seemed out of all proportion to the merits of the cause. The sense of grievance, carefully fostered by the pioneers of feminism, gave the impression of being more manufactured than real.

The apathy of politicians was destined to be rudely disturbed by outbreaks of aggression so naïve and startling in character as to paralyse the normal operations of the law.

At first the authorities were inclined to regard them with a tolerance born of contempt. But later it became evident that militant feminism was a force that had to be reckoned with. Concrete illustrations of the poet's "*furens quid femina possit*" were of daily occurrence. Brickbats were thrown, windows were broken, churches were set on fire, while the sacred persons of Cabinet Ministers had to seek police protection from the more violent manifestations of female rage.

So short is the public memory that it is almost forgotten in what wild scenes of disorder our gentle sisters called attention to their wrongs. Many were content with civil martyrdom, and languished in gaol. Collisions with the police became almost "common form." Dishevelled amazons vented their puny wrath on stalwart custodians of the public peace, to whom the whole thing must have been a picnic compared with expressions of public feeling in Poplar or other less-favoured purlieus of the metropolis. Much of the agitation descended to the level of comic opera, while the public, for the most part, gazed with petrified amazement at the unfamiliar scene.

Englishwomen, unlike their Continental sisters, do not take naturally to a rough and tumble, and have little in common with the *petroleuses* of the Commune, who so ably assisted the forces of disorder in Paris in '48.

Apart from physical disabilities, women are hampered by hats, and the general impedimenta of an equipment ill-adapted to warfare.

None the less, we must in common fairness admit that they put up a remarkably good fight, and women showed themselves ready to die for a cause that the rest of an unregenerate world found it very hard to take seriously. They had raised the banner of revolt and they dared men, misguided devotees of the established fact, to wrest it from them.

To men's credit be it said, they made no united effort to do so. They allowed judgment to go by default on a question that had never seemed to them to be of more than second-rate importance. Women got what they wanted, because it had ceased to be worth man's while to withhold it from them.

It is the tragedy of all great causes that they flourish most in opposition.

So soon as the alarums and excursions of war had sounded a new and more terrible tocsin, interest in the woman's question naturally waned, nor has it ever reverted to its pre-war level of public importance. It has come to be regarded as a spent force, a mere academic diversion amid matters of far greater national moment.

The most sacred cause is damped by indifference.

It may, of course, be asserted that no cause can be damped that has been won. What women demanded has been granted to them. We would not willingly rob women of any of the fruits of victory, but it must not be forgotten that it was not in concession to a right justly maintained and nobly demonstrated that women got what they wanted, but rather in the spirit that a bon-bon is reluctantly yielded to an importunate and petulant child. The nation as a whole had steadily refused to take the movement seriously. It was not felt that the future of civilization was bound up with female suffrage or the establishment of civil equality between the sexes. Prophets of gloom there were who felt that civilization could not stand the racket, that the intrusion of women into the national counsels spelt the doom of society. But of serious opposition there was little enough.

But there were none with sufficient prophetic insight to visualize the actual event. None foresaw that this mountainous labour was to produce a mouse of such very disproportionate dimensions. Two or three women in Parliament, a handful of women on public bodies, a few female doctors, and a Portia or two is all that this fine frenzy, this tremendous epic of militant feminism, has been able to produce.

There are those who tell us that this is only the beginning. A more candid if less kindly criticism might be disposed to regard it as the end. We are possibly witnessing not the inauguration of the era of feminism, but its obsequies.

Nor is the cause for this very far to seek. The movement was foredoomed to sterility when it became apparent that the vast majority of women did not wish for the freedom that was being forced upon them by the militant sisterhood. Nor was the entry of women into Parliament, the crowning achievement of the sex war, heralded with the enthusiasm that generally acclaims the dawn of a new epoch. There was no triumphant pæan of rejoicing that trousered legislators were at last to have the sceptre snatched from their palsied grasp. This monumental innovation, which in a less sophisticated era might have been regarded as the first step in the process of constitutional decay, was the subject of a mild jest or two, a "nine days' wonder," and then it was buried in the obscurity that awaits all causes that do not go to the roots of the public weal.

Women made very little use of the opportunity offered to them. Instead of a "monstrous regiment" invading the sacred benches and putting to flight the forces of reaction, a mere handful of women decorously trod the historic floor, while their legislative protests were a zephyr compared to the blast that was expected of them.

Nor is it clear that any beneficent changes in public policy have resulted from this devastating departure from constitutional practice. Things are very much as they were, or rather more so, as the Irishman said, and we are left pondering on the strange ways of Providence and wondering if the whole affair is not a comic interlude in matters of more serious public interest.

Never was there a more perfect example of tearing a passion to tatters than this carefully-engineered protest against the alleged wrongs of women. Many a humble-minded seeker after truth is puzzled to know what all the pother was about. Many an ardent reformer is still seeking for evidence of that "oppression" which lashed a few misguided women into such a ferment of revolutionary zeal.

Women as a whole have steadily resisted this conspiracy to "unsex" them. While they have, in some cases, taken advantage of the opportunity offered to them in fields of action hitherto confined to men, they have for the most part kept to the beaten track that custom and tradition have marked out for them. Nor does their success in unfamiliar regions of social and civil action encourage the belief that the area of feminine enterprise should be extended. But this is, perhaps, trenching on dangerous ground.

So far, we have only touched upon the history of the movement. Its remoter field of ethics provides a ground where angels would tread lightly.

A movement is like a man in that it is known by its fruits, and it looks as if the Woman's Movement were doomed to the Nemesis that sooner or later overtakes all attempts to be one up on Mother Nature.

We skirt round the perilous argument that the sexes are physically unequal, and that in this particular the dice have been heavily loaded in man's favour. Many a domestic hearth provides ample evidence to the contrary. Nor is mere physique much to the point. What lies in the way of perfect achievement is spiritual obstruction, not material.

While it is true that we get an occasional metathesis

of the sexes, and men and women are born into a sex to which they do not properly belong, for all practical purposes the sex line is clear and unmistakable. Nor has the attempt to confuse it borne any but dead-sea fruit.

It is not the loss of the conventional picture of womanhood in its milder, more ministerial moods that we deplore. In this respect men have learnt to give as well as receive, and if the sex war has deprived woman of her wings, it has no less deprived man of certain god-like qualities with which a more degenerate age was wont to endow him. It has made him less heroic, but it has made him more human.

Such considerations as these, however, do not go to the root of the matter. It still remains a mystery how two beings that fulfil each other by the contact of opposites, that reach their highest self-expression by the polarity of sex, can be "equal." There are no products of the creative process less equal than man and woman. It is doubtless flattering to man's vanity that women should claim to be on his level, which at least implies a rise and not a descent in the scale of being, but this claim can never touch those qualities that belong to man as man and woman as woman, of which the gods themselves cannot dispossess them.

Nor can woman hope to revolutionize the architectonics of Nature by a mere approximation to the opposite sex, in which she becomes a bad imitation of man, and exchanges qualities that belong to her sex for those that do it violence.

The mere fact that woman can do some of the things that man does, whatever supererogatory merit she may claim for it, no more implies equality as between man and woman than the same principle does between a cat and a dog.

In both, the existence of common characteristics leaves the vast area of difference untouched, and it is safe to affirm that nothing will serve to bridge the gulf short of a new creation. But there are other things that have grown out of this revolt of graver import than the mere psychology of the matter. The young men of to-day are taking woman at her word, and are allowing her to reap the logical fruits of her doctrines, however bitter.

Thus we see men sitting in 'buses and the underground while women stand. Moreover, there has been a distinct decline in the standard of public courtesy.

Chivalry may be an exploded creed, but it added certain spiritual sanctions to life that no age can afford to dispense with altogether.

We do not wish to keep women on a throne that she can no longer occupy with comfort or dignity, but neither do we wish to see her becoming the mere hack of circumstance, or fighting a battle for which she has not been provided with the needful weapons. We love her too much for that, and would protect her from the worst consequences of her lapse from true femininity.

But let us be thankful that Nature and common sense have stepped in to provide the necessary reactions. The dust of battle has settled, and in the calm in which the whole question is now enveloped it is possible to take its true measure.

The cause itself was injured by the violence of its first exponents, mere excrescences of their sex to whom man was the malignant symbol of a tyranny he was blissfully unconscious of exercising. That women should have lost their lives in such a cause is an irony we do not care to contemplate. We can only take refuge in the reflection that, so long as man is man and woman woman, they will continue to develop along the lines that Nature has laid down; nor can the most violent revolutionary zeal avail to deflect them from the path which has led them throughout the ages to find their chief solace in a more perfect understanding of each other.

SEVEN DEADLY SINS OF WOMAN IN BUSINESS

BY ANNE W. ARMSTRONG

NOT long ago I called on a woman who is doing, as we women in business and professional life love to say, "a big piece of work." Her importance, achieved in an incredibly short period, was attested by the location of her New York offices and by the crowded reception-room in which I was asked to sit down and wait. "Could you state what you wished to see Miss A. about?" her secretary had asked in a rather toplofty manner. I could not, and this answer, strangely enough, seemed to give me precedence. I was conducted almost at once into Miss A.'s presence.

She sat at her desk, facing the door, a youngish person, unostentatiously dressed in a white blouse and dark skirt.

"Will you sit down?" she invited, though invited is too strong a term to express her impersonal, detached tone. I took a chair near the door, feeling I should not obtrude myself farther than was necessary, not, at any rate, until Miss A. completed what must be, I thought, an urgent report.

After pencilling a number of annotations on the sheets before her she tucked them away in a filing cabinet in the most deliberate manner and, seating herself at a typewriter, typed away for some ten minutes. Then she rang, told the messenger she would see Mr. So and So now, gave the man some instructions when he appeared, and dismissed him.

I was immensely impressed. "Is it possible," I thought to myself, "that we women in business are taking ourselves so seriously as all this?"

At last Miss A. glanced in my direction and, without the ghost of a smile, indicated she could give me her attention.

I stated my purpose in calling. I wanted advice. I was thinking of making a change and entering the business field in which she herself was a pioneer, though I must confess that during my long chilling wait I regretted the impulse which had brought me to see her.

To my amazement, Miss A. entered at once into my project, assuring me there was plenty of room for others besides herself, that the opportunities in the field were indeed almost limitless, and that there were particular reasons why it was one suited to women. She traced modestly her own beginnings, the discouragements she had met, the obstacles she had had to overcome, but insisted that the difficulties had been exaggerated and should prove no deterrent, even going so far as to offer to take me under her tutelage without charge. She was, it turned out, when it came to what she was doing, not only human but disposed to be thoroughly helpful.

As we shook hands in parting Miss A. suggested I should see a Miss Brown, I may call her, who was also (Miss A.'s words) "doing a big piece of work," in a related if not identical line. She offered to give me a note of introduction or to telephone that I was coming, but I declined both courteous offers, feeling, not without amusement, that I should have a better opportunity to observe what Miss Brown's "big piece of work" had done to her if I went unannounced. There was no anteroom, no opportunity to send in my card. At the end of a spacious, rather empty-looking office I saw a woman I judged to be Miss Brown, a forthright capable-appearing person, of what we used to designate as the school-mar'm type before the teaching profession came so largely into the hands of the pretty, girlish, smartly dressed young teachers of the present day. Miss Brown was explaining something in a thoroughgoing manner to a gentleman who was listening with meek attentiveness. Although it was about eleven in the morning and she gave no evidence of having just come in or being on the point of leaving, Miss Brown wore her hat. The fact of her wearing her hat in her office was, as I had learned years before, eloquent.

I paused inside the office door, waiting till it was convenient for Miss Brown to come forward or send the girl sitting at a typewriter near by. It was evident that Miss Brown was aware of my presence. She kept snapping her eyes in my direction as she went on with her discussion. The girl at the typewriter lifted her eyebrows in my direction once, with a vague inquiry in her otherwise expressionless face, then resumed her pounding.

I advanced cautiously, trying to make it apparent I did not wish to interrupt. "I'll wait," I had started to say to the girl at the typewriter in a low voice, "till Miss Brown—"

But Miss Brown had sprung from her chair and with a movement of shaking her flounces, though she had none to shake, challenged me, "What is it you want?"

"Well, not," I answered, suppressing a smile, "to sell you insurance—or anything else!"

Miss Brown stared at me for an instant, then taking a step forward, reiterated, "Well, *just* what is it you want?"

My reason for coming to see her proving not wholly unflattering, Miss Brown consulted her watch, her calendar, the girl at the typewriter. "Well, I can't

possibly see you to-day," she said finally. "I have an important conference at two o'clock, another at four. And to-morrow—" There were other important conferences on the morrow. "But day after, promptly at three, I might give you a few minutes."

Next morning, however, her secretary called me up to say that it would be inconvenient, after all, for Miss Brown to see me at the time appointed. "Miss Brown would prefer next week."

I failed to avail myself of this opportunity to see Miss Brown again, but I must say I blessed her memory. I shuddered to think how often I must have prated of "important conferences," and sought to give the impression that my time was more valuable than Judge Gary's.

II

The habit of taking ourselves too seriously grows, no doubt, out of taking our jobs too seriously. What every woman in a business organization knows is, that if a woman earns, say four thousand a year, she must make the showing of a man drawing ten. In our nervous anxiety to succeed, straining every faculty to the uttermost, we overlook the part our lighter, the more purely feminine side of our nature might play. Women in business are constantly surprised, not to say shocked, to find how much time men "waste," how much frivolous interchange goes on among them. If business men work hard, in spurts, they play not only at lunch time and on the links, but all through the day apply to their toil the lubricant of agreeable intercourse with one another. In a word, they have made of their business life, if not actually an exciting, at least a pleasurable affair instead of a sad necessity. Gossip and jokes enliven their most important councils and a raconteur among them possesses a valuable business asset.

Yet we women in business are afraid to take time to be gracious, almost afraid even to smile. I do not refer, of course, to the vast number of girls and women who are in business only for a season, till they marry or the family situation improves, but to that smaller, though ever-increasing, proportion who, either through necessity or choice, expect to make business a career. It is those who work so feverishly. The business world may conceivably grow to be a far more beautiful and joyous place than it is to-day. Yet they add neither beauty nor joy. They rattle the dry bones. They increase what is already, with all men's efforts to freshen it, the too great aridity of the business atmosphere.

Nor is business alone damaged thereby.

A business woman, herself a shining example of success in whatever she undertakes, remarked one day:

"I wonder if we women in business are not overreaching the mark and failing, where we fail, not because we are unintelligent or untrained, but because we are too much in earnest, too conscientious, and above all, too hard-worked."

"The great fault of women," she added pungently, "is excess of virtue. Those who strike the happy medium are really the most successful. When we women play more, we shall create more."

Another business acquaintance comes to my mind whom I met first soon after her graduation from one of our leading women's colleges and entrance into her first position. Brilliantly endowed, she was a lovely creature at that time, wore simple but becoming clothes, was sparkling, responsive, generally charming. I heard of her from time to time and after some years met her again. She was dowdy, ill-groomed, tense in her manner, and self-centered to the last degree. She still gave evidence of what is termed a "steel-trap mind," talked fluently and ably about her work and the problems involved, but was interested in nothing else in the world and had lost every vestige of her former attractiveness.

A masculine associate in the business house where she started her business career, in discussing the change, said to me, "We all admired her so much. She was a girl of rare promise. But we saw it coming a long while ago. Her gayety and enthusiasm grew to be sharpness, then hardness, and now it is—well, I might say, hysteria. And the sad part is, she seems to think this furious attention she gives things, the high-speed, ruthless manner she has developed, are aids to business success.

"As a matter of fact," he went on to say, "I happen to know she was asked to resign from one position and shut out from another for which her name had been considered, solely because in her ardor to make good she has developed a personality few care to encounter."

III

In taking our jobs so solemnly, we have, of course, little time to indulge in sports or social diversions of any kind. Largely unawakened, as a class, to the fact that it is the quality rather than the quantity of service we render that counts in business, in order to give it heaped-up and running-over measure of ourselves, we let our tennis go by the board and only the most audacious among us dare go in for golf. I played golf myself for years before I entered business, but have never touched my mid-iron or brassy since. We seem to think that we can keep physically fit by no more exercise than the daily gentle whirl in our office chair or a little marching about indoors from floor to floor. At most we allow ourselves the tame diversion of driving back and forth to business, when walking might furnish a certain exhilaration to our sedentary day. We bring to business exuberant health and spirits, and more often than not in a few years grow seedy, stodgy, or obese, haggard and with frayed nerves, as the case may be.

Being constituted as we are, we business women need to give our health even more intelligent attention than business men do theirs. Not that they, with the dietary crimes they daily commit, their high blood pressure and chronic sleeplessness just when they reach the big job, are any too good as guides. But what we do, as women, is to trifle even more flagrantly with the mechanism that keeps us going.

I mentioned one day to the president of a big business that a fine young woman in his employ had recently been committed to a state institution for observation.

"Miss R. is the third," I said—not accusingly, but as a matter of interest—"that's been committed within a short time, all of them ten to twelve years in your employ. Did you know that?"

"What is the diagnosis in these cases?" he quizzed, after a pause.

"Overwork, I believe."

"Nonsense!" he said. "Nonsense! Mighty few people, in this company, anyway, work too hard. But a lot of them don't have enough fun. That's the trouble. There isn't enough fun in business itself except in a very few jobs, like your own," he laughed, "to furnish the requirements of the human system. And yet these humdrum deadly things have got to be done. The only solution I see is to fill up on fun of some sort outside. And if you knew the inwardness of these cases you speak of," he went on, "you'd find they're simply cases of starved lives. It's not what people do in business that hurts them. It's what they don't do outside. It's the reason," he ended, "I'm in favor of decreasing working hours as rapidly as is feasible. Most people have got to find satisfaction for their human cravings outside of business, and they need time to do so."

The president was right, I found out later, at least in regard to two of the cases in question. These young women, when the prospect of marriage had receded, had narrowed themselves zealously to their narrow routine jobs, in the hope, no doubt, of finding there a compensatory interest. Not only had they

had no social life to speak of, even less had they attempted to keep abreast of events, read fine fiction or poetry, cultivate an appreciation of nature or the arts. In a word, they had drunk scarcely a drop from any of the great wells available for human refreshment during years and years of pouring over columns of figures and of filling customers' orders. But columns of figures and customers' orders will not, it appears, yield all that the mind and body of women in business (being yet women) need to keep them healthy. Business houses abound in nice girls past their first youth who are growing a trifle "queer" as the result of a too steady and unmixed business diet.

It is so easy, I admit, to sink into a rut, to consider we have time for self-cultivation only along the lines of business, and as tired business women to develop even more childish and barren taste in what entertains us in our hours of relaxation than has the tired business man. Let anyone who challenges the truth of this last statement secure the yearly program of almost any one of the innumerable business and professional women's clubs that have sprung up all over the country.

The American business man has long held the world's record of being, to people of *esprit*, the dullest of dull companions. Observe him on one of the present popular Mediterranean tours, where he is conveyed, without having to exercise his higher cerebral centres, from the Casino at Monte Carlo to the Parthenon, from the Church of the Holy Sepulchre to the Great Pyramid of Gizeh. Observe, and with compassion rather than gibes, how he seeks, and is sought by only his own; how he is happy and at home with himself only when he resumes his endless discussion of prices and production costs, or what he believes may affect one or the other. It was when waiting together at Port Said to cross the Canal that I asked one of these captains of American industry how he liked Athens. "Athens. Athens. Oh, yes, I got the best shoeshine there I've had on this trip!"

But let the American business man take note he now has a rival. We women in business propose to become even more dull, more thoroughly confined, if possible, to one subject of conversation. Why, however, should we not leave him his precedence in at least this one province? The more so, that we may again be on the wrong track.

Very recently a woman in New York was elevated to one of the highest positions any woman in business has yet attained. It is, I think, of real significance that interviewers who seek her in her office find, and apparently are surprised to find, a vase of pansies on her desk and a Martha Washington sewing-table in one corner. The fact that she has not permitted that side of her nature which flowers in pansies and sewing-tables to wither and die has helped her, I do not doubt in the least, to her present high post. She has been, according to all accounts, a very busy business person since she entered business fresh from High School more than twenty years ago. But she has taken time on her way to becoming president of a great corporation to read, to ride, to shoot. She has even taken time for the humanly enriching adventure of matrimony.

IV

In striking contrast to this picture, a slim dark-eyed woman, no longer young, of distinguished bearing, and with every evidence of an exceptionally intense nature comes up before me. For convenience I shall speak of her as Miss Black. She entered the huge business organization where she still works till late every night and on Sundays as well at a time when the presence of women in a business organization, except in routine jobs, was far more keenly resented than it is to-day. Being perceptive in some directions beyond the common, she soon perceived that any open move on

her part to secure control of the important department of the business with which she was connected would be defeated. She developed cunning subterranean methods of securing her ends, became in time a master-strategist. She was not primarily concerned with outwitting men, not especially antagonistic to them as a sex; from my observation and knowledge of her, was never overweeningly ambitious for recognition and reward. But she craved contact with the most intimate affairs of the business. All the tremendous store of emotion she had to bestow, diverted from other possible objects, she bestowed on it. She loved the business for itself, everything about it, from bottom to top— all its dustiest details. She invested it with the charm with which she might have invested a lover, guarded its interests with the fierce devotion she might have given a husband and children.

To-day, after thirty-five years of this, business has entered into her very bones and tissue. She eats and drinks, wakes and dreams business. Meddling in every business department, she magnifies trifling business errors into monstrous proportions. She never consents to take a holiday, unless of the briefest, and when she hears of an associate running off to Europe or elsewhere for rest and recreation, it is certain to draw from her some such ironic comment as, "How nice! I never find time myself for such junkets!" If she does take a few days off and goes to some city, she cannot enjoy the theater, opera, or even shopping, for rushing back to her hotel to see whether "long distance" wants her. Poor woman, she is as restless and unhappy, in fact, on these occasional jaunts as a mother who has left a small child at home and fears it may tumble into the fire or swallow a fishbone. She feels she never for an instant can take her fingers off the pulse of the organization, and when confined to her home from frequent illness, notwithstanding her doctor's orders, constantly dictates to a girl at her bedside, only stopping to talk over the telephone to this executive or the other.

Miss Black has given herself unstintingly to business through a lifetime, given her youth and maturity. In return? Well, she has seen man after man pass her, often attain his rank through her coaching, while she is subsequently expected to report to him, a man it may be without a tenth of her knowledge of the business but drawing thrice her pay. She has always been too proud to fight—as men frequently have to—for a proper stipend, but has brooded without doubt over the fact that one has never been proffered her. She is an embittered joyless woman, whose barbed tongue scourges associates, paralyzes subordinates, and diminishes or even destroys their usefulness to her.

Yet possessing more than ordinary attractions of mind and person, with a generous and ardent nature and superior breeding, Miss Black held every possibility within herself of a rich rounded life, to say nothing of an openly recognized, highly remunerated position in the great organization she has served.

We have long been familiar with the effects when men have deified business. It is only lately, through figures that arrest our attention here and there in the business field, we have had opportunity to study what happens when we women prostrate ourselves before the same jealous god and allow devotion to become obsession—a sin, I maintain, even at the risk of being charged with distinguishing sins that do not differ—that differs at least by degree until it takes on the guise of a separate and signal vice.

V

Granted Miss Black is an exceptional case—we are more familiar with this figure in the making than as a finished product, verging on the pathologic—there is, on the other hand, nothing at all unusual in the spectacle of women in business sharply antagonistic—as

sharply as they dare be—to their men associates. Every business woman, doubtless every business man, recognizes the type.

These are usually, like Miss Black, women of superior ability, and perhaps have played brave parts in the feminist movement. It is for the honor of the sex, rather than as an individual matter, they feel it incumbent upon them to demonstrate at every turn that the feminine brain per se is in no wise inferior to the masculine. There is something gallant in this attitude, and I should be the last to charge it against them except that their gallantry stops too often with their own sex.

There was a Miss Barnard with whom I had frequent contact. She was one of those "fierce athletic girls" Walt Whitman predicted for the republic, superb physique, vitality, and what I may call a lordly air and even stride. No staying overhours for her! Miss Barnard dispatched her business responsibilities with lightning rapidity, had plenty of leisure for horseback riding, tramps, music—whatever she chose. In addition, she was a first-rate administrator, respected and liked by a large corps of girl assistants because of the patience and justice she exhibited in her relation to them as supervisor.

With the men she dealt with daily it was altogether different.

Miss Barnard once confessed to me that the greatest surprise of her life was in finding so many muddle-headed men in business. She had supposed, before she entered it, that every man who attained any business prominence whatever was mentally keen, as she expressed it. She had once looked with awe on every one of the masculine figures imposingly arrayed at the speaker's table at a Chamber of Commerce dinner. She now knew better. "Nothing," she said, "raises my gorge like seeing these little men in business give themselves such big airs—and purely on the ground of their sex, their historic position as males." Miss Barnard delighted, in fact, as I more than once witnessed, in taking them down.

But she paid a high price for this delight. She had made the mistake of letting the little men, as well as larger men, know how she felt, and she had failed to take masculine solidarity into account. It was impossible to get Miss Barnard's salary raised beyond a certain point, or to secure her promotion to one of several higher posts that yawned for a person of just her capacity. The men in a position to determine these matters, while freely acknowledging her competence, without exception heartily disliked her. "She's too smart, that's what's the matter with Miss Barnard!" one executive said of her scornfully.

It was not, of course, excess of brains that had damaged Miss Barnard in this executive's estimation. It was her well-known habit of showing up some man in the organization as a dolt on a business problem she herself could grasp with ease.

That there was another side to Miss Barnard was proved when one day, to the surprise of everybody, her engagement was announced to a business associate, a man of character, and like herself, able, but a man she had by chance been thrown with socially, giving him opportunity to discover engaging qualities she had never thought it worth while to add to her business equipment.

Above every other, an instance stands out to me of a woman even more highly endowed than Miss Barnard, a woman of superlative mind, with broad outside interests added to a positive genius for business. I do not cite this woman as a case of failure. She would lead a full life if she never saw the inside of a business house again. Her relationships with both men and women outside of business are ideal. And the one thing, I am convinced, that has prevented her from reaching as high a station in the business world as any woman has yet attained, is the technic she employs in her business relationships—relationships with masculine associates, to be explicit.

True, her technic is tied up with her honesty, with some of her sturdiest attributes. She has been unwilling to practice in business those arts which no woman who aspired to social leadership would dream of disdaining. She has failed to establish a camaraderie with her masculine associates, at once gay, dignified, impersonal, and perfectly possible for her, had she agreed to its importance.

The man who sits beside us at dinner may be a frightful bore, but quite apart from any humanitarian impulse, the last thing our social training permits us to do is to give him a hint that we are aware of his dullness. On the contrary, we exert ourselves very particularly, help him score wherever he can.

Why do we feel that the fine art of making people happy about themselves is so out of place in business? Certainly we can not overlook much longer the number of women with social background—I can count a dozen in New York City alone, without stopping to think—who have gone into business, and as a result, not of "pull," but of actual performance, have quickly outdistanced business sisters who could, as they say, run rings around them in business knowledge.

The thing we women in business are prone to do is to look on our male associates as rivals, instead of as partners. Let me be plain. I do not charge this iniquity to others more than to myself. I know very well I should come up and take my place on the mourners' bench. We should, no doubt, be judged rather leniently on this score. Most of us have had a fairly hard time of it to gain any recognition at all. We are still unable to dissemble our satisfaction in business triumphs, however small. But what we're apt to forget is, that it's a good deal of a fight for the man, too, who gets anywhere in business; that he is faced with many, if not all the obstacles that impede our own progress; has as much, nay more, at stake than we have. Leaving out of consideration family responsibilities, which nevertheless, broadly speaking, are heavier than our own, failure to succeed in business spells ignominy to him. To us, as yet, it spells nothing of the sort.

There are, to be sure, often those airs of his, those airs which Miss Barnard found so insufferable.

But are we, after all, patient enough with the men? Consider their predicament! When we women invaded business we invaded one of their last strongholds. Heaven knows we were not invited, except to do monotonous routine work they wished to escape themselves. We came of our own volition. And the average business man is still smarting under our all-too conspicuous presence in a house he thought he had built for himself. We must give him time. More than one business man still has the feeling that business—in its higher reaches—is no place for women. More than one doubtless shares the feeling which an executive expressed in referring to the rapidly increasing number of women who are succeeding in business positions formerly regarded as incapable of being administered except through masculine wisdom. "When it comes to taking orders from a woman, I'd as soon," he said, laughing, but in all earnestness, "take orders from a Chinaman or a negro."

It behooves us to be indulgent!

VI

It was this same frank and merry executive who reminded me that women in business talk too much—not gossip, far from it.

If American business men talk only of business when they leave it, during business hours, ironically enough, they are willing and eager to listen to a little sprightly chatter on almost any subject under the sun, provided it has nothing to do with business. They have, in short, as I have previously hinted, developed a social art of sorts under the business rooftree. What they will not tolerate, from my experience, is one of

those lengthy disquisitions we women sometimes seek to deliver, in order to impress them with our seriousness of purpose or our acquaintance with the field we represent. A sage bit of counsel given me when I entered business by a woman wise in the ways of the business world was, "Be brief! Boil down every business matter you have to present to the fewest possible words."

"They wear you out, telling you things you don't need to know," the good-natured executive referred to insisted now, still laughing. "There's Miss G. in the Purchasing Department, an excellent woman, I admit, but—" He held up his hands. "I flee her like the plague!"

"But business abounds," I countered, "in long-winded men."

"Oh, yes! But don't forget," he warned, "that your sex is still on sufferance in business. You can't afford to imitate quite all our vices."

VII

And I'm not sure but that, after all, unfortunate as is our drift when we regard ourselves as men's rivals and competitors, the deadliest of all our sins is imitation of man.

Time was, only a few years ago, when a woman proposing to make business or any of the serious professions her career thought she must don masculine attire. Few went the lengths of Dr. Mary Walker, but many adopted severely cut suits, masculine collars and cravats, cultivated a brusque address, and even adopted stentorian tones. It is almost as hard now to find one of these near-men among our thousands upon thousands of business and professional women as to find the proverbial needle in the haystack. When we do come upon one, chances are we discover a rather wistful example of thwarted ambition. We have learned at least one lesson: that imitation of man, when it comes to our clothes and our manners, does not necessarily lead to business and professional triumphs, and may as likely as not defeat them.

But most of us are still striving, either unconsciously or through deliberate self-interest, to absorb and imitate the business man's point of view, though it seems, sadly enough, that we play the sedulous ape more often to his weaknesses or his hardnesses, his prejudices and his limitations, than to his virtues.

I have rarely heard any business man so blunt as a woman executive who recently remarked that she had no time to listen to employees' grievances and had delegated a subordinate to hear all the "sob stuff." I was especially distressed in this instance because, so it happened, I had been instrumental in securing her job for her. I had recommended her to her present "boss," under the impression that she would put more humanity into a group of factories where the handling of workers had been along the old bullying, but no longer so successful lines.

What she did was promptly to fall into the worst defects she found in her new environment. Though her higher education should have made her proof against such hysteria, she at once began to echo loud and empty talk about "Bolshevism." This must have been foreign to her nature. Surely it was a betrayal of her scholarly training.

It takes no mean courage, I may add, to express in the business world one's feminine faith. It is hard to admit having ideals in a realm where ideals are looked on so frequently with suspicion. I remember that in so trifling a matter as taking in hand a bleak office-building lunchroom that looked as if it belonged to a penal institution, introducing fern-boxes and cretonnes, I was jeered from more than one quarter. "What's this, the Ritz, you're giving us?"

These women jobs are, all the same, ours to do, I believe. It was his woman secretary, I have understood, who introduced tea into the office of the hard-pressed president of one of New York's great banking houses. I suspect she was twitted, that it was dubbed "British side" when she imported this admirable custom for use in an American business house. But *she* knew what the president and some of his associates needed—a breathing space by way of the tea-caddy just before the final conference each afternoon.

A highly temperamental business executive, who is regarded as the foremost man in his line in this country, said of his secretary, a winsome young woman, "I've had more accurate secretaries, in the matter of shorthand, but upon my word, I wish I could pay Miss W. ten thousand a year! She's worth it. It's the atmosphere she creates around her. I don't hesitate to say she increases my output."

But so few women seem to see that it's the woman in them, above everything else, that business needs—needs, frankly, more than in mere matters of tea, cretonne, and flowers on the desk. More than one woman close to a big executive and enjoying his respect has abrogated her ancient right to warn as well as comfort.

The motto that so long fed our complacency—"All's right with the world," is out of date. It is a certainty that all's not right with the business world. But it is equally certain that all's not wrong. The amazing thing is, that it's no more wrong than it is. Both sexes are highly involved, directly and indirectly, yet the point of view of only one sex has entered thus far, to any appreciable extent, into the conduct of business. Is it too unreasonable to hold that neither society at large nor the business world itself will profit greatly by our entrance into it, until we women, no longer content solely as understudies, shall offer, at whatever hazard, our own contribution—all we have gained through our special inheritance and experience—until we seek to supplement, rather than duplicate the parts in business that men play?

29

THE PROBLEM OF WOMEN IN INDUSTRY

ETHEL M. JOHNSON

Assistant Commissioner, Massachusetts Department of Labor and Industries

WHEN we speak of the problem of women in industry, we usually have reference to the conditions under which women work, their hours of labor, night work and wages; the effect of these conditions upon the health and welfare of women; their social effect; and the measures taken to protect women from injurious conditions of employment in their own interest and in the interest of society.

We gain some idea of the importance of the problem from the number involved. If we use industry in its broadest sense, embracing all forms of gainful occupation, then the problem of women in industry numerically is the problem of eight or nine million women in the country as a whole.

Whether the existence of this great army of women wage earners should be a source for pride in the growing economic independence of women or grave concern as to the future, depends upon much more than the mere numbers represented. Before we can form an intelligent opinion on the subject, we need to know something of the kind of work these women are doing, and something of the workers themselves.

Are they mature, responsible women, equipped through education and training for earning a livelihood? Or are they, many of them, young girls and inexperienced women who have been precipitated into industry with little or no preparation, and with little knowledge of what is before them? And what of the work they have entered? Are they in skilled employments, in positions of responsibility, awarded adequate compensation? Or are they largely unskilled workers, receiving in many instances, wages inadequate to meet the needs of healthful living?

We can get a general answer to some of these questions, enough perhaps to enable us to sketch a composite picture. In Massachusetts, for example, nearly one-third of the working women are foreign born. Approximately two-fifths are under twenty-five years of age. One out of every five is married. Nearly half of all the women wage earners in the country—approximately 3,500,000—are employed in industrial pursuits, in factories and workshops, in mercantile and mechanical establishments. In some of the manufacturing states the proportion is much greater. It is these women, rather than those engaged in professional service, in business for themselves or in managerial positions who constitute the problem of women in industry.

Concretely, this problem is the

30

problem of the girl in the five-and-ten-cent store, of the woman who irons shirts all day in a steam laundry; and the widow with small children who goes out at night to scrub the marble corridors in an office building.

Very few of these women are organized. Economists have estimated the number of women in the United States that are organized as 390,000.[1] That is less than one out of every twenty women wage earners. Many of the women workers, because of their youth, their inexperience, and because of home demands, can not be organized. Men, through collective bargaining, have been able to control to some extent the conditions of their employment, to limit their hours of labor and to raise their wages. Women, lacking organization, have been helpless in this respect until special legislation has been enacted for their protection.

In Massachusetts, before the 48-hour law was passed, and before all the occupations now covered by legislation limiting hours were included, the State Board of Labor found women employed in certain occupations from seventy to eighty hours a week. Before the Minimum Wage Law was enacted, the investigations made by the Special Commission on Minimum Wage Boards disclosed the fact that thousands of women and girls were working for less than $5.00 a week.

Although conditions h a v e improved since then, many women still receive low wages. In 1920, when the cost of living was higher than it has ever been, more than 12,000 adult women in Massachusetts industries worked for less than $12.00 a week for full-time employment. It is only when we try to translate such wages into terms of room rent, food, carfare, clothing, doctor and dentist bills, that we get their real significance.

Women's wages are still far below the wages of men. For the manufacturing industries in industrial states the weekly wages of women are approximately half those of men. Although the organization of men and the lack of organization of women doubtless contributes to this result, it is not the only factor. Nor is the situation primarily due to the failure on the part of employers to give equal pay for equal work. To a large extent the work that women are performing in the factories and workshops is not the same work that men are performing.

Women are employed largely at simple machine processes that require not so much skill as dexterity and patience, nimble fingers and a docile mind willing to give attention to a single monotonous process, such as placing a bit of metal on a die, releasing a lever, and repeating the operation again and again; watching myriad strands of thread being wound on rows of whirling spindles, mending the broken threads, removing the filled spools and doing this over and over, day after day and week after week. The heaviest work, the most hazardous work in industry is performed by men. This is one reason for the difference in wages. Another reason is that much of the more skilled work in industry is performed

---

[1] These figures are for 1920 before the general exodus of women from some of the industries entered during the war. The figures today are probably nearer 300,000.

by men. This is partly a matter of training.

When we provide, through our public schools, as extensive opportunities for trade training and executive training for women and girls as for men and boys—when we offer schools for forewomen as well as for foremen—then we may hope to see women advancing more generally to higher positions in industry. As long, however, as we are content to have them enter industry without preparation, or with just a smattering of training—just enough machine work to enable them to perform a simple, repetitive process—so long we shall have women and girls thronging the lower levels in industry and competing against one another for substandard wages.

Before we can secure adequate training to fit women for responsible positions in industry, however, we must secure a change in the attitude of the public and in the minds of women themselves with regard to the importance of providing as thorough and serious preparation for work in the case of girls as in the case of boys.

Within the last generation the number of women gainfully employed outside the home has increased more than 100 per cent, while the number of women in the entire population has increased only 70 per cent. A significant fact in connection with this change is the increase in the number of married women who are entering industry. For many women the factory job is becoming a permanent job, a job in which the single woman remains, a job to which the married woman returns with the care of a household added.

Yet, the popular conception—and the conception that is still largely reflected in the schools is that woman's work outside the home is of purely temporary nature, a stop-gap to fill a vacant year or two before the Prince Charming appears. We need romance, of course, but we should not permit it to blind us to the economic facts.

This then is the situation. Women in industry, to a large extent, are crowding the unskilled and semi-unskilled employments. They are doing this because they lack the training for skilled work and because little opportunity for such training is afforded. Their wages are low, because they are unskilled, and because they are unorganized. And the fact that they are unorganized and that it is very difficult to organize them makes them helpless in controlling the conditions of their employment.

The ballot does not aid them much as yet. For one thing it is too recent an acquisition. Then, too, many of these women are young, too young to vote; and many of them are immigrant women, with little knowledge of American customs and American standards. Yet their sons and daughters are the citizens of tomorrow. And their ideals or lack of ideals will have a definite part in shaping the future of the country.

Whatever the ultimate solution of the problem—if there is an ultimate solution—whether it will come through effective organization or through adequate technical training or extensive programs of Americanization work, or through a combination of all, the fact remains that at the present time the only protection available against industrial exploitation for thousands of working women is that afforded by the laws regulating their hours of labor, restricting night work, and establishing a minimum level below which their wages may not fall.

Such laws have been secured only after years of struggle. They have had to meet the opposition which every attempt to place human interest above immediate financial interests has always encountered. But merely to have good laws on our statute books is not sufficient. In the case of labor legislation more than any other form of legislation eternal vigilance is essential.

The supporters of these measures sometimes nod; but the opponents never sleep. Attacks on the constitutionality of labor legislation for the protection of women and children are made in the courts. This was the action in the case of the Federal Child Labor Law, the Minimum Wage Law of the District of Columbia, and of Arizona and the Oregon Hours of Labor Law, and the New York Night Work Law.

Attacks are made through efforts to curtail appropriations necessary for effective enforcement. Most insidious of all, however, are the indirect attacks through attempts to secure the appointment of unsympathetic officials to administer and enforce these laws.

Although the strongest opposition to protective legislation naturally comes from employing interests, it is not confined to these. There is included among the opponents, a group of well-meaning women whose enthusiasm for equality exceeds their knowledge of industrial conditions, industrial history and industrial legislation. These women, if they could, would sweep aside all of the special protective legislation in their effort to achieve what seems to them a short-cut to equality, but what in reality would prove a long and rocky road to disillusionment.

The task of inducing sane and intelligent thought on the subject of women in industry, and of securing fair treatment for the measures providing protection for women is one which requires the assistance of all unselfish and public-spirited men and women.

EQUALITY OF WOMAN WITH MAN: A MYTH

A CHALLENGE TO FEMINISM

BY JOHN MACY

MERELY to buttonhole the Woman Movement for a moment and ask it a few questions is to bring down upon one's head a cataract of abusive and irrelevant retorts, to be accused of oldfogyism, of misogyny, of disappointment in love, of wearing the scars, or the bleeding wounds, of the pecking hen. To give tentative answers to the questions, to suggest that woman has insuperable limitations, natural inferiorities is to be charged with the heinous crime of being a "mere man," or to be dismissed with a derisive jibe as impertinent, though probably not so witty, as Max Beerbohm's punning description of the suffragette parade as the "army of the unenjoyed."

Well, this article is the view of a mere man, because a man writes it. Everything written must be written from the point of view of a man or of a woman, since, obviously, very few neutrals and children write for publication. I may say, however, that much of my information and emphatic corroboration of my opinions come from women, their conversation and their published writings. In discussing this article and a possible book with several women of various social grades and ages, staid matrons, flappers, cocktail-drinking radicals, school teachers, working women, intellectual idlers, home-bodies, and ladies of the world, I found to my surprised delight that almost all the women with whom I talked approved my ideas and were eager to pour oil upon my typewriter. This attitude could not be wholly accounted for as female flattery of the male parading a pet idea. Our sisters do not like one another. It is not simply a matter of jealousy or envy, for many of my charming friends have beauty or talent or social position which lifts them above mean rivalry. Perhaps some of them have a sense of superiority. At any rate there is an intrasexual antagonism, a critical hostility among women more sharply and dentally feline than the animosity and irritable friction between the sexes.

It was no mere man but a lovely, wise, and fully emancipated woman, a musician and teacher, who after a discussion of her girl pupils and her older contemporaries, concluded with the desperate generality "Oh, women are a mess!" And when I was searching for a word which should analogously match "feminism," it was a brilliant woman, a talented sculptor and poet, who coined the word "Masculism," a word which is not in the dictionary but I dare say will be in the next editions. If I am making an attack, there is an amusing irony in the fact that some of the explosive shells are being fed into my battery by fair hands.

But I am not making an attack. I am issuing a challenge to the feminist movement, as it is at the present hour, to give an account of itself, to indicate clearly its future course and ambition, to make an honest inventory of its powers to go forward to some definite destination worth striving toward. And I am also proposing the development of a counter corrective movement to be called "Masculism"—lady, I thank thee for that word!—a Society for the Prevention of Cruelty to Men. This new movement or cult will seek to restrain the wild women from losing themselves in the woods and perhaps to help them along some desirable road.

"Masculism" is not misogyny, not woman-hatred. That is as insane, as morbid as misanthropy, the hatred of man as a sex or of man as Mankind. All we have to work with is men and women, and all we who are past redemption have to work for is children, the men and women of to-morrow. Human nature may be feeble stuff, but it is the best we have; and most intelligent healthy-minded people seem to believe that, though it contains capacities for disastrous error, it contains also latent unrealized possibilities for good, and that some of its faults are transitory, remediable, eradicable.

II

Let us see what the woman movement has accomplished up to date. During the past fifty years America, and most European countries except the Latin, have witnessed the progress, the partial triumph, of Feminism. Women have won victories which every intelligent person must applaud or at least concede without blind reactionary opposition.

Equal suffrage is now an old story in thirty countries, America, Germany, Russia, the Scandinavian nations, England, though in England the equality is not quite equal, since women may not vote until they are thirty, a manifest injustice which progressive men and women are trying, with certain ultimate success, to remove. The practical political question, the answer to which would require a longer article than this, is what good the vote is doing women and what good are they doing with the vote?

Aside from the franchise, and much more important, certain economic and social disabilities which women suffered for centuries have been rectified, largely through the efforts of enlightened men. There was a time, a long time, when, whether a woman could or could not call her soul her own, she was absolutely forbidden to call her property her own. And the man had exclusive proprietary rights in her children. In Italy as late as 1917 a woman had no free and clear title to her houses and lands. To sell an estate she had to make the transaction through her husband, brother, or other male representative. In almost every country to-day the man's right in the woman's property, the "courtesy" right, is balanced by the dower right of the woman in the man's property; it is a fifty-fifty game, and it may even be that in some states the woman's hold on real estate, especially on the homestead, is stronger than the man's. Many men take advantage of the position which women now enjoy in this relation by putting their property in the wife's name. The legal status of women throughout the world is a vast subject which has not been thoroughly studied, so far as I can discover, perhaps because the status is confused and is rapidly changing. It would be a good subject for one of the new sisterhood of barristers to investigate while she is waiting for clients.

Other ancient disabilities to which women have been subjected are enumerated by that splendid woman, Ellen Key, the leader of feminism in Sweden, who died recently after fifty years of incessant labor for the emancipation of women—and of mankind. These are some of the worst of the iniquities now happily abolished or at least mitigated:

The double standard of morals as affecting divorce, the woman having no way of freeing herself from the errant man, the man being able to put away the sinning wife.

The right of the man to collect his wife's wages from her employer.

The control of the public schools by

men and the ineligibility of women to serve on boards of education.

The disbarring of women from the higher education and the learned professions and arts, and also from the better-paid salaried positions and independent business enterprises.

The special obedience and subservience of women to clerical authority.

The literal application of the vow of obedience to the husband.

The indignity and belittlement of the single woman.

Marriage as the only means of livelihood for the woman without property; enforced married or unmarried prostitution.

The practical necessity of lying and cajoling to win consideration and comfort.

The slavery of unregulated child-bearing, and bondage to housework, partly due to lack of modern conveniences.

The uncritical acceptance of the superior wisdom of man.

The taboo upon wholesome exercises and athletics as "unladylike."

The absolute authority of the father in selecting a husband for his daughter.

The strict surveillance of courtship and lack of opportunity for young women to try out acquaintanceships, learn something about the characters of their lovers, and follow their hearts.

The premium placed upon frivolity and weakness instead of on serious thinking and strength of mind and body.

Prescribed ignorance of the things a young woman most vitally needs to know.

The taken-for-granted position of the daughter, as well as the wife, as a household servant.

The unquestioned right of the man to indulge in physical abuse of wife, daughter, and for that matter, of the son too.

The ruthless outlawing and persecution of the unmarried mother (in which as often as not the older women were more cruel than the men).

Complete misunderstanding of the nervous system and emotional life of women, due largely to the backwardness of physiology, psychology, and medical science.

Rule-of-thumb mode and code of life with no consideration for the woman as an individual, a person, a special case— a lumping codification that restricted men as well as women.

The misapplication, misdirection, and general squelching of woman's natural abilities and capacities for self-expression and service.

The assumption that the sexual relation was primarily intended for the gratification of men.

The conversion of woman's passion and rebellious desire for more freedom into ingrowing hatred and meanness of spirit.

The aggravation of sex antagonism and the discouragement of sex co-operation and mutual support and fulfillment.

The subordination of maternal authority to paternal, with a resulting depression of woman's wisdom and power to rear her children and a consequent maleducation of the succeeding generation.

The wearing out of a woman's body before the fullest possible development of her intellectual life.

And more items of the same debasing kind. Truly a formidable list of crimes against nature and civilization. No matter what the virtues of the "good old times" may have been, nobody, not the most stupid conservative and praiser of the past, will wish to return to these outrageous conditions (some of which in a measure still prevail), conditions which inspired John Stuart Mill's magnificent essay on *The Subjection of Women* and Ibsen's "Doll's House," and a vast literature, expository, argumentative, and artistic, of revolt against hoary tyrannies. It is to be remarked, by the way, that the greatest expressions of Feminism, the most eloquent and effective pleas for emancipation of women, have come not from women but from men, though women have made some noble and imaginative contributions.

37

III

No, we shall not go back, we must go forward. But forward in what direction? Whither are we, not drifting but driving? It seems to some of us that the woman movement is running loose without guidance or clearly foreseen purpose, and that such freedom as has been won is in danger of being abused, or frittered away or degraded into pell-mell aimless license and undisciplined lawlessness.

When the clamor of women for the vote and other rights began to swell in irresistible volume, some of the arguments for and against their demands were a maudlin riot of ignorance, unreason, and misrepresentation of fact. For example, opponents of woman suffrage contended that woman has a weaker intellect than man, is not instructed in public affairs, and is not "logical," but is swayed by her emotions. As if millions of the male mutts who vote were not hopelessly ignorant, indifferent to the fundamental political and economic issues, incapable of reading and understanding a clear statement of fact or a sound argument! Watch the idiots spoiling their hats, listen to their bellowing at the bogus oratory of a politician whose election will not do them or the public the slightest good, or may perchance promise a fat job. That argument against votes for women is fatuous while the ancient Latin proverb still holds good: *Quam parva sapientia regitur mundus*—with how little wisdom the world is governed. Even if women were all morons who did not know the difference between a Republican and a Democrat (there isn't any), they would still have a right to a voice in the government under which they must live and to which they contribute with their labor or their money. And such an argument is equally imbecile when directed against any effort of women to enlarge their opportunities, to secure a free, fair, and open field of endeavor and enterprise.

On the other hand, some of the claims of the advocates of votes for women were preposterous and untrue to biological fact. Some women maintained that their sex was as a whole equal in capacity, and the same kind of capacity, to the male sex. And the winning of the vote seems to have confirmed the blind zealots in this pitiful fallacy. Hark to Miss Alice Paul, Chairman of the Executive Committee of the National Woman's Party, as her words are quoted in the New York *Times:*

"The Woman's Party has continued to emphasize that it opposes protective laws for women, such as minimum wage laws, believing that such measures presuppose an inferiority that the party does not acknowledge exists."

Let me hasten to say that some of Miss Paul's remarks and some of the items in the program of the Woman's Party are intelligent. But the idea embodied in the quoted sentence is a pathetic delusion. If it represents the attitude of the Woman's Party, then the Party is deplorably misguided. The inferiority *does* exist. Women do need special protection in the matter of wages and hours of labor. They are handicapped by the maternal function and by periodic illnesses associated with that function. All workers need whatever protection they can secure by organization on the economic field with the support of such legislation as they can compel or persuade political authority to enact and enforce. And men and women workers must stand together to get what they can. But men have a better chance, more strength singly and in union, than women have to fend for themselves without the aid of political action. The program of another female organization, the National League of Women Voters, recognizes, not the inferiority, but the special needs, the physiological burden of women, by demanding "the extension of the period of operation of the Maternity and Infancy act with adequate appropriation."

The inferiority *does* exist. The comparative weakness does exist. The special function with the temporary impediment to other activities does exist, actually or potentially. When women pretend to a kind and degree of power which they do not possess, though they have a kind and degree of power, patience, endurance, fortitude all their own, they drive one back to the stupid old masculine slander that women cannot think straight.

Woman is her own worst enemy. That is, some women are. One hardly knows which is worse, the stand of women of reputed intellect, like Mrs. Humphry Ward, against the political progress of their sisters, or the insolent and unwarranted pretension of women to do everything that a man can do—and a little more. The only things that a woman can do that a man cannot do are sing soprano (some freak males can do that), keep a smooth face without shaving (some women cannot do that) and bear children (some unfortunate women cannot or will not do that).

The extreme feminist who in her new-found partial freedom lets her hysterical enthusiasm play ducks and drakes with facts is doing the sororal world no good; she is harming the "cause" of women and the cause of men and the more important dependent cause of children. She is at best ridiculous and at worst a thorn in the flesh of conservatism that makes it not yield but balk. Woman is her own worst enemy. That is, some women. And man is her best friend. If he is not her hope and salvation, he is an indispensable ally. If she irritates him, she will get a fearful setback. And some of her false starts indicate that about now the doctor prescribes not a setback but a period of rest and reconsideration. The shrill, febrile, scatter-brained waste of voice and energy is getting to be a pesky nuisance damaging to lucidity of thought and rational planning. Unfortunately in the woman movement, as in all other movements, it is too often the flushed and clamant lunatic that gets a hearing, and the little docile women trot, trot, trot in multitudes after a leader who

is running amuck. The case of Feminism is especially confused and complicated. For some of the most prominent feminists are hard-favored vinegar-faced shrews who have it in for the men more malignantly than Mrs. Poyser, the creation of a great and wise woman, George Eliot. Other more comely women are quite unconsciously morbid, expending their sexual energy in a crusade that leads to no Holy Land but leads away from the land of heart's desire. There is some serious truth in Beerbohm's smart-aleck joke. But this is not a matter for jest. I quote from Dr. H. W. Frink's *Morbid Fears and Compulsions:*

A certain proportion of at least the most militant suffragists are neurotics who in some instances are compensating for masochistic trends, in others are more or less successfully sublimating sadistic and homosexual ones (which usually are unconscious). I hope this statement may not be construed as an effort on my part to throw mud on woman suffrage, for on the whole I am very much in favor of it. As a matter of fact it is nothing to the discredit of any movement to say that perhaps many of its conspicuous supporters are neurotics, for as a matter of fact it is the neurotics that are pioneers in most reforms. The very normal people who have no trouble in adjusting themselves to their environment, are as a rule too sleek in their own contentment to fight hard for any radical changes or even to take much interest in seeking to have such changes made. To lead and carry through successfully some new movement or reform, a person needs the stimulus of chronic discontent (at least it often seems so) and this in a certain number of instances is surely of neurotic origin and signifies an imperfect adaptation of that individual to his environment.

To make this passage clear to readers who may not happen to know the scientific words—"sadistic" means desiring to dominate by violence, to inflict pain. "Masochistic" is just the opposite, it means desiring to be dominated by violence, to endure pain. Thus according to the new and still groping science of psychopathy and psychoanalysis, the most brilliant, aggressive, *enragée* woman leader may be unconscious not of what she is doing but of why she is doing it. And the better-balanced and wiser woman, Ellen Key or Dr. Anna Howard Shaw, often makes her fanatic sisters impatient. The temperate self-controlled woman, though she may be passionately devoted to the improvement and progress of her sex, refuses to take part in a violent warfare on male man and mankind generally.

But the violent woman too often prevails—for the moment—and it is she who needs curbing, who should be spanked and put to bed. She is the trouble maker who has it in for the men. She has often manifested herself as a rabid temperance crank (abetted by old women in trousers). Her motive in depriving men of liquor, and even of tobacco, seems to her righteous and noble, and she is apparently on the side of hygiene and sanity. But unconsciously she is impelled by the desire to spoil a man's pleasure, whether it be evil or innocent. The case is parallel to Macaulay's explanation of the Puritan's objection to bear-baiting, not because it hurt the bear but because it gave pleasure to the populace. In her zeal to break up the other fellow's game she (with her emasculated or Puritanic brother) is utterly unscrupulous in her methods and her juggling with truth. Though she lies outrageously she is sure that Heaven and all the angels are behind her. I once knew a woman who tried to force through a most unreasonable and vicious proposition. She was sure that God was with her. Mark Twain happened to be against her and he remarked in his even, deadly accurate style, "These women make me darned tired who try to take God in as a silent partner without his consent." I am not sure that he did not say "people" instead of "women," for this kind of sincerely dishonest aberration is not the exclusive sin of one sex. But it is a vice to which women seem to be greatly addicted, partly because they are not restrained and men permit them an abuse

of liberty and privilege which they would not tolerate in other men.

A recent example was the appearance of a crowd of women at the hearing in Washington in April before a committee of the Senate sitting to hear testimony on the wet-dry controversy. The ladies, headed by Mrs. Henry W. Peabody of Boston, had, as the New York *World* put it, "few exact figures but were loaded with generalities." Mrs. Peabody said, "These women who appear here to-day represent from 12,000,000 to 18,000,000 in the Protestant churches of America. . . . We represent the homes and schools of America."

The lady had not a single credential to prove how many people she and her companions represented, and her sweeping inclusions of all the homes and schools in America is capable of immediate disproof. Senator Reed of Missouri questioned her rather sharply, but nobody flatly disputed her, because a white-haired lady still enjoys the immunity from attack which is accorded by old-fashioned courtesy and chivalry, a chivalry, largely lip-service and hypocrisy, but in part sincere gallantry which women are doing their best to destroy.

The woman as kill-joy, as snooping, sneaking, malicious trouble maker, or innocently unconscious sadist enjoying the discomfort of others, is as old as the human race. But woman's new freedom and extended range of activities seem to give her more ample opportunities for mischief. She can make a wide public display of her will to interfere which used to be confined to home and father. A neighbor of mine on a New England farm defined this trait or tendency of the female, that is, of some females, "There's lots o' women who if they can't find enough trouble lyin' round the house go out in the back yard and dig up some." Woman's back yard now is the whole world. It was the same shrewd Yankee who, having sized up his wife, was confronted with the problem of a younger woman, his daughter who had all the ways and manners of the town flapper.

In these days of movies, magazines, and Ford cars, the village girl is no longer isolated from the corruptions, sophistications, and up-to-date-ness of the city. "That gal of mine," he said, "is doggone smart, but she ain't got brains enough to carry it."

IV

This brings us to the real brow-furrowing problem—the younger generation. We are passing, or past. What is the new woman doing with the new girl who is to become the newer woman? Not one single essential thing which grandmother did not do at least as well for mother, which great-grandmother did not do at least as well for grandmother. True, daughter has a much better chance than her foremothers to become a stenographer and marry her employer if she is good looking. If she is unbeautiful she can be fairly sure of supporting herself. And comely or not, she can bid the men go hang with more assurance than the elder women felt, or she can make use of men for her own purposes more boldly and frankly than was customary in times past. She has a slightly protective superficial information which her foremothers did not possess or did not dare confess or discuss.

But what vital thing is her mother doing for her? What new courageous, expansive outlook is opening before her? What step is she to take ahead of her mother which shall make the newer woman better and happier than the old? None that is discernible to the naked eye of the present. The new freedom means simply a breaking down of old discipline without any adequate compensating extension of vital experience or growth of mind. The new mother is falling down badly on her job. And that job, if the race is merely to endure, not to speak of improvement, development, progress—that job is in the home, in the household, bearing and bringing up children intelligently. That is the job for most women, though it is perfectly proper for some women, especially the less attractive ones, to go their solitary ways.

It used to enrage the extreme feminists to be told that a woman's "sphere" is the home, and they heard that dictum parroted so many times that it is no wonder they resented it. Nevertheless, it is true. In chasing after the paper ballot women have neglected the paper that records the household accounts. That is, some women have. While listening to Professor Quackenbosh's lecture before the Women's Club on Recent Developments in the Pedagogical Psychology of Infantile Neuropathic Abnormality women have forgotten that the school begins at home and that a large part of their job is to make themselves expert elementary teachers. That is, some women have forgotten. In fighting for a mythical equality with men, women have lost a decisive battle, the gentle, subtle conquest of children, a conquest which has for the spoils of war an attainable and priceless equality, equality with the children themselves. Some women have become expert in argument on the platform and have failed to cultivate the art of persuasion in the nursery. Some idle women have become champions at bridge whist while Willie played solitaire. Some women have been delegates to the convention of the International Women's Christian League for the Prohibition of Baseball on Sunday or the Unity Alliance of Christian Women for the Abolition of Cigarettes, while they delegated to nurses, dry or wet, the delightful, instructive task of caring for their children. "Oh, nurse," cried Reginald, "who is that beautiful lady?" "Darling," said the beautiful lady, on a flying visit home, "I am your mother." While dabbling in the fine arts, or even honestly working at them, some women have allowed domestic arts and science to become, so far as their knowledge goes, lost arts. Much American home cooking is an unsavory assault on the digestive system. The face of ignorance is saved only by manufactured foods and fool-proof appliances, mostly devised by

men.   And by the way, since we may as
well rub it in hard, a man cook can beat
a woman cook hands down in the invention and preparation of palatable dishes.
The chef is superior even to the excellent
Mrs. Rorer and Mrs. Farmer.

The suffragettes had a slogan: "Come
out of the kitchen," the commendable
purpose of which was to rescue women
from the killing drudgery of pots and
pans.   One of the slogans of the Association for the Promotion of Masculism
shall be: "Go back to the kitchen quick,
but to a kitchen properly equipped."

But, ah, the free, foot-loose soulful
woman will live her own life and devote
herself to art and literature, to psychology, so that she may converse glibly of
"inhibitions" and "complexes" and the
interpretation of dreams, without dreaming just what her own complex, that is,
pain in the left gizzard, really is.   She
must lead her own life.   Very well, leave
her lead.   But let her face the fact that
women in the arts and sciences are second-rate.   As one very successful woman novelist said to me, "When I read
what men write, I don't see how we have
the cheek to try."   And yet literature is
the one art in which women have done a
few supreme things.

In music woman is often a fine per-
former, for example Madame Careño,
and Maud Powell, and the great women
of the stage, operatic and "loquent,"
are the equals of the great men.   Indeed
it is possible that there are more good
actresses than good actors, since beauty
is half the show, and women are naturally and habitually players of parts, his-
trionic assumers of roles, makers of gesture for effect.   There has never been a
woman composer of first rank, seldom
one of second.   Creative impulse is
often present, but the creative power,
the lofty and broad imagination, is
lacking.   It is idle to plead that in this
art woman has not had a chance.   Woman has always been encouraged to
study and practice music because the
male brute liked to hear her play and
sing and see her dance.

There is no great woman sculptor or
painter.   We hear about Rosa Bonheur
and Mary Cassatt, Cecilia Beaux, and
Malvina Hoffman because of their positive merits and also because there are
few women so talented.   The museums
and studios for a century have been
full of girls.   Some of them have done
good work, and many women are making
their living by competent painting and
illustrating.   But there is no emergent
genius.   There have been fine lyric poets
from Sappho to Christina Rossetti—I
dare not mention living poetesses.   But
no woman has written a sustained epic
or drama of great merit.   In scholarship, at least in the absorbent, acquisitive school and university stage, women
by diligent application have sometimes
rivalled men and run off with the prizes.
But it is so unusual that when a woman
takes a "first" it gets in the papers.   It
is news, as when a man bites a dog.
But only biographers take the trouble to
remember that Peel, Halifax, Gladstone,
and others took double-firsts.

No woman has made a crucial discovery in science.   Madame Curie, to
whom all honor and homage, was educated by Monsieur Curie.   Dr. Alice Ham-
ilton, Professor in the Harvard Medical
School, is eminent in industrial medicine
and bacteriology.   Florence Nightingale
and Clara Barton did lay the foundation
of modern scientific nursing, and in that
noble profession woman is at her best,
for it is essentially maternal.   All the
surgical methods, appliances, antiseptics,
anæsthetics are the discoveries and crea-
tions of men.

Ellen Key, who may be depended on to
make out the best possible case for the
achievement of women, says, "Many
women are active in the sphere of invention, without a single woman's name
having been thus far connected with
an *epoch-making* invention.   Especially
where constructive ability is necessary,
women have as yet not been eminent;
they have created neither a philosophic
system nor a new religion, neither a
great musical work nor a monumental

building, neither a classic drama nor an epic."

In religion women have been great created and worshipped figures, if not creators. Among the saints and martyrs is none greater than Catharine, Theresa, and Joan of Arc. In Catholic churches and homes more prayers are addressed to the Virgin Mary than to God Himself. In other religions and mythologies (of which most women are ignorant because they would rather read "Advice to the Love-Shorn" and "How to Keep Your Husband's Affection, Though Worthless" than a fascinating book like Frazer's *Golden Bough*), in the great poetic religions the mother is the symbol of life, the very earth is a vast fertile benevolent womb from which we come and to which we return to be reborn. But the master of the universe is He, Zeus, Jove, Jehovah, Allah.

The one art in which woman is most fully mistress of herself and of life is literature, especially memoirs, friendly letters, prose fiction. Fiction consists primarily of the study of human character in love relations and the family life, which woman has abundant opportunity to observe, and of command of the prose of daily life, which she possesses in pure form. She is not critic, not philosopher, but she has the gift of humorous and emotional story-telling. Every country has had distinguished women novelists. But women have still to give us many portraits of women which *they themselves* find as true, as profoundly analyzed, as beautifully drawn as the women of Meredith and Hardy, of Balzac and Flaubert, of Tolstoy and Tourgenev and Dostoyevsky.

Sappho is reputed to have been beautiful, and I have known women who made verses and pictures only less pretty than themselves. But there is truth in Ambrose Bierce's epigram: "Women of genius commonly have masculine faces, figures, and manners. In transplanting brains to alien soil God leaves a little of the original earth clinging to the roots."

VI

Let us be done forever with this nonsense about the equality of the sexes. They are not equal in nature and never can be. If the woman argues—and it is proverbially useless to argue with her—that she wants a chance to show what she can do, the answer is, Certainly, madame, all the chance in the world, for you, and for the man and for the child, opportunity for everybody to cultivate the best that is in him or her for the good of the individual, for the good of the race. But in heaven's name let not the woman try to compete with man, for the more chance she has, the freer the world grows, the more chance man will have, and he will always keep slightly ahead of her.

It is good for the world that individuals and the sexes cultivate divergent yet complementary aptitudes and do not all try to do the same thing. Ellen Key notes two ideals, two directions of the woman movement, the second of which she approves: "The older program reads, 'Full equality of woman with man.' In the 'state of the future' both sexes shall have the same duty of work and the same protection of work, while the children are reared in state institutions. The movement in the other direction purposes to win back the wife to the husband, the mother to the children, and, thereby, the home to all."

Professor William James, who derived much of his philosophy from a direct study of common life, used to quote with amusement the wise saying of an old farmer: "There's mighty little difference between one man and another, but what little difference there is is mighty important." So it is with the sexes. Let us foster the important differences. Men and women are much alike, perhaps too much alike, both belonging to that curious species of animal Homo Sapiens, the Human Being. They have about the same faults and virtues in varying degrees. And to every commentary upon the Gentle Sex is one conclusive reply:

"So's your old man."

Feminism Destructive of Woman's Happiness

By GINA LOMBROSO FERRERO

Daughter of the late Cesare Lombroso, famous criminologist, and wife of Guglielmo
Ferrero, the Italian historian; author of *L'Anima della Donna* (*The Soul of Woman*),
a book which recently excited sensational interest in Europe, and other works

*The feminine heaven is higher and more difficult
to attain than the masculine heaven, but it is
futile to rebel against this fate.*

*Feminism wishes that woman should enjoy all
the benefits enjoyed by men, thinking that
she will add the happiness which she has enjoyed to that which she will enjoy in the
future.*

WHAT does feminism wish? What
is feminism, that doctrine, that
movement, which for nearly half a
century has predominated as a subject of
discussion in books and political reviews
and outweighs all other factors in domestic
and social organization? If one searches
through the official literature of feminism,
if one turns to the women who have
headed or who head this movement,
one will receive the most conflicting and
contradictory answers. I myself have experienced this; my book, *The Soul of Woman*, has aroused the anger of the feminists of all the nations of Europe and also
of America. Some women wish to win for
women the right to do all that men do;
others wish women to develop more completely their femininity; some demand a
more rigorous morality than that of men;
others free access to all professional careers now monopolized by men; still others
ask for legislation to protect the working
woman.

There is one point in common between
all the feminist movements in all countries
—the demand for woman of all the rights
possessed by man, the determined effort to
bring woman to the enjoyment of all privileges enjoyed by man, on the understanding that in this way woman will enjoy
all pleasures she formerly enjoyed as well
as those which only man enjoys.

That the movement has succeeded in imposing its program no one can deny. All
the barriers against which Feminism has
struggled, all the barriers that seemed to
bar women from happiness, all the differences of mission and profession formerly
standing between men and women have
fallen. Woman today has the vote as well
as man, she can study in the same way
and as much as man, she can become a
priest or minister in certain religious communities, she can be a chauffeur, a diplomat or an astronomer, she can aspire to all
positions and to all honors, she can participate in all games and sports enjoyed by
man. It can even happen, as Miss Lenglen
has shown, that a tennis champion can earn
vast sums of money.

But when I am asked if these victories
have increased woman's happiness, I reply
that I doubt it. Never before has woman
been so active, never before has she so
protested against man, against society,
against the world as at present, and in no
country have these claims and struggles
been more intense than in the countries
where the victories have been greatest. An
Italian proverb says: "He who is contented does not move." Hence it does not
seem to me rash to conclude from this
agitation that despite these victories woman is not contented, rather, that she is
less contented than before, when she indulged in no agitation whatsoever.

How and why is it that woman is worse
off, or, at least, is not so well off as before? Why has she not attained all that
she desired and why do the things she desires and the things she has desired and
obtained give her no joy?

It is not peculiar to woman, but is common to all humanity, to desire things that
give no pleasure when they are obtained.
It is given to only a very small minority
of the human race to know itself—that is,

to know its own deep-lying aspirations; and as we physicians know from every-day experience, those who are sick have a tendency to lean toward a different, often opposite direction from that which would bring them joy, happiness, health and comfort. The sick person—and woman in this case can be considered as a sick person—is and always has been a very poor diagnostician and also a very poor physician for herself, for she tends to blame for her own troubles purely passing causes which have brought those troubles into relief and seeks a remedy for them in all the pleasurable sensations that she can recall. If I may cite a personal incident, I will relate a typical case in point. My little boy had been attacked by a stomach trouble which made it necessary for him to fast for several months. After the first month he began to manifest strange desires, now for some game, now for some play that he had seen months before, and finally for a coat of mail of Joan of Arc, and he nearly drove several of our family group insane supplicating us to obtain it for him. He could not sleep at night and prayed as one prays to God for the coat of mail. Oh, the coat of mail! If he could only have the coat of mail! Then all his troubles would be over. Nothing that he had ever had could give him the joy that the coat of mail would give him. Of course, as soon as he obtained the coat of mail the illusion passed and he began to cry heart-brokenly, doubly disappointed because the coat of mail had not effected the hoped-for miracle, and because he had nothing else in view. This desperate feeling lasted until another desire arose of the same kind and ending in the same way, and this alternation of moods lasted until he was allowed to eat a good substantial slice of bread.

Woman suffers in the same way as my child suffered, but the remedies that feminism proposes and has already proposed to her to alleviate her sufferings very much resemble the toys that my child yearned for so desperately—diversions which once obtained give her no pleasure and even perhaps intensify the evils which she desires to combat.

The lack of fixed objective, the moral discomfort from which women are suffering today, had its inception almost a century ago, and culminated in the triumph of industrialism, of machinery, which broke down the old moral, social, intellectual and artistic traditions, the barriers which separated classes and sexes, minimized the importance of ingenuity, economy, manual skill, and the moral virtues in which woman excels, and by increasing, if only momentarily, the acquisition of wealth, increased the possibilities of intellectual and material enjoyments, in which man excels. The rôles of the two sexes have thus been inverted. In the Middle Ages, with their fixity of classes and sexes, with their need of economy, with their narrow limits, restricting intellectual, material and sensual pleasures, woman, whose pleasures are essentially moral and spiritual, whose aspirations are fixed, whose need of abstraction is negligible, was favored by exterior conditions; and man, whose aspirations are essentially material and intellectual, was sacrificed. Today, with the predominance of different and even antithetical exterior conditions, the situation is reversed: Man can expand freely and woman is sacrificed. That is to say, man has undoubtedly derived pleasure from these changed exterior conditions and woman has suffered.

Errors of Feminism

It is to the credit of feminism that it perceived this gain and loss, and revealed it to the world. It is to the blame of feminism,

1. That it did not realize that man had derived pleasure from the new conditions, not because these conditions had in them any special value, but because they favored the real qualities and the real aspirations of man;

2. That it did not realize that the changed exterior conditions made woman suffer, not because they increased man's pleasure, but because they did not correspond to the special qualities and aspirations of woman;

3. That it persuaded woman that her sufferings were due to the specific evil intentions of man;

4. (Consequence of the first and second error) That it turned woman toward the

copying of man, persuading her that that which makes man happy or unhappy must also make woman happy or unhappy;

5. That it led woman, instead of resisting with all her strength the changed conditions, whereby she would have rendered great service to humanity and to society, retarding and diminishing the triumph of machinery, to help this movement, to exaggerate it, to despise past times and past conditions, which had so greatly favored woman.

As an excuse for feminism, it must be said that it is not easy to go back to remote origins for one's troubles and to induce others to do so, nor to resist a powerful current, while it is quite easy to persuade one's self and others that one's troubles derive from the evil intentions of others and that it suffices to copy exactly some one else who is happily situated, in order to be happily situated one's self. In the case of feminism, copying man has a special objection, in that woman and man are different and suffer and derive pleasure from different things, just as two individuals of the same species may differ from one another. In the one case, aspirations which are strong and permanent are, in the other case, minor and transitory.

The pleasures of glory, of independence, of riches, of power (easier to win today than yesterday), are enjoyed also by woman, just as the discomfort arising from rigid monogamy, from too much dependence and from the lack of power is also felt by woman. These sufferings are incidental and impermanent in woman, while aspiration to love, desire of being loved and of loving, of reuniting herself to continuous life, are in her stable elements; in man, on the contrary, passing and irrational aspirations to love are incidental and impermanent, while aspirations to power, glory and wealth are permanent and powerful impulses. The heroes and heroines of Ibsen represent this difference strikingly. Borkman, Sollness, love Kaia, Hilda, but they do not hesitate to sacrifice them to power, glory, wealth, while Hilda and Kaia are ready to sacrifice these desiderata, which they also prize, to love.

Woman was formerly sacrificed and repressed from the time of her birth, compelled always to obey her father and mother at first, then her brother, her husband, her son later on. She was restricted in her control of the house and the family; she was barred from knowledge, arts and sports; barred from the pleasure of traveling, of independent action; molded on a single pattern difficult to vary, but ill-adapted to many; destined to be forever and only "the servant of others." She suffered from these repressions, but she suffered much less than a man would have suffered and, at all events, suffered less than the woman of today suffers, because those repressions, to which she seemed to yield of her own volition, this willing service which became to her second nature, exalted her extraordinarily in the esteem of men, and gave scope to those true, enduring and complete loves which former periods have recorded, and which repaid her a thousand times for the sufferings of which she was the victim.

Isolation After Victory

Yes, woman has today the vote, glory, power, independence, often has wealth, freedom to do what she pleases; but she does not have love and affection, no one to think of her and of whom she can think; she is alone, alone and desolate. In the crowded streets which she traverses two or three times a day, among the human anthill in the restaurants where she eats, in the shifting lodging of the burning city quarters where she lies at night separated by a thin partition from hundreds and hundreds of other human beings; in the suffocating public offices, in the ministries, in the private offices where she works, where she dictates, where she teaches, where she lectures, in the crowded movie shows where she seeks diversion— woman is alone, much more desolate than in the lonely little room of former days, more alone than in a convent cell, more alone than in a provincial town, in the country, in the lonely room where formerly she was wont to rest and work.

The fact is that those beings that swarm around her, that jostle her on the street cars, that suffocate her in the office, that deafen her in her room, that bewilder her in the theatre, are alien to her. The people who surround her vary every day and have no interest in her joys and sorrows, nor has she any reason or duty to be interested in them. As alien and variable as human beings are the inanimate objects that surround her, the bed in which she sleeps, the machine on which she writes, the window that gives her light, the table at which she eats. All these objects are not hers, they are only entrusted to her, they may change every day, as her superior or inferior or her neighbor at table may change. Nothing around her is permanent or fixed, nothing accompanies her in life, and nothing and no one can be the confidant of her thoughts. She is a mere automaton in the office, confronted by unfitting work, which she cannot galvanize into life, of which she understands neither the reason nor the utility; a mere automaton at the theatre, or at the movie, where she goes to benumb her mental suffering. She is isolated at home where every one thinks only of himself; she is alone in the ever varied and variable cities where she goes for pleasure or instruction; from one moment to another she may disappear without any one to weep over her or regret her disappearance. She has nothing of her own that is fixed, linked to herself, to think of or that will think of her, to wait for or that will wait for her, nothing to act for or that will act for her. Objects and human beings surrounding her change and have the right to change without her having the right to weep for them or to regret them.

This isolation, this variability, which bring no sorrow or suffering to man, who is wholly self-centred; this indifference of the world to the individual, which pleases man, who hates emotions and bothering about other people, is unbearable to a woman, who yearns to have communication with others, who aspires to love and to be loved, to have something or some one to devote herself to and something or some one to her devoted. To her, indifference is worse than intense hatred, continuous change worse than absolute fixity, isolation worse than complete solitude, for hatred can be converted into love, and in solitude, in fixed conditions, she can clothe the plants, the animals and the things around her, even they are not her own, with

her own sentiments, she can love them and imagine herself loved by them.

The world wonders why the woman of today, launched on a campaign to triumph over the austerity of masculine and feminine customs, over the infamous practice which forced young girls to sell their own bodies in obedience to their parents' command, to win a love more sacred, loftier, purer, than the old, has fallen into the most unpoetic sensuality, in her claim to the right of maternity and free love. But this is the logical consequence of the victories won and of the isolation resulting, and from which she cannot escape except by yielding to the grossest sensuality, although this is the form of love that she least enjoys.

The fact is that it was easy for her to win the vote, to attain the same education as man, to gain access to masculine professions, but she did not succeed in realizing the rest of her program, which she did not proclaim from the housetops, but which she secretly cherished and desired more than all the rest—viz., *to persuade man to love her outside and beyond the limits of the traditional point of view, outside and beyond the limits of virtue, outside and beyond consideration of the services that she might render him and outside and beyond the senses, at the very time of their enjoyment.* Was the attainment of this part of her program possible? Will it ever be possible, in a more or less remote period? I am absolutely convinced that it will not.

Feminism has persuaded woman that the traditional morality to which she was previously bound, the severe repressions to which she was trained, the loftier sacrifices demanded of her, as contrasted with man, the little house corner in which she was confined, were rules and restrictions imposed by man for the pleasure of causing suffering, a survival of that love of suffering which pervaded the world in the Middle Ages under the influence of austere Catholicism, that they were traditions and rules established by men out of hatred for women. This is not the case. Moral rules and traditions represent the minimum of sacrifice which experience judged necessary to guarantee to each and all the satisfaction of given instincts within a community in which other individuals live who have the same or different desires. The traditions which ancient civilizations imposed on woman, favored qualities and habits necessary to enable woman to attain the satisfaction of her deepest and most sacred instincts, to permit her to have some one to love, in whom she could centre all her life. Man can be selfish, for he does not depend on others for the satisfaction of his desires. Woman cannot be selfish. Without being ready to serve others, to be useful to others, one cannot excite desire as woman wishes to excite it; without repressions, sacrifices, demonstration of one's altruism, one cannot console or love as woman desires to console and love; without winning the esteem and the admiration of man, she cannot win from him continuous affection. To persuade man to depart from the traditional point of view, to persuade him to love her outside the limits of virtue, and irrespective of the services that she can render him, did not prove difficult, for that is his favorite point of view. But once the man has ceased to love the woman from the viewpoint of the usefulness that she can have for him, he adopts the viewpoint of beauty, of provocativeness, the viewpoint, that is, of the pleasure that he may derive from her.

I know that feminism did not wish man to judge woman from the viewpoint of culture, of schooling, of ability, strength, responsibilities assumed, the capacity she shows for working outside the home: these are qualities that man appreciates in other men; qualities that win his respect, but not his admiration, much less his love for a woman.

Love is related to sentiment, not to intellect, to moral or physical, not to intellectual qualities, to the qualities useful for the race, not to those useful to individuals, to the qualities which most differentiate the two sexes, not to those that are held in common and in which the sexes are alike. Nor can the desires of one sex change in any way the desires of the other, any more than our desire can endow the sheep with the courage of the lion, or the lion with the gentleness of the sheep. Psychological laws have their own logical necessity, as fixed and inevitable as the law of physics. As soon as the old tradition was broken under which man loved woman because of his admiration for her altruism, her gentleness, her devotion to him, and he ceased to desire woman because of his gratitude for the services that she could render him, he cast woman aside as a permanent companion and saw in her only the female who could excite and satisfy his senses. How and why has the feminine mode of dress become so provocative, as much so if not more than for a few years during the French Revolution? Why do women of every class and rank try so hard to imitate the courtesan? Because woman today feels that men now love her as a courtesan, because she feels instinctively that this is the only way now left to her, viz.: to excite, instead of the admiration and respect to which she was able previously to aspire, some strong though transitory sensual passion.

IMITATION OF MEN

For similar reasons she imitates man. In this imitation, it is true, there is a professional necessity. Once woman like man holds a position in a bank, sits among Government ministers and preaches from church pulpits, runs her own motor car or navigates the air in airplanes, or competes with man for championships in sports, she must also copy his mode of dress, as the "postwoman" and the street car "conductoress" copied it during the war-time period. Once woman has become accustomed to the masculine attire required by her professional needs, it cannot be wondered at that she should continue to wear it in ordinary life, nor that, if it gives prestige, it should spread also to non-professional women.

But if, on the one hand, woman copies man because of logical professional reasons, she copies him much more because she feels that man is avoiding her; because she feels her prestige diminishing; because she perceives that man is now preferring the company of other men to hers; because, by imitating him, she hopes to keep her hold on him. Did not man complain that he could not bring his sister with him to the country because her clothing hindered her, or to the club because smoking was indulged in there? Now, by adopting trousers and smoking, woman hopes that men will bring forth no more excuses for leaving her at home. Woman today has won the right to bob her hair, to dress in men's attire, to have her own clubs like man, to insult man like a courtesan, to dress—or rather, to undress—like a courtesan, to change love and clothing like a courtesan.

But is this a sign of victory or defeat? Is it a sign of triumphant superiority or of recognized defeat? The superior person does not copy his inferior, the conqueror does not copy the vanquished; quite the reverse. The middle-class citizen does not dress like a workman; the workman dresses like the middle-class citizen. The model, consciously or unconsciously, reveals the aspirations of the copier. The courtesan copied the virtuous and respectable woman, when the latter attracted man by her modesty and virtues, when the chaste and virtuous woman enjoyed the prestige of an attraction greater than that of the courtesan. Man copied woman, her way of thinking, her dress, in those periods when woman enjoyed the greatest prestige and when he did not dare to approach her without making himself in some way worthy of her. Woman today copies man because she feels it necessary to copy him to get closer to him, because she thinks him superior, because she wishes to enter into closer relations with him, to fuse her being in his. Woman copies the courtesan today because she feels that man loves in her what is most different from him, what is most feminine in her, and not wishing and not being able to display her most diverse and most feminine traits in the intellectual field, she is compelled to display as much as possible her physical differences.

Protests are heard today against the fashion which daily shortens the length of women's skirts or invents the tailor-made costumes which are an approximation to man's attire; but fashion inevitably follows the general trend of the times and lends itself to the help of woman following her own point of view.

But all this cannot endure. All this is artificial and degenerate. The present fashions are ephemeral; they make woman ugly and do not win for her the love she longs for. I believe that a general change of tendency is not far away, and I believe that this change will first arise in America, where feminism was born and where it has now reached its climax, and hence, logically, where more than anywhere else it must begin its decline. I see signs of this not only in the wide distribution of my book, *The Soul of Woman*, which embodies an attack on feminism; not only in the many letters received from America from women who express their weariness of a life empty of affection, but also and much more in the special orientation of American feminism, which has resolutely begun to take steps to avert the menace of immorality which had overflowed immediately after the barriers had been removed. It was from America that that feminism came which seeks to persuade woman "to renounce love" as a weakness which should be left to those stupid women who have no other arrow in their quiver, a surviving atavism over which intelligent women should triumph, as an error taught by the traditional type of education which they must uproot and leave to the weak, for the intelligent woman, the woman who studies, the superior woman, will find in independence, in wage-earning, in glory, greater joys than in love.

OLD STANDARDS THE SOLE SOLUTION

I believe the roots of love too deep-lying and too necessary for woman's true mission in life to enable this movement to win success; I believe that the urging of men and women to follow the same careers and the same ambitions has grave dangers because of the competition to which it will give rise, and the hostility which this competition will engender between man and woman; but I believe that from this feminism it will be easy to pass to a different tendency which will solve all woman's problems.

A very intelligent French woman who directs one of the most important juvenile associations of France wrote me a somewhat discouraged letter about the new generation of girls. It is impossible, she said, to educate and enlighten girls by appealing either to their heart or their intellect; and it seemed as if it would finally become necessary to appeal only to their selfishness. I place considerable hope in selfishness.

The woman of today is tired of all these artificial games in which she has trifled her time away in these last years; she longs, as it were, for a slice of plain bread to satisfy her hunger. Once convinced there is no other way to love and win love than by a return to the old morality, she will resign herself thereto much more quickly than the world imagines, and the greater the excesses of flirtation will become, the more willingly and rapidly will she come back into the old hive, for such excesses will always and increasingly alienate those permanent affections which she yearns for more than anything else in life.

Yes, it is true that the traditional woman corresponds to the ideal that man has built up around woman, but it also corresponds to the ideal that man must have of woman in order to be able to give her, not a moment of violent, transitory love, but protection and constant affection. If woman wishes to love and to be loved, there is no other way in which she can attain this.

Let us even admit that what man loves in woman is a mirage; yet if woman wishes to be loved, she must incarnate that mirage. The man can be what he is, for he does not depend on others for his desires and aspirations; but woman, who aims above all to bring joy to the man she loves, must continually strive to reproduce in actual life what man desires her to be. And it is not enough for woman individually and separately to represent this mirage; she must compel all women to whose class she belongs to approach this ideal, otherwise the whole class become disqualified.

Thus will woman attain happiness. A distinction is needed here. No movement, no party, no society can propose as a definite aim the happiness of its members, a happiness that may be placed in the most contradictory aspirations; it must be restricted to precise aims, useful for all; it must plan to guarantee the satisfaction of those general instincts which exist in all

its members and are useful to the mass, in the measure in which this satisfaction is possible to all, without harming others. In the same way society seeks to guarantee all its members food and work and lodging sufficient for the support of life, and for protection against hunger and cold, which are real, certain, general needs, without which the happiness of the individual is impossible. So giving woman a way of having some one whom she can make the centre of her life and who makes her the centre of his life, means assuring woman of the appeasement of her first natural instinct, a guaranty if not of happiness, at least of the satisfaction of those needs without which her happiness cannot exist. Man does not have these needs, because his happiness is easier of attainment, and this explains why in all climes and among all races man has always been envied by woman.

The feminine paradise is loftier and more difficult to attain than the masculine paradise! The way that leads thereto is long and stormy, strewn with briars and sharp and painful thorns. From time to time during the course of history woman rebels against this fate; furious to perceive that man can reach his own heaven with so little effort, she wishes to invade man's paradise. But when she reaches it she finds that heaven worse than the earth which she previously inhabited. The fish that breathes in the waters cannot breathe in the air; nor can the butterfly, accustomed to live on flower pollen, satisfy itself on fruit. The heaven of every individual is a measure of his own nature, nor can the fact that it is easier or harder of access have any influence on the possibility of changing it.

Love is the fixed, unchangeable aspiration of woman. Love is the glowing sun of her heaven—not love in its vulgar and sensual form of physical attraction, but as conceived by woman, having some one to think of and who thinks of her, some one to devote herself to and who devotes himself to her, as in the case of a mother and her child. Let woman make this her aim, and it will appease her longings better than freedom, independence, the franchise, wealth, power, or glory.

Second Thoughts on Feminism

By Iona Mure.

IS womankind on the road to extinction? We hear a great deal to-day about the *rapprochement* of the sexes, but it is noticeable that it is woman who is doing the approaching. Why feminism then? Masculinism would be a more apt definition of this sinister cult devoted to the reproduction of the female in the likeness of the male, at the expense of her age-long entity, for the " new woman " looks uncommonly like the old man and is " *plus royaliste que le roi.*" What a pitiable admission of male predominance. If we are only a spare rib all the more reason to appear something quite different—as Eve was well aware, when, considering amongst the fig leaves the disadvantages of publicity, she devised that gesture of expediency " *femme incompromise.*" Unfortunately it is very difficult to go on being misunderstood in these expansive times. Has woman forgotten that the serpent was the first publicist that she responds so blithely to the overtures of his hydra-headed descent?

This so-called emancipation is an abdication, so it is not surprising that some of our chief feminists are men, delighted at the prospect of being rid at last of all opposition to their own standards and relieved of irksome responsibilities. Was there ever a more fallacious slogan than " women's rights "?

It took something tangible in the shape of an apple to tempt Eve, but her simple descendants permit themselves to be exploited with a vote, and the assurance that we command man's respect as a responsible factor in the body politic. Now who will trouble to feed or clothe the body politic, to say nothing of comforting it in sickness and in health? As for respect—no doubt we shall be accorded ample opportunity to cultivate the civic virtues. Surely the most myopic of womankind must at length see that if we pursue this defeatist policy we shall be reduced to utter independence. What an exchange for a birthright of privilege!

We must execute a *volte face* before it is too late, man has already travelled a long way from the touching simplicity of his grandfathers, so addicted to discoursing on " the sex " over their port wine, while " the sex," gone to covert in the drawing-room, made plans for their male relative's good—and goods. It is true that in those days one was expected to be a " fine woman " or else replete with all the domesticities (preferably the former) to merit masculine consideration, but I daresay a display of " womanliness " was generally adequate.

Has woman forgotten the technique of that super-art femininity? Let us return to our primitives and something may yet be done in the way of self-preservation. I am confident that man, the confirmed idealist, will meet us half-way in an endeavour to portray his dearest delusion, " the eternal feminine."

Woman, the essential artist, has inspired all the arts, winged a thousand songs, lent the colour of her personality to the painter's brush, harmonised the musician's reverie, and firing the spirit of adventure, shaped the mariner's course for the horizons of his dreams, or flung the banners of conquest across the world, requiring no medium other than the imagination of man.

Let us stick to that! To those of my sex who fancy that our notable achievements in world-history-making argue an ability to compete with man in an executive capacity I would point out that it was not owing to her eminence in the shipping industry that Helen launched a thousand ships—but perhaps that is an unfortunate instance to have chosen by way of example!

We must by every means prolong the external feminine and another Villon may yet arise to sing of the girls of to-morrow and divert the attention of his fellow poets from steam-engines and hoboes to their traditional theme. Yes, even the ballad mongers neglect the " new woman," and no wonder when in reply to would-be squires: " ' I'm going *a-voting*, sir,' she said." Not an expedition to promote social amenities, unless with opportunist politicians seeking a prey. How far we have wandered from the good old ways when the favourite pastime of every " gentyle knyghte " was succouring damsels in distress, but even Lancelot would turn a deaf ear to the clamour of grievance that arises from women's organisations and flee their deputations. Let us revert to the system of being distressed one by one and provide the chivalrous male with his legitimate opportunities. The movement would be popular judging by the heartiness of the cinema patron's applause when the belle of Bunkumville, delivered from all the customary perils of the scenario, fades coyly away in the respectful embrace of her 100 per cent. he-man rescuer. The pity of it that poor travesty of romance—but we have to do with the potentialities.

Every woman has it in her gift to endow some man with the vision of lordship, and kindle his ardour for life's great emprise, the quest for the kingdom beyond the hills and the treasure at the rainbow's end. Our militant spinsterhood would do well to ponder the flight of the butterfly, elusive as the play of light and shadow, spreading its wings just out of reach.

If the woman of to-day finds the inspirational rôle inadequate as an outlet for her energies, and insists on active participation in governmental affairs, instead of tamely adapting herself to masculine ways and means, why does she not use her formidable voting power to revive the matriarchal system, honoured by the ancients, and, I believe, still in good working order in Thibet. A deputation might with advantage be sent to the upper Himalayas to report on the merits of that institution. I submit, however, that our dominion is greater when functioning through influence than when based on aggression.

VOLUME 155

JUNE 1927

Harpers
Magazine

FEMINISM AND JANE SMITH

ANONYMOUS

IT IS surprising, to the casual observer, that in the discussions of feministic theory, formal and informal, which he has heard or taken part in very few have consented to be anything like fundamental. Talk and books alike seem to rest their argument on political or social conditions which, in the nature of things, must constantly be changing. There is no reason to suppose that if Greece and Rome passed we shall endure; and no man can say how, or when, we shall perish. What is certain is that our best chance of preserving our civilization is to separate, in all weighty matters, the essential from the accidental; and, in determining our attitude, to rest, as far as possible, on facts that are not going to change with political, or economic, or even ethnic fashions.

Nothing is more striking to the same casual observer than the failure, on the part of feminists and anti-feminists alike, to bring sex, as such, into the discussion; their tendency, in other words, to argue forever about the social or economic by-products of the physical fact without once examining the physi-

cal fact itself to see what it implies. Whether discussion of child-insurance and maternity relief is considered more delicate than discussion of the marriage-relation, which stands causally behind these other problems, I do not know. Very likely; for we seem to sidestep any reference to "male and female," though we may prate as much as we like of romantic love, or repression, or complexes. Yet it would seem to be clear that you can get at no satisfactory solution of the political, social, or economic relations between the sexes without considering the respective roles which Nature has assigned them in the fundamentally and eternally important business of reproducing the race. Nature is concerned—as far as male and female go—only with that. What creative evolution may eventually do to modify the process of reproduction now existing it would be idle to speculate upon. Certainly, as far as we know, ever since the human race has been what we call human, children have been begotten, conceived, and born in one way and one way only. To the race in general, the average man is significant chiefly as a potential or actual father, the average woman as a potential or actual mother. Passion is thrown in as a bait and a lure, to one end alone.

Psychology (in the non-laboratory sense) counts much more for the average person than pure science or pure philosophy. Even a biologist is human outside his laboratory; as a feminist is human when he or she steps off the platform. The average person does not think about his own human relations so much as he feels about them. It is not from the point of view of pure science that you can discuss these things, because all sorts of complicated reactions enter into the decisions and opinions of the average person. The writer is attempting to discuss them only from a widely human—a merely psychological —point of view. Nor is this intended for an exhaustive discussion: only as a reminder of certain facts that many special pleaders, on both sides, have omitted to mention. The great omission, as has been said, is the omission of any reference, direct or implied, to the respective roles of the two sexes in reproducing their kind.

It is an interesting fact that the most rational lists of the "twelve greatest women" with which we were not long ago afflicted mentioned only women who were unmarried or childless. Some people who sentimentalized motherhood were even, I believe, offended thereby. The fact is interesting only in passing, as a straw to show which way the winds of the ages blow. Anyone who has ever given thought to the matter would have expected it. Through all the ages, the respectable wife and mother has been a very rare achiever of distinction in any field of creative work. The "great" women (in the sense of artistic or intellectual success) have been for the most part either unmarried or childless— or frankly contemptuous of the conventions of their world. This fact, as I say, need not detain us. The sex is merely running true to form. What is more

important is that a large number of the women who are most vociferous about what used to be called "women's rights," about the whole question of women's "equality" with men, are either unmarried or childless. There are, of course, notable exceptions; but the reader, I believe, will agree that a large number of the feminist agitators have never borne a child. The writer would respectfully submit that a woman who has never borne children, while she may be perfectly qualified to speak about the rights and needs of the exceptional woman, is positively unqualified to speak about the needs and rights of the average woman. Of plain Jane Smith, married and a mother, she knows very little.

The mystical attitude is a dangerous one to adopt towards any subject. Yet it is the attitude that determines the sacramental idea; and the sacramental idea is far older and far more nearly universal than any Church. It inheres in the commonest counsels of the race; it lies at the bottom of all such familiar tags as "you never can tell till you've tried it," and "must be experienced to be appreciated." A sacrament is the outward and visible sign of an inward and spiritual grace—that is, at least, the definition of the Christian Church. But, to take it more widely, a sacrament is a physical fact which has a spiritual significance that could not be apprehended without the physical experience prescribed. You do something or other with your body in order to learn something with your soul. The Church made marriage a sacrament fairly early; it never, with its secular bias against women, made childbearing a sacrament. To most people ecclesiastical notions of sacraments make very little difference nowadays. Yet most people cling to the belief that there are certain experiences you must have yourself in order to reason properly about their significance. No one, I think, would put a monk or a nun on the jury that was considering a *crime passionel;* no one would accept a teetotaler's decision as between two brands of champagne. Mrs. Jane Smith, mother of children, may be less well equipped intellectually to discuss feminism than Miss Mary Jones; but she knows something that Miss Mary Jones cannot derive from an intellectual process.

II

One does not suppose that Jane Smith is usually—taking the planet over—particularly well able to reason. The average person is not. But, if she can reason, she is possessed of fundamental facts to go on, with which Mary Jones is not provided. Let us suppose, for a moment, that Jane Smith is articulate, and dispassionate; not bewildered, or resentful, or sentimental. She is likely enough to be all three—especially the last, for on no fact of life has more sentimentality been misspent than on motherhood. Partly, in our Western world, no doubt, a matter of defense: the Church thrust women all along the line into an inferior position, and women had to find such consolation as they could. Certainly the cult of the Blessed Virgin must have been a great help to a repressed and downtrodden sex. Nothing, it must be admitted, is as simple as all that; but the statement may pass as suggestive of a truth. Returning to Jane Smith, let us suppose her, as we said, articulate; able, to some extent, without religious or egotistical prepossessions, to state her case in the light of her own adventure, to view herself as a human being who has undergone certain normal and universal experiences.

She knows, first of all, that childbearing is a physically humiliating experience: such a surrender of bodily integrity as the other half of the race knows nothing of and can hardly imagine. The social attitude to motherhood may differ widely with civilizations. To the Chinese woman, to the Hindu woman, it may be the sole great source of legitimate pride. To the English or American woman it may, on the other hand, be

an occasion for the sympathy, if not the pity, of her friends. We will not deal with these accidental points of view. We are giving Jane Smith an English name, as a matter of convenience; but we are for the moment regarding her simply as a female human being, paying no attention to climate, religion, or social status.

Stripped of the prestige value which may or may not, at any given epoch, in any given country, be attributed to the feat of maternity, childbearing remains, as we said, a humiliating experience. Jane Smith, who has been a mother, knows it. The maternal instinct is strong in most women; and few mothers would ask back, if they could, the price that they have paid. Hypatia's refusal to "suffer tortures fit only for slaves to bear" would find, perhaps, no far-reaching echoes. Nor is it the fact of pain that gives Jane Smith pause when she considers the implications of her role in life. Pain is not confined to her sex, and she knows it. No woman suffers in childbirth as countless soldiers suffered in the late war; though it must be remembered that the pain of childbirth is the only absolutely inevitable pain which Nature has provided for those who live what Nature considers the normal life. People may die even, suddenly and without suffering. It is being done constantly. Pain is likely to come to all of us during our three-score years and ten; but it is sure to come to the woman who marries and has children. The cards are stacked against her.

Still, as we said, pain is so nearly universal a fact that we will not dwell on it. People, moreover, both men and women, often deliberately incur or accept pain for reasons of altruism. It is not pain that makes Jane Smith feel that she knows more about the position into which her sex is thrust by the Universe than the childless woman can know. It is rather, as we said, the humiliation of the experience. Modern science has mitigated the suffering and the dangers of maternity, so that the modern woman who can afford nurses and specialists need dread the mere childbearing no more perhaps than the Red Indian woman does. Her more delicate and complicated system may suffer more after-effects than the savage woman's; but on the other hand she has chloroform and ether on her side. What science has not done, cannot do, never can do is to make it a decent business. The race avoids pain when it can; any woman will choose the best care she can have at such a time, for the sake of the future as well as the present, for the sake of her children as well as for her own; but the fact remains that, were it not for natural cowardice, Jane Smith would prefer the solitude of the Apache woman's labor to the ministrations of obstetricians. The only way in which Jane Smith, mother of children, can put up with her memories is to discard them. This, with the astonishing gift humanity has of forgetting the unpleasant when it is once over, she manages to do. But her experiences have inevitably, if she is a reflective person, modified her attitude to herself. She will never, having borne a child, feel the same creature again. Passion may be a shared thing; in any case, if a woman loves a man truly, she is willing—and glad—to be his wife. But the long period of pregnancy, ending with the shattering fact of labor, is something that she must put through alone. She must be ugly, weak, miserable as an isolated individual; and at some hour or other of her prolonged purgatory, she is going to observe, reflect on, vividly and keenly ponder, her husband's immunity. If she is not sentimental, she will not make the mistake of glorifying herself as the sole parent and producer of the child to be born. Some women do that, taking unto themselves all the pride of parenthood. But Jane Smith has an honest mind; she is not going to consider her child more hers than its father's.

Jane Smith is also—remember—perfectly normal: ready to "accept the universe"; she is not going to resent the inequality of the physical burden. The fact that it is absolutely inevitable will in itself reconcile her to it. She believes that the race must go on, and she knows that it can go on only if women everywhere endure what she is enduring. She is not, I repeat, going to resent male immunity, any more than—sensible soul—she resents the precession of the equinoxes. Both are, as far as humanity is concerned, inevitable. But she is going to understand absolutely what was in Euripides' mind when he made Jason cry out against the way in which the race has to be reproduced. She is not going to agree, with her whole mind, for, remember, she has accepted the universe; but she is going to understand Jason's purely masculine point of view better than most men ever can. She is even going to see that to be included in another human being might revolt the imagination, as including another human being within oneself can revolt it. She has had the experience of a complete captivity; she has been the helpless habitation of another human creature; she has been invaded, to the uttermost recesses of her being, by a life not her own. These things do not happen to woman without profoundly modifying her outlook on life, especially her outlook on the problems of her sex.

Love and respect, which make all the difference between rape and the consummation of marriage, make also all the difference between happy and unhappy motherhood. Jane Smith, remember, is normal, is not morbid, is ready to play her part, and is asking only to base her theories on ascertained fact. She sees clearly that if women are to hold their heads high—and they must hold their heads high, for everyone's sake—they must find real compensation for the physical humiliation of marriage and childbearing. Love, which makes all things mystically clear, cannot be too heavily counted on; for it is too much to hope that most marriages, the planet over, will be garments of the great love. Women must go on bearing children, though they are not heroines of grand opera. Children themselves are not the whole answer, for they are the father's children as much as the mother's, and he has paid no such price, physically speaking, as she has paid.

What Jane Smith discovers, as she ponders, is that Nature has evidently never been preoccupied with making the sexes equal in either dignity or liberty. A child is begotten from the positive impulse, the overwhelming desire of the father; whereas conception is a passive role. To put the case extremely: a woman, as we all know, may conceive a child not only against her will, but when her aversion from the man amounts to horror; she could even conceive a child in a state of complete unconsciousness; whereas no child has ever been begotten except from strong desire—albeit merely physical—on the part of a man. Nature, which is interested solely and supremely in getting the race reproduced, has done only what is needful in the matter. She has stopped short of gratuitous favors. That the race should go on against all discouragements, moral, social, sentimental, it was necessary that some instinct should be well-nigh irresistible. Nature endowed the male with that instinct. It was not necessary to her purpose that the female should be endowed with it as well. It was necessary that women should be, generally speaking, capable of feeling sexual attraction; otherwise we should have the potential mother eternally eluding the potential father. But the mere fact that passion on the woman's part is not in the least necessary to the conception of a child shows where Nature chose to lay her stress and bestow her consideration. Not only did she make the male stronger than the female; she made the reproduction of the race a matter, initially, of his impulse and his volition. She saw to it that fatherhood should in no wise incapacitate him physically. She gave to the female the subservient role.

These facts—the mere alphabet of marriage and parenthood—once looked at for what they are worth, not confused with social or sentimental issues, may well give Jane Smith furiously to think. She comes inevitably to the conclusion, first, that male and female are not, in certain ways, equal; and that female "equality" is the fruit of male pity, or the attempt on the part of sensitive and high-minded men to redress artificially a balance that can never be redressed really. Nothing that women have won, in any society, whether it be chivalrous homage, or financial irresponsibility, or the vote itself, has been won except because men let them win it. On the merely moral side of the matter, Jane Smith will not ponder long, because moral superiority, or inferiority, or equality—whichever it may be—is a very difficult thing to determine. She will probably let it go at saying that men and women are both human beings, and have the defects of their respective virtues. She is interested, remember, merely in finding out what Nature has irrevocably decreed; and Nature has never been in the least preoccupied with morals. She will, on the other hand, linger over the question of the comparative mental powers of the sexes. That, indeed, is the chief point of conflict, for even Miss Mary Jones does not usually argue for the physical equality of the sexes. Miss Mary Jones takes it out in announcing that women are intellectually equal to men. That is the crux of the matter, for feminists and anti-feminists alike.

Jane Smith, then, takes account of stock. She sees her sex given the subservient and the painful role in the reproduction of the race. She sees that whether or not the family be the sole natural unit of society, during the helpless period of the offspring's existence the family has to be, if only temporarily, the unit. The male is given his physical immunity in order that he may be free to provide sustenance for an incapacitated mother and for helpless young. She shrewdly suspects that since he must have the strength for three, or four, or five, since he must not intermit his natural work, whether he is working for food directly, or indirectly in the form of money, it is his strength and his share in the impersonal work of the world that Nature is interested in. In other words, she suspects that immunity was granted to the better candidate, and that even had the case been reversed, the immune female would have been of less use than the immune male. She does not pretend to speak authoritatively of Nature's belief in the matter; she admits that the causal relation may be different—that the woman may be the lesser person because she has not this immunity. The results, however, seem to her extraordinarily similar. Either the woman is inferior because the passive role (in the full sense of "passive") has been thrust upon her, or the passive role was given her because she was inferior to the male. Remembering that enforced surrender of vital integrity, that subservience and obliteration, Jane Smith shrewdly suspects that Nature, framing her for one tremendous purpose, and one only—since the fulfilment of that purpose incapacitates her largely for other tasks—did not waste on woman more strength than she needed, for her peculiar function. In other words, that Nature gave immunity to the sex which could use it best; that if men are left free to do the varied work of the world, it is because they are more fitted for it. And that comes very near, in Jane Smith's honest reflection, to an admission that men are definitely superior. One would certainly expect Nature to handicap the creature that is less fitted to respond to the multitudinous demands of the human society—to withdraw from the world the person the world least needs. Jane Smith is not interested in setting the sexes over against each other; but she realizes, too, that the mere fact of superior physical strength makes for superior mental power. And she does not believe that Nature gave the subservient and suffering role to the female

sex merely by way of a compliment, for it would be a very back-handed one. Jane Smith, in her heart of hearts, finds herself suspecting that women, as a sex, are not "up to" men, as a sex.

III

Jane Smith, as I said, is not a morbid, or a sentimental, or a resentful person. She wants only the facts. She will then proceed to square her self-respect with the facts—not the facts with her self-respect. She has probably been bred up in some religion; and most religions grant women souls. Jane Smith is quite sure that if men have souls, she has one, too. If any final spiritual dignity is attainable by human beings, that final spiritual dignity is as much her goal as her husband's. She knows, of course, that all men are not born equal, and that many women are superior to many men. She is not going to sentimentalize her own role, but neither is she going to minimize it. If Nature gave men the physical immunity that frees them to do the work of the world, she gave to women qualities that enable them to preserve, for children and husband, certain priceless elements of existence. The atmosphere of conflict is not the atmosphere to develop those qualities; and the home is not the place where conflict should be necessary. Conflict, and the strength for conflict, belong in the world outside the home. Without sentimentalizing maternity, without, on the other hand, sentimentalizing male immunity, she realizes that her role is ultimately and absolutely important. To be necessary to the fundamental purposes of humanity is dignity enough for a human being. Jane Smith, in her more moral moments, desires not to challenge the male on his own ground but so to harmonize her role with his that male and female, husband and wife, shall present, as it were, a complete working organism for the service of society. She is no saint; and if she is willing to complement the male role instead of usurping it, it is because she knows that complementing it is the most that, in the end, she can manage with real success; that when Nature itself proclaims her subserviency, her only game is to accept it and make of it a beautiful and dignified thing.

Nor is Jane Smith a reactionary, or a traitor to her sex. She will, I think, welcome any honest achievement of women: she will be the first to applaud those who stand out from the ruck. She will want the women who prefer independent and impersonal endeavor to the more personal task of marriage and motherhood to be successful and praised of men. She will never forget, however, that the woman who has chosen independence of this sort is not the average woman, and cannot decide the problems of the average woman. She realizes that the fundamental problem is not what women can achieve when they evade the duties Nature has imposed upon the sex, but what women can achieve when they fulfil the complete natural destiny. In other words, that the attitude of society at large to female capacity must be determined by the capacity of the wife and mother; and that claims of equality are valid only if the wife and mother issues them and makes them good. It is Jane Smith's firm, if reluctant, belief that the wife and mother—taking the race as a whole—will neither issue the claim, nor make it good; that the present "emancipation" of women has no more permanent significance in human history than had the Kingdom of the Amazons. She would not have women medievally confined—though she will also be well aware that many medieval women carried far heavier responsibilities of a business and administrative kind than most modern women; that they managed estates, held courts, and dealt in politics, to an extent that in this age would be considered extraordinary; that, indeed, the deepest immersion of the female in important affairs has come in periods when her personal submission to the male was complete.

It will be strange if Jane Smith does not in the end wonder whether talk of "equality" will not give place to a sharper definition of differences; whether the maximum efficiency of women as well as men will not be reached by admitting certain inferiorities to begin with, and dealing with life on that basis. Certainly she finds her own dignity, her own self-respect more or less after the fashion of the Christian when he repeats the words "whose service is perfect freedom." The Christian knows that the service of God is not, in many senses, freedom at all. It is only to the man who accepts God without after-thought or reservation that His service is perfect freedom. It is only when Jane Smith accepts her inequalities, her inferiorities, as fundamental and inalterable that she can proceed to envisage herself as free. Freedom is freedom within possibilities; and accepting the universe is the beginning of self-respect. If the sex persists in considering its inequalities as accidental, not fundamental, the war for equality must needs go on. But Jane Smith has decided that Nature has given the lie to those extremer pretensions. She refuses to waste her time on them, therefore.

Since every law of life involves a human duty in relation to it, Jane Smith, who has experienced marriage and maternity, will naturally ask herself what duty of hers is defined or conditioned by the state of affairs that she has found. Let no one be shocked if she comes, at long last, to the conclusion that the reins of government in any normal household can be held ultimately by only one person, and that, as far as she can honestly see, the male would seem to be, as physicians say, "indicated." Men have never shown much disposition to usurp the distinctly female responsibilities; and she will not be hard put to it to keep the governance of the domain that is obviously hers. She will have little time or opportunity, if she wished, to regulate the work her husband does outside the home: for his impersonal responsibilities are not to his wife but to a stranger. In every household, however, there are questions to be decided which are neither peculiarly woman's nor man's field, yet which affect them both nearly. These are decided by consultation, agreement, or compromise. The only case that presents any difficulty to Jane Smith's reflections is the case of positive disagreement. It is in the nature of a decision to reject one alternative and accept another; without such acceptance, such rejection, there can be no decision—the matter, whatever it is, is left hanging. Practically, that will not do.

To Jane Smith, who has accepted Nature's discriminations against her, comes now the necessity of accepting the logical sequel. Since there are moments when one opinion must prevail, it would seem to her indicated that the opinion of the superior person should prevail. That it may not always, in any given case, be the superior opinion is more unfortunate than significant. Nothing is so destructive as indecision; and it is obvious that if decisions are to be made, there must be some ultimate court of appeal. There cannot be two ultimate courts of appeal. She sees society, in every land, holding the male responsible to the outer world for his wife and minor children. The person who is held responsible is the person who must decide. Jane Smith will probably make up her mind, in the end, that the male has more legitimate pretensions than the female to the dominant role. She may never put it to herself that it is her moral duty to obey her husband, but she will put it to herself that the interests of order and efficiency are best served by his having the final word.

IV

We said that Jane Smith would be the last to grudge to the special case its special opportunity. That is true. She wishes the utmost possible fruition for every woman's gift. Jane Smith is not anti-feminist: far from it. She is not, I think, particularly enthusiastic about women in politics, because she recognizes there the likelihood of a dilemma. The really valuable person in affairs of government—as in every other field—is the trained person. The man who really counts politically is the man who has prepared himself arduously for a political career. The woman who would count politically must also be willing to give her most serious attention, her best years, to some activity that prepares her to govern. The wife and mother cannot do this. During the years when she should have been in closest contact with public problems, she has been given up to problems, equally vital but wholly different, within the home. The women who can really train themselves to be politically valuable are the women who have not spent their youth and early middle-age upon purely personal interests and duties. Jane Smith is a tolerant creature, and loyal, besides, to her own sex; but she notes with apprehension the tendency of the exceptional woman who achieves political standing not only to view public questions from the point of view of her sex, alone, but from the point of view of a minority of her sex. Jane Smith, for example, views with amused alarm the tendency of the feminist to fight for laws that ignore her—Jane Smith's—most fundamental discoveries. She will not support legislation that thrusts all the women of the world into a position that few women, comparatively speaking, hold. She feels that the normal woman, doing her normal job, is no more a business or a political animal than she is a fighting animal. She sees Miss Mary Jones arguing in high places for "rights" that the sex as a whole cannot effectually claim, for responsibilities that the sex as a whole cannot effectively discharge. No law can be fair to all individuals, and Jane Smith thinks it better that Mary Jones should suffer an undeserved eclipse than that the average millions should be thrust into a position which they cannot fill. She is quite willing to have Mary Jones herself a senator, but she is mortally afraid that Mary Jones, being quite unable to speak for her sex at large (yet usually determined to do just that), will make the sex at large ridiculous by attributing to it powers that it has not.

Jane Smith does not sentimentalize or idealize men; but she sees them obviously fitter, by natural opportunity, for certain tasks than women. Mary Jones does not prove the political value of women any more than the Battalion of Death proved the military value of women. Yes, if Jane Smith is English or American, she will probably cast her vote—for she not only accepts the universe, she accepts the present period of history. If she quietly asks her husband how she shall vote, it is not because she considers herself disqualified to think about these things; it is because every honest voter makes up his mind after much consultation and argument with his kind, and as much tapping as possible of the sources of expert information. Jane Smith is an honest woman, and she has tried consulting her own kind, in vain. She probably prefers her own husband's opinion to the windy echoes of the opinions of other women's husbands.

Undoubtedly Miss Mary Jones could tell her, fluently enough, how to vote; but she is a little afraid of Miss Mary Jones, who seems to her to base her partisanships on misconceptions, if not on ignorance, of Jane Smith. She is not at all sure, that is, that Mary Jones is really speaking for Jane Smith, or can intelligently represent her. She comes near to believing that the father of her children understands her political needs better than the cleverest and most altruistic spinster. Moreover, in her long pondering on masculine immunities, she has come to admire—I will not say envy—most of all the immunity from sudden gusts of emotion and prejudice which even the sanest woman will not escape. She credits men, to be sure, with emotions and prejudices; but she feels that these are usually traceable to something at least more stable than a state of nerves. She who has borne children knows how deeply physical conditions reach down into the nervous system. She knows, too, that the creature to whom physical health is the first of all duties—for the sake of children about to enter or recently entered upon their earthly career—is not the creature best equipped for dispassionate mental effort. The mother's chief duty for long stretches of time is to inhibit her "nerves," and to emulate the placidity (to say nothing else) of the cow. When one considers—as Jane Smith does— that under the best possible conditions each child means one year out of a woman's life: months of pregnancy, during which she must protect the life within her, weeks of labor and its aftereffects, weeks or months, probably, of feeding the child from her breast: a period during which most women, given up to this special duty, can hardly be assigned with advantage to any duties more impersonal or public—when one considers these things, one will not lightly say that women stand in a similar position to men for dealing with the affairs of the world.

There has been latterly, in discussion of the equality of the sexes, a certain stress on the word "economic." Economic equality would lay on the woman a financial, legal, and social responsibility equivalent to the man's. This conception of justice need hardly detain us, even though it should momentarily prevail. Jane Smith, the world over, is not going to be able to hold a job as her husband can. Even if she finds employment outside the home, when she can, she is perforce going to belong to the type of casual worker who is the last to achieve the real rewards of labor, the last to be considered important. Even if she sticks through thick and thin to that job, she cannot stick to it as uninterruptedly as the male. Even if the government takes over her children at birth (one of the extremer solutions) she still has to reckon with those intervals when she must pass her job on to someone else, and drop temporarily out of the running. Nor does she see any likelihood of any government's permanently succeeding to the parental role. Both she and her husband know that to no individual, to no system, to no law, can the child ever be so important as to its parents; and in the end the human race will see (as it has hitherto always seen) that the truest economy lies in getting the maximum solicitude for the least expenditure. Parental affection is too profound, too universal a thing not to be capitalized by any successful state.

Feminists will point to the woman who has borne her children young and has reached a comfortable middle age, with health, leisure, and money to attend to intellectual or political affairs. These women, unimpaired in health, free, rich, who have also been able to keep up a continuous intellectual development, are proportionally very few. Not many men who have passed the decade from twenty-five to thirty-five in invalidism bulk big in affairs thereafter. Even leaving actual ill-health out of the question, the seclusion, the special concentration, and the special interruptions of the childbearing years have no better parallel than invalidism. And when Jane Smith considers that for most mothers of children, who cannot hire people to take over their job, the rearing of the children borne adds another decade to the original one, she sees her sex handicapped through half of active life. In the name of common sense, she is not going to turn over the administration of her country to such. Her rough and ready reasoning would run: the normal woman living the normal life is incapacitated for the management of national affairs; and it is dangerous business to let the unmarried and the childless woman be spokesman for the women she does not really represent. The fact that many men in public life are not husbands and fathers counts less. In the first place, most public men are husbands and fathers; and if the fantastic case arose of a Senate and House (for example) composed almost wholly of bachelors, people would sit up and take notice and object. Jane Smith herself would object; but first of all to object would be Miss Mary Jones.

To be sure, as we have said, Jane Smith goes farther. With all her loyalty to the exceptional woman, she does not believe in the equality of the sexes, as a general proposition. She sees no warrant in Nature for such a belief; and Nature is the one thing that cannot be bucked. If Nature has assigned her, in no uncertain terms, a passive and subservient part in the game of life, she feels that her strength lies not in trying to get that assignment reversed, but in perfecting her own role, in being as virtuous, and various, and intelligent, as she can, within her obvious limitations. The superwoman is as useless a criterion as the superman. Jane Smith, facing facts, makes up her mind —reluctantly, it may well be, and after a bitter struggle—that the fair rewards of feministic doctrine have nothing to do with her, and can come her way only theoretically. Therefore, she rejects them.

The Enfranchisement of the Girl of Twenty-one

By Anthony M. Ludovici

It is not change or reform that ought to alarm us, but the fact that hardly any change allowed to take place in England today appears to bear any known relation to a general scheme or an ultimate general end, clearly visualized. To know exactly what one wants and courageously to devise the means whereby it may be brought about, is surely admirable. It not only inspires friends and supporters with confidence and hope, but also imposes even upon enemies the duty of more narrowly defining their position. Nothing good, however, can possibly result from listless drifting, and those who practise opportunism so consistently as to exploit every current and move with every tide must in the end alienate all allies, discourage all adherents, and satisfy only the indifferent—until the rocks are reached!

Now what is happening in England today in regard to the relation and specialization of the sexes is an example of such drifting, which cannot fail to end disastrously, because no one is clear about the inevitable result of the reforms that are being prosecuted.

Just as our grandfathers and great-grandfathers dealt blindly with the forces which brought about the Industrial Revolution, and by so doing created many of our most difficult problems and most intolerable scourges, so we now, by refusing to frame a conscious and deliberate policy in regard to the problem of the sexes, by allowing the ship of state to cruise at the mercy of every crank who agitates the tiller, are preparing disasters for generations to come, which touch the very heart of life.

What is needed most urgently, therefore, is a general awakening to the principal issues at stake. Even if, after such an awakening, an erroneous policy continues to be adopted, even if after the end-result of present-day reforms has been clearly visualized, the modern trend is confirmed by the consensus of contemporary opinion, it would surely be better to know whither we are tending than to march unconsciously towards a goal the nature of which no one can define, and the desirability of which, therefore, no one can judge.

Thus, although I may appear to some to entertain

unjustifiably pessimistic views regarding the value of modern feminism, it seems to me that, in my endeavours to reduce the whole of the tangled problem to a plain and definite issue, I may, despite, or precisely on account of, the opposition I provoke, be promoting the end most urgently needed—a more clear-sighted policy all round, both on the part of the feminists, their opponents, and the more or less indifferent public beyond. At least a plain statement of my views may help to promote a greater definition of policy and aims on the part of those who are now irresolute; it may awaken those others who are preparing a future the evils of which they have not troubled to explore.

The question for the people and the Government of England is, What do they precisely want to achieve? What is the end they contemplate? They evidently wish to transform woman. Have they any clear idea regarding the sort of being they hope to see evolved out of the creature on whom they are now practising their newfangled experiments? The facts of evolution have shown that little is impossible in the matter of fresh adaptations, and their resulting transformations. When once the end desired is clearly presented to consciousness, there is hardly any modification, within reason, which slow development may not bring about. But are present reformers aware of any definite end to which they are tending? I can hardly believe so. At all events, I cannot believe that the public behind them are, for if they were modern, feminism would be short-lived.

It is not the impossibility of making women more like men which is the burden of my criticism of the feminists, but the obvious likelihood of this end being achieved if it be really desired, and if the means to secure it be conscientiously and perseveringly pursued. I do not question the efficacy of the feminists' methods so much as the soundness of their taste. I ask if the masculinization of the female is desirable.

Hitherto the qualities in both male and female which have favoured the efficient performance of their specialized functions have been more or less successfully preserved by a severe demarcation between their respective interests and duties. Attempts to break down this frontier, such as the feminist movement of the seventeenth century in France, and the earlier feminist movements of ancient Greece and Rome, all came to naught, because of the dramatic and total evanescence of the societies in which the experiments were made. But this does not mean that the present attempt will necessarily fail through the same cause. It may or it may not. If it does not, then we have to ask ourselves what advantages are to be derived from the forcible destruction of differences in social function which, after all, are but the reflection of the specialized physical functions which each sex stands for. It is essential to be clear about this matter. It may, in the end, prove to be only a question of taste. But we should not forget that the taste of one age determines, to a very large extent, the conditions of existence for the ages that follow.

The House of Commons quite erroneously, as I believe, extended the franchise to a certain section of women without first pausing to ask whether the nature of the best and most normal woman would be impaired or improved by a development of those qualities which go to make a good πολίτης, or politically functioning citizen. The Government now proposes to increase this error of omission by giving the vote to younger women without first considering whether, in view of their greater malleability and pliability, the consequences of this Procrustean imposition will not necessarily be much more severe.

We cannot have it both ways. The pleasure of fireworks would not be increased by doing away with the inconveniences of groping about in the dark. That is probably why nobody dreams of having a pyrotechnical display at noon. In less obvious matters, however, the modern town man, with his vitiated sense of reality, conceives it to be perfectly possible to enjoy the advantages of two utterly conflicting states. He sees nothing odd or mistaken in the policy of urging reluctant and desirable women into politics and in wishing woman to remain as his father and grandfather knew her—equipped for the efficient and successful creation of happy and durable home conditions, and the perfect relationship which consists in maternal and filial devotion.

My own criticism of the present trend, therefore, is quite briefly as follows. A large and most important department of human life is dependent upon the hearty and voluntary concurrence of the female with Nature's scheme. The female, however, can only give her hearty approval to that scheme and play her part in it efficiently and well, if her emotional equipment is unimpaired, and, above all, not impoverished.   An enormous number of the necessary actions and reactions of home life receive their original impetus from the emotional riches of the female. She it is who chiefly weaves the precious web of attachments which make the home the focus, the core, of the nation and ultimately of the Empire.   And the richer her emotional equipment is, the more efficiently is this task of construction accomplished.   From the day of her betrothal to the moment when she takes her last grandchild to her arms, all the trials and difficulties of her rôle in life are alleviated and taken as a matter of course, because she approaches them, not with cold and intellectual detachment, but with deep emotional impulses of all kinds.   To force upon her a permanent preoccupation or interest in which intellectual detachment—a certain *froideur*—is an essential prerequisite, is, therefore, to develop a side of her nature which will prove an obstacle rather than an aid in the discharge of all those other duties connected with her specialized functions.   It means that, in order to turn her into a creature capable of philosophic calm and indifference, something belonging to her old nature must perish or decline, for intellectual detachment and emotional direction are mutually exclusive.   When the first is developed, the other must suffer.

This may or may not be a desirable end.   But has it ever been clearly conceived as the end to which modern tendencies are pointing ?   The introduction of women into politics, into the atmosphere of courts of law, Parliament, etc., may be the necessary and inevitable expression of the modern world's wishes.   But the really important question is whether the modern world actually desires the inevitable consequences.   Does it wish to impoverish the emotional nature of the best and most normal women ?

If, however, it did not understand the consequences nine years ago, when it gave older women the vote, it can hardly be hoped that it will do so now.   For if the best women of thirty and over still remain to a very large extent under the sway of their emotional equipment, it is quite certain that women of more tender years, standing on the threshold of the career which will be made or marred according to the richness or poverty of their emotional gifts, are, or should be, wholly under the direction of the latter.   So much of vital importance has to be decided and done by them which only their emotions can help them to decide and do efficiently, that any other form of guidance may actually be dangerous.

But politics represent interests and problems which are the least suited to an emotional approach. The most alarming vices of democracy, its most regrettable consequences, can all be traced to the difficulty of excluding emotionalism from an activity in which a mentally undisciplined and untutored mob may constitute itself a determining factor. Democratic politics tend in any case to degenerate into a demagogic exploitation of popular emotions, unless there is always a balance in favour of the intellectually detached, the rational, and the philosophic elements in the population.

The female franchise clause of the Representation of the People's Act of 1918 certainly levelled a serious blow at all those elements which tend to counterbalance the emotionalism of modern politics. But if the franchise is now to be extended to 4,000,000 girls between twenty-one and twenty-five, then the intellectually detached and rationally minded elements in the population will be wiped out, and democratic control, at least in England, will commit suicide by becoming utterly irresponsible and ridiculous.

What is the alternative ? To deprive the young women of their emotional direction, and thus fit them for their new political activities ? This end is certainly possible. But, when once it has been clearly visualized, will any sensible person solemnly assert that it is desirable? It will mean the destruction of normal women as we know them and value them, and meanwhile—during the period of imperfect adaptation—the total degradation of the political life of the country.

But the truth is that modern men are not aware of this alternative. They are not sufficiently clear about sex matters in general to be able to see that in this question it is impossible to have it both ways. They have committed one grave error, for which they cannot fail sooner or later to be punished. They have generalized so wildly about " woman " that in the end they can no longer see the individual trees for the wood. They took " woman " to be an inclusive term, capable of being applied indiscriminately to every member of the female sex. And thus when a handful of intermediate types—each with five-eighths female and three-eighths male elements in her constitution—arose and posed as representatives of the " women " of the nation, and clamoured for the vote, the right to sit on juries, and the privilege of being treated for most social purposes as men, modern Englishmen thought they were confronted by the whole of the female sex. They imagined that " women " really wanted the things these " intermediates " agitated for. And why ? Simply because the agitators happened outwardly to look like women !

With all the cold detachment of incomplete beings, these feminist pioneers and leaders rightly claimed that their emotions never once disturbed the even tenor of their thoughts—nay more, they undertook to prove that they could be as neutral as wax figures endowed with brains when confronted by any political or intellectual problem which required dispassionate attention, and they actually persuaded the male section of the population that they represented " Woman " ! Such deceptions are unpardonable, but surely it is far more unpardonable to be taken in by them. The agitators and pioneers of the Woman's Movement were largely of this intermediate type, capable of packing their emotions and their passions into their cigarette cases if the necessity arose. That explains why, in the thick of the old Suffragette fights, thousands of bewildered women of the more normal type protested that they did not want the things the " intermediates " clamoured for. But the bulk of these normal women were inarticulate and unorganized, and so the nation was not impressed by them.

It is the same today. The agitation for the " Flapper vote " has followed the same lines. To suppose that the handful who really want it represent the majority of girls of twenty-one is to allow oneself to be hoodwinked by a mere disguise, a sartorial trick. It is, however, much more serious than that in its consequences. For it means that ultimately, if we wish to make our young women fit for politics, or if we wish to save our political life from Nemesis, we must endeavour as quickly as possible to transform all our desirable and warm-blooded young women into intermediate types—cold, impoverished, listless, passionless, and abnormal creatures, standing half-way between the masculine and feminine poles, and therefore possessing none of the best qualities of either.

PUBLIC OPINION—WOMEN IN INDUSTRY

Margaret G. Bondfield, M. P.

ON THE general question of organization for women there was complete apathy during the nineteenth century, not to say antagonism, on the part of certain sections of men trade unionists. Some of the earlier discussions of this question make indescribably quaint reading today. In Mrs. Drake's book, "Women in Trade Unions," a paragraph occurs describing the agitation in the nail-making industry, in 1882. "Mr. Hill, secretary of the Oldswinford Nailers, tried to arrange a compromise. The men's object was only to 'restrict females to certain classes of labor, but not to stop them from working.' He suggested that 'if women would only keep to the proper size of nails as suggested in the report of the government commission, and not make above size one,' they would not want legislation.' He further advised women, who were thrown out of work in this way, to enter domestic service." Disputes continued as to the proper size of nail for women to make until at last a resolution was brought before the Trades Union Congress that "where women do the same work as men, they shall receive equal pay." The men's representative explained "that he had come to the conclusion that nothing but better pay for women could cure the evil, and they had therefore resolved to organize women as soon as possible."

It is quite true that one of the most talked-of strikes in the early nineteenth century was that of the women bookbinders against the British and Foreign Bible Society, and in this the men supported the women. The general attitude of the men, however, was similar to that of the nail-makers, and it was not until the second period of trade-union activity—that which followed the unrest of the early seventies — that trade unionism for women made much headway.

In 1874 the Women's Trade Union League was founded by Mrs. Emma Paterson, with the object of stimulating the organization of women in trade unions. Between this year and 1887 the League was successful in encouraging the formation of a large number of small women's unions in different trades. In the latter year it became a Federation of Women's Unions, and so gained a great influence on women's questions not only in the trade-union movement, but in Parliament and in the formation of public opinion. It was largely owing to the work of the League during the last years of the nineteenth century and the beginning of the twentieth century, and to the Sweated Industries Exhibition organized by the Anti-Sweating League, that public opinion was at last aroused on the whole question of the sweated conditions under which women were working, and this began to be reflected in legislative action.

In 1901 the Factory Act was amended, and in 1909 the Trade Boards Act was passed, which at last set up machinery for the establishment of minimum wages in the most sweated industries.

Concurrently with these activities, the Shop Assistants Union was working both industrially and politically, and secured the passing of the Shops Act.

During the war the question of the status of women's labor took on a different aspect. The fight for the raising of the minimum standard still went on, but, owing to the increased economic power of the workers, and the great demand for women in all branches of industry, the demand for equal pay for equal work which had always been the women's remedy for the evils of unfair competition and underpaid labor, became more specific and developed into the cry of "the same rate for the job." The importance of the problem of women's employment and its relation to industry as a whole can be realized by the fact that the Cabinet set up a special War Cabinet Committee on Women in Industry, with terms of reference covering the whole field of women's industrial problems. Its report was not considered satisfactory by organized women and Mrs. Sidney Webb signed a minority report recommending the adoption of the principle of the national minimum, the occupational rate, and the rejection amongst others of the principle of a separate male and female rate and of the determination of wages by family obligations.

Acute as were these problems during the war, those which arose through the demobilization of thousands of women on the signing of the Armistice were in a sense more important because more likely to be permanent. The pressure brought by the women workers themselves and the realization of the injustice done to them in being cast aside when their services were no longer required, resulted in the reappointment of the Central Committee on Women's Training and Employment (originally set up at the outbreak of war to administer the Queen's Work for Women Fund, raised by public subscription to relieve distress among women arising from the war). It was now faced with the new problem of distress among women as an effect of the transition from war to peace conditions.

On January 5, 1920, the Minister of Labor reappointed the committee with the following terms of reference: "To consider, devise and carry out special schemes of work and training for women unemployed or women whose earning capacity and opportunities were injuriously affected as a result of conditions arising out of the war." More important still, a sum of money was added to the balance in hand from the National Relief Fund, and it was run in close cooperation with the Ministry of Labor.

Similarly, the government cooperated in the formation of the Society for the Oversea Settlement of British Women, which deals with the many problems incidental to the migration of women to the Dominions.

On all these committees and in all governmental inquiries representatives of organized women were recognized and were in many cases appointed members of the respective committees.

The corresponding development of opinion within the trade-union movement itself will be dealt with in a subsequent article.

Side by side with this comparatively slow awakening of the public conscience on the question of women in industry and its reflection in governmental activity, was the more spectacular political agitation of the women for the vote. The trade-union and labor movement in England has always supported and worked for the principle of equal franchise for men and women, but the women trade unionists have never been purely feminists, because, even in the case of the National Federation of Women Workers, which was a purely women's society, they have always believed in and worked towards the ideal of men and women working side by side, and on equal terms, or in their own union. The feminist agitation is not in any sense representative of trade-union or Labor opinion and it only touches the industrial side of women's development on the question of protective legislation, where the feminists demand that there shall be no protective legislation for women until it also applies to men, while the trade-union and

labor women take the line that, while wanting equal protection for men and women, it is for them to hold what they have been able to gain in the way of special legislation for women to raise the standard of women's employment and conditions as high as possible, in order to bring them more on an equality with the men trade unionists.

This feminist attitude has never found expression in the legislation of the country, nor has it had any effect upon the policy of the trade unions and the great mass of labor and working women. The Women's Trade Union League and the Women's Group of the T. U. C. (which has replaced it), the General Council of the T. U. C.—the supreme body as regards policy of the trade-union movement—and the Standing Joint Committee of Industrial Women's Organizations, representing the trade union women, the whole of the women in the cooperative movement, and the women in the political labor movement—totaling in all over a million women—all of them are quite definitely in favor of protective legislation for women.

Thus, during the last hundred years, women in industry in Great Britain have slowly won their way towards recognition as an integral part of industry, and have played their part in arousing the public conscience and securing that it shall be reflected in the legislation of the country.

Woman's Morality in Transition

By JOSEPH COLLINS

A Doctor of Medicine and Neurologist Practicing in New York; Formerly Professor of Neurology at the New York Post-Graduate Medical School; Author of Various Works on Medical, Literary and Other Subjects

PROPHECY is an essential part of the physician's art. In practice it is called prognosis—forecasting what the future has in store for the patient. Habituated to making such estimates, he is tempted to try his hand in other fields. Hence, I am easily persuaded to say what is likely to be the result of the advent and activities of the New Woman; what the effects of the dissemination of the ideas and conceptions for which she is held responsible will be on morals, manners, marriage and man. The expert in prognosis must have large and varied experience. The person who ventures to outline the future activities of the New Woman nust be an observer of the present and a tudent of the past, sympathizer with women, familiar with their psychology.

Though it may ot be generally admitted that the New Woman exists, no one is so obdurate is to maintain that woman is the image f man and not the image of God, or deny that she has wrested from unwilling man the privileges that he arrogated to himself. By ways and means which are neither clear nor obvious, she has won a loodless victory of independence for her x and a measure of freedom which assures her equality with man in the great hings of life. Now she has a secure place n the sunlight. It has not come about

Wide World

DR. JOSEPH COLLINS

gradually and insensibly, but overnight, as it were, in the span of one generation.

The acceptance of the new ideal for woman had its birth with the century. Man and his institutions, secular and civil, have striven from time immemorial to enslave woman; that is, to deny her the rights and privileges to which she was entitled. While doing it he has indulged himself in what is known in psychology as rationalization, which means giving rich reasons for poor motives. He has claimed that she was a clinging vine that needed support, protection and pruning; that she was modest and tender-minded; that her intellect was dominated and directed by her emotions; in short, that she was a child in everything save body; that she was to be cajoled, coerced, caressed, conquered, trimmed, disciplined and corrected just as children are. She was to do what she was told when she was told. Sometimes she did, but more often she pretended. Hence her reputation for mendacity, intuitiveness and resourcefulness. She might look upon ripe, succulent, gustatory fruit, but she was not permitted to pluck or eat it save when man said she could. His passion for standardization was first vented upon woman. He standardized her morals and her manners, her activities and her aspirations, her indul-

33

The two figures at the left represent women's fashions between 1848 and 1860; the two at the right those between 1860 and 1864

gences and inhibitions. He never made a greater failure in anything he ever undertook. He was bound to fail, for he started by affronting the Science of Life.

Man and woman are identical in their origin, genesis and destiny. They have one purpose—to reproduce their kind. Subduing the earth is incidental and contributory, that their descendants may have a propitious and pleasant place in which to propagate. To promote this purpose man secretes one specific element, woman the other. All other differences are minor and inconsequential. The soil is more important than the seed. Hazard or a comet may bring seed, but if soil is lacking sterility will prevail. Woman is the soil, man the seed. Man's attitude of mastery toward woman is the best example of inferiority complex that exists. Woman is far from satisfactory, but the hiatuses of her mind, the indentations of her emotions, the intermittences of her heart are the result of the artificializing procedure to which man has subjected her with few spasmodic interruptions since the beginning of time. And now it is a thing of the past.

Woman has obtained her freedom. What is she going to do with it? It is too much to expect she will use it wisely and prudently. If she can learn by experience, one day she will have wisdom. Of one thing we may be sure, she will not be willing to be the mirror of man, his servant, his slave or his shadow, save when she is in the throes of love. The transitoriness of passionate love is known to all save youth. Transmuted into affection, admiration and respect, it becomes the most inexhaustible source of the effects, the most indestructible building material of happiness, the Staff of Life second only to bread.

"New Woman" is an infelicitous designation. There is, of course, no such thing. Woman has forced the bars of her cage, cast the manacles off her ankles, shed th artificial skin in which she was encase and immobilized. She is the same today ¿ she was in the days of Ruth and Esther Penelope and Nausica, Ninon de l'Enclos and Charlotte Corday. She knows the same weaknesses and desires, has the same in tellectual equipment and the same emotiona reactions. For countless centuries she ha been told that she has qualities that she does not have; that she likes things for which she has an unconscious abhorrence that she has anatomical and physiological limitations that seriously handicap her in the race of life.

The World War came. Her life was pulled from its hinges with a jerk, and for five disintegrating years she had to adjust herself to a manless world in which habi' and wont were at the mercy of constant. changing conditions. She had to do many things that she had not thought hersel capable of doing, because she had never been permitted to try them. She was praised, blamed, discussed, accepted, acclaimed, rejected, but she rushed forth to accomplish a duty which was opposed to her previous monotonous routine. She found thrills, fulfillment and joy in this new life which broadened her viewpoint and made her take inventory of herself. The result is modern woman. Consciousness of her value had already been half awakened by the previous generation of mothers who had felt the stirrings of Feminism. She found in the war the field in which she could practice becoming what she thinks she has become—independent of man, a power unto herself. She has gestated new ideas and brought forth new methods of thinking and learning. She is now convinced that she has reached equality with man in so far as mental and practical achievements are concerned, and she has set out to prove it. In every field of activity she has made a splendid showing, save soldiering. The end of all wars may be in sight when women are sent to the colors and men stay home to tend domestic duties and cultivate the fields. Woman's sadistic and cruel mind will prompt her to such undreamed-of methods of torture for the enemy that people will prefer living in peace with their neighbors much rather than battling with them.

With the spread of the new ideas which make woman mentally the equal of man, there has come a new code of morality, or rather a new distribution of moral ideas between the sexes. Woman, finding that she could assume the duties of man in the professional sphere, insists on sharing his alleged rights and long-established privileges in the moral one. In her discoveries of herself she has stumbled upon the fact that far from being what man has always asserted she was, timid, prudish and monogamous, she is bold, immodest and polyandrous. She is making short business of adapting the existing code of morality to her new interpretation of it. As a result, many women no longer consider it essential to enter matrimony in complete ignorance of what it implies of duties and pleasures. They insist upon formulating their own conception of the marriage bond and have ceased to accept its laws as man made them. Undeniably the effect is prejudicial just now for the future of the race and the lasting quality of marriage, as it was meant by the Church and as centuries have accepted it. When woman was subjected to the autocratic pleasure of her husband, and knew that by refusing her loyalty and fidelity to him she would be an object of scorn to the world—and by shirking her duties toward the race she would heap upon herself condemnation of the Church and punishment in the hereafter

At the left the two figures show women's fashions in 1879; the two at right those of a few years later

Women's dress in 1887, when the bustle was in fashion

in its disfavor. Society, after all, reduces itself to the family, and a family is the only justification for marriage. If it were not for children, and especially now that we are becoming more and more convinced that we make our own hell on earth, why should people want to marry when they can have the joys of matrimony with none of its onus? Thus, the creation of a new family in the bosom of the old one justifies amply the sacrifices of personal freedom and independence that marriage implies. The failure of the modern woman to recognize her duty toward the Sacrament which Paul thought preferable to burning may turn marriage into a jolly fair where

—the future of the world was thought safe. She has changed all this, and unless the tide turns and brings woman back to her first and fundamental duty, that of bearing children, there is no prophesying the future.

It would be idle to condemn woman or even to look for harmful effect in the fact that she no longer feels herself subservient to man in marriage or out of marriage; indeed, actual observation and personal experience may serve as an acceptable selection when the time for marriage comes, and the new code of morality which proclaims that what is good for man is equally good for woman has no ill omen in itself for the future. It will become a subject for fearful apprehension should woman refuse to admit that her lot in life is fundamentally different from that of man, but the fire-like rapidity with which she has adopted modes and mannerisms which identify her with man encourages us to believe she will return just as fast to a more equilibrated medium.

The attitude toward marriage which makes divorce a common, everyday occurrence, accepted by society, quasi-recognized by the Church and condemned only by the conservative has much in its favor, and more

one will be so absorbed getting in and out of it that there will be no time or desire for procreating a family. The warning not must be given to women, but it is within themselves that they will answer it. A profession is not incompatible with marriage and children, but woman too often chooses to make it so.

Man, be he pietist, puritan or pagan, must eventually realize that woman of the future is not going to sit back supinely and observe him suck life's honeycomb. She is going have pleasures and pastimes equivalent his. It is likely that they will be much same in view of the way she has taken tobacco and alcohol during the past f years. To be cognizant of her indulgence will sometimes harass him and often humiliate him, but it will not drive him cra: When, however, she will insist upon having the same amatory license that he gran himself then he will go off his head, be parent, brother or husband, unless he see things in a very different light from that which he sees them today. In head-hidi' man has the ostrich beaten "to a frazzl He knows that he is polygamous by natu: but he tells himself and believes that w man is monogamous; he knows that pa sion can sway him as the wind sways the reed, but he tells himself and believes that only "bad" women are equally swayable by creative instinct; he knows that the vagrant and purposeful thought of man has always been and always will be concerned with sex to a tremendous degree, but he tells himself and believes that woman has no such thoughts and that if she does she has "fallen" or is on the way; and he believes that the experience that makes him ruins woman. Man must undergo a change of heart to keep pace with woman's change of mind.

No one can have extensive and intimate contact with the rising generation of women and not know that the old code of sex morality has suffered and is still suffering profound modifications. There are many reasons for it and not one of the least is the dissemination of the doctrine and practice of birth control. Without here passing judgment upon it other than to say that in my opinion it is one of the most dangerous weapons of the age, since it tends to promote sterility of the good and fertility of the bad, it must be admitted that it has done more to destroy purity than temptations or tests. All that which spells enlightenment has had much to do with its vogue also.

Modern women know life at the age of 18 as well as, if not infinitely better than, their mothers knew it when they had reached late maturity, borne a number of children and encountered successes and failures in quantities sufficient to temper their souls. They have definite ideas about right and wrong, pleasure and pain, morality and ethics, privileges and duties. The manner in which these ideas are developed and directed will make for good or for evil. A woman of 40 today is as young as her sister of 20. Old age has been receding in a long stride when youth forced it beyond the half century limit. This extends the period of woman's activity to a considerable degree. What she will make of it is still a question heavy with doubt, which time alone can answer.

What may be called morality in general does not seem to have been affected by the New Woman. Lying, murder, stealing, bearing false witness are held in the cus-

The capes and puffed shoulder effects that characterized women's dress in 1897

Wide World

A woman's formal afternoon costume in the style of 1927

twisted with our thread of life, nothing but the scythe of death can cut. The divorce record in all countries save those under the dominion of the Roman Catholic Church attests it. It may please the Bishop of the Episcopal Church of New York to say that trial marriage is not marriage at all, and that companionate marriage is nothing but a brazen proposal to sanction irregular relations, but dogmatic as he is there is nothing in his past performances to suggest that he is infallible. The sooner religion reconciles itself with the new ideas and the new powers the better it will be for religion and for those to whom religion is necessary, that is, to the people by and large. I cannot see that the New Woman is particularly concerned with religion, but when she becomes so, I venture to believe that she will insist that it shall absorb and assimilate the new ideas and take cognizance of the new powers.

There can be no doubt that home and family are beginning to suffer from the dissemination of New Woman ideas. Revolution inevitably entails suffering, but there has never been a revolution from which advance and good did not flow. If one believes that when woman deserts the kitchen and forsakes the nursery the future of the home and the family are imperilled, then the advent of the New Woman is a menace, for they are the foundation of the structure called Life. The solution of the matter is squarely up to women. The bearing of children is their function, their privilege and their duty. Nurturing children and bringing them up may often be entrusted to others with greater success.

The whole question is based upon the intelligence of the individual woman. Therefore, it simmers down to a question of personality. A woman of superior intelligence who makes a success of business or profession will understand by taking thought, if she does not by instinct, that she is still the responsible member for keeping home

tomary detestation. Covetousness, pride and ingratitude are possibly held in greater esteem than they were, though hell was full of the ungrateful as recently as Don Quixote's time. That the woman of the future will insist upon the modification of marriage goes almost without saying. Marriage can no longer be the Gordian Knot which none can untie, and which, being and family together. And she will succeed in this as well as in her self-chosen work. The woman of average intelligence is likely to combine a desire for independence with a need of man's support and affection, and she will tolerate in practice the duties against which she rebels in theory; and the woman of low intelligence is not more fitted for the job of home-maker than she is for business or trade. The future of the race seems to depend more today on quality than on quantity. It may be just as safe, perhaps more so, if it is restricted to a higher type of woman who is aware of its importance than it would be were the old rule followed that a woman who has no talent for anything in particular should be married as early as possible. It takes more talent to be a successful mother and wife than to be a competent physician.

Women do not change their natures with their names at the altar; those who are born with a need to discover wings for themselves will not be satisfied with a Ford or a Rolls-Royce. Those who have no such urge are content to walk, and walking perforce is no sign of progress.

It is a great mistake, however, to think that woman can ever be completely independent of man, no matter what she wishes to believe or have others believe. The movement of emancipation begun by women has gone too fast and too far and many have misunderstood the question. Their great aim appears to be Freedom from Man. What woman should want in reality is to be delivered from the shackles into which man has put her, her intelligence, desires, ambitions and talents. She wants to have a manner of self-expression which does not necessarily mean emulation or competition with man. She wants to be permitted to use fully whatever male attributes she may have in her make-up which give her physical strength and endurance, mental power, active energy and a desire for creation; but she cannot rid herself of the feminine qualities which are generally the superior in number and power in her constitution. The modern woman seems desirous to shed these female traits, but she acquires nothing in their stead when she goes in for manly activities without being fundamentally built for them. The result is in its gross exaggeration those hybrid creatures who have succeeded in making themselves caricatures of men without achieving anything which would redeem them or reconcile society to their existence. In its finer form we have the modern woman trim, neat, positive, self-

supporting, assured of her ability to carry on the work of her choice, at the same time wife, mother, daughter, lover. It is to her

Wide World

A one-piece dinner gown and bobbed hair in the fashion of 1927

that we look with hope and satisfaction. She is man's companion, not competitor; she has enough energy—a male characteristic—to stimulate her to worthy achievements, but she has not forsaken her feminine appeal.

The most discouraging thing about the New Woman is that she is willingly a slave to the most tyrannical of all masters, *La Mode*, whose seat of government is Paris. Let Fashion decree that she should wear her hair and skirts long, and she would run to cover like a frightened rabbit. Even if it should prescribe the red flannel underwear of our grandmothers instead of the silk of our present grandmothers, she would make prompt genuflexion. Until the New Woman denies this Master I despair of her.

The way in which woman has developed in the last twenty-five years has been so rapid in pace and breath-taking in scope that it is still too soon to pass definite judgment upon its meaning and possible consequences. It cannot surely be called a progressive change in the nature of woman, for woman has not changed fundamentally. It is more likely to be a stage of transition toward a different conception of woman's sphere in the world, a transition accompanied with exceptionally definite displays of independence and freedom. Because of

this very definite attitude woman displays toward her new conception of herself, the change in itself is not permanent; it could not be and yet be so self-assured, self-satisfied and at the same time so conscious of itself. When woman has found her real place in the world, a place which will be as different from that cherished by her grandmothers as it is from the place she is assuming now, she will no longer feel this sort of growing pains which make her seek for appeasement in every new fad and idea.

Eventually she will have to adjust herself to herself. That will be more amusing to witness than the present struggle at being something that she is not in reality, and it is safe to say that it will be more picturesque. If any one has doubts that woman is the image of God, seeing her frequently in her present-day get-up will confirm them. She is now going through a transitional stage toward a new conception of woman's sphere and she is displaying all the grotesqueness and more that children show in the awkward age. Give woman a chance to handle love properly and she will make a great contribution to life. She should not be called upon to do it alone. Man should help her. It is the only way he can make amends.

Woman's Encroachment on Man's Domain

By ANTHONY M. LUDOVICI

AUTHOR OF *Woman: a Vindication, A Defence of Conservatism* AND OTHER BOOKS ON SOCIAL AND LITERARY SUBJECTS; FORMER GENERAL STAFF OFFICER, BRITISH ARMY

NOTHING is easier in the investigation of extensive social changes than to confound cause and effect, influence and result. For the gradual emergence of a particular social form is frequently promoted and accelerated by the very conditions, whether psychological or physiological, which, after the event, it is believed to have brought about. Let any one reflect, for instance, on such apparently obvious results of the New Woman movement as the claim of sex-equality and the decline of domesticity among modern women, and consider the difficulty of determining how much of both anteceded the movement by many scores of years, and actually favored its progress.

Women as the most conservative of beings are prone to acquiesce in any established state of affairs. We may, therefore, go very far astray if we conclude too hastily that their claim of sex-equality and their present success in achieving social and industrial parity with men have been the outcome of an original and purely feminine struggle for emancipation. Ought we not first to inquire how often—aye, how incessantly—during the last hundred and eighty years the modern world, in England, France, Germany and America has either assumed this equality or made the most strenuous efforts to bring it about, at least in practice, if not in theory?

The essential factors in the maintenance of any position of authority or privilege are responsibility and protection. Over those we protect and are responsible for we may claim authority and privilege, and they readily grant us both. When once, however, we leave people to self-protection or self-responsibility, the position of authority and privilege is automatically abandoned. Now, long before the recent cry of sex equality was taken up by the Feminists (I say "recent" because the earlier Feminist movement of the seventeenth century in France died with the Revolution), Europe and especially England, which set the example in the most extreme form of epicene industrialism, had abandoned any idea of distinguishing between men and women in the world of labor. Far from being protected, women were in most cases exploited more heartlessly than men, because they were more feeble. Far from the male legislators of civilized nations recognizing their responsibility in regard to women and their domestic traditions, the latter were ruthlessly assailed and broken up by drawing the women in thousands away from their homes. No thought was given to the consequences of the exploitation of female labor either from the standpoint of the nation's domestic life or of its children. It was only gradually that legislation was introduced to protect the married and single female from ruthless abuse; so how could a thought have been given to their homes and their children?

To ascribe the Feminist cry for equality and independence to the exertions of the modern woman or to suppose that the growing distaste for domestic duties is the outcome of her influence would therefore be preposterously inaccurate. Both the sex-equality and the indifference to domesticity were tacitly assumed over a hundred and eighty years ago by our ancestors, who inaugurated the Industrial Revolution and who imposed their hard credo in practice on the women of civilized nations by sheer force. By the side of such a reform as this, with its abandonment of the factors, protection and responsibility, such literary and hortatory efforts in favor of woman's independence as J. S. Mill's pamphlet, *The Subjection of Women*, are mere child's play. They are hardly more than a faint and barely perceptible gesture, confirming the deeper and stronger tendency of hard facts.

Moreover, we have also to remember that industrial and urban conditions themselves, which in the last hundred and eighty years have developed on such an enormous scale, have, if only by the emasculating tendency of the occupations which they offer to men, gone a long way toward destroying the difference in social functions between men and women. The constant spectacle of men working at tasks which every woman knows

21

she could easily undertake (and there are thousands of such tasks in any urban or industrial community, as the World War proved), carries much more conviction than the best-worded essay on the inferiority of men or the equality of the sexes. At the same time the steady degeneration of men, which began with the Industrial Revolution, has also given women every reason to abandon their old attitude of subserviency and discipleship toward them.

It would, therefore, obviously be most imprudent to say that the claim of sex-equality and independence, or the decline of domesticity among women, was the outcome of the New Woman movement. It is this difficulty of distinguishing between cause and effect which makes the writing of contemporary history so full of pitfalls.

Taking the words "encroachment on man's domain" in their broadest sense, and considering the phenomenon as a whole, apart from the great impetus it has received from comparatively recent and conscious Feminist efforts, and from the exigencies of the World War, it would appear that the chief psychological results of feminine influence have been:

ON MAN—(a) *A decline of the chivalrous spirit*, with its correlative loss of respect for and interest in woman, except on the physical side; hence an accentuation of materialism in the relation of the sexes. The clerks, typists and other bread-winners, who travel to work in big cities, are not men and women meeting by chance and glad of the fortuitous encounter. They are competitors, equals, in the struggle for existence, resenting each other's rivalry even in the sphere of seating accommodation. The sitting men do not even shift their eyes from their papers to contemplate the strap-hanging girls before them. Furthermore, when once the latter are known as rivals and equals, they cease to be judged by a different standard. Equals are judged by a common standard. So that when, to take but one example, a man sees his alleged equal, whether in a train or at a ledger, open a vanity bag and powder and paint her face, he seems to be seeing through a trick and beholding a weakness. Whereas formerly he accepted the end-result of secret titivation joyfully, he now despises those who, while contending with him in the arena of bread-winning, have recourse to such transparent expedients. It is probable that this decline in chivalry extends to all women.

(b) *A decline in sensitiveness and of natural reaction in the presence of women;*

hence the ability to resist to a far greater extent than his male forebears constant association and contact in his daily and hourly life with girls who are dressed in the scantiest attire. The development of modern fashions in women's morning, afternoon and working attire alone is a sign that far more potent stimuli can now be borne without prompt reaction than formerly. The constant association of young men and women in offices and workshops would be impossible if this were not so.

(c) *An accentuation of the hedonistic impulses*, due partly to the fact that most girls are now money earners, and that the cost of entertaining them is therefore frequently halved; and partly to the fact that girls are more free and therefore more easily secured as companions. More thought is given to having a "good time" with women than of founding a home and family. Even with the woman chosen in marriage pleasure takes precedence of normal functioning and responsibilities. The disproportionate increase of restaurants, theatres, dance-rooms and entertainments of all kinds in recent years presents one aspect of this change. Birth-control is another.

ON WOMEN—(a) *A destruction of their versatility.* The traditional difference between men and women in Western Europe in the eighteenth and nineteenth centuries, before the intensive employment of women in masculine callings, was the greater versatility of the female mind, its wider range of interests. By escaping the besotting influence of narrow specialization, characteristic of most male callings, women had retained a catholicity of tastes and interests, which often made their men appear empty and dull at their side. This difference is now disappearing. Women are beginning to show the effects of narrow and routine specialization, and are thus becoming intellectually and emotionally flatter and duller. The decline of the arts of conversation and the increasing cultivation of indoor and outdoor distractions of doubtful intellectual quality (the loud speaker often functions throughout a whole meal now), are only the more apparent consequences of this change, the most disastrous being the fact that modern women everywhere have ceased to give birth to a generation of great sons.

(b) *A development of her capacity for sublimating physical and spiritual impulses by other than religious means.* The New Woman finds that the pleasure she derives from constant entertainment and her bread-winning activities leaves behind it a feeling of dissatisfaction, which she tries to relieve. Since her rationalism often denies her the solace of religion, she turns with increased avidity to the expedient of vicarious experience. This consists in reading romantic literature (chiefly novels) about women who undergo what she wishes she could undergo but does not. A sign of this development is the extraordinary output of fictional literature, and the fact that those who demand it are chiefly women. As, however, a neurotic solution of this kind must amount to a fantastic escape from reality, there is a tendency, both in the novels and those who read them, to hold a view of life which is unrealistic and false and which makes the modern woman a much more romantic creature than her "less practical" sister of a century ago. The increase in divorces is one of the signs of this romanticism.

(c) Through their improved economic resources and lack of traditions in money control, as also through their increased freedom, *women have also acquired a pronounced accentuation of the hedonistic impulses*, which, however, as we have seen, does not necessarily lead to happiness. I have already discussed the evidence of this in the section on man.

(d) *An accentuation of the masculine elements in her spiritual make-up*, while the feminine elements become more and more recessive. Thus the paradox is reached that for women Feminism really spells Masculinism. Exposure to the vicissitudes and asperities of the struggle for existence brings out the combative, predatory and latent male side of female nature and represses and impoverishes its dependent, peace-loving and sequacious side.

The chief pathological results affect women. There is only one of importance affecting men and that is the continuous selection now operating in favor of men of inferior attractiveness. Owing to the presence of attractive girls wherever he works, pronounced instincts and sensitiveness are an obstacle rather than a means of advancement to the young man. That man succeeds best and is most trusted who can most easily resist the constant stimulus of feminine attractions or most certainly repel the female. Thus in all businesses, industries and public offices selection is now operating in favor of the more or less unattractive male at the cost of men more vigorously endowed and more naturally alluring. Any other conditions would make modern business impossible. The pathological results, as they affect women, are:

ANTHONY M. LUDOVICI

(a) *Abnormal growth of the adolescent.* Owing to the masculine aspirations of Feminism the process of assimilation to the male is made to start early. In girls' schools, even in the latter part of the last century, girls were already being treated as boys. Not only were they given the male's intellectual curriculum, which, according to many authorities (Dr. Stratz of Amsterdam, Dr. Menge of Heidelberg, Dr. Sellheim of Tübingen, Arabella Kenealy and others) placed a too heavy strain on their constitution, but they were also drilled and taught rough games and exercises. In the last thirty years these methods have been intensified, with the result that much harm is being done to the female adolescent. The exorbitant demands made on young bones and muscles by boyish athleticism lead to a premature ossification of the pelvic structure and to morbid rigidity in the pelvic and upper femoral regions in the adult. Darwin pointed out sixty years ago that sailors have smaller hip measurements than soldiers, the former from early youth having more violent bodily exertions than the latter. Thus does early muscular strain become compensated in a sex in which pelvic development is not vital. Dr. Gaillard Thomas pointed out some years ago that only 40 per cent. of American women proper were physically fitted to become mothers, and the late Stanley Hall (in *Adolescence*) has published a mass of statistics to show the alarming unfitness of Anglo-Saxon women for maternity. Professor G. L. Englemann and other eminent gynecologists in various countries confirm this view. Sterility or agonizing confinements are the inevitable outcome of these conditions and are the price paid for the refusal to recognize a radical difference between male and female.

(b) *Increase of cancer and other diseases.* The modern woman who insists on luxury, on the one hand, and on freedom, on the other, limits her family, when she marries, to one or two or has no children at all, and frequently refuses to breast feed even those she does have. Now there appears to be no doubt that ailments peculiar to women are more common in spinsters, sterile women, or women who have had long spells of unfruitfulness in wedlock or have failed to suckle, as shown in the works of leading British, French and German medical authorities. Thus Birth Control and the decline of breast-feeding which characterized French Feminism of the seventeenth century and which, through the New Woman's revolt against the female's burdens (see Paul Bureau: *L'Indiscipline des Moeurs*, pp. 161-163), have also characterized modern Feminism, are probably leading to many disorders, some of which have been definitely traced to the abnormal conditions now prevailing and others which will also in time probably be traced to the same cause.

(c) Owing to the increasing neglect of domestic interests and pursuits among women, *food conditions and the state of food preparation in most countries where Feminism has prevailed are notoriously bad* and are growing steadily worse. The art of cooking gradually becomes a fool's game and in its place there appear innumerable patent and proprietary products, the preparation of which demands no skill and no trouble. These products are but poor substitutes for the natural foods of our ancestors, but as they leave the women ample leisure in which to gad about or else to earn money outside the home, no one complains. Quick soup and gravy makers, pudding and cake powders, tinned foods of every description (ready for consumption), custards, porridges and jellies that require only the addition of water, and a multitude of commercial jams and other preserves, now replace, though they do not equal, the preparations of former times. There is no doubt that the health of the various nations is suffering from them. This is particularly true of England, as in this country the bad feeding merely confirms in the adult the evil effects of bottle-feeding in infancy. Evidence of this is to be found in the feverish interest now prevailing in all Feminist countries regarding the illnesses due to bad dieting and the means of dealing with the evil.

The social results are too manifold to be enumerated in detail, but the chief are:

(a) *A marked increase in luxurious tastes in every class.* Never before in the history of the world have sumptuary laws been more urgently needed than they are today. Everything—health, progeny, normal feeding and functioning—is sacrificed to clothes, entertainment, motor cars and "pleasure." By being free, that is to say, emancipated from home ties, and, if married, from maternal ties, the modern woman is like a *nouveau riche*, tasting expensive idleness for the first time. The consequence is that luxury and excitement are the order of the day. The large streets of big cities are now but a succession of drapery palaces, competing for the custom of crowds of women who spend more on their clothes than their grandmothers spent on their whole keep, and extravagance and display are the vices of every class of the nation. Those who can ill afford display, whether in cars or clothes, stint themselves in essentials in order to be in the swim. And as almost all women smoke nowadays, there is no end to the expenses that have to be met before essentials are thought of. (Typical signs of the times are the huge profits of drapery stores, the dramatic rise in tobacco shares and in shares in other luxury articles).

(b) *Increased freedom in irregular relationships.* Owing to the spread of the knowledge of Birth Control methods, there is undoubtedly among young people an enormous amount of laxity which never comes to light. Occasionally a suicide or a murder reveals the past history of such a relationship, but even more rarely now do certain other consequences do so. It is probable that much of the cynicism and *insouciance* of modern young women, which make the present age an extraordinarily brutal one, is due more to such experiences than to the love element of human relations. See innumerable novels and plays which are supposed to portray the modern girl.

(c) *A tendency for politics to become*

Whistler's painting, "The Little White Girl: Symphony in White Number 2," exhibited at the Royal Academy, London, in 1865. Here again an artist's psychological insight is shown in a conception of girlhood that is challenged by the young woman of today. (Reproduced from *The Works of James McNeill Whistler,* by Elizabeth Luther Cary. New York: Moffat, Yard & Co.)

hostile to men. It may be that the recent political tendency to exclude the middle and to concentrate on the two extremes, Conservatism and Labor, may be due in some part to the influence of the women voters and to the kind of appeal which they can best appreciate. It is conceivable that an untutored electorate, or at any rate an electorate new to its work, would incline to recognize only sharp and rude distinctions. The way in which British politics has now become almost a duel between the Labor and Conservative interests, without any attempt being made either in the press or elsewhere to make a more moderate appeal, might thus feasibly be interpreted as partly the consequence of female suffrage. Be this as it may, there appears to be no doubt whatever that politics is now becoming more and more emotional. The inherent vice of democratic control has always been that it ultimately degrades politics into a science of emotional appeal through the instrumentality of demagogues. Since the advent of the woman voter, who is hardly equipped for anything beyond an emotional orientation in the political world, there can be no doubt that there has been a sharp accentuation of the emotional element in politics. This has been reflected even in the House of Commons itself, where debates have become more and more rowdy; at elections it comes to the fore in the increased bitterness of the antagonism and the more fantastic nature of the promises made by the candidates. A recent example of this was the election of young Oswald Moseley at Smethwick, commenting on which The London *Times* said, "personalities played a bigger part than politics."

a matter of extremes and ever more a matter of emotion. It is perhaps a little early to appreciate the effect of female suffrage, and, as for female members of Parliament, they have been so few that their influence is hardly noticeable. As regards the women M. Ps., however, this much is clear, that as most of them hitherto have been old or past middle age, the little influence they have had has been Puritanical and

Evils of Woman's Revolt Against the Old Standards

By HUGH L. McMENAMIN
RECTOR OF THE CATHOLIC CATHEDRAL, DENVER, COLORADO

WHAT is woman's place in the social order? Is the modern woman, the so-called "New Woman," filling that place with credit? What may society justly demand from her? Is she supplying that demand?

A study of man reveals the fact that when God created men and women He made them the complements of each other, one supplying what the other lacked, mutually dependent, but both forming a perfect whole. That same study reveals the spiritual equality and the physical inequality of the sexes. It reveals that, while to man has been assigned the aggressive, progressive and governing power in the world, to woman has been assigned the conservative and refining power. Hers is the social and aristocratic influence, and following her divinely given impulse she shrinks from conflict, but entwining her affections around those she loves with tender devotion, she has filled the world with homes, the foundation stones upon which rests our present civilization. She has filled it with sweet and tender recollections, with elevated sentiments and religious impulse. She has been the friend, the companion, the affectionate counselor of man in every Christian age.

That same study reveals to me that woman is dependent upon her warrior husband for sustenance, and God and Christianity are averse to subjecting her to the brutalizing influence of competition with man. She is physically and temperamentally handicapped, and the result will be an injury to the race. It reveals to me that man shall rule over woman. "He shall rule over thee," was decreed not by man but by man's Creator, and before the Christian era, in pagan lands, man perverted that decree by making woman his slave. But with the passing of the centuries and the injunction, "Husbands, love your wives," there was born in the heart of man that love for woman which made her his companion—not his slave—that tenderness that threw the protection of his strong right arm around her frailer figure, that chivalry which caused him to stand aside and

let a Titanic carry him to a watery grave while she rowed on to safety, that admiration, respect and esteem which placed her on a pedestal, before which he comes to learn lessons of culture, refinement and morality. For what reason, think you, did God give her those finer sensibilities, that higher moral tone, those loftier ideals, those gentle aspirations, if it be not that she should set the standard after which we should shape our conduct? We have the right to demand it from her. She has a duty to fulfill the demand.

While I write, two events are taking place near me, both of them indicative of the trend of thought that is developing the "new woman." In Colorado Springs a national "Equal Rights for Women" convention is in session; here in Denver a newspaper is conducting a "bathing beauty contest." In Colorado Springs a group of women are confusing an equality of rights with an equality or identity of duties and privileges. If woman is ever emancipated from the protecting care of man; if she insists upon being man's competitor; if she disregards the limitations of sex and claims the right to do all that man may do with equal propriety; if, in a word, she descends to man's plane and is considered merely as a rival, then it will not be long until the theory of companionship will be discarded and women will relapse into the pagan condition of servitude, for when woman forfeits the right to be ruled by the tender rod of love and guardianship, then will she be ruled by the iron rod of tyranny. Agitation, human legislation and modern paganism may attempt to place the sexes on the same political, commercial and social platform, but it never can. Sex limitations forbid it.

We have defined woman's place in the social order. Is the so-called "New Woman" filling that place with credit and is she supplying society's just demands? Let us see. We hear a great deal in these days about the "double standard." It is undoubtedly true that a great many are influenced, led on perhaps unconsciously, by the sophism and false principles of the

86

age which condones immorality in man and makes mere respectability his code of morals, but holds aloft to woman the sacred laws of God; which judges the enormity of the sin by the sex of the transgressor, as if forsooth sin had sex. Now, while we abhor such a condition of affairs, we breathe a prayer that the "double standard" remain, for, if it should be changed by the woman of the present generation, it will not be by lifting man to her standard, but by her descent to his. The tendency is downward, not upward. The "New Woman" has neither the influence nor the inclination to lift man up. She has forgotten that she has been fashioned by God and nature to be the refining influence in the world and that her standard of life and conduct should be such that there will always be something for man to strive for and to imitate.

Look about you. The theatre, the magazine, the current fiction, the ball room, the night clubs and the joy-rides—all give evidence of an ever-increasing disregard for even the rudiments of decency in dress, deportment, conventions and conduct. Little by little the bars have been lowered, leaving out the holy influences that held society in restraint. One need be neither prude nor puritan to feel that something is passing in the hearts and in the minds of the women of today that is leaving them cold and unwomanly. I know it is said that if a man may indulge freely in alcohol so may she; if he may witness prizefights so may she; if he may harangue a crowd from a corner soap box so may she; if he may go about half naked so may she. But the moment she does so she has stepped down from the pedestal before which man was accustomed to worship and he is left without an ideal.

There are many who would have us believe that she does not differ from her mother or her grandmother. It is significant that she is on the defensive, for she does not claim to be better. We may try to deceive ourselves and close our eyes to the prevailing flapper conduct. We may call boldness greater self-reliance, brazenness greater self-assertion, license greater freedom and try to pardon immodesty in dress by calling it style and fashion, but the fact remains that deep down in our hearts we feel a sense of shame and pity.

When women can gaze upon and indulge in the voluptuous dance of the hour; when young girls can sit beside their youthful escorts and listen to the suggestive drama of the day and blush not; when they spend their idle hours absorbed in sex-saturated fiction; when women, both married and single, find their recreation in drinking and petting parties; when mothers clothe their daughters in a manner that exposes their physical charms to the voluptuous gaze of every passing libertine; when they can enter the contract of marriage with the avowed purpose of having no children; then surely the "New Woman" is different, and it is a libel on the generation that has gone to hold the contrary. In the words of a prominent churchman, "If this be the 'New Woman,' then God spare us from any further development of the abnormal creature."

The "New Woman" has not yet reverted to the pagan practice of deifying the vices. She does not yet call them virtues; but how far has she not departed from the standards of twenty-five or fifty years ago, from that innate modesty, that reserve, that sense of delicacy which must ever be an essential characteristic of female excellence? In that other day woman retained at least a sense of shame, and though they fell, they found themselves ultimately on their knees sobbing out their broken-heartedness. The "New Woman" has no sense of shame and she endeavors

REV. HUGH L. McMENAMIN

to save her self-respect by putting a halo on her wickedness. She attempts to hide her sordidness under fine phrases—"Art for art's sake," "To the pure all things are pure," *"Honi soit qui mal y pense"* ("Evil to him who evil thinks"), and the like. Having delivered herself of these platitudes, she proceeds to wallow in the turpitude of vice and then attempts to convince the world that it is the artistic, the beautiful, the esthetic in the play, the film, the dance, the dress, and not their vile suggestiveness that attract, but she succeeds in deceiving neither herself nor us.

The public sense of decency has been so perverted that spectacles like *The Black Crook*, to which a few degenerates crept in shame a half century ago, are models of decency compared to those to which mothers take their sons and daughters today. We have now reached the condition that finds our modern sociologist condoning crime and endeavoring to give it respectability by the simple expedient of legalizing it and by teaching that "codes in morals are as changeable as style in dress"; that "sin, so-called, is but the tyranny of society." Witness the "companionate marriage" discussion and its necessary adjunct instruction in the use of contraceptives. Note their logic. Our modern sociologist observes a growing laxity in morals and an increased freedom between the sexes— a laxity which society frowns upon and a freedom which oftimes creates an embarrassing condition for the woman. But instead of bending his efforts to correct the laxity and curtail the freedom, our modern sociologist attempts to give the condition respectability by calling concubinage by a new name and prevent the possible embarrassment by teaching the use of contraceptives. Similarly, our modern sociologist observes that not a few married couples, unwilling to make the mutual sacrifice necessary for the permanence of any marriage, become dissatisfied and separate, and thus deprive their children of a home. So our modern sociologist conceives of a union in which there will be no children until the couple discover that they are going to be happy together, forgetting that it is impossible for any couple to endure the intimacy of married life without the bond of a babe. Ninety per cent. of the divorces granted in the City of Denver last year were granted to childless couples.

The fact that the most enthusiastic exponent of this new attack upon decency is the "New Woman" reveals her distorted nature at its very worst. Men will not turn to such for inspiration.

"BATHING BEAUTY" CRAZE

Witness the second event I referred to— the "bathing beauty contest." This contest will have been held before this article is in print. Nine out of ten of the "beauties" have never touched water deeper than that in their bath tubs. They are to be assembled in a public park, in the scantiest of attire, and will be exhibited on a platform to the gaze of the assembled libertines of the city. Denver has an annual stock show; I see no reason why the exhibitions should not be joined. This "bathing beauty" craze, together with present-day ballroom and street attire, reveals a dominant characteristic of the "New Woman." She would attract by the lure of her person rather than her personality, and men are accepting her at her own valuation—"Only a rag and a bone and a hank of hair." Evidently the "New Woman" is not supplying the demand that society has the right to make of her. She is not a refining influence.

Modern economic conditions, with the mania for speedy profits, have been a powerful factor in producing the "New Woman," inasmuch as they have dragged her into the commercial world and made her economically independent. It is quite impossible for a woman to engage successfully in business and politics and at the same time create a happy home. A woman cannot be a mother and a typist at the same time, and unfortunately she elects to be merely a wife, and out of that condition have arisen those temples of race suicide—our modern apartment houses—and the consequent grinding of the divorce mills.

Modern conditions have made woman more independent, if you will, but that independence is not benefiting the race. The woman who goes off to work with her husband each morning and returns in the evening to keep house for him has assumed a burden too hard to carry and one that will make it impossible for her to make him happy. In addition to that, such an arrangement forces them into an unnatural, childless union which is disastrous to them and to the race.

FANATICAL FEMALES

The Rev. JOHN LEONARD COLE, Saranac Lake, N. Y.

ANCIENT and modern history is strewn with them. Shining like bright stars of courageous faith amid feeble lamps of ordinary cautious mortals—or with the sheen of fool's gold (according to one's viewpoint) —women have certainly illumined the path of human history. In some cases it has required the lapse of a few centuries for men to decide that the light they shed was the true brilliance of worth and not the glitter of folly. But that is better than the sort of meteor-like career which is dazzling to-day, then gone out forever. Now and then, of course, "when she was bad," she has been "horrid"; but, when good, she has been "very, very good." And her goodness has had the leap of faith in it, the thrilling, dauntless abandon that puts to shame much of the nicely reckoned, safe and sane virtue of mankind.

> UNDER a novel title Mr. Cole has studied from a new angle the dominant traits in women whose deeds were truly great. He shows that what is deemed "foolish" may be wisdom in its highest degree.

The Widow With Two Mites

Take that woman who clutched tight two very thin pieces of copper and crept round through a crowd of pompous, broad-robed Sadducees near the women's court of the temple of Herod in Jerusalem. Her aim was to reach the treasury chest in front of the court, leave her two mites, and slip away unnoticed. It was so small a gift that she did not desire to have any more people than necessary see her (fact was. a Rabbinical rule said no one should give one mite). So she concealed herself as much as possible. slipped round the sweeping gestures of the ostentatious givers, and finally got up to the funnel-shaped mouth of the chest that received contributions for the temple and for the poor. There she dropped in her two mites "which make a farthing" and crept back hoping no one had seen her.

But one had seen her. An eye which delighted in just such quiet and magnanimous deeds as that caught sight of her, and a voice that thrilled to relate such acts of genuine goodness in unexpected quarters called attention of some bystanders to her in words which men have treasured ever since (Mark 12:43).

Ordinary common sense would have dictated a reservation of at least one of those mites. Any masculine observers who stood that day "over against the treasury," any except that one, would more likely have said, "How foolish!" She was not compelled to give either; one, in ordinary prudence, she should have kept to "live on." But—"that's like a woman, reckless and extravagant."

"Just like a woman" is sometimes an unintended compliment. This one, forgetting her supper, her lodging for the coming night, forgetting the morrow, forgetting everything save her temple, her God, and the poor people, cast in "all that she had." She may have been a fool; but she was "God's fool."

Ruth the Moabitess

Then, to go back well nigh a thousand years, here is another widow, younger, but far from "merry"; a Moabite woman, in all the rich and luxuriant beauty of the Oriental type. Little more than a girl, she had just

90

lost her husband; her sister had just lost hers; her mother-in-law was just widowed too. To this bereaved, immigrant mother-in-law she is saying, as the older woman starts back to Bethlehem in Judah, "Entreat me not to leave thee, nor to return from following after thee; . . . The Lord do so to me, and more also, if aught but death part thee and me."

Calm and dispassionate judgment says that Orpah, who kissed her mother-in-law goodbye and turned back toward Moab, the ancestral home, the place where other husbands and children waited, was the sensible sister; that Ruth, setting off with a woman thrice and freshly bereaved to face ridicule as a "foreigner" and small chance of marriage in a Jewish land, was another "foolish" woman. She, too, ventured "all she had," her "very living." And yet somehow men have kept saying over, as most beautiful, those words of Ruth the Moabite woman, not as the ravings of a lunatic, but as the sentiments of one of the truest, purest, and most loyal souls who ever lived. Even if her adventure had not "turned out all right" (lucky gleanings, Boaz, courtship, marriage, illustrious descendants), posterity would say that of such faithful love ought kings, prophets, and saviors to be born.

The Woman With the Nard

Now, look at another woman who, in H. G. Wells' phrase, "forgot herself into immortality." She is nameless. She did a thing just as reckless as these other women. It happened in leper Simon's house at Bethany. One whom she had come to adore sat eating there. Like a woman, she wanted to do something for him. So she fetched in an alabaster flask of pure nard perfume worth three hundred shillings—or sixty dollars—maybe her life's savings; and she poured it over his head. That time there act-

ually were male critics at hand—rapid, cool calculators; mere adding machines. They knew in a minute how much cash value had been "wasted"; and they growled openly about unwise extravagance,—how it might have been spent much more logically, and more efficiently. But there it is again. Ignoring logic, save the logic of her heart, the woman just heedlessly gave her very best and, altho her lavish outpouring would never stand the test of practical reason, the voice of the fair critic said, "Let her alone." And posterity has kept and admired that "memorial of her."

Edith Cavell

Another of the stars in the galaxy of women who risked everything, bestowed all their "living," loved with absolute recklessness, shone out in Belgium when an American Red Cross nurse gave this statement to the world, after a few days of thinking and praying under the clear light of eternity; "Patriotism is not enough. I must have no hate or unforgiveness in my heart toward any one." The bullets of a German firing squad promptly cut off the voice of Edith Cavell, but not before another "foolish woman" had made her calm appeal to a world full of hate and suspicion and distrust; not before another fanatic had sounded the clear call to a better order of international life, and had sealed it with the "last full measure of her devotion."

"A wild, impossible thing," the experts in psychology and the experts in national defense said. So they said the leap of the monk Telemachus into the arena was the deed of a hare-brained fanatic. But the cruel games were never renewed after that day.

When they give, these women give all. When they believe, they believe without mental reservations. When they love, they love with no lukewarm flame, but a burning and consuming passion. Where men proceed with reason, step by step, woman leaps with intuitive faith, a brave ignoring of "ways and means"; she risks everything, welcomes adventure, happy to attempt the impossible. Men may sing "one step enough for me"; woman does not seem to require even one step. "Encircling gloom" becomes bright with the light of her own clear shining confidence in her Goal and her Guide.

Professor Sabin

To cite one more, modern: here is the first woman to be elected to the National Academy of Science, Mrs. Florence Rena Sabin, professor of histology at Johns Hopkins Medical school. "All her living" she gave to one of the most difficult scientific studies,—that of living blood cells. She took blood from her own arm; day after day she counted corpuscles in an ounce of blood every fifteen minutes. Bending over a microscope, 9 A.M. to 5 P.M. day after day till eyes ached and body was fatigued,—interminably counting and observing carefully. Any reasonable man would say, "A waste of time—no practical results." As yet there is little. But she toils on, convinced that the end of the adventure will reveal some hidden chemical secret of the body, particularly the cause of the growth and decline of blood cells. Mrs. Sabin calls her laborious work "romantic," "an adventure," and sometimes even "fun." She has this oft-recurring fanaticism of women for the unseen, —this uncalculating devotion to "a cause." "When a problem begins to clear," she says, "so that the conclusions are evident and so that all the paths to it are clear, then I lose interest and want to try something else."

There it is again,—going in for something not clearly manifest; giving one's best to a quest of the apparently impossible. Modern, as well as ancient; American as well as Hebrew; these women seem to have within them something that impels them to "cast in all their living" for the object of their devotion. It may be suffrage; it may be a warless world; it may be industry Christianized; whatever it be, they "go in for it" for "all they're worth." So much so that by well poised intellects they are repeatedly called fanatic. Says Doctor H. W. Frink in his *Morbid Fears and Compulsions:*

A certain proportion of at least the most militant suffragists are neurotics who in some instances are compensating for masochistic trends, in others are more or less successfully sublimating sadistic and homosexual ones (which usually are unconscious). . . . It is nothing to the discredit of any movement to say that perhaps many of its conspicuous supporters are neurotics, for as a matter of fact, it is the neurotics who are the pioneers in most reforms.

So far from being, then, a matter of mud throwing at women, this being teetotally enamored of and devoted to a great cause, this casting caution and logic to the winds to promote it,—is rather a matter of heroism, the stuff that heroes and heroines are made of. Close at hand they may seem disagreeable; in the perspective of the years they are the honored ones.

When woman gets to studying the application of the Golden Rule and religion to the human relations in industry with all this sublimely audacious faith and energy, maybe something rather radical will occur. Interesting it is, at least to notice that the secretary of Copec ("the Christian order in Politics, Economics, and Citizenship) is a woman; and Miss Lucy Gardner puts it squarely this way:

The great question Christianity has to face to-day is, "Do we believe that our life can be so ordered that the human race can eat and live and travel from place to place on a code based on the teachings of Jesus Christ?" The answer is Yes or No. We are here because we believe it can be.

Men have hemmed and hawed, analyzed and investigated, for years on these matters of politics, economics, and citizenship. When a few Cavells and Sabins and Ruths come along with the bold devotion of all their powers to the actual changing of "things as are" to "things as ought to be," something is likely to happen.

Just now these "possessed" women seem to be bringing their precious alabaster cruses to the business of stopping war. They speak plainly on that matter, and seem willing to devote their "whole living" to bringing into actuality the long-delayed peace and reason. Practical men and experts like Admiral Fiske get impatient:

They have an insatiable desire to interfere in matters which they do not understand. . . . Of all existing matters, the one that women understand least is war. . . . War is a business of mathematics and machinery and scientific appliances and noise and discomfort and bloodshed and many other things from which women instinctively recoil. Not only do they recoil from even the idea of war, but the extreme delicacy of their nervous system makes many of them incapable of even thinking about war in a rational way. . . . The proof of this is the obvious fact that most women confuse a desire for a reasonable preparedness for war with an actual intention to make war. . . . The only possible hope of escape is some action by men that will bring the women to realize realities.

Ever since the level-headed scribes found fault with that Bethany woman, men have been trying to get women to "realize realities." Fortunately they have not entirely succeeded. Mankind would be buried under a deeper mass of sordid materialism than it is were it not for these women's determination to believe in, pray for, and work for—dreams. In this matter of war it is hard for women to talk reasonably. Olive Shreiner writes in this unreasonable way:

Men have made boomerangs, bows, swords, or guns with which to destroy one another; we have made the men who destroyed and were destroyed! . . . We pay the first cost on all human life. . . . There is perhaps no woman, whether she have borne children or be potentially a child bearer, who could look down upon a battlefield covered with slain but the thought would rise in her, "So many mothers' sons! So many young bodies brought into the world to lie there!" . . . No woman who is a woman says of a human body, "It is nothing." Men's bodies are our woman's works of art. Given to us power to control, we will never carelessly throw them in to fill up the gaps in human relationships made by international ambitions and greeds.

It is likely that Pilate considered his wife incapable of looking at things in a "rational way." But his name would have gone down to history with less execration attached to it if he had heeded a message sent over to the court room by his wife concerning a dream she had had enjoining him to "have nothing to do with that just man."

The daughter of a great psychologist explains this heroic and unselfish idealism of women after this fashion. In *The Soul of Woman* Ginia Lombroso says:

Man, like all other living organisms unstamped by potential maternity, is egocentric . . . woman is alterocentric; that is to say, she centers her feelings, her enjoyment, her ambition, in something outside herself; she makes not herself but another person, or even things surrounding her, the center of her emotions, and usually this person is some one she loves and by whom she wants to be loved; husband, father, son, friend.

When "this person" or "things surrounding her" do become the center and soul of her world, the object of her dreaming and working and giving, something is likely to happen. She herself may gain the characterization of "unbalanced"; but that to which she has given herself is likely to be materialized. Will Durant has been complaining of the loss of prestige by philosophy and ascribes it to philosophy's loss of the spirit of adventure. The old time boldness of its major prophets like Socrates and Plato has been swallowed up, he thinks, with petty discussions of epistomology. It may be that some venturesome woman is needed to impart fresh daring to philosophy. Perhaps the philosopher who will reestablish philosophy as lord over all the sciences and arts will turn out to be Xantippe, her energy and fiery faith looking outward toward the solution of life's mysteries instead of inward toward a misunderstood husband.

And if the prophetic fire has departed from organized religion; if it be true that now as in the days of Eli there is "no frequent vision"; if the Church has become overoccupied, like philosophy, with minor matters of mint, anise, and cummin, it may be that the impact of the "new woman," with all her undying capacity for vision and self-immolation, will bring the revival of religion and make itself felt against the principalities and powers of this materialistic world-order even as Deborah made Jehovah's power to be felt by Israel's enemies. It is certain that some of the strongest citadels of this sordid and pagan age have been shaken from their stolid solidity by the vigorous Christian idealism of a woman preacher in London by the name of Maud Royden.

Of course the unpardonable sin of these female fanatics, from Moses' mother, possessed of the crazy idea that her boy could be saved from the Egyptian's massacre, down to Jane Addams with her absurd idea that every woman's boy can be saved from becoming cannon-fodder, is uncompromising idealism. That determination to hitch their wagon to a star, backed by sacrificial devotion and willingness to pay any price, can move heaven and earth. Men may deplore it, but the Lord of men approves it with delighted surprise, "O woman, great is thy faith!" A *New York Times'* editorial, referring to Mr. Briand's defense of his foreign policies before the Chamber last November, said, "In order to be practical the idealist need not feel his way forward timidly. He can take the bold step provided he realizes the consequences and is prepared to pay the price." That editorial pronouncement shows where these women belong who have been, and still are, moving the world up out of the fog of gross skepticism into the light of "practical idealism."

It suggests, too, why, as John Macy said recently in Harper's, "The equality of men and women is a myth." At the end of his argument, he quotes William James: "There is mighty little difference between one man and another, but what difference there is is mighty important." "So it is," writes Macy, "with the sexes. Let us foster the important differences."

This little and evidently important difference is a willingness on the part of women to be "fools for God's sake." However man may surpass in logic, in this unreckoning and spendthrift quality of idealistic love and faith he will have to acknowledge woman his superior. Did one ever hear of a man, even in India, leaping on the funeral pyre of his departed wife?

A strict analysis of the origin of the word "fanatic" reveals that it means "inspired by divinity." It may be, then, that "female fanatics" are in closer touch with heaven than the level-headed males; and it is only reasoning from history and present observation to conclude that they are exerting on this earth a tremendous pull toward heaven.

THIS TWO-HEADED MONSTER—THE FAMILY

BY HENRY R. CAREY

"IF WE leave this town, and go to live in that village hole, I am going to quit you flat!"

Through an open, brilliantly lighted window came the wife's voice, sharp, aggressive, and defiant. Yes, I will admit it, I stopped under the window that hot summer evening and listened with both my ears. There was something arresting in this woman's excited tones—something which told me that here was no ordinary altercation, no customary threat. Thunder and lightning were in the air within doors as well as outside. A short silence ensued during which I could hear the husband shifting in his chair and rustling his newspaper. Cigar smoke curled thickly from the open window. Finally the answer came:

"You know the law in Pennsylvania, I suppose. A woman who refuses to accompany her husband when he changes his residence lays herself open to a charge of desertion and to an action for divorce."

I could hear the sharp click of the woman's heels as she paced the floor. "It's a horrible, old-fashioned, man-made, despotic law! Children or no children, business or no business, divorce or no divorce, law or no law, I simply will not go." This time there was a longer pause, during which the tobacco smoke continued to slip in thin wraiths from the window.

At last, "Very well," answered the man quietly, "that settles it. When the month is up here I shall move, and you can go where you damn please. If you will not follow me, where I follow my business, I shall have to divorce you and find another mother for the children."

I continued my walk, not in the most pleasant mood. There was no denying that such an episode as this gives one furiously to think, and it is not always easy to cogitate on sultry summer evenings. Here was a woman actually breaking up a home by refusing to change residence with her husband. If this sort of thing was at all common our country had gone forward, or backward, with a vengeance. It was at any rate a great change from the days of our forbears, whose wives traveled with them or perished. As I strode along in the moonlight I recalled a little scene—another domestic row—which I had witnessed long ago in Paris. How differently that had ended! My American college acquaintance had been living on the Boulevard St. Germain, just where it crosses the great student highway into the Latin Quarter. His young French wife was the most delightful little witch who ever came out of Marseilles. They had been gloriously happy for two years, while he worked on his book and she kept house, mending his clothes and keeping a zealous watch over their common purse. Tiffs, of course, they had had. French women, one almost believes, occasionally manufacture minor quarrels, carry them to their artistic climax, and then melt deliciously, in a halo of reconciliation, into the arms of their men. However that may be, when the fight is over the last state of that union seems to be better than the first. There is a new emotional bond between the partners. This time, however, there seemed to be a serious disturbance between my friends, as I happened upon them in their special cozy corner of their favorite restaurant. I never did find out what it was all about, but they were more excited than I had ever seen them before. Suddenly, however, the radiant Marseillaise leaned across the tiny table and caught her husband's hand in her pink fingers.

"*Chéri*," she crooned, "your good friend is arriving. It will not do to go on. I am sure you are right anyway. Let us order a third glass and a second bottle. We shall all drink to the success of your book in good *Château Lafitte* and we shall top it off with coffee and cognac. After that we shall go home and I will do for you both my little Spanish dance while you play the guitar. When your friend leaves we shall sleep soundly and cozily, and to-morrow we shall see our way clearly out of this mess." With that she leaned over and implanted on his cheeks two good French smacks, in front of us all. The incident was closed. When I met them a week later, at a dance in the Latin Quarter, domestic harmony was written in every line of their smiling faces.

"She got her way after all," grinned my friend, as they whirled off together in one of those intricate steps of the Boulevard St. Michel.

Since then I have often compared in my own mind these two domestic skirmishes. After all, which kind of feminism works best within the man-woman relationship, the American variety, or Feminism—French Style? One begins to understand why the women of France have so often said to the feminists of other lands, "We have no need of the vote, for we rule our men already, far better than you." True, many Frenchmen have their escapades outside of the family life, and at such times, at least, the French wife does not rule. That, however, is beside the point. American escapades are unfortunately common too. No wife in any country rules an unfaithful husband while he is on a spree. Her innings come in his lucid intervals.

But the French husband returns to a wife who, like his mistress, governs him by charm, whereas the American goes back, as often as not, to irritation, sex competition, divorce, and every incentive to return to his Lily of the Field. Thus, assuming that the legalized man-woman relation is worthy of encouragement, for the sake of children and the race if for no other reason, the French woman is often more successful than the American wife, for she has found the secret of holding a man and of preserving harmony. French women thrive upon charm. American wives copy their dress and use their perfume; but they do not adopt the wonderful manners and easy yielding to male authority by which the French woman so often achieves her purpose and so successfully staves off the disruption of the family. American men cannot be permanently governed by gowns and perfume alone. Paradoxical as it may sound, they must be ruled in the long run by feminine surrender and submission. Such were my thoughts as I strolled through the moonlight on that summer's evening. I asked myself again and again, "Which of these women won, and which lost? Which family came out ahead? Which did the more for posterity and the race? The children of which union will make the better citizens?"

II

I have often wondered, too, why American divorces are increasing so rapidly. Has the high and quickly increasing divorce rate anything to do with the new independent ways of American women? Feminist writers have long foreseen that woman's emancipation is a possible threat to family life. A well-known feminist, writing at about the turn of the century, expressed the following mingled hopes and fears:

"The liberation of woman in every one of its aspects profoundly involves the destiny of the family. It signifies in all the larger activities of life the relative individualization of one-half of human kind. This means, of course, a weakening of the solidarity of the family group, so far as its cohesion is dependent on the remnants of medieval marital authority. Will the ultimate dissolution of the family thus become the price of equality and freedom? Or rather, is it not almost certain that in the more salubrious air of freedom and equality there is being evolved a higher type of family, knit together by ties—sexual, moral, and spiritual— far more tenacious than those fostered by the regime of subjection?"

Let us see what the "more salubrious air of freedom and equality" in the most salubrious air of America has done to knit together "the higher type of family" by ties more "tenacious" than the old. As far back as 1886, when the Woman's Movement in America was well under way, the United States led every country in the world (for which figures are obtainable) in the number of its divorces proportionate to population, with the one exception of Japan. For more than a quarter of a century, prior to 1925, the increase of divorce in the United States was far greater than the growth of population. The number of divorces per thousand of the population was more than three times as large in 1925 as in 1887. Apparently the new equality-cement for marriage has not quite come up to expectations, at least in America. The rise of the New Woman in America has been accompanied by an astounding growth in the American divorce rate.

Wholesale divorce is thus a distinctively American phenomenon. If we wish to explain it, therefore, we must look for a distinctively American cause. We must seek its reason for existence in some clearly American aspect of family life. Is it due to the comparative brutality or neglect of American husbands? But American husbands have the reputation in all foreign countries of being the most faithful, indulgent, and even cringing in the world. Is it caused by the American woman's politi-cal freedom? Hardly, for women have liberty as citizens in many foreign countries where divorce is not a rapidly growing phenomenon: women may vote even in China. But just notice this: a wife's financial independence of her husband is a characteristic of family life far more marked in America than elsewhere. Nowhere has a married woman's economic emancipation been carried so far. An American wife is remarkably free to earn money and to spend it; in a word, to live a life comparatively independent of her husband. Of course there are cases of husbands whose unproductiveness forces their wives to earn outside the home. But the fact remains that public opinion permits the American wife to make money whether or not it is really needed.

This rather new state of affairs seems to have come in with the Industrial Revolution. When the factory took away woman's home occupations, one by one, she started to pursue her employment and livelihood within the walls of factories and offices. She, like her husband, became a wage earner, and began to bring home cash wages. Unfortunately, but perhaps naturally, she considered them as her own. Family budgets were changed so that there was now not one fund but three, the husband's, the wife's, and the house account. Marriage was no longer a co-operative adventure. Gone was the old division of labor, in which the husband filled a single family treasure chest and the wife kept the key. Questions of mine and thine arose within the partnership. Our American doctrine of liberty and equality, pushed to a fatal extreme which has affected the discipline even of our children, began to threaten the age-old unit of society. When liberty and equality came in at the front door, fraternity and maternity flew out the window. The fine spiritual bonds, which used to knit together the old families, weakened and disappeared when the economic tie was severed. And we have learned—let us hope not too late—that the income-dependence of the wife upon the husband, and the home-dependence of the husband upon the wife are the indispensable cohesive forces without which the American family threatens to scatter to the four winds. Take these away and you have left only the yoke of mutual sentiment, which often dies too soon, and the common interest in children, who too frequently never appear at all. The home is becoming, not a club, but a place to sleep in.

The new woman, according to an American feminist, Dorothy Dunbar Bromley, prizes her economic independence because it enables her "to terminate a marriage that has become unbearable"; but the trouble is that this new financial freedom and the ease with which American divorces are obtained tend to make woman, instead of the court, the judge of what is unbearable, and the new woman is quite capable, especially if she is earning a salary, of considering even children unbearable. Thus, a distinctively American cause of divorce seems to be the American woman's financial independence, a phenomenon occurring to the same extent nowhere else in the world.

A poor man married to a rich wife is generally recognized as the most abject of creatures. He is the butt of jokes in every comic paper. Why? Simply because the realities have been turned upside-down, and authority has been shifted, with economic leadership, from the man to the woman. Try as they will, such a couple are apt to become ill at ease. American diplomats are not the only men whose careers have been ended shortly after marriage with an American heiress. We all know of such cases. In my own experience, there is a young doctor of splendid promise whose patients are leaving him one by one. His hours for consultation are becoming shorter and shorter. The monotony of daily golf is robbing him of the infinite variety of medicine. Sooner or later comes the gentle command, "My dear, I have decided that we are going to spend the winter at Hot Springs."

Exit career, close on the heels of proper masculine authority. Such a situation seems to most of us unnatural. But it is only a higher development of woman's ordinary economic semi-independence, which appears to the writer almost equally unnatural.

But there is another curious thing about American divorces. The overwhelming majority of them are, and long have been, granted, not to men but to women. During the year 1926 in Paris, judgments of divorce were handed down to more than two hundred American couples. Of these only a dozen husbands brought successful suits. Thus, about sixteen American women sought and received legal freedom, to one American man. (The very latest news from the Paris divorce mill tells of a well-known feminist who has petitioned for her liberty on the ground that her husband has "refused to serve her in his home"!) But perhaps this feminine nature of American divorces in Paris may be explained on other grounds than the freedom-urge of the new woman. Perhaps it is due to the collusive manufacture of divorce "evidence" by gallant American husbands; or just possibly to the overwhelming comparative wickedness of the American male (a rather doubtful assumption, to say the least).

Let us turn, therefore, to divorces in America, where collusion and the manufacture of evidence, not to mention immorality, are supposed to be far more restricted than upon the shores of Gaul. Which is the divorcing sex in the United States? The Government Census Report for 1925 shows that in the divorce business husbands are trailing far behind. In 1925, 30.1 per cent of all divorces in the United States were granted to men; 69.9 per cent to women. Here, at least, the interpretations usually given, male depravity and the fact that divorce is in some states more easy for women, are by no means satisfactory. And they fail utterly to explain why since the late eighties, a period of pronounced feminist agitation, the preponderance of wives in America who receive divorces has been slowly but unmistakably increasing. The bare fact remains that for more than a generation American wives have been exceedingly aggressive in legally disrupting the family. They are becoming more so with each succeeding year. In America, divorce is a growing female institution.

Since 1922, moreover, there has been an increasing proportion of divorces in which children were affected by the decree. In 1925, in probably one-half of such tragedies the lives of American children were involved.

Very possibly, then, we can isolate a second factor in American divorce— some feminine attitude of mind, not found to the same extent in other countries. I here raise the question whether that peculiar mentality is not the craze for independence which we have learned to associate definitely with the feminist movement and its egocentric doctrines. Recently, a London daily paper published a questionnaire, intending to discover why unmarried British girls had abstained from wedlock. Mr. Meyrick Booth has pointed out that not one of the young spinsters who replied even mentioned the fact that women, as such, owe a duty to the community; that the maintenance of the home life of the nation is their specific task. One and all, the answers showed a self-centered tone, extreme love of personal freedom, and a total lack of "the sense of feminine function." Many of these girls had had chances to marry, but had let them slip because their suitors were not in a position to give them large incomes or numerous luxuries. Most English girls, says Mr. Booth, do not in the least realize the deep antithesis which must exist between independence and sex love. A passionate love of freedom, however valuable it may be in other directions, is one of the worst possible qualities with which to enter upon a state which demands much self-discipline. Yet British girls fly to the idea

of "equality" to protect themselves against any possible possessive claims on the part of man, and to the idea of birth control (and now to the nursery school) to make sure that the claims of maternity shall not interfere too largely with freedom. Mr. Booth asks the question, "What is there of *love* in this outlook? Does not the very essence of feminine love lie in the idea of surrender?" It seems to the writer that much of this criticism applies with equal force to American women. It may be hoped that they will soon begin to think more sympathetically concerning the needs of their husbands, though, judging by the single vacuous feminine tirade which was the only answer in England to Mr. Booth's thoughtful article, the prospect is not encouraging. However, I hopefully invite American women to discuss my contention that the second great cause of the American divorce evil is the American woman's desire for independence from husband and family. I hold that the female custom of divorce in America is the outward sign of the inward craze for liberty, liberty unrestrained.

Divorce, too, seems to be more frequent in cities than in rural districts. I am inclined to lay this in part to the fact that in the country the man-woman relation has much of its old and more natural aspect. The farmer husband is still contesting with Nature and he is, therefore, more apt to control the important questions of family policy. Interestingly enough, the same natural relationship returns, even in cities, in times of physical struggle. When the car breaks down, when there is a fire or an earthquake or war, the husband is unquestionably the commander, since the family is again dealing with the hard facts of nature. It is only in the periods between such emergencies that the softer sex steps out of its feminine sphere. "The despotism of mere brute force," some woman exclaims. But muscular power is and always will be an important part of life. It cannot be ignored.

Yes, this woman movement has its good points; but it is going altogether too far. On the material side, for countless years woman's chief function on this planet has been to attract and hold a man, with the object of reproducing and educating children. Man's job has always been to feed the family. It is not natural that the role of woman should be so suddenly modified.

III

In order to test my idea that notions of feminine independence are tending to break up marriage, I resolved to collect the opinions of my friends. Since practically all of them are happily married and form their judgments jointly, I knew it would be impossible, for purposes of comparison, to get the separate theories of husband or wife. I decided, therefore, to ask for a composite picture of their views, and with this in mind I dared to send them a questionnaire! I do not know whether my wife and I had more fun in writing this masterpiece or in chuckling over the answers. One very good friend, on receiving the queries, became so worried concerning our domestic relations that he suggested that he should pay us a visit, apparently in order to patch things up! Others took the thing as a huge joke, still others were furious and declined to answer; but a large number responded nobly, obeying my injunction to avoid wise cracks and such like fooleries, and providing me with valuable and thoughtful answers.

We first asked them which one of the pair had authority to decide questions of family policy in cases where there was a complete *divergence and deadlock of honest opinion* between husband and wife—a difference due, not to mere pettishness, but to real conviction. We also asked which one *should in theory* possess such authority. To this they replied almost unanimously by unconsciously dodging the question. *They* never had disputes, it seemed, which

could not be settled almost at once by sweetness, light, and reason. Sometimes one gave in, sometimes the other. It was, therefore, not necessary to discuss who had, or should have, authority. It was not needful to have a rule one way or the other. They were glad to say that in *their* family each parent had *equal* authority. The implication was that my views were horribly old-fashioned, and needed overhauling. So much for the general theory.

The answers to the next question, however, showed a painful discrepancy between theory and application. *"In case of an honest disagreement as to the next place where you are to live, or concerning the manner in which your children are to be disciplined or educated, should the husband or wife have the deciding vote?"* The good-natured victims of our questionnaire later told us that they had argued long and laboriously on these points. For of course they had to agree before they could send in an answer. One couple produced no replies because, they said, they agreed on nothing. Finally, most of them turned out a shower of conflicting solutions. "The man should determine the new place of residence, since he is usually the income provider, and because his business controls the situation of his home." Or, "The father should be the judge of the proper discipline and education for the children, because it is his place to do so, he being the firmer disciplinarian." Or, quite contrarily, "The woman is more in the house than the man. Her wishes, therefore, should govern in choosing the location of a new home." Or again, "The woman naturally knows more about the children, hence she should decide how they are to be disciplined and educated."

Next we inquired, *"Do you think that the economic dependence of wives, where it exists, safeguards the continuance of marriage, by insuring family harmony through the necessary surrender of the wife in cases of prolonged dispute?"* This question generated more heat than light.

It brought forth cries of "Shame on you!" especially in the replies which had been left chiefly in the hands of the wives. One man wrote that the economic dependence of wives is indeed a safeguard of marriage, but a poor one.

Our last question ran about as follows: *"Do you think that the growing desire for personal independence, as observed in American wives, has any bearing on the rapidly increasing American divorce rate?"* This produced the most amazing responses of all. A typical answer ran like this: "Yes, feminism is increasing the American divorce rate, but what of it? If a man is not willing to allow his wife complete freedom to do as she pleases, isn't it better that the family should break up? Divorce is surely preferable to such submission to male authority."

Here, I felt, was a striking confirmation of my hypothesis that feminism tends to destroy the family. Theoretically, these couples never had serious disagreements. Actually, it cost them hours of discussion before they could decide whether a man or his wife should settle the simplest questions of everyday life, even though the discussion was in this instance purely academic! Here were the germs of endless domestic trouble, yet there seemed to be no sort of rule or understanding for settling such disputes. The economic dependence of women, though admittedly a preserver of matrimony, was immensely unpopular, apparently because it interfered with complete female emancipation. And divorce was actually preferred by the modern educated American woman to the slightest show of authority by her husband! Now, our friends are doctors, lawyers, business men, teachers, and their wives. They are thus representative of intelligent American opinion. Practically none of the wives, be it noted, contributes to the family support. Yet so inoculated are these people with the doctrine of feminine independence that they are willing to consider the possibility of divorce in case masculine au-thority should become established. The idea seemed to me a bit extreme. I wondered what their attitude would have been had they possessed most of the family income, like the wife of my friend the Doctor, or had owned their own business, or their own separate establishment.

IV

While I was turning these interesting answers over and over in my mind I remembered a sentence from the early feminist already quoted. She had characterized the liberation of woman as the "relative individualization of *one-half* of woman kind." Why only *one-half?* Why shouldn't man, I asked myself, be liberated too? Why should he go on with the drudgery of his office routine, while the ardent feminist slights her household duties? If independence of this sort is good for a woman, it is as good or better for a man. If a wife is too busy outside the home to give her husband more than half herself, why should he not divide his affections also? So, acting on the theory that it is a poor rule that will not work both ways, I took the recent words of a well-known feminist writer in this magazine ("Feminist—New Style"), and made a free translation of them into masculinese, just to see how they would sound.

I called my imaginary male revolutionist the Twentieth Century Man, or "Virist—New Style," and this is what I found him saying: "Virist—New Style is moved by an inescapable, inner compulsion to be an individual in his own right. It is obvious that a man who plans intelligently can salvage some time for his own pursuits. He is convinced that he will be a better husband and father from the breadth of outlook he will gain by functioning outside the office. He means to drop the grind of the office and spend part of his week as he pleases, possibly about the house, carpentering, painting, and tinkering with the car, possibly somewhere else. Men are highly conscious creatures who feel obliged to plumb their own resources to the very depths. It would, therefore, be ridiculous to insist that men who are gifted with genuine talent for such pursuits as painting, writing, or acting, should neglect these interests by too constant attention to their income or business. The same applies to those men who are born with marked ability for one of the trades, such as that of mechanician. They too must follow their star, even if it be only the lowly ambition completely to overhaul the family washing machine. Virist—New Style will proceed on the principle that a person of intelligence and energy can attain a fair amount of success by the very virtue of living a well-balanced life. 'Come out of the office' is a fine slogan, especially after working hours. Virist—New Style detests working after hours, but if his wife is properly appreciative he will do so, and he will, of course, expect her to relieve him, in turn, of some of his home duties. He knows that it is his American birthright to emerge from a creature of toil into a full-fledged individual who is capable of molding his own life. And in this respect he holds that he is becoming woman's equal, at least in the art of recreation. If this be treason, ladies, make the most of it!"

Now Married Maidens—New Style, be honest! How do you like Selfishness—New Style when the masculine version is presented? Do you not see that men would like independence too, but that so far duty has held them, in most instances, to their appointed tasks? How do you like the prospect of your husband's wasting his special business or professional talent, and seriously affecting his income, by doing work at home which someone else can do far better? Isn't it still true that specialization spells efficiency, and if it is wise for a man to specialize to produce income, is it not yet more advisable for a woman to specialize, to give her family those home values which are far more precious than money?

If you wish to realize your feelings, should you suddenly begin to see such propaganda everywhere, as men saw womanist propaganda a few years ago, suppose you try the experiment of reading this article to your husband. I will bet that before you are through a sly twinkle will creep into his eyes. He will nudge you gently in your emancipated ribs, and he will remark blandly, "Well, let's make this a fair two-sided proposition, independence from home and husband for you, freedom from office and wife for me. Suppose we try it?" No, if we still care in the least to preserve family life, the thesis of the married feminist will not stand, if the masculine converse is so much as stated.

Question your husband farther and, if you succeed in drawing him out, you will probably learn that he regards much of the independence of married women with pronounced disfavor. It will hardly be maintained by honest-minded women that this feeling is due to jealousy of female accomplishments in spheres outside the home. You will learn from your husband that he feels that where men are married to intellectual tomboys family life lacks a certain spiritual richness which was characteristic of marriage years ago, and of which men are now being robbed; that if a woman does her duty by the race and raises, with tender care, two or three children, she has all the career that she needs, and her outside interests will then take their proper place as hobbies or pastimes. That the children of the new woman feel spiritually starved does not make the situation any better. As to the man, such a situation tempts him to turn instinctively from the aggressive woman who scorns to give him her time, her thoughts, and herself, to some other feminine companion. A husband's sense of loyalty to his wife weakens as her independence grows. All too easily a man turns from a woman who is his wife only in a technical sense to one who will give herself with that completeness which alone can call forth his single-hearted and unselfish devotion. If you say that this looks like a tendency toward sexual anarchy, you have it exactly right. It is the natural result of a failure, now chiefly feminine, to see in marriage a mutual enterprise. It is the inevitable outcome of the egocentric philosophy which the modern girl is learning in school and college. She cannot have her cake and eat it. She cannot be a man and hold a man. If she is seeking to abolish marriage, we must give her credit for knowing exactly how to go about it.

V

Do we really object to this gradual approach to a condition of free love (a term coined, by the way, in the United States)? If not, well and good. We know just where we are, with the advanced feminists who frankly want it, though perhaps they know not why. Quite possibly these women are right. If so, wives have only to continue their displeasing independence, and man will soon learn from them a new male independence which is really a throw-back to the old. Sloughing off the thin veneer of civilization, so painfully acquired, he will easily slide downhill to that delightful primitive polygamy which still haunts his dreams, and to the Romany life of ancient days, vague memories of which still make his office seem at times a worker's prison. Let us not, however, drift in this direction without at least noting our course beforehand.

But if we do look with uneasiness on the growing divorce rate and all that it may lead to, then, though there is no panacea to cure it, two steps will help us to regain the lost ground. First, married women should decide voluntarily to give up the independent breadwinning function wherever economically possible. With this goes the corresponding determination of men to assure wherever feasible a decent family income, the economic subordination of their wives, and the male authority which goes with it. Second, married women

should realize that their desire for unrestrained freedom is a direct cause of divorce in America, and a treason to their primary function as women, which is to keep the family intact and to carry on the race to higher and higher levels.

Of course a wise husband will keep his authority in reserve. He will govern his home by reason and persuasion. He will not parade the Fasces. He will know that his wife should have as much freedom within marriage as is possible without reversing the natural occupations of the sexes. He will not expect her to tell him where she goes and what she does. He will not attempt to dictate what she must wear, or to control her religious beliefs. Conversely, he will hope for similar toleration on her part. But with all this proper moderation, he will keep alive the precious truth that a wife who will not surrender where there is an honest and lasting difference of opinion involving the fortunes of the whole family is, from a man's point of view, not a wife at all.

Feminists, note this well! It is the double-headedness of the modern American family which is causing it so frequently to split down the middle, leaving the children more or less exposed. The heads are at war with each other. The house divided against itself does not, we observe, stand. Marriage dissolves in feminism as sugar melts in acid. No one expects married women with the priceless gift of leisure to spend their time entirely within the home. But let them avoid the mistake of assuming the man's part. Let them fill a terrible gap in American life by devoting themselves to the many good causes which do not, as a matter of fact, pay cash dividends. Let them dedicate themselves to the task of showing their men that there are finer interests in life than dollars and cents.

I want to leave this thought in the modern married woman's mind. Co-commandership in a family, and unbridled self-assertion in a woman are the quickest ways to break up a home. There is a deal of truth in the saying that a woman who wins an argument with her husband is likely to lose her man. It is a self-evident proposition that where two persons in *equal* authority seriously disagree there is *no* way of settling the issue save by calling in a third party. A business partnership of two members dissolves, and no great harm is done. The two equally powerful Roman Consuls of ancient times settled their differences by blood and iron, and the Roman rulers soon invented the Triumvirate, with a third member who could act as umpire. When nations disagree and a court of arbitration is set up there are never less than three members. The function of the third or neutral member is to prevent a deadlock. Marriage might in some respects have been better arranged had it included a colorless third or neutral party with diplomatic functions; but as things are, the deadlocked American marriage partners have no recourse but to air their troubles before the Domestic Relations Court or the Divorce Tribunal. The only way to avoid this intrusion of a third party is for the husband to resume command of the pair. Assuming that women still desire the welfare of their children, and that children are to receive the care to which they seem to be entitled, divorce must be knocked on the head. And the quickest way to kill divorce is to restore to all loyal husbands, in these times of prosperity, that natural authority which is theirs anyway the moment anything goes wrong. If they use their authority unwisely the courts are still at hand. But if they behave themselves, it is surely a pity to destroy a family because the wife, who would not tolerate effeminacy in a man, insists on masculine activities for herself. The charm of the sexes for each other lies in the differences between man and woman. Any step which tends to make them alike in function, manners, or appearance is a step away from nature and towards sexual chaos.

There is an African bird, the Hornbill, which during the nesting season walls up his mate with mud or clay in her nest in a hollow tree. Only the tip of her beak protrudes. Through this the male industriously feeds his spouse, while she cares for the family. That bird understands domestic unity and the division of labor which spells success. Let us admit that he is masterful. But it is known that he is extraordinarily devoted, and it appears that he is determined not to let "liberty" destroy the rights of the family. When his mate has performed her maternal functions and given her offspring a good start in life, the mud wall is broken and she is free to resume her personal occupations. But she is never permitted during the child-raising period to contribute to the family income. Nor is there any evidence that she objects in the least to the presence of a solid reminder of her duty to serve her race in Nature's good old way. Consider the ways of the Hornbill, O Man, and be wise!

Common Problems of Professional Women

By Ruby A. Black

PROFESSIONAL women are becoming aware that individual achievement is not enough to overcome the prejudices against women in the professional world. They are learning, in increasing numbers, I believe, that united effort is necessary to make their status all it should be in the competitive economic field. They are seeing their problems as the problems of women, to be faced by women and to be solved by a solidarity of women, so that every woman will not have to combat and overcome as an individual the same old handicaps which hundreds of others, as individuals, have battled against, either victoriously or futilely, before her.

As chairman of the Research Committee of the Professional Pan-Hellenic Association, I helped make a study of what professional fraternities of college women are doing for professional women, what they have found to be the problems peculiar to women in their respective professions, what they have done in an attempt to solve these problems, and what they think should be done. We sent questionnaires to such fraternities representing the professions of education, medicine, law, journalism, physical education, public speaking, music, dramatic arts, physical education, home economics, business, and chemistry.

Among other things, we sought to learn whether or not these organizations of uni-versity-trained professional women had found problems which they believed to be common to women in all professions, whether they thought the Professional Pan-Hellenic Association, as an organization representing practically all the professions in which college-trained women may be found, could contribute anything to the solution of these problems, and whether any of the organizations had attacked the problem of the combination of a home and work outside the home, meaning by this not only the problem of the married woman with a job, but also the problem of the maintenance of a home by the unmarried professional woman.

Of the seventeen fraternities responding to the questionnaire, thirteen expressed the opinion that such an organization as the Professional Pan-Hellenic Association could contribute to the solution of the problems common to women in all professions.

Two ignored this question, one answered "probably," and one placed a question mark in the space left for the answer. Thus it would seem that the professional fraternities believe that there are common problems to be solved, and that they can best be solved by united effort.

That there is a live interest in the problems of women in the professions is evi-denced by the fact that every fraternity except one reported projects for the advancement of women in their respective professions accomplished, under way, or in contemplation. The one fraternity reporting no such project represented the teaching profession, in which women have been entrenched longer than in most of the other professions.

The most frequent projects undertaken by professional fraternities were in the form of aid to students, such as scholarships, loan funds, fellowships, and prizes. Eight fraternities had established, either nationally or locally, some form of financial aid to students, one is now planning such a project, one has established an endowment fund for the purpose of providing such aid, two other endowment funds are in process of establishment, and two are offering prizes to students in the professions they represent. One of these prizes tends also to contribute to the solution of problems of women in the profession represented, as it is offered annually for an article representing research on some aspect of the status, opportunities, advantages, and achievement of women in the profession represented.

One fraternity has made a survey of the opportunities for women in journalism, the profession it represents; three others are now making surveys, and two plan to undertake such surveys. These surveys take varied forms, some of them covering

106

the positions now held by women in the profession represented, some of them covering the positions held by members of the fraternity, and some of them covering the whole field of openings for women trained for certain professions.

Two fraternities reported that they have done or are doing some work in vocational guidance among students, one of them having furnished speakers for vocational guidance conferences in colleges, and the other offering such service, along with others, in connection with a faculty advisor system.

Only one fraternity reported any organized attempt to get at the problem of the combination of a home and a profession, and its effort in this direction was rather limited, depending upon the calls received for part-time jobs by the placement bureau it has established.

The journalism fraternity has established and has been operating for seven years a placement bureau which has found hundreds of positions for women in the profession it represents, and has also extended the opportunities for women in journalism by calling the attention of employers to the training, experience, and availability of women for positions which women had not previously held. Another fraternity contemplates forming such a bureau.

One fraternity reports that it is attempting to raise the standards of the profession it represents, and doubtless others are making similar efforts. Another reports that it is concentrating on the improvement of the training offered women in the profession it represents.

APPARENTLY there was some hesitation in answering the question as to the problems common to women in all professions. Some did not answer at all because they had undertaken no general surveys, and some appeared not to answer because they had no opportunity to consult their national councils, and did not wish to express personal opinions. The answers which were made, however, were striking in that they so frequently mentioned much the same problems, indicating not only that women are increasingly conscious of the fact that women do face definite problems common to women in all professions, but that they find much the same difficulties facing them in the varied professions represented.

The answer most frequently given to this question was that women as a whole have not achieved equality of opportunity, advancement, and pay in the professions. Six of those answering this question mentioned this problem. Several spoke of the lack of co-operation among women, and of the need for more thorough development of a professional attitude among women. Vocational guidance, placement service, suitable recreation, the combina-

tion of a home and work, overcoming the handicaps women suffer because of the large turnover resulting from marriage, better housing facilities for professional women, and the elimination of an inferiority complex among professional women so that they will have the self-confidence to live up to their utmost capacities were other problems mentioned as common to women in all professions.

Some of the replies made to this question are notable because of their similarity and their difference.

For example: Phi Delta Delta law fraternity, after mentioning the lack of equal opportunity for placement, advancement, recognition, and compensation, then commented:

"Women's chief problem is within themselves. They may possess the training and ability to make decisions in connection with their work, whether professional or business, and yet they will not, as a general rule, take the responsibility of making such decisions, and instead of acting on these questions or problems independently and receiving proper recognition, they take their suggestions to their superiors for approval.

"Women deliberately raise the question of prejudice, often unconsciously, it is true. If they will only ignore that prejudice, discuss their work and hopes of progress in it with their masculine associates on the assumption that no possible prejudice exists in their particular line of work, they frequently will discover that their masculine associates forget it, too. Women are too prone to blame all failures on their part to the sex prejudice whereas it is probably responsible for only a small part."

Another side of the same picture was presented by Phi Delta Pi, physical education fraternity, which commented:

"Very often it seems difficult for the business and professionally-trained woman to receive from the public and administrative officers equal recognition with men of relatively the same ability and training. This is discouraging and often causes bitterness, which is apt to be damaging to one's efficiency. Men are usually chosen in preference to women for the higher positions. Why is this so? Is it because it is men who make the selections, or do women not make good administrative officers? * * * * * Possibly in their zeal to perform the details of their work they do not take time to theorize about its greater possibilities. I do not know. I am just expressing what occurs to me at the moment. I do know that the lack of recognition and the consequent unhappiness is a handicap to the earnest and ambitious woman."

This representative of a fraternity attributes the very lack of self-confidence and responsibility of women to the prejudice with which they are surrounded. It would appear that women are working in a vicious circle which should be broken.

Phi Chi Theta, business fraternity, which has undertaken a survey of wide scope to find out the type of positions held by its members, the difficulties they have encountered, information of help to those in business and college, and the advisability of a central information and employment bureau, reports that the worst handicap women face is the turnover as a result of marriage. To this many men interviewed by the representative of the fraternity attributed the failure of women to obtain equal pay and advancement. She also found a general lack of faith in the combination of a home and a job, and considerable tendency to refuse to employ married women. If this is the key problem to women's advancement in the professions, then there is clearly an enormous work to be done (1) in improving the machinery for maintaining a home without the constantly present supervision of some member of the family; and (2) in educating both the employer and the employed so that neither will assume that the fact of a woman's marriage is evidence that she is attempting to carry two jobs.

ANALYZED to the final degree, the common problems facing women in the professions, as indicated by these responses seem to be:

(1) That group of problems which involve certain changes in the world in which women work, including:

(a) Equalization of the opportunities, advancement, and compensation of women with that of men doing equivalent work, including, of course, the elimination of prejudices against the employment of married women, since women and men will not be equal in the economic world unless marriage and parenthood constitute no more a bar to a woman's employment than to a man's;

(b) Improvement of the machinery for woman's having both a home and a job, whether she is married or not.

(2) That group of problems which involve changes within women themselves, including:

(a) Development of a more professional attitude among women;

(b) Creation of a greater solidarity and co-operation among professional women until they reach the point where they no longer face problems which professional men do not face;

(c) Elimination of that fear of prejudice and lack of self-confidence which hampers women in the full development of their capacities.

At its last conference, the Professional Pan-Hellenic Association adopted a report on this investigation with the recommendation that the association form a Standing Committee on the Status and Advancement of Women in the professions, to continue the study begun by the Research Committee, and to work toward a central clearing house of information about women in the professions, and toward a united effort to face and solve the problems common to women in the professions. This report with its recommendations was prepared by a committee consisting of Lois Gates Gorman, one of the two women attorney-examiners in the Interstate Commerce Commission, Esther D. Longstreet, a business woman, and myself, a newspaper woman.

Miss Longstreet made a special study of the work done by professional organizations of women other than Greek-letter professional fraternities for women, and found that several important studies have been made or are in progress by such organizations, seeking to reach some solution of the problem of increasing the opportunities and improving the status of women in the professions.

SEX INFERIORITY

RUTH ALLISON HUDNUT

THE idea of a superior and inferior sex is subtle and far-reaching. It is camouflaged and denied. The so-called superior sex sends out a barrage of flattery extoling motherhood, wifehood, beauty, sweetness, innocence, and declaring that no work is as sacred as the home-maker's, but strangely enough a man with these virtues or aptitudes is regarded as "feminine," an opprobrious term when applied to him. It might be argued that male virtues in the female are also condemned, but is this true? Honesty, courage, strength, intelligence, dominance are among the traits man likes to call his own. A woman has to have them in overwhelming measure to secure for them recognition. When she does she is considered a "man" and the term is not one of contempt.

An examination of the modern novel reveals how universally women are still tacitly thought to be the inferior sex. In a recent study of the status of women in the modern novel, covering some sixty odd novels chosen at random from well-known contemporary American and English authors, I found sex inferiority permeating the material. It was an idea held by both sexes, disclosed by a general preference for male children, by the remarks of the characters, and an emphasis on woman's appearance rather than on her intelligence.

Illustrations will make these points clear. Many babies were born in the Irish community in which the Callahans and Murphys resided, and all the young mothers hoped for boys rather than girls.[1] Mrs. Bradley cared more for her sons than her daughters and with some reason, for the sons were cleverer.[2] Mr. Grammont "despised and distrusted women generally," and made clear to his daughter that it was a grave error for her to be a daughter instead of a son.[3] Bernard, father of three children, wondered what he had really secured from life and was comforted when he thought of his only son.[4] Richard Callender wished a divorce from his first wife partly because her one child was a girl, and he and his mother passionately desired a boy to inherit the family fortune. When his second wife was pregnant everyone hoped and prayed for a son. It had to be. It was.[5] Maartje never caressed her daughters, but Selina saw her fondling her son and thought, "She loves him best."[6] This same preference for the male was shown by Pervus De Jong when he told Selina of his first marriage. His wife died in childbirth, the child also. It was a girl, but then he was always unlucky.[7] Evelyn, thinking of the baby she was going to have hoped it would be a boy.[8]

In none of the novels were there passages of a similar nature indicating a preference for female children.

Ina "revered her husband's opinions above those of all other men. In politics, in science, in religion, in dentistry she looked up to his dicta as to revelation."[9] The Professor did not expect to find mind in his wife. His romance with her was

[1] Norris, Kathleen, *The Callahans and the Murphys,* pp. 102–103.

[2] Sedgwick, Anne D., *The Little French Girl,* p. 45.

[3] Wells, H. G., *Secret Places of the Heart,* p. 182.

[4] Gale, Zona, *Preface to a Life,* p. 193.

[5] Bromfield, Louis, *Possession,* pp. 311, 312, 335, 465, 486.

[6] Ferber, Edna, *So Big,* pp. 61–62.

[7] *Ibid.,* p. 100.

[8] Parrish, Anne, *To-morrow Morning,* p. 249.

[9] Gale, Zona, *Miss Lulu Bett,* p. 74.

one of the heart. His romance of the mind and imagination was with a man.[10] Govett thought "the minds of women . . . . were totally different from the minds of men. Simpler. Without exterior obligation."[11] Joe Easter assured the man who ran away with his wife that there was no ill-feeling. "No woman that ever lived is worth giving up a real friendship for," he said.[12] Sondra was socially superior to Clyde and for that reason he looked up to her. She sensed his submissiveness, "that of the slave for the master, and in part liking and in part resenting it, since like Roberta and Hortense, even she preferred to be mastered rather than to master. . . . ."[13] Although Gabriella had an immoral and worthless husband, "against men as men she had never thought of cherishing a grievance. All her life she had looked to some man as to the saviour of the family fortunes, and her vision was still true enough to perceive that, as a human being, Archibald Fowler was finer and bigger than his wife, that Billy was finer and bigger than Patty."[14] The doctor was convinced that women could not produce ideas, but he thought they might be encouraged to respond to ideas and become for men "mistress-mothers," persons who would care for them, their work, their honor more than for aught else, receptacles for the creative male mind.[15] Sempack, the philosopher, wrote a letter of advice to Mrs. Rylands about her husband. He told her to consider their differences. "You are a finer thing than Philip but you are—slighter. . . . . He has the mak-

ing of a far bigger and stronger and more effective person than you can ever be. . . . .[16] Philip is your job. . . . . I see no other job in the world for you to compare with it or to replace it. . . . . Women are for men and children are a by-product."[17]

A reference to a man as a woman is considered an insult. Frank Shallard of today is as incensed as Arthur Kay of yesterday at being called a female. Frank was glad to leave the ministry in one way, for other men could no longer think of him as "an old woman in trousers."[18] But preachers even if only "old women in trousers" gained the respect and worship of the women—perhaps because of the trousers. Elmer's mother wanted him to become a preacher, because she had such awe of them.[19] Elmer never tired of standing around looking "impressive and very male for the benefit of lady seekers." And all of them responded whether "spinsters with pathetic dried girlishness" or "misunderstood wives."[20]

Even the most successful and dominant women have moments of weakness in the novels when they think themselves inferior because they are "only women." Sharon, the revivalist, the one woman who really dominated Elmer Gantry, and the leader in their partnership said to him, "I'm a woman. I'm weak. I wonder if I oughtn't to stop thinking I'm such a marvel, if I oughtn't to let you run things and just stand back and help you? Ought I?" Elmer was quite overcome by her good sense and assured her that perhaps it would be wise. Of course she was as clever as he, but a woman was not built to

[10] Cather, Willa, *The Professor's House*, p. 258.

[11] Hergesheimer, Joseph, *Tampico*, p. 182.

[12] Lewis, Sinclair, *Mantrap*, p. 269.

[13] Dreiser, Theodore, *An American Tragedy*, vol. I, pp. 376–377.

[14] Glasgow, Ellen, *Life and Gabriella*, p. 181.

[15] Wells, H. G., *Secret Places of the Heart*, p. 76.

[16] Wells, H. G., *Meanwhile*, p. 107.

[17] *Ibid.*, 112–113.

[18] Deland, Margaret, *The Kays*, p. 10; Lewis, Sinclair, *Elmer Gantry*, p. 386.

[19] *Elmer Gantry*, p. 29.

[20] *Ibid.*, p. 190.

carry on things the way a man could.[21] Two men who heard Sharon speak admired her gift of oratory, but one of them observed, "Same time though, tell you how I feel about it: woman's all right in her place, but takes a real he-male to figure out this religion business."[22]

Imogen said to her aunt, Miss Creswell, when they were both in danger of succumbing to the magnetism of Peter Kharkoff, the Jew, a kind of superman, "If there's one thing I hate more than another it's the worshiping woman.   Every callow curate has his fatuous worshipers, every vicar, every bishop, every known man, be he writer, painter, pianist, politician, or merely one of the Rudins of the world, a talking windbag." Yet this very modern young woman finally succumbed to the Jew's charm and worshiped like the others, saying to him weakly, "D'you know I think I must be a very weak vessel? Perhaps most women are."[23]

Ellen Tulliver was a successful woman, yet during the war she thought of herself as "merely a woman whose men were at war, a woman who could do nothing, who must sit behind and suffer in terror and doubt."[24]   And at another time she termed herself "only a poor, weak, feminine creature."[25]

Joanna Godden was a dominant woman, managing a large farm and controlling her hired men, yet her baby boy was too much for her. He made a scene at a fair, and Joanna could not handle him. "The spectators were predominantly female— they whispered and nudged and clucked— four male years were able to hold them at bay." Suddenly a man stepped into the crowd, picked up the yelling child

and carried him off under his arm, while "the three women followed, trotting helplessly."[26]

Bernard told Alla, "You're as honest as a man," and thought it was a compliment.[27] Berazov also thought he was praising Imogen when he said, "I'm almost afraid of your honesty. . . . . Why are you being so honest? That's not like woman."[28] Bernard believed any woman who was competent and independent was a "man."[29] Jessica also felt that because she had these qualities she was too much of a "man" to please the ordinary male.[30] Although Dorinda's stepson was a cripple and dependent on her, "he shared . . . . with all males who were not milksops, the masculine instinct to domineer over the opposite sex."[31]

If women have not men's brains, if they are weaker and subordinate, waiting to be absorbed, they must have some appeal that will induce the masculine sex to absorb and master them. The novel shows that appeal comes through beauty, something that must be cultivated, the chief object of successful womanhood. "The girls of the world are divided into two classes: the pretty ones" and those "who are not pretty. The latter have undoubtedly their compensations. They have pretty hands, hair, or shoulders, they have brains, or talents, or charm. They have no bloom to lose in early middle-life, and frequently they have actual beauty to gain:" yet "life has done them an incurable injustice."[32]

In comparing the importance of brains

---

[21] Ibid., p. 216.

[22] Ibid., p. 223.

[23] Hichens, Robert, The Unearthly, pp. 196, 452.

[24] Bromfield, Louis, Possession, p. 357.

[25] Ibid., p. 396.

[26] Kaye-Smith, Sheila, Joanna Godden Married, etc., pp. 93–94.

[27] Gale, Zona, Preface to a Life, p. 321.

[28] Hichens, Robert, The Unearthly, p. 386.

[29] Gale, Zona, Preface to a Life, p. 320.

[30] Herrick, Robert, Chimes, p. 174.

[31] Glasgow, Ellen, Barren Ground, p. 475.

[32] The Callahans and the Murphys, p. 174.

versus beauty for female characters of the novel, beauty was three times as important in the earlier novels and twice as important in the later novels as brains. Although both men and women writers emphasized beauty, the former did so more often than the latter, and the latter were more inclined to give weight to brains.

The novel, that mirror of life, written from the training and experience of human beings, is cluttered with sex inferiority. Men and women writers speaking through male and female characters show a definite concept of male superiority. The idea must be a handicap to women, a retarding force in attaining equality with men. If men consciously or unconsciously look upon their own sex as possessing the greater intelligence and brains, they will be loath to give women equal economic opportunities. As men now control the economic life of the nation and economic power resolves itself in the ultimate analysis into the right of self-maintenance, men are in a dominating place. This higher position causes their superiority complex which helps to keep women secondary, and the whole resolves itself in a vicious circle.

Chivalry and Labor Laws

IN several recent legislative hearings certain well-groomed ladies from the National Woman's Party have fought shoulder to shoulder with the manufacturing interests against special labor laws for women. The manufacturers have welcomed this feminine support with great gusto and the press has given generous headlines indicating that the women reformers are divided among themselves. Behind the public hullabaloo there has not been an adequate body of facts on either side of the discussion. The trade unionists and social workers who support labor laws for women have given reasoned testimony for their belief based upon long experience, but the left-wing feminists have talked well and marshaled enough individual instances of sex discrimination to impress the public.

As *The Nation* has frequently pointed out, the leaders of the Woman's Party do not oppose labor legislation as such but only labor laws which apply to women as a sex. The question at issue is largely one of social philosophy. The left-wing feminist tends to see society as a sex struggle in which man exploits woman, while the laborite looks upon the same milieu as a class struggle in which employer exploits worker. The rub comes when the two struggles overlap and labor concedes the sexual *status quo* by appealing to the chivalry of the employer and the community for special labor laws for women. The intelligent labor champion does not make this appeal because he likes to make it; he prefers to win justice for woman as a worker through organized power but he will take justice for woman as a woman if he cannot get it in any other way. The appeal for woman as the weaker sex arouses the ire of the left-wing feminist. Chivalry is for her as bad as poverty because it perpetuates the prejudices which have kept women in subjection. Moreover, she claims that women workers actually lose by special labor laws because such laws throw them out of work and limit their employment opportunity.

This claim has been analyzed with great care by the Women's Bureau of the Department of Labor in a new study, "The Effects of Labor Legislation upon the Employment Opportunities of Women." The published facts knock into a cocked hat the arguments of the Woman's Party that shorter-hour legislation for women in the manufacturing industries has taken away opportunities to work. The investigation shows that most women who are gainfully employed are not affected one way or another by special labor legislation for their sex, but in five important manufacturing industries which employ women in large numbers the legal limitation of hours for women only has "not brought about any degree of substitution of men for women."

The investigation proves that in the matter of laws against night work for women the Woman's Party has some justification for its claim that men have supplanted women as a direct result of the laws. Likewise certain laws designed to protect women have caused the substitution of men in such tasks as running street cars and operating elevators. But these are individual instances and custom has done much more than law to eliminate women workers from night shifts, street cars, and certain types of elevators. On the whole the cases of individual injustice to women workers caused by special legislation seem unimportant compared to the resultant improvement of industrial standards.

COCKSURE WOMEN AND HENSURE MEN

IT SEEMS TO ME THERE ARE TWO ASPECTS TO WOMEN. THERE IS THE demure and the dauntless. Men have loved to dwell, in fiction at least, on the demure maiden whose inevitable reply is: Oh, yes, if you please, kind sir! The demure maiden, the demure spouse, the demure mother — this is still the ideal. A few maidens, mistresses and mothers *are* demure. A few pretend to be. But the vast majority are not. And they don't pretend to be. We don't expect a girl skilfully driving her car to be demure, we expect her to be dauntless. What good would demure and maidenly Members of Parliament be, inevitably responding: Oh, yes, if you please, kind sir! — Though of course there are masculine members of that kidney. — And a demure telephone girl? Or even a demure stenographer? Demureness, to be sure, is outwardly becoming, it is an outward mark of femininity, like bobbed hair. But it goes with inward dauntlessness. The girl who has got to make her way in life has got to be dauntless, and if she has a pretty, demure manner with it, then lucky girl. She kills two birds with two stones.

With the two kinds of femininity go two kinds of confidence: there are the women who are cocksure, and the women who are hensure. A really up-to-date woman is a cocksure woman. She doesn't have a doubt nor a qualm. She is the modern type. Whereas the old-fashioned demure woman was sure as a hen is sure, that is, without knowing anything about it. She went quietly and busily clucking around, laying the eggs and mothering the chickens in a kind of anxious dream that still was full of sureness. But not mental sureness. Her sureness was a physical condition, very soothing, but a condition out of which she could easily be startled or frightened.

It is quite amusing to see the two kinds of sureness in chick-

115

ens. The cockerel is, naturally, cocksure. He crows because he is *certain* it is day. Then the hen peeps out from under her wing. He marches to the door of the hen-house and pokes out his head assertively: *Ah ha! daylight, of course! just as I said!* — and he majestically steps down the chicken ladder towards *terra firma,* knowing that the hens will step cautiously after him, drawn by his confidence. So after him, cautiously, step the hens. He crows again: *Ha-ha! here we are!* — It is indisputable, and the hens accept it entirely. He marches towards the house. From the house a person ought to appear, scattering corn. Why does the person not appear? The cock will see to it. He is cocksure. He gives a loud crow in the doorway, and the person appears. The hens are suitably impressed, but immediately devote all their henny consciousness to the scattered corn, pecking absorbedly, while the cock runs and fusses, cocksure that he is responsible for it all.

So the day goes on. The cock finds a tit-bit, and loudly calls the hens. They scuffle up in henny surety, and gobble the tit-bit. But when they find a juicy morsel for themselves, they devour it in silence, hensure. Unless, of course, there are little chicks, when they most anxiously call the brood. But in her own dim surety, the hen is really much surer than the cock, in a different way. She marches off to lay her egg, she secures obstinately the nest she wants, she lays her egg at last, then steps forth again with prancing confidence, and gives that most assured of all sounds, the hensure cackle of a bird who has laid her egg. The cock, who is never so sure about anything as the hen is about the egg she has laid, immediately starts to cackle like the female of his species. He is pining to be hensure, for hensure is so much surer than cocksure.

Nevertheless, cocksure is boss. When the chicken-hawk appears in the sky, loud are the cockerel's calls of alarm. Then the hens scuffle under the verandah, the cock ruffles his feathers on guard. The hens are numb with fear, they say: Alas, there is no health in us! How wonderful to be a cock so bold! — And they huddle, numbed. But their very numbness is hensurety.

Just as the cock can cackle, however, as if he had laid the egg, so can the hen bird crow. She can more or less assume his cocksureness. And yet she is never so easy, cocksure, as she used to be when she was hensure. Cocksure, she is cocksure, but uneasy. Hensure, she trembles, but is easy.

It seems to me just the same in the vast human farmyard. Only nowadays all the cocks are cackling and pretending to lay eggs, and all the hens are crowing and pretending to call the sun out of bed. If women to-day are cocksure, men are hensure. Men are timid, tremulous, rather soft and submissive, easy in their very henlike tremulousness. They only want to be spoken to gently. So the women step forth with a good loud *cock-a-doodle-do!*

The tragedy about cocksure women is that they are more cocky, in their assurance, than the cock himself. They never realise that when the cock gives his loud crow in the morning, he listens acutely afterwards, to hear if some other wretch of a cock dare crow defiance, challenge. To the cock, there is always defiance, challenge, danger and death on the clear air; or the possibility thereof.

But alas, when the hen crows, she listens for no defiance or challenge. When she says *cock-a-doodle-do!* then it is unanswerable. The cock listens for an answer, alert. But the hen knows she is unanswerable. *Cock-a-doodle-do!* and there it is, take it or leave it!

And it is this that makes the cocksureness of women so dangerous, so devastating. It is really out of scheme, it is not in relation to the rest of things. So we have the tragedy of cocksure women. They find, so often, that instead of having laid an egg, they have laid a vote, or an empty ink-bottle, or some other absolutely unhatchable object, which means nothing to them.

It is the tragedy of the modern woman. She becomes cocksure, she puts all her passion and energy and years of her life into some effort or assertion, without ever listening for the denial which she ought to take into count. She is cocksure, but she is a hen all the time. Frightened of her own henny self, she rushes to mad lengths about votes, or welfare, or sports, or business: she is marvellous, out-manning the man. But alas, it is all fundamentally disconnected. It is all an attitude, and one day the attitude will become a weird cramp, a pain, and then it will collapse. And when it has collapsed, and she looks at the eggs she has laid, votes, or miles of typewriting, years of business efficiency — suddenly, because she is a hen and not a cock, all she has done will turn into pure nothingness to her. Suddenly it all falls out of relation to her basic henny self, and she realises she has lost her life. The lovely henny surety, the hensureness which is the real bliss of every female, has been denied her: she had never had it. Having lived her life with such utmost strenuousness and cocksureness, she has missed her life altogether. Nothingness!

EMOTIONAL HANDICAPS OF THE PROFESSIONAL WOMAN

ELEANORA B. SAUNDERS, PH.D., M.D.

The Sheppard and Enoch Pratt Hospital, Towson, Maryland

I RECALL a nurse, estimable, worthy, and efficient, who had, however, only one viewpoint—her own. She erected a barrier against coöperation with associates, was strict in discipline, "absolute" in her ideas of right and wrong, rigorous in regard to the social relations of the nurses—in fact, they called her "cut steel". We may speak of such a woman as inflexible or repressed—praiseworthy, but difficult.

Here is another case, also that of a professional woman, who developed a love affair that ended in pregnancy, with isolation, social estrangement, feelings of being cut off, and a yearning for some one who understood. A flight to work was the only thing that made life tolerable. The isolation, the silence and seclusiveness, continued over a period of sixteen years. Then when her son, having been taunted in the street about his parentage, demanded full enlightenment, the long silence was broken with an acute attack of what psychiatrists call "confusion". At this time she spoke rather more freely, but then drifted back into the silence that had endured for years. She recovered from the psychosis, during which she had not been communicative and in which she did not develop full insight or understanding, only to lapse again, but this time into a less rigid condition than before.

The lives of these two women present a striking enough contrast, yet one may say with some truth that each in her way was attempting to solve the same life problem.

Lack of ease in personal adjustment, self-dissatisfaction in women, accompanied by a determination to forget, to make the best of things, may be an evidence of determined self-control. The reactions in such cases may be rigid; they may seem to be lacking in understanding and sympathy, with an appearance of harsh indifference that represents a struggle

119

within themselves. Because of their own emotional stress, they may seem intolerant of those who present to their official attention a problem similar in nature to that which brings up painful associations in their personal lives.

Inability to live out emotional reactions through adequate channels makes for efforts to forget and attempts to push the disagreeable thoughts from attention. Women in this situation often seek a means of flight, so to speak, from themselves. Work for them may be a form of protection. Many women disappointed in love or marriage take up nursing or go into a sisterhood. This flight to work serves as a substitute for an outlet at the emotional level, and gradually there is a lessening of the capacity to feel keenly. In some cases there develops an unwillingness to take part in any activity that may bring about a painful emotional stirring. A prolonged effort to forget may develop into a determination not to "feel" anything. A narrowing of interest in pleasurable activities, a guarding against the feeling of pain, lead to a difficult personality, with an appearance of lack of sympathy and failure of perspective. So often we see a rigid, austere forewoman, or charge nurse, who demands that a cut-and-dried plan be followed in her own life and in the private lives of all those under her.

Such experiences lead one to believe that greater efficiency in work and in personal ease, added security in mental poise, and a lessened liability to mental illness may be brought about through an adequate expression of the emotions and by the removal of the handicaps that result from pent-up emotions.

Under the heading "emotional handicaps of the professional woman", I wish to discuss some of the evidences of a lack of adequate emotional outlet in women of this class. These manifestations may assume the symptom expression either of physical disabilities or of mental maladjustments. A search into the cause, however, will disclose an emotional factor at work—a body-mind interrelationship in cause and in effect.

If we conceive of the psychobiological development of a woman as a growth of mental and physical capacities, we will recognize that there must be a unification of functions in the mental and physical realms. The components must be developed harmoniously if there is to be ease of activity. We sometimes think of these components as personality— that is, the equipment with which one is born plus that which is accumulated as the result of experience. These personality traits may be considered as instinctive and acquired, but there must be an harmonious relationship among them to make for that ease of adjustment which we call health. All the components of personality should grow and develop as a whole, if there is to be the maximum efficiency.

From studies of mental life we have learned that the integration of the parts makes for ease of adjustment to the surroundings, the organism, in a kind of two-way activity, acting upon, and in turn being acted upon by, the environment. Experience is a series of reactions and adjustments to the environment, and modifications of it, which mean, in our more or less complex social and economic existence, the necessity for accommodating both the individual to his environment and his environment to him. In this process of adjustment, there is a give and take that leaves impressions of greater or less intensity upon the individual. White says, ''Adjustment to the world of reality is by no means a passive molding by external forces. The individual is reaching out and trying to mold the world to suit himself. In this effort he develops attitudes which, like habit, grow and in their development cause the pushing back of expressions of emotion.''

In the attempt at adjustment through a period of years, many alterations of personality may be effected; certain traits may be stunted, others developed. We speak of a calm, impersonal, professional attitude. This is evidence of an effort to mold the personality to fit the environment. The events of to-day may be the means of recalling hidden or forgotten experiences, even those of early childhood, which are surrounded by a painful emotional tone. Unusual reactions to minor or insignificant events may represent far more than the feeling about the particular situation in question.

Our reactions to casual events, our first impressions of people, our associations of one person with another because of some similarity, may link the present with our past.

Pleasant or painful emotions may be brought to the surface by some trivial or apparently irrelevant occurrence. The pushing back, the forgetting, the burying of painful emotions or events, may make for inflexible attitudes, the result of the instinctive urge or desire, we may say, to spare ourselves pain and to fit into the requirements of the group. When a woman fails to meet these requirements, there are feelings of inferiority on her part. When she feels the lack of approval of the community, the loss of esteem of the group, she is apt to lose her self-esteem. To be comfortable, she must grow and in a great measure appear as do others. This may be a so-called conventional requirement, but there is an instinctive desire to be like other women. The history of the development of the human race is full of evidence of this instinctive desire to meet the demands of the group. Fraser, in *The Golden Bough,* gives numerous instances of it among primitive people. Trotter, in *The Herd Instinct,* and Flügel, in his *Psychoanalytic Study of the Family,* illustrate this urge among the people of a more cultivated level.

Success is measured by ability to fit with ease into the requirements of the community. There may be individuals in whom this conformity to the group is accomplished with great discomfort. There are others who are unable to accommodate themselves to social requirements, and efforts to force such accommodation make for an outcropping of the opposite tendencies. The cause of the nonconformity may be of long standing. Many of woman's instinctive cravings or desires are unsocial. While her ethical self longs to live on an acceptable plane, her instincts may demand satisfaction at another level. The inability to harmonize the ethical and instinctive desires makes for a struggle that is often relentless. This struggle may actually be a sort of groping in the direction of right, even in cases where the behavior on the surface appears antisocial.

The delinquent, the psychotic, the psychoneurotic, the criminal all represent inability to fit in with the group. These expressions of conflict within the self or with the so-called conventions meet with sympathy or censure according to our conception of the degree of responsibility we place upon them. The cause or motive of the inability to fit in with the conventions is too often neglected or misunderstood by others who have been more successful in life. Disability may even result from attempts to appear like those others who have met with greater success. A failure may actually represent a great effort to find the solution of a struggle. Many women have found social conventions out of harmony with their instinctive needs. We must remember that while ethical or social standards vary in different communities, the basal or primary instincts remain constant.

In our modern civilization, a new problem has been presented to women in the breaking down of old economic and social barriers and the opening up of new opportunities. The traditional limitation of activity, the necessity for protection and support, are being challenged on all sides. Belief in woman's capacity has varied from the point of view that relegates her to the field of household cares with adequate protection to that which places her on an equal footing with man on a high plane of economic efficiency. But her biological cravings remain constant.

We think of a personality as flexible or as rigid according to the extent of its capacity for sympathetic identification with, or ability to see, another's point of view. There are those who remain pliable and understanding, and there are others who have apparently forgotten youth and its longings and who appear as automatic, though efficient human machines; they have apparently lost all human qualities. The development of some one capacity has been accomplished, but at the expense of a dwarfing of many of the personality components. Intellectual and official acumen have been gained at the cost of emotional ease. The demands made by civilization upon women's capacity for self-control and self-denial are often so great that feelings are pent up without an adequate outlet. In primitive people and in children there is a freer expression, with far less of the conventional suppression. This damming up of emotions makes at times of special stress for irritability and ease of anger reactions. We often hear these women say, "Everything went wrong. It was just an accumulation of things." Out of this attitude there frequently arise feelings of inability to cope with situations. A fear of unsuccessful attempts at competition, secret misgivings, fears, and a sensitiveness to comparison bring about a feeling of lack of fair play.

Secret longings, rigorously repressed, often reappear in the form of delusions of persecution and hallucinations of sight and hearing projected into the outer world and thereby, as it were, disowned. A well-rounded development of personality, with adequate emotional expression for the inner cravings and desires, makes for ease of adjustment and understanding of the longings of others. The rigid personality is usually under stress of emotion which is kept hidden and cannot afford to recognize the right of this emotion to satisfaction in others. The painful content of thought and feeling make a kind of forgetting necessary. Ideas fraught with painful emotion must be avoided, and as a result are not seen in the self or in others. These women are not able to establish a proper feeling tone about things and events that bear upon their pent-up emotion. Biased opinions of things of which they are ignorant preclude clear thinking. As a result, many situations bring up facts which they are unable to review without great personal stress. Opinions and reports or impersonal official questions are often colored by an over-reaction to the situation, whose intensity depends on purely personal experiences.

Disappointments, failures to acquire longed-for love objects, marriage, ambition, or anything really wanted may bring about an exaggerated tendency to anger or irritability. Those who are very tense and pent-up may show an anger reaction or testy attitude with the slightest provocation. Often associations of thought without any disturbing event may bring about a noticeable change of mood. We hear them say, "I got to thinking." Pondering, wishing, ruminating over the past, make for moods that have little tolerance for the irritations of the hour. Sensitiveness to offense, feelings of discrimination, bring out reactions of a longing for desired attentions and satisfactions. I recall a nurse who is now forced by age and physical infirmity to accept a menial position, when formerly she was in one where she commanded a greater degree of prestige. At the present time she is irascible, offers objections to every suggestion, and is very critical. She scolds, argues, and finds an outlet for an otherwise unexpressed emotion in resentment toward her superior nurse. Necessity for accommodation to unpleasant situations creates a degree of tension that finds easy expression in scolding.

I am sure many of you have come in contact with women of highly organized make-up, who, when fully occupied and interested in philanthropy, are cheerful, but let there be a lull in diversion and they become introspective, with an increased interest in themselves. The leisurely classes of American women bear witness to this fact, and the war record of many invalid women shows the healing property of a vital interest. Widowhood, loss of money, or the like, may reduce a luxurious invalid to the stern necessity of earning a livelihood and coincidentally a return to health.

In women of this type ideas surrounded by painful feelings may be hidden and crop out in another guise or form as invalidism. There may be a conversion of the mental conflict into physical symptoms. In many women the stress of competition is a burden. The fear of being supplanted grows with the feeling that more youthful associates, with greater capacity, may take their places. For them illness is an honorable flight.

A stenographer of fifty in a very progressive manufacturing establishment felt herself in many respects incompetent to keep up with those about her who had a much greater earning capacity and superior training. With each added evidence of her inability to compare favorably, there were attacks of invalidism. The death of her father, the illness of her mother, were added burdens. She depended upon an indulgent chief until the company changed ownership; then there were evidences of greater inferiority. With this she began to develop a condition resembling writer's cramp. She was at last admitted to the hospital, where for a period of six months she worried over her lack of income, her gloomy future, her loss of prestige. Every added evidence of stress brought out new manifestations of bodily disease. In some of these so-called invalids there is a tyrannical attitude. The following is a case in point:

A. K., a nurse, is a member of a neurotic family, the women being zealous Catholics, the men somewhat more desultory. The patient developed a feeling of responsibility for the laxness of her brothers. After a disappointment in a love affair, she attempted nursing, but did not find it satisfactory. With the development of a rather casual physical disease, she learned that comfort may be derived from the attentions given an invalid. This idea became somewhat fixed, and she resigned herself to ease and luxury and became definitely tyrannical, selfish, and antagonistic. There were many complaints of indigestion, gall-bladder disease, nervousness, and an inability to work.

For a period of twenty-five years, she has made many demands on an indulgent family and has shown a childish satisfaction in their attentions. She makes unlimited demands in regard to food and medicine. Much of the time she is in the home of relatives, but at infrequent intervals she is admitted to hospitals, where she is mandatory, critical, and petulant. Her complaints are of a somatic nature and refer to "nervousness and to terror dreams of snakes, of water, and of falling".

Interest and enthusiasm make drudgery a pleasant duty, but an unloved occupation brings daily stress and exhaustion of spontaneity and buoyancy of living. The necessity of daily application to duty in an occupation that is distasteful or that is not satisfactory is another source of discontent. After a period of successful work, one patient made an unsatisfactory marriage. There was a daughter and subsequent desertion. Being forced to earn a livelihood, she found work as a secretary. Here she was for a time happy, but, on a change of directors, she felt pushed aside, considered her work of little importance and of a monotonous type. Financial straits forced her to live with her elderly parents. Her father, an invalid with tuberculosis, her neurotic mother, and her young daughter made demands on her time when away from work. Her evenings in the home after the daily routine was completed offered no recreation or personal satisfaction. She developed a depressive reaction with many distressing notions of the death of her parents and of her daughter, associated with a feeling that she had killed them or that she had in some way permitted their death by violence. Again, she hallucinated their voices as if in pain near her. After a prolonged illness, she made a more successful adjustment of her life, with increased attention to her recreations and to securing work of a more satisfactory nature under more comfortable conditions.

Here is another case of a resort to invalidism when all other outlets had failed, this time on the part of a non-professional woman who had tried and failed in the rôle of wife and mother:

D. G., Sicilian, staunch Catholic, married the man of her family's choice, but continued to love another—of her own choice. There were five children, but with the lapse of time the husband became interested in his work and was indifferent to the patient, who longed for attention. When she realized that her husband was finding consolation in the companionship of another woman, she began to be more childish and whimsical in her demands and to create situations in which she could force the attention of her husband and of her children. She became intolerable in the home on account of the demands on their time and her petulant arrogance made it impossible to placate her whims. Her daughter reports an incident in which eleven eggs were prepared for breakfast. Each attempt was met with a criticism of its being too salt, too cold, too well done, and so on. The day was filled with such experiences. There were many complaints of somatic discomfort and later ideas of "queer" bodily sensations: "I can't get well", "My face is drawn", "I have a jumping feeling in my stomach." There were many requests for examination which were used as a means of attracting attention. Along with the tyrannical demands there were many threats of suicide when foiled.

There are those who pass their early years in an environment of invalidism and who learn by imitation to react with sickness in the face of difficult situations. There is a patient now in the hospital whose father had tuberculosis, whose mother was neurotic, and whose grandmother was an invalid as the result of a hip injury. This patient learned the habit of somatic interests. With an unsuccessful marriage after a professional career of about two years, she began to express many hypochrondriacal tendencies upon encountering emotional stress or any difficult situation.

I recall a young woman, a librarian, whose father, a confirmed invalid with imaginary heart disease, ruled his children with the cry, "Now, you will kill me!" The patient apparently compensated for this attitude with an unusual interest in athletics up to the time of a disappointment in her lover, who deserted her. She then passed through a period of intense depression and drifted over from lamentations upon her loss to ponderings about her bodily functions. She had an unusual capacity for describing the sensations associated with physiological processes.

Success and confidence give way to doubt and misgivings when there begins to be a realization of loss of prestige, capacity, or position. Conscientious types of women develop an emotional stress, which, if not disposed of at the conscious level, frequently takes on certain physical manifestations. The invalid, unloved wife who demands attention and creates situations that command it is a case in point. A very efficient professional nurse married a physician, less powerful in his make-up than herself. After a short time she learned that his interest had drifted to other women. She became depressed, had many feelings of shame, and felt herself looked down upon by the community. She was unable to face the fact that she had lost her husband. She became tense, and somewhat suspicious and irritable. In her illness there was a dilapidation of habits and a recrudescence of erotic interests.

Often women of more mature years realize that competition with youth and its effulgence of energy results in a comparison unfavorable for them. Humiliation because of their waning power makes them unable to accept the fact that they are losing. They cannot realize that it is their failing capacity, but project the responsibility to another. They develop the feeling that they are being kept back and that there are those who "work against" them. The aggressive types, when they begin to feel secret longings and misgivings, may become more and more uncomfortable. They begin to feel that the environment or some force outside of their own thinking is affecting them. They feel slighted and tend to become suspicious. They "know" that people are working to their discredit; then they may begin to hear accusing voices of friends at a distance. Sometimes these voices suggest women they know, sometimes it is an enemy. They blame external forces for the shortcomings within themselves, as a well-known psychiatrist has said. Many of these women develop secret attachments to some man for whom they work. Often they feel he is indifferent when perhaps he does not know of their feelings. As a result, they are pained by his attitude toward them, and they begin to hate him. They think something comes from him to do them harm. They feel themselves against a stone wall and cannot realize that the trouble is in themselves and not in the other person. Then the "malign influences emanating" from persecution, danger, and so forth, necessitate the development in them of means for protection and defense.

C. L. was a professional woman of outstanding intellectual capacity, single, aged fifty-seven, a teacher and research worker. The patient's mother was epileptic, her father neurotic, and her favorite brother psychotic. In early life she felt herself an unwanted child. She developed a tremendous urge toward scientific investigation and research work and spent much time in Europe and America doing valuable work with tissue cells. Her interests were along intellectual lines without emotional outlet. She began to feel that her associates were trying to steal the results of her work. Then she thought these men were attempting to circulate stories of immorality on her part. She was convinced that her young woman assistant, who was somewhat modern in social habits, would bring discredit upon her. She then began to believe that she was being watched and followed. There were definite ideas of assault, and she resorted to many means of protection. When placed in a hospital, she was certain that men tried to get into her room at night. Then there were delusions of grandeur, in which she thought that she was to be held responsible for a World War. She also thought that her death would in some way avert or postpone such a condition indefinitely. After five or six years she committed suicide, having said on many occasions that she would do so for the purpose of saving the world.

E. W., aged fifty-eight, single, was an artist. She was the second of three children in a Quaker family. The father was psychotic. The patient had a tremendous urge toward full satisfaction of her emotional life, but was restricted by her parents, who were satisfied with much less. After a disappointment that resulted in a broken engagement, the patient at nineteen developed an attack similar to the father's illness.

The successful marriage of her sister brought about feelings of inferiority on the part of the patient. She talked of "others who deprive me of what is my right. They keep me from it. They interfere." In her periods of excitement she talked of loneliness and of wanting love. Later she began to develop more definite tendencies to projection. She thought strange men and women were trying to assault her and that they put "words in my mouth and thoughts in my brain".

The cases quoted so far all illustrate the way in which the natural longings for love and power that have failed to find adequate outlets in real life may be deflected into other channels in the attempt to find relief. Thus a thought or an activity less painful than the true cause of the distress may be substituted for it.

I recall an only child, devoted to her father, with some hostility to the mother, who was always timid and at five developed a fear of being "penned in closed spaces". Later there was a fear of animals, then of injury by sharp objects which might come in contact with exposed parts of her body. During an illness in which she was very emotional, there were erotic ideas about her father, later associated with religion and God. There were feelings of unworthiness, dissatisfaction, and great depression.

Another patient is the daughter of a rigid, devout widow. At puberty her mother talked much to her of the uncleanness of sex, of the dangers of physical exposure during the menstrual period, of conventional restrictions, and of means of protection against "immoral people". The patient developed a tendency to masturbation, and when she reached the age of puberty there were feelings of inferiority, of being looked at, and of being unclean. She developed the habit of hand washing which was necessary "to keep me clean". There was first a fear of contamination from the physical standpoint, then the uneasiness shifted into the spiritual realm with the necessity for greater religious fervor and confession. Attendance at church was discontinued on account of the danger of contamination, and the patient was almost completely incapacitated. While employed in a clerical position, she became so much preoccupied with the hand washings that it was impossible for her to do acceptable work. She became increasingly more submissive, prudish, preoccupied, and shy.

Ideas of an obsessive nature may represent a kind of compulsion, in which there is an additional feeling of being forced to do or think certain things. There seems to be an accumulation of tension, with calm after the impulse has been carried out. This has been frequently given as the reason for tendencies to burn or steal, and other activities of an unsocial nature, to which the patients feel themselves driven. A similar impulse may be seen in persons who in walking along the street must not touch certain objects or who must carry out a given activity a certain number of times. Cases illustrating this obsessive tendency could be multiplied indefinitely. The following are typical: A patient who was the ward of a philanthropic society began at five to show evidence of a childish sex curiosity. At eight there were evidences of sex interest. At nine or ten there were attempted sex relations with boys. At nineteen there was a fancied or real assault followed by emotional outbursts of a hysterical nature. The patient was tense, had feelings of shame, and was very unhappy on account of a tendency to sex ruminations. There was almost a compulsory tendency to masturbation, with active daydreams and night terrors associated with thoughts of normal and perverse expressions of her sex life.

In a period of great stress, a conscientious woman left in charge of a business establishment developed a fear that certain duties had been left undone. She had no peace until she had gone around to inspect each point to be sure everything had been closed up for the night.

Another patient, who was very much disappointed in her husband, refused to think of his inconstancy and alcoholism, but began to worry about whether or not the glass of water which she demanded frequently was exactly full. She became agitated and was often in a kind of frenzy, repeating to herself, "Is it full? Will it hold another drop?" It required much urging, and sometimes coercion, on the part of her children to get her to drink the glass of water. Then she was momentarily satisfied, but the same process had to be repeated many times during the day with other glasses of water.

A student, sixteen years of age, with a very strict upbringing, began the habit of taking three steps backward, then three to the side. This was in time followed by a tendency to rhyming and other repetitions of similar nature.

A very competent craftswoman, after a disappointment, developed a ritual about the articles in her room. Everything had to be placed in a certain position a certain number of times. Shoes were placed under the bed, removed, and replaced four times, before she could leave them. Another patient was forced to arrange everything in very orderly fashion. These ceremonies and evidences of great indecision may often refer to early sex experiences to which may be added a sense of guilt or apprehensiveness. An elderly patient admitted that her indecision in regard to dressing, shopping, or the daily routine dated back to a childish preoccupation with masturbation, and frequently the tendency, "Shall I? Shall I not?" referred to the early childhood habit rather than to the daily activities.

Slander, anonymous-letter writing, risqué jokes, and blackmail are often manifestations of pent-up emotions which find an expression in a childish manner. These may represent early experiences with sex subjects. There may have been sex secrets or frank sex acts in childhood with which there is associated in later life self-censure, shame, or diffidence. The letter writing and slander may represent expressions of sex emotion in which there is an element suggestive of the habits of primitive people with a desire for exhibitionism. Frequently these manifestations are based on sex curiosity. The opposite condition, prudishness, represents a protection against the same desire.

A woman, thirty-seven, single, was brought up in a very quiet home with religious surroundings. She had a tremendous emotional drive, but was pent up in her love life. She found expression in paintings too poor to afford real satisfaction. She accepted a position as a secretary, but could not adapt herself to the surroundings. While associated with a minister in a philanthropic movement, she developed an attachment to him and began to show evidences of jealousy of another secretary. She began writing anonymous letters and sending telephone calls. She was somewhat crafty in arranging these calls so that there could be no means of identification. Other evidences of very erratic behavior necessitated her being placed in a hospital for mental diseases. Here she excused her behavior by saying that it resulted from jealousy and a determination to get even. We read almost daily in serious context, or in the comic strip, references to such cases. A review of our domestic-relations courts will afford many instances of similar nature.

Flight from intolerable situations may be accomplished through the use of drugs of various kinds. In this habit there is a tendency to rationalization. One person "drinks to avoid company, another to make him more at ease with company". Many of these cases are simply mental illnesses. Artists not infrequently tend to indulge in alcoholic drinks, and many women of the leisure class resort to the same means of relief. Nurses and doctors have a tendency to drift into the habit of hypodermic medications of various alkaloids, such as cocaine, morphine, and hyoscine.

Sometimes the craving for these stimulants comes on only at intervals when the underlying tensions become intolerable. An artist, unhappy in her marriage, reported that from time to time she was driven to the necessity of taking, over a period of weeks, absinthe and whisky to the extent that she was unable to realize the conditions about her. She went into her apartment under the care of her maid and protected herself from painful thoughts. Then, after a period of time, she appeared more at ease, and was able to go on with her work for several months.

Another patient, very unhappily married to a periodical drinker, developed also the habit of alcohol and drugs. Separation from her husband and removal into surroundings where it was easier for her to obtain an adequate emotional outlet made it possible for her to attain satisfaction in the occupation of her choice.

Another patient who was very unhappy and somewhat hysterical in her emotional outbursts was given hyoscine. She gradually became more and more dependent, and at last developed a hyoscine habit. She said that after the administration of one of these tablets, she had a period of almost complete unconsciousness for three or four hours, after which she was able to go along with a fair degree of ease for several weeks.

In the ordinary day of the average person, much time is given to the daily occupation, but a good deal of this work is actually done in a kind of automatic fashion. Typists and other kinds of artisans have developed a habit of relegating their work to the lower centers, and often spend much of their time during the day in fancies and daydreams while they carry on the daily routine.

The psychology of choice of occupation, the mental effects of the stimulating qualities of certain types of occupation, and the blunting effects of other monotonous duties have attracted the attention of the applied psychologists of the day. With the more monotonous types of work, there is a disposition to drift into daydreams or the building of air castles. These fancies are frequently upon a childish basis, and are often out of keeping with adult thinking in the world of reality. Conflict between these daydreams and the actual reality may make for unexplained irritability. Stekel, in his *Polyphony of Thinking,* has used the comparison of an orchestra in which there is not complete harmony of the parts.

The success with which women meet their personal problems is a measure of their success in the world at large. Their difficulties with associates are frequently a reflection of difficulties within themselves. The discovery that their problems are not confined to themselves, but that nearly everybody has to fight the same battle more or less is often a means of gaining more understanding and from this more sympathy for others. Draining off emotional tensions little by little in sharing with others their troubles in sympathetic understanding has proven a help to many. Women often reach a solution of personal difficulties by resolving those of others. A vicarious or indirect approach may be more tolerable to them and may mean much less wounding of pride or loss of self-esteem.

With greater sympathy, there is less criticism of the motives and attitudes of others, and in this way they become more nearly adapted to the situation which may refer to themselves in some manner. This may mean the development of freedom from feelings of shame and inferiority, with resulting additional harmony within the self and with the daily life.

While much of our thinking is by a process of "feeling" rather than through the medium of words, a great deal may be brought to expression with some one who understands. In this way pain and bitterness are lost. To develop a talking basis of confidence and frankness is a great factor in the release of emotion. Much material that has previously been subjective becomes more objective, less a part of ourselves, and, therefore, less painful.

Creative work of a pleasurable nature, such as painting, music, writing, designing, and so forth, in place of indulgence in fancy or in daydreams, is a distinct source of satisfaction and should be developed in some form. The little inner personal pleasures that afford satisfaction should be cultivated just as is business efficiency.

►► What More Do Women Want? ◄◄

By CREIGHTON PEET

IF, as Emily Newell Blair reports in a recent issue of the OUTLOOK, our feminists are "discouraged," I shudder to think what we have in store for us should they ever "succeed" and become actually triumphant about it.

I cannot agree with Mrs. Blair that there is no institution in this modern American world "which bears the imprint of women," and that they "seldom rise to responsibility and power." It is true that there has never been a woman president of the Bethlehem Steel Corporation, or a lady captain of a big transatlantic liner—and it is also true that they are unjustly discriminated against in the matter of salary. But their "power" and "influence" are limitless. Who wants to run a silly old steel corporation when you can influence the emotional, intellectual and artistic life of a nation? Never before in the history of the world has the feminine or female point of view so strongly impressed itself on the life of any community as it has on the United States today.

As a trifling male, I find myself surrounded from morning to night with books, magazines, movies, plays, department stores, advertisements, motor cars, house furnishings and (unless I wisely escape to a man's club) with extraordinary and blasphemous food combinations, all of which are devised and concocted especially for the feminine fancy. Never before have the arts—from symphony orchestras supervised by idle ladies, to cheap popular magazines telling them how to hold a husband with one hand and make a lovely marshmallow and tomato salad with French dressing with the other—been so woman-ridden. Never before has the male point of view been so conspicuously unimportant. Nobody cares what music or books or magazines or movies or food or decorations men prefer. And as for drinks! Ah, gentlemen, a toast to the sex which invented the gin-and-chocolate-malted milk mixture, and first thought of making beer nicer by adding ice cream! A toast, I say, and drink it down—if you can!

It is true that the men of America, as a group, have very little interest in symphony music, opera, books, plays, art exhibitions or any other civilized manifestations. They no longer take part in them, or patronize them. The ladies, being just as competitive as the rest of us, keep their husbands at work earning enough to pay off the installments on newer and bigger radios and automobiles—while *they* spend the money.

Frankly, I think the men have been fools, not because they allowed the women to become equal to them in influence, but because they allowed them to become so vastly more powerful than themselves. The aspects of American life which are completely feminized are the most vital. Business, after all, is business, and goes through its ups and downs without anything more than temporary effects on the community. The literature (or lack of it) and amusements influence the whole character of a community.

But let us begin at the beginning. The American home, or what is left of it, is decidedly feminine in character and appearance. Everywhere can be sensed the invisible hand of the household editors of the women's magazines. I realize that in some cases these editors are men, but their appeal is entirely to women. In such instances they function merely as mechanics, interpreting and reflecting women's tastes and interests. Certainly the average American household is more feminine than the dusty, junky, red-plush-fringe days of our grandfathers. For all our factory-made life, there always seem to be little things around a house to be arranged—small individual adjustments, decorations and fixings. Somehow even these seem to have become feminine, and frequently this is all right.

PASSING from the home in general, we come to the library table loaded down with great masses of printed matter known generally as "women's magazines." How much women themselves have to do with their manufacture is beside the point. The fact is that they are contrived and compounded particularly for the female population. The stories and articles are adjusted to the feminine viewpoint. A friend of mine writing for one of the most powerful of these journals had his story returned with the suggestion that if he reversed his male and female characters—giving all the adventures, risks and exploits to the lady and making the gentleman merely a clothing dummy in the background—it could be used.

And it was, after he had made the proper adjustments. Even back in college, some years ago, I remember that the class was warned by a lecturer that fiction intended for women's magazines must be carefully planned to avoid any shocks or jolts, as a goodly proportion of the readers of such magazines were mothers or about to be mothers and could not stand anything violent. I have no desire to go about shocking delicate women; I merely want to point out that it is impossible to say that women have no influence in the American community.

Suppose we go out for supper to a tea shoppe run by the neighborhood's lady poor-relation who must make her own way. The place is usually cleaner than the ordinary smallish restaurant, which is a good deal to be thankful for—but the dear lady who runs the place has a terrible tendency to put sugar in her vegetables, sugar in the soup and sugar on the meats, not just a little, but enough to ruin them. The whole scheme of the place, from the "art" decorations leering out of every nook and cranny, to its spectacular salads designed with an eye to tasty color combinations, and its seductively rich desserts, is designed to appeal to the feminine fancy.

Now suppose we walk out to a movie, or a play, if we live where they have plays. All about us we see gigantic sign boards plastered with the words "sin," "love," "marriage," "secret," "past," and "woman." Now let me call your attention to the fact that these entertainments, although manufactured by men, are produced entirely with the idea of pleasing the feminine portion of the population. Movies and plays yapping about "sin" and "sex" are not calculated to appeal to the proverbially pornographic male, but to the modern miss who wants to find out how to have safe fun followed by Grade-A matrimony.

Look back a hundred and fifty years in the history of English literature and drama, and you will discover that while just as many characters were married as today, dramatists found other sources of interest than the question, "Whom shall I marry?" It's an interesting question, I grant you, but it becomes a little monotonous day in and day out. No doubt it is fair enough, however. Women bulk large in modern American intellectual life; they make up our audiences and read our books; and undoubtedly their interests deserve attention. I am merely trying to demonstrate that women *do* have an effect on our cultural life, from Eugene O'Neill's Nina Leeds who moaned about her sex life for five hours at a stretch in his *Strange Interlude,* clear down to Norma Shearer in her *Free Soul.* Turning to the recent stage productions we have Philip Barry's *Tomorrow and Tomorrow,* and Katharine Cornell's production of *The Barretts of Wimpole Street* showing how love came to the life of Elizabeth Barrett Browning. In every case the subject is a woman, and she simply can't get her mind off her sex life, or her romance, depending on the period and genre of the piece.

Now to get to the business of buying and selling. Since women have charge of spending most of our money, our billboards, advertisements, department stores and the wrappers in which things are enclosed are designed especially to appeal to the ladies. Motor cars are sold on their upholstery, their finishings and their streamline effects—and some of them are about as handsome as anything our modern mechanical world has produced. Although I find myself snubbed and ignored in department stores— salesgirls work on the principle that men are a little stupid, don't know what they want, and haven't any money to spend anyway—I must admit that some of our big stores are not only handsome but extremely efficient and marvelously well run, and this has been due to the women whom the store managers are trying to please and attract.

And finally, Mrs. Blair, you say that the young women just out of college, used to seeing women working, are now no longer fooled by appearances of equality, but are going to demand the genuine thing. Perhaps. But I think that the first reaction of the girl who grows up with the idea of going to work as soon as she is out of school occurs when one of her schoolmates makes a good marriage to some nice young man with an adequate income. The young lady's reaction is this: "Say, *that's* a wonderful racket! Why didn't somebody tell me about this before! Work all day in a stuffy office! Ride home in the subway!" With which she plucks herself off a convenient young man.

In some ways the Nineteenth Amendment is as futile in accomplishing its aims as is the Eighteenth. Perhaps we ought to stop amending the Constitution.

Are Ten Too Many?

By Marjorie Wells

*A young mother of an old-fashioned family states its case,
reckoning its assets and liabilities and finding it profitable in peace and happiness*

I SUPPOSE I am old-fashioned. I am quite sure many of my friends and neighbors think so, while some of them do not stop at so kindly and sympathetic a judgment. I am aware sometimes of their pity, condescension and amusement, and even of contempt and a veiled antagonism.

The reason is that I have a large family, stretching already as far as the eye can reach and with the end not yet in sight. In an age when two or three children are considered the civilized and respectable achievement, I have ten to date and am still unchastened and unrepentant. I am even mildly ostentatious about it, and find a reprehensible satisfaction in projecting my oversized family like a bombshell into polite society, where it is variously greeted with congratulation, consternation, interrogation or condemnation. The friendlier reactions concede that this is indeed an old-fashioned family, supposedly endowed with indefinite but admirable old-fashioned virtues and advantages. But I am aware of other attitudes beneath the polite surprise or careful congratulations of casual conversation. There are those who clearly count me as no better than a deluded female, unkindly outlawed from the pleasures and privileges of modern life by an unfortunate biological habit. There are some who would weep for me and with me, if I gave them but half a chance. There are others who probably think me a scab and blackleg, traitor and backslider, in these days of feminine emancipation.

I HAVE no intention of apologizing for my family. I have never done so nor tried to keep it a secret, which would in fact be difficult. I am, indeed, candidly and brazenly proud of it. A large family is liable to have that effect upon its perpetrator and proprietor. All ordinary parents are publicly proud of two children or even three. Most parents become a little reticent about five or six. But when the score mounts up to nine or ten, parental pride gets a second wind. There is something monumental about such a family, and it is asking too much of human nature to expect its parents to keep it entirely to themselves.

But I sometimes feel like speaking out against the undertones of unpleasantness which often answer my parental pride. Especially I resent the insinuation that I am somehow related to the old lady who lived in a shoe, who had so many children because she didn't know what to do. In this age of grace and gossip, ignorance must keep company with stupidity in order to preserve itself entire. There is a clinical candor about our reading, our conversation, and even the advertising in the most respectable of our family magazines, which makes it difficult to retain the innocence of ignorance unless one is firmly determined upon it. Ordinary curiosity has been enough to introduce me to Dr. Marie Stopes and all her works, and the name of Margaret Sanger is not as unfamiliar to me as might be supposed. I am, in fact, reasonably sure that I know as much about keeping the stork from the door as do most of my friendly and unfriendly critics, and that I know vastly more about practical biology than most of these young modernists who regard me with such a pitying and patronizing eye.

So IN the natural course of events I come upon Mrs. Sanger's latest book, *Motherhood in Bondage*, and am thereby much tried and exercised. It is a tragic and terrible book. It is made up principally of letters — hundreds of them — from women and some few men overburdened with the bitternesses of too much parenthood. It is a grim collection of hard luck stories, every one of them outlining a human tragedy. It is a compilation of case records in marital misery, full of pain and poverty and protest against the blind inhumanity of natural law. Its purpose is clear, even though it is published in a country where there are still some things which must not be talked about. The letters are chosen and grouped to prove that families should be made to measure and not left to luck or the lack of it. It is overpowering in its picture of human misery and entirely sincere in its conviction that something should be done about it, but its specific plea is for public approval and dissemination of a practical doctrine of Birth Control.

I AM really not much interested in this particular question. It seems likely that the curse of Anthony Comstock might well be lifted in this age of reason, but it also seems likely that a certain amount of damage might result from too much eating of the tree of knowledge. It strikes me as a delicate problem, as delicate as some of those which every parent knows who tries to bring youngsters safely through adolescence. As I have suggested above, the vast majority of parents have access to all the knowledge there is on this subject, and the fact that it is sometimes a little difficult to get at is probably a moral safeguard rather than a national calamity. Knowledge is an excellent thing, but it won't cure all our personal or social diseases. It never has. And it is often, much too often, turned to evil account.

But my complaint against Mrs. Sanger's book is that it lacks a certain letter. I have never felt the urge to write to Mrs. Sanger, but I think now that I should have done so. I should have written in the following fashion and thereby contributed my share to the great American tragedy.

141

DEAR MRS. SANGER:

I am only thirty-eight years old and have been married less than fifteen years, but we already have ten children and I am beginning to feel that there is no reason why I should not have ten more. When we married, my husband was earning just ten dollars a week as a schoolteacher, and at the end of ten years he was getting less than three thousand a year and we had seven children. We have never had any income except what we could earn, so I have always done practically all my own work, including the cleaning, cooking, washing and everything. For years we hardly ever went to a theatre or concert or took a vacation. Four years ago my husband lost his job and had to start in an entirely new line, but the children kept right on coming. Now we have ten of them and the oldest not yet fourteen, while the youngest is about six months. During the time before the last one was born my husband was taken ill and had to go away to a hospital for a serious operation, and my mother was also taken ill and died. I had to let my own work go in order to help nurse her. Through all this trouble I wondered many times what would be the effect of it all on the new arrival.

When I was married I knew very little about marriage and all its responsibilities, and had to learn as best I could by experience. Just now I have a cold in the head and the boys have kicked a football through the living-room window and the dishes aren't washed and the coal man has sent a bill with "Please Remit" on it, and what's going to become of us I don't know.

Perhaps Mrs. Sanger would have published this confession; perhaps she wouldn't. The point is that while its facts are all true, its implications are all false. I don't feel sorry for myself, and I never did. There's nothing the matter with my family, and there's nothing the matter with me that I can blame on the family. There's nothing the matter with the latest arrival, who is a healthy, happy, good-looking little rascal and the pride and joy of the whole household. Other people may feel sorry for us because we have practically the largest and noisiest

family east of the Mississippi, but we don't feel sorry for ourselves. We have a tremendously good time with our family, and we don't much care who knows it.

THE trouble with all this loose talk and careful propaganda about Birth Control is that it implies, more or less subtly, that the large family is in itself a dangerous, undesirable and even reprehensible performance. It is inferred and even stated that overproduction involves a tempting of Providence, an invitation to poverty, and a gamble with maternal health and childhood happiness. It ignores all chances that the large family may have positive and intrinsic advantages of its own, and its own rewards and compensations for all the toil and trouble attached to it. It implies — without actually saying so — that the small family is the right family and the large family the wrong family, and that therefore people like myself are in some sense a public nuisance or a public menace.

· So although I have been steadfastly uninterested in Birth Control propaganda as such, I find myself compelled to have some ideas on the subject. I have, in fact, been publicly debating the problem in a definitely practical fashion through fifteen years and by means of ten children. Every new bud on the family tree has been not only a hostage given to fortune but a challenge and even an affront to all these people who seem to know what is good for me and good for my children and good for the human society in which we all find ourselves. Mrs. Sanger might conceivably approve of my family, but only as an exception to prove her rule, for we are fundamentally on opposite sides of the argument. I am doubtful of my abilities as a debater, and therefore when the subject came my way I have kept quiet. But there is nothing quiet about a family of ten. It is an assertive, obvious and concrete argument in itself.

But apart from particular cases and present company, I feel that the vital consideration in the Birth Control discussion is the matter of proper proportion. Nobody denies that there are many mothers who have more children than they know what to do with. Everybody must agree that the world holds too much misery which is a by-product of unrestricted child-bearing, particularly now that Mrs. Sanger has filled a book with it. But it should be remembered that other books of human misery might be filled readily enough with the dreadful things wrought by tight shoes, aspirin tablets, radio sopranos, home cooking and cocktail shakers, without actually proving anything except that it is all too bad.

Mrs. Sanger has collected abnormalities and horrors in such quantity that the whole of humanity seems tarred with the same brush. In effect she preaches that uncalculating parenthood is a sort of universal disease, which can only be relieved by the universal practice of her pet doctrine. She is deeply distressed by all the troubles she has seen, so that her theories have become badly scrambled with her emotions and she attempts to be both sympathetic and scientific at the same time. Therefore she at last makes the usual mistake of women who attempt the guidance of public opinion, and tries to transfer to public responsibility what is essentially and inevitably a private and local problem.

I have said that this seems to be a matter of proportion, and it is certainly so in a private sense. Every married woman must draw up her own balance sheet of debits and credits in this business of motherhood. Every married man must do the same. Children are both a liability and an asset, and in order to reckon the net values of the family — natural, moral and spiritual — the parents must have an honest show-down with their own consciences and convictions. What they do about it is their own business, and should have nothing to do with the current fashions in families or the legal status of this doctrine or that. When the sub-surface agitation in favor of Birth Control begins to assume shape as a popular notion that three or four or five children are enough, it takes away from the most conscientious parents something of the freedom to which they are entitled.

It is a matter of proportion. Each and all of us have our own scale of values by which we measure the worth of the pleasures, privileges, duties, comforts and satisfactions of life. Our attitude toward children, real and potential, will reflect pretty closely what we think and feel about these various elements. It really has nothing to do with the rights and wrongs of Birth Control. Birth Control, rightly or wrongly, is no more than another device which we use or decline in deference to our sense of what is important. We ought, in honesty to ourselves, to resent the suggestion that it is anything more, that it is an article of faith for the scientific age. We ought, in a word, to feel free and be free to take it or leave it alone.

So though I do not believe in Birth Control, neither do I disbelieve in it. To announce that I believe in it means that I believe in it for somebody else, which seems to me to be none of my business. It happens that I don't believe in it for myself, under present circumstances and conditions, but that also is an entirely personal conviction and one which has no relation or importance to any other woman's problem. But I do believe that the contraceptionists are unwittingly making things uncomfortable for the large family, by giving scientific encouragement to the human liking for scandals. People do love to think the worst of their neighbors, and there is no such likely target as the parents of a large family. There ought, I think, to be a closed season for such parents, during which it would be a breach of the peace for mere theorists to add bedevilment to their burdens. Bachelors, maiden ladies and scientific reformers should in particular be warned to stay off the matrimonial grass where they have no proper business.

It is a long time since any one made out a case for the large family. The argument has all been on the other side. I find at least four general arguments in favor of the small family. (1) Its cultural advantages. (2) Its possibilities for health and intelligence. (3) Economic necessities. (4) Racial hazards and obligations. To keep my conscience clear I must make some sort of a settlement with each of them.

The eugenists tell us that the small family is the really civilized achievement, in the face of all experience that one child or two may be totally unpleasant products and that the small family is perilously near to extinction with the first epidemic of whooping cough. They argue that the small family gets its full rations of educational and other advantages and turns out a higher type of citizen thereby. The answer is that it doesn't. Other things being equal the large family gives better social training than the small one, and offers more stimulus to imagination, enterprise and intelligence during the most critically formative years. My own children knock the corners from each other, sharpen their wits on each other, and practise the social virtues on each other. They must necessarily learn to work together and play together. They must take small responsibilities early, and their affections and ambitions have small chance to get self-centred. It is possible that they may go short some day on the high-priced privileges of education and travel, but it won't matter much. They are learning already how to find their way about and make themselves a place in the world, and they are learning it at home.

In regard to the second point I take refuge in the record. My children are perfectly healthy and reasonably intelligent, and the later ones seem to have a slight edge on the earlier experiments. The suggestion that they might have been more so had there been fewer of them does not much interest me. Children, it seems, are healthy and intelligent principally according to the health and intelligence of their immediate ancestors and the parental progression in mutual development and usefulness, and if there is any rhyme or reason to the matter the later child has the best chance. Concerning my own health I am equally free from anxiety. I weighed a scant hundred pounds on my wedding day, but since I have increased by nearly four per cent per annum the family regards me as a good investment.

THE third argument concerns the economic probabilities. To this my answer is that we have never yet been justified by our income in extending our family. We have extended the family, and then done what might be done to bring the income up to scratch. We were as financially embarrassed by one child as we are by ten, and we shall probably continue that way. Nothing in our married experience leads us to suppose that a small family guarantees financial independence or a large family forbids it; the two things simply don't have any cause-and-effect connection. We have no certainty as to what the morrow may bring forth, any more than do our more cautious neighbors, but we are sure of this, that the constant challenge and spur of increasing responsibilities and necessities have been fundamentally good for us. If we ever amount to anything — socially, financially, and particularly as to character and worth — my husband and I are agreed that we shall blame it on the children.

I am not entirely clear about the racial obligations involved in the doctrine of the small family. Very few people seem to be clear on the matter, with the exception of Havelock Ellis and a few others whose opinion, I suspect, is a fairly academic one. But I understand that a certain Mr. Malthus, aided and abetted by higher mathematics, has demonstrated that the human race, unless checked in its mad career by Act of Congress, is due either to be squeezed to death or starved to death. This is important if true, though it is probably not my business. But it may not be true. History is full of the dead bones of prophecies that have come to a sad end and the future is full of unknown quantities to upset all human calculations. Further, I am impressed by the obvious standstill and even retrogression of population increase within my own range of experience. Despite all my own contributions to the cause, the generation to which my children belong is falling short of its predecessors. There are families of my near acquaintance that are literally dying out; and nobody knows why. Civilization, I suppose, is taking its own toll by many secret ways, without much direct help from statisticians and scientists.

ONE other thing I have discovered by dabbling a little in vital statistics. The apparently alarming population increases of the past generation or so don't mean all that they seem to. Many children were born, for our country attracted chiefly the young and hardy; few old people died, for the dying generation belonged to a previous period of much smaller population. But now the numerical advantage shifts up the line, aided as it has been by the lengthening of the expectation of life during the past generation, and a lot of people must die soon as the consequence of having been born in the busiest times of the last century. Looking around a small circle of acquaintance, particularly in our cities, I can't see that the coming generation will do more than compensate for the ordinary wear and tear of time on the ones that are passing. My friends and acquaintances aren't having any too many babies to take the place of all the uncles and aunts and grandparents and such whose time is nearly over. So much for statistics, which don't mean much anyway.

To get back to my own family, which — as usual — is in danger of neglect whenever I mess around with speculations, the four popular arguments in favor of the job-lot of children simply don't apply, so far as I am concerned. And I am aware of substantial arguments on the other side. I leave out of the discussion certain spiritual considerations which are entirely personal, and I prefer to ignore all unconvincing statistics about everything. I rest the case for the large family on the simple fact that children are desirable because they are pleasant and stimulating things to have around the house. They vastly increase the happiness of life. Happiness is made up of responsibility, ambition and achievement, of mutual appreciations that are a bond and blessing for two people who understand each other, and of numerous intelligent appreciations. A family of ten children will supply these in quantity and variety.

Children are, of course, sometimes a nuisance and always an embarrassment. They keep you out of bridge clubs, poker games, golf tournaments, uplift movements and the movies, and even out of the divorce court. They insist that you shall make a reasonable attempt to live happily with your own husband or wife, which is not a very dramatic, exciting or fashionable ac-

complishment. They demand that you shall devote most of your time to plain and unvarnished hard labor, but if this is undesirable or abnormal then the world was very badly designed on the first morning of creation. And they keep it up without much interruption until they pack up and leave you, which is an eventuality to be regarded as philosophically as possible.

I concede that my philosophy, such as it is, ignores such charming contingencies as inherited lunacy, disease, and abject poverty; also pathological abnormality, confirmed criminality, and inherent immorality. These things do not belong in my personal problem; they belong rather in Mrs. Sanger's book. But I claim that the code of normal people is not to be determined by the behavior and condition of the unfortunates.

For myself I am deeply thankful for all those enriching accidents which permit me the pride and delight of an old-fashioned family. I admit that I am fortunate — fortunate in having good health, a home in the country, kindly and forbearing friends, and a calm and perhaps cowlike disposition. For some of these advantages I thank the children themselves, and my family doctor is inclined to agree with me. And since I am fortunately free of some of the bogies that are frightening family folk out of their proper rights and responsibilities, I can enjoy my family as the veritable "heritage and reward" of the Biblical phrase. For I have found that a real family of children pays an adequate daily dividend of satisfaction and delight, and if you don't believe it you may ask at least one woman who owns one.

The
ATLANTIC MONTHLY

NOVEMBER 1931   VOLUME 148

A WORD TO WOMEN

BY ALBERT JAY NOCK

A LONG time ago — all of three years, perhaps longer — I saw a floating item in a periodical to the effect that 41 per cent of our national wealth is controlled by women, and that the percentage is rising. Curiously, this bit of news did not make much of an impression on me at the time, but the recollection of it kept coming back to me afterward, and more frequently as time went on. After being pestered in this way for three years or more, I bethought myself of an acquaintance who has facilities for looking up data on such matters, and asked him to get chapter and verse for me, which he very kindly did.

It appears that a firm of investment bankers operating in Chicago and New York had made an investigation into the division of our national wealth between the sexes. They did this purely in the way of business, of course, to determine the amount of stress that could profitably be laid on female clientage. The general conclusion was that at the time the survey was made, say four years ago, nearly half our national wealth was controlled by women, and that the proportion was tending to increase steadily and rather rapidly.

Some of the incidental findings turned up by the investigation are interesting. It found that ninety-five billion dollars' worth of life-insurance policies were in force in this country, and that 80 per cent of their beneficiaries were women. This alone would considerably help along the rising proportion of female control unless there were somewhere some offset which the survey did not show. An even more interesting finding is that by wills probated in New York City, over a given period, fifty estates out of seventy were left by men to women, and forty-four out of sixty-nine were left by women to women. It found that women were taxed on three and a quarter billion dollars of income annually; men, on four and three quarters. One hundred and thirty-nine women paid taxes on incomes in excess of a half million, as against one hundred and twenty-three men; while forty-four women paid on net incomes in excess of a million, as against forty-two men. Women were found to be majority or almost majority shareholders in some of our largest corporations, for instance the Pennsylvania Railway, American Telephone and Telegraph, United States Steel, Westinghouse Air Brake, and National Biscuit Company.

It should be remembered, too, that American women have a good deal more purchasing power than this survey shows, because many of those who legally own nothing are on fairly liberal allowances from male members of their families, and many more are wage earners who spend their wages as they please. Women's collective virtual control is thus considerably larger than their legal ownership indicates. This surplus of petty wage earning and of what might be called delegated control is not a matter of interest to investment bankers, so the survey did not attempt to take account of it; yet its aggregate must be quite large. There seems little ground for doubt that, taking virtual control with legal control, our women now have more purchasing power than our men have. Four years ago they were within 9 per cent of equality in legal control, and quite rapidly on the rise; and surely the amount of delegated control which they exercise, plus their wage earnings, would be enough to carry the sum of their purchasing power well over the mark of 50 per cent.

II

In Europe one notices a general prevalence of the notion that our country is a paradise for womankind. Europeans think we operate our institutions greatly to the advantage of the female sex. Some years ago a highly placed English dignitary — I think it was the present Dean of St. Paul's — spoke of the United States as 'an ice-water-drinking gynecocracy.' The popular idea on the Continent appears to be that our women do as they please without let or hindrance, and that they have reduced our men to the Levitical status of hewers of wood and drawers of water, if not to that of mere skulkers upon the face of the earth. Continental women — those, at least, with whom I am acquainted — indulge this notion with interested curiosity, in which one sometimes discerns a touch of envy. A more conservative opinion is that, while our women have managed to gain an unshakable ascendancy, they have also managed to establish a roughly satisfactory relation of live-and-let-live with their male entourage, mostly by way of concession, which is not as a rule too onerous and not perhaps utterly degrading; a relation, however, which, with all the good will in the world, a male European would find hard and repugnant.

The wonderment is how the American woman has done it. This more than anything, I think, is what has always made our women an object of special interest to the European mind. I never saw anything to make me suspect that Europeans of either sex like our womenfolk or admire them especially or even much respect them, but they have always showed great curiosity about them, somewhat like our curiosity about the habits of the sea bear or the peculiarities of the lemming, or the traits in other creatures whose main interest for us is that they keep us wondering how they accomplish what they do, and do it apparently with no great fuss or effort, nor any consciousness that they are doing something unusual and striking.

One sees Europeans regarding casual specimens of our petticoated produce, more often than not pretty poor specimens, and wondering what on earth they have in them to have worked themselves into their highly privileged status, and to have got this status accepted without objection or complaint. The European would say that such a notable collective manœuvre betokens first-rate ability somewhere, and he cannot see that they have it; his own womenfolk, by and large, seem much abler, wiser, more mature of mind. Cleverness will not answer; he acknowledges that American women are very clever, but no one can be *that* clever. Nor can such a piece of strategy be put through nation-wide on the strength of feminine fascinations, even granting that American women are endowed with these beyond all other women, which he thinks highly doubtful. All the horde of foreign 'observers,' novelists, dramatists, journalists, lecturers and the like, who beset our shores, usually with some sort of axe to grind, always show that this problem is in the forefront of their minds. They treat it with gingerly deftness, as a rule, and hence their observations are seldom valuable, but they always exhibit a lively curiosity about it.

The best that European opinion has done with this problem, as far as I know, amounts to saying more or less kindly that our women are shockingly spoiled and that our men spoil them. In its view the American man of family appears, by his serious side, as a kind of composite of Silas Lapham and Mr. Potiphar. By his lighter side, he appears when on parade with his frolicsome daughter (or wife or sister, as the case may be) much as he does in Mr. Georges Lauwerijns's utterly delightful ballet called *Hopjes and Hopjes*, which anyone going to Brussels should time his visit to see and hear. European opinion holds what it regards as our men's weakness, their easy-going good nature, their sense of essential inferiority, responsible for letting themselves be choused out of their natural and Scriptural rights over the women of their households.

There is something in this, of course, and there was formerly much more in it than there is now. Mr. Potiphar and Silas Lapham are real enough, but they belong to an earlier day. Mr. Lauwerijns's figures are modern and not greatly exaggerated — the simple-hearted and likable old boy who never learned how to play, out on a lark with his gay daughter who is rather fond of him in her careless fashion, is on good terms with him, and exploits him scandalously. Mr. Sinclair Lewis has perhaps a little over-vulgarized a somewhat similar pair, in his excellent portrait of Mr. Lowell Schmaltz and his daughter Delmerine. But there is no longer any point in discussing the distribution of responsibility. In citing the American man's traditional easiness with women, European opinion may have had everything on its side in the days of Daisy Miller, and may still have something on its side. What it has or has not, however, is no longer of more than academic interest, because a new factor has come into the situation since Silas Lapham's and Daisy Miller's day — the factor of economic control. It may be said, no doubt, that men were culpably shortsighted not to foresee this factor's coming in and to take measures against it; but that is little to the point now, because the mischief, if mischief it be, is done, and there is no help for it.

The thing now, I take it, is to measure the strength of this new factor, and to observe some of its bearings. I venture to suggest this because no one, as far as I know, has ever taken the American woman's proportion of ownership and her probable preponderance of purchasing power into account as affecting her freedom of action, and as in consequence putting certain definite marks upon our society which do not appear on any other. I am no such hidebound disciple of the Manchester

149

school as to pretend that the American woman's position is to be accounted for in economic terms alone. I say only that her economic status has a great deal to do with defining and establishing her social status, her social privileges and immunities, and that in this relation her economic status has never, as far as I am aware, been competently considered by any critic, native or foreign; and since one magazine article will hardly go around the whole subject, it may properly devote itself to this single aspect of it, even at the risk of appearing limited and partial.

III

To-day processes the refractory raw material of yesterday's heresy into the standard tissue of orthodoxy; and to-morrow re-processes its remnants into the shoddy of commonplace. Side by side with this procedure, and apparently related to it, go odd changes of fashion concerning delicacy and indelicacy of speech. A dozen years ago, it was most indecorous to say anything suggesting the doctrine that those who own rule, and rule because they own. We all knew that the doctrine was sound, but, like a sound doctrine of certain biological functions, there was a convention against speaking of it, above all against letting anything about it appear in print. The correct thing was to say that those who vote rule, and rule because they vote — standard eighteenth-century political theory. The fashion has changed now, and everybody speaks quite freely of the relation between ownership and rulership. Even our more progressive institutions of learning no longer make any difficulties about the fact that actual rulership of a population rests finally in the control of its means of livelihood, and that this is vested in ownership.

Our government 'buys,' we say, an island from a foreign government. One flag is hauled down, another is hauled up; one set of officeholders decamps, another comes in. But the island is actually owned by three men, and the same three men who owned it under the foreign government continue to own it under ours. They are the actual rulers of the island's population, because they can make it do what they please, — which is the essence of rulership, — since they control the source of its livelihood. Some years ago a Greenbacker or free-silverite, I forget which, discussing private land monopoly with Henry George, said, 'Give me all the money in the world, and you may have all the land.' 'Very well,' said George, 'but suppose I told you to give me all your money or get off — what then?'

Ownership means the ability to make people obey your will under the implicit menace of shutting off their supplies, or what we call in war time an economic blockade. I do not suggest this as an academic definition, but we all know that it is what ownership comes to. It seems clear, therefore, that the distinctive character of a preponderating ownership would be pretty faithfully reflected by the society in which that ownership was exercised. Hence, when Europeans see our society as deeply effeminized and wonder why it should be so, the most competent answer, surely, is found in the amount of economic control that is in our women's hands. How it got there is of no present consequence; it is there, and apparently there to stay. How is it possible for a society not to be effeminized when its women have so large a power of imposing upon it their collective will, of impressing upon it the distinctive mark of their collective character, their criteria of intelligence, taste, and style?

I suspect that the extent to which women direct our national development in the realm of the spirit is quite imperfectly realized. Putting it bluntly, they control education, they control the church, the forum, publishing, drama, music, painting, sculpture. That is to say, in the United States the musical director, preacher, publisher, lecturer, editor, playwright, schoolmaster, always instinctively addresses himself to the quality and character of interest peculiar to the female portion of his constituency. In Europe he is under no pressure to do so. In fact, this is the most noticeable difference between the practice of these activities here and in Europe, and I think the most significant as well. It is surely more than a coincidence that the increase of women's control of our practice has gone on in a fairly direct ratio to their increase in purchasing power. A study of woman's rise to her present position discloses too many such coincidences for us to take stock in the presumption of coincidence. Her demand for political equality, for instance, was pushed hard and earnestly for nearly a century, but one observes with interest that nothing came of it until the time, almost to the day, that she arrived at equality in purchasing power; and then she got what she wanted with relatively little effort.

Now, in any society, the status of the pursuits I have just mentioned, the status of what goes on in the realm of the spirit, is the measure of that society's actual civilization. Exercise of the instinct of workmanship alone, no matter how energetic, is not civilizing; there must go on with it a balanced and harmonious exercise of the instinct of intellect and knowledge, of religion and morals, of beauty and poetry, of social life and manners. A society may be very rich, it may have any number of industries, railways, hygiene establishments, sport centres, banks, newspapers, telephones, finance companies and the like, and remain quite uncivi-

lized. These things are in a sense the apparatus of civilization, because under proper direction they make for a diffused material well-being, and civilization can get on better if it has this as a basis; but they do not in themselves constitute civilization or even make directly and immediately toward it.

IV

My main design in writing this article is to address a word of exhortation to our feminists. Modern feminism has contented itself with asserting the thesis of women's ability and right to do everything that men can do. Perhaps some of our more thoughtful feminists have looked beyond this thesis, but I know of none, from the days of Fanny Wright and Susan B. Anthony on to the present, who has done so. Feminism has been content with demanding the right to vote, to practise politics and hold public office, as men do, and to enter commerce, finance, the learned professions, and the trades, on equal terms with men, and to share men's social privileges and immunities on equal terms. Its contention is that women are able to do as well with all these activities as men can do, and that the opportunity to engage in them is theirs by natural right.

This thesis is wholly sound. Every objection I ever heard raised against it has impressed me as *ex parte* and specious — in a word, as disingenuous. There is no doubt whatever that women can do everything that men can do: they have always done it. In the thirteenth century, women were not only studying and practising, but also lecturing, in the Faculty of Medicine at the University of Salerno. Joan of Arc made no special impression on the people of France as a military figure; they were quite used to seeing women under arms in the mediæval wars. As late as the sixteenth century, Louise Labé got a bit bored with the routine life of a well-to-do merchant's daughter at Lyon, so she reached down the gun, sallied forth in men's dress, and fought through the siege of Perpignan. Then, having had her little fling at an active outdoor life, she went back to Lyon, married, and made her home the centre of a brilliant literary society, and wrote some of the most beautiful verse ever done in the French language, or, for that matter, in any language. She also wrote an excellent manual of housekeeping in a practical and sententious style rather reminding one of Cato's treatise; which seems to show that she was quite as handy with the broom and the rolling-pin as she was with the pen and the smooth-bore.

Then, as a type of the first-class executive and diplomat, there was Saint Radegonde, in the sixth century. Our feminists ought to look her up as the patron saint of feminism, and I say no more about her in the hope that they will do so; she will be a rich find for them. In the realm of public affairs, the women of the French and Italian Renaissance are too well known to need mention. Even the gun-moll, generally supposed to be a product peculiar to our time and country, has a very early prototype. In the sixth century two spirited hussies, mere youngsters, princesses named Chrodhilde and Basine, pranced out of Saint Radegonde's convent at Poitiers in dudgeon against the management, gathered a band of cutthroats around them, and shot the town to rags. The streets of Poitiers ran red with blood, and the forces of law and order had a frightful time putting down the riot. Indeed, the two princesses never were put down. They rode off somewhere beyond the reach of extradition — some mediæval Miami, probably — and lived to a green old age, full of ginger, and wearing the halo of popular renown. That was many centuries ago, but even to this day the Nuns' War is mentioned with uneasy respect throughout the Poitou.

At any period in history, I think, one may find women 'living their own lives' in the feminists' sense, about as satisfactorily as men were living theirs; doing, if they chose, just what men did, and doing it just about as well. One must observe, however, that these women were relatively few, they were always exceptional, and — here is, I think, the important thing — they were all marked by one sole invariable differentiation: they were economically independent. I say 'all' rather inadvisedly, perhaps, for I have not looked into the pocketbooks of all the notable women in the world, from Semiramis down; but out of curiosity I have lately examined the circumstances of a great many, here and there, and have found but one exception, Joan of Arc. She was a poor girl; but her enterprise was of a very special kind, not likely to be affected by her economic status, though if she had been well-to-do she might not, quite probably would not, have lost her life in the way she did. Given a certain amount of resolution, women who were economically independent seem never to have had much trouble about 'living their own lives'; nor, apparently, do they now.

It may therefore be said, I think, that the efforts of feminism have never been, strictly speaking, in behalf of the rights of women, but in behalf of the rights of poor women; and all the greater honor to feminism that this is so! Those who were not poor or dependent seem always to have been able pretty well to do as they liked with themselves, and, as our expressive slang goes, 'to get away with it.' It must be remarked that, for our present purposes, the wage-earning woman is not to be classed as economically independent, for she holds her place on sufferance of an employer. By economically independent I mean those who are fixed quite securely in the owning class, as were the eminent women of the Renaissance, for instance.

It would appear, however, that feminism in America has not many more fish to fry in the way of its historic contention. If our women of the owning class very much want anything, they are able to concentrate upon it an amount of purchasing power which constitutes an economic demand hardly to be resisted; and their getting it would be likely to accrue to the benefit, if it were a benefit, of the dependent members of their sex as well. A rather trivial instance of this is seen in the latter-day style of dress. We remember that when women took to the wholesome fashion of wearing almost no clothes at all, especially on our beaches in summer, all the institutional voices of our society spoke out against them. The police and our prurient and officious local Dogberrys made trouble for them, and employers held a blanket threat of dismissal over the head of girls who would not conform to more conservative notions of propriety in dress. But there was enough purchasing power concentrated on the style to hold it in force and to bring all objectors to terms; and the poor and dependent women profited accordingly. Putting it broadly, Fourteenth Street could not have held up the style, but Park Avenue could and did, and Fourteenth Street shared the benefit.

Hence feminism can no longer get up an argument on the thesis that women can do anything that men can do. All interest in that contention has died out; everybody has stopped thinking in those terms, and our militant feminists are reduced to pushing minor issues, to smoothing out relatively petty inequalities of legal status, and the like. This is important and should be done; but I suggest that while it is being done the more progressive and thoughtful spirits among our feminists should consider the thesis that women can do something which men cannot do.

V

Women can civilize a society, and men cannot. There is, at least, no record that men have ever succeeded in civilizing a society, or even that they have made a strong collective endeavor in this direction; and this raises a considerable presumption upon their inability to do either. They can create the apparatus of a civilization, the mechanics of that diffused material well-being upon which a civilization is founded. Men are good at that; they are first-rate at founding industries, building railways, starting banks, getting out newspapers, and all that sort of thing. But there is no record of their handiness at employing this apparatus for a distinctly civilizing purpose. Indeed, it is very doubtful whether, left strictly to themselves, they would employ the greater part of it, the part that bears on what we call the amenities of life, for any purpose; they would incline to let it drop out of use. The standard cartoons and jokes on the subject all tend to show that when the missus goes away for the summer, the gent lapses contentedly into squalor and glories in his shame; and these may be taken as an allegory reflecting matters of larger consequence.

In the greater concerns of life it is the absence of the impulse toward civilization that justifies women in their complaint that men are forever children. Men feel no more natural, unprompted sense of responsibility than children feel for the work of civilizing the society in which they find themselves;

153

hence in respect of all life's concerns, even its very greatest, women have been figuratively cuffing and coaxing this sense into their heads, figuratively overhauling them, not so much for unwashed ears and unblown noses as for the persistent *tendency* toward these, the indefeasible disposition to accept a general régime of unwashed ears as normal and congenial, and to regard any complaint of it as exorbitant.

A while ago I took occasion to write something which bore on this point, and it elicited a very tart letter from a lady, asking me what I meant by 'civilizing a society.' I have no notion that the letter was written in good faith; still, the question is a fair one. Words, as Homer says, 'may tend this way or that way,' and nothing is ever lost by making sure that one's use of terms is always perfectly clear. We have already mentioned mankind's five fundamental social instincts — the instinct of workmanship, of intellect and knowledge, of religion and morals, of beauty and poetry, of social life and manners. A civilized society is one which organizes a full collective expression of all these instincts, and which so regulates this expression as to permit no predominance of one or more of them at the expense of the rest; in short, one which keeps this expression in continual harmony and balance.

To civilize a society, then, means that when this harmony is imperfect, when the expression of one or more of these instincts is over-stressed, the civilizing force should throw its weight in favor of the under-expressed instincts and steadily check the over-stress on the others, until a general balance is restored. Social development under these conditions is, properly speaking, a civilized development; and a civilized person is one who manages the expression of his individual five instincts in just this way, and directs himself into just this course of orderly individual development.

Men have, of course, managed this individual development in themselves; though even here, unfortunately, it is seldom clear what part a distinctly feminine influence has played in its direction. Men apparently, however, have neither the ability nor the aptitude to organize and direct a collective development of the kind; and women seem to have both. Men's collective influence has never, that I can discover, even tended significantly in this direction; women's often has. It would therefore appear as certain as any generalization can be that, while women can do everything that men can do, they can also do this one thing that men cannot do: they can civilize a society.

The correspondent whom I mentioned a moment ago intimated that in my interest in this matter I was entertaining myself with a mere logomachy, and that my reflections upon it were all moonshine. In a personal view, one does not mind this; one should be always glad of criticism, just or unjust. But the personal view is unimportant. The important thing is to observe that in the long course of human experience, whenever a society has gone on the rocks, as sooner or later all have done, it was invariably the collective over-stress on one or more of these fundamental instincts that turned it out of its course and wrecked it. One may look back upon any of these societies, — England of the Commonwealth, France of the *Grand Siècle*, any you please, — identify at once the over-stressed and the neglected instincts, and follow through the record of progressive over-stress and progressive repression, running directly on to final disaster. Similarly, one may work out the prospects of an existing society with almost actuarial exactness by observation of these symptoms, as critics have often done. Hence one is concerned with the degree of civilization attained by the society in which one lives, not on such grounds as my correspondent might regard as more or less fanciful, but upon the solid ground of security. An uncivilized society has in it the seeds of dissolution, it is insecure; and the lower the degree of its civilization, as measured by the means I have indicated, the greater its insecurity. The race is always instinctively in pursuit of perfection, always looking beyond an imperfect society, putting up with it perhaps for a long time, but in the long run invariably becoming dissatisfied with it, letting it disintegrate, and beginning anew with another.

Our American society, mainly on account of its wealth and material prosperity, has always come in for an uncommon amount of observation and criticism. Every complaint of it on the part of both native and foreign critics, as far as I am aware, is reducible to the simple thesis that it is not a civilized society. These critics do not use this precise formula, — not all of them, at least; some of them do, — but it is the sum of what they have to say, and this is as true of our most kindly critics as well as the most unkindly. It is the sum of Mrs. Trollope's observations at one end of the long array, and of Mr. Dreiser's and Mr. Sinclair Lewis's at the other. There is a complete consensus that our society leaves the claims of too many fundamental instincts unsatisfied; in fact, that we are trying to force the whole current of our being through the narrow channel set by one instinct only, the instinct of workmanship; and hence our society exhibits an extremely imperfect type of intellect and knowledge, an extremely imperfect type of religion and morals, of beauty and poetry, of social life and manners.

I am not concerned, at the moment,

to comment on the soundness of this criticism; I say only that this is the sum of every criticism that has been passed on our society. Try this formula on any observer, native or foreign, and you will find, I think, that it covers the content of his opinion.

VI

Thus one is led rather seriously to wonder whether, in encouraging our women to do only the things that men can do, our feminists have not been encouraging them to take quite the wrong way with themselves. For my own part, I suspect it may be so. One may easily see how our society, if it had to, might get on without women lawyers, physicians, stockbrokers, aviators, preachers, telephone operators, hijackers, buyers, cooks, dressmakers, bus conductors, architects. I do not say we *should* get on without them; that is another matter entirely. I say only that we *could* get on. We *cannot* get on, however, without woman as a civilizing force. We cannot get on — at least, I see no way whereby we can get on — unless women apply the faculty which they have, and which men apparently have not, to the task of civilizing our society.

In encouraging women to do only what men can do, our feminists have encouraged them to put still greater stress on the instinct of workmanship, the one instinct which all critics say is already over-stressed to the breaking point; and this virtually decreases the stress on those which are already intolerably under-stressed. It causes a still more violent disturbance of balance between the claim of workmanship and the claims of intellect and knowledge, religion and morals, beauty and poetry, social life and manners. Considering the available indexes of these several claims, it would appear that our critics (I venture, after all, to give my opinion in the matter) have a good deal on their side. The development of a sense of spiritual activity as *social*, as something popular and common, in which everybody may and everyone naturally does take some sort of hand — this development seems really not to have got very far.

There is, for example, a great deal of music in America; yet compare the development of our sense of music as a social expression with that which you perceive at work naturally and spontaneously in almost any German village! Similar observations may be made with regard to our literature. We all remember Mr. Duffus's examination of the state of the book market, and we are all aware of the extremely exiguous and fear-ridden existence of anything like a serious periodical literature among us; well, compare this state of things with what one finds in France, or indeed in any Continental country, for I believe our rating is reckoned lower than any of them — as I remember, we stand eighteenth on the list of nations in this particular, though I am not sure of the exact figure; it is, at any rate, shockingly low. So one may go on, through the whole roster of spiritual activities. It appears, then, that further stress on the over-stressed instinct, and further repression on the others, are not what will do us any good.

Here, I think, comes in the point that feminism is in a position not only to direct *interest*, but, for the first time in the world's history, to direct as much purchasing power as men have, or perhaps somewhat more. We have already seen that, in a commercial sense, women's interest controls all our organized expressions of spiritual activity. Take the advertising matter in any newspaper or magazine, and consider the proportion of it that is aimed directly at women's purchasing power, and you can see at once how far publishing policy must reflect specifically feminine views of life. Consider the proportion of woman's purchasing power represented on the boards of our orchestras, in the contributions to churches, in the maintenance of schools, forums, lectureships, and you will see at once the direction that their policies must take. It is a commonplace of the theatre that the verdict of women will instantly make or break any production, instantly establish any general mode or tendency, instantly reverse one already established. Test the question of women's commercial control of organized expression anywhere in the realm of ethics, manners, art, anywhere in the realm of general culture, and your findings will be the same.

Hence it would seem that there is here a great social force out of which our society is at present getting but little good. I believe it is a much greater force than our feminism has any idea of; and this is my justification for suggesting so directly to feminism that it should recognize and measure this force, and then do everything possible to give it a better direction. Our society cannot be civilized through women's attainment of the ends that feminism has hitherto set before them, laudable and excellent as those are. It can be civilized by giving an intelligent direction to the interest and the purchasing power of women. At present these are exercised very irresponsibly and casually in the direction of civilization, largely because women have been over-preoccupied with the idea of doing what men can do. Modern feminism has unquestionably encouraged and abetted them in this preoccupation; and hence it seems competent to suggest that feminism should henceforth concern itself with recommending a higher and much more rational ideal of social usefulness.

156

IS FEMINISM DECADENT ?

YES, by Captain Bernard Acworth.

As brevity is the soul of wit, so is precision of reasonable debate. What is meant by feminism and decadence? Feminism, surely, means the enfranchisement of the feminine mind in public, as opposed to domestic, affairs. Decadence means the systematic and deliberate debasement of political and moral conduct to standards progressively declining below the highest abstract standards available—in our case the Christian standards, the ethical " Gold Standard."

The mind of a woman is ego-centric, and refers debatable questions to the woman's natural self—in fact, to nature. This natural ego-centricity is concerned little, if at all, with abstractions; justice, mercy, morality, and honour itself, being to a woman personal, and therefore ephemeral, matters, dependent on circumstance and relativity, rather than on eternal verities. In short: a woman is without abstract standards which, in her heart, she despises as unpractical on those rare occasions when she can apprehend them. Thus Mrs. Jekyll and Mrs. Hyde are always room-mates, and generally bed-mates. Do they ever fail to consult one another? I think not. The " goodness " of a woman is thus dependent upon environment, upon desire and affection.

In a true man, on the other hand, Dr. Jekyll and Mr. Hyde—the supernatural and the natural—occupy different rooms in the same building, and are scarcely on nodding terms. Hyde is always powerful and Jekyll generally weak, but they remain apart. Thus, when judging himself or society, and giving judgment the force of law, an unfeminized man apprehends abstract truth and, to do the poor wretch justice, he generally sides with the angels, no matter how miserable a sinner he knows himself to be; and this is not hypocrisy. In short: man is the servant of the Abstract and woman of nature and materialism, if publicly released from the control of the Jekyll in man.

Heretofore man has ruled England, the quality of that rule depending upon the relative strength of his spiritual and natural components. To-day woman rules with the consent of man's natural self.

In politics, abstract principles, from their nature changeless, are openly ridiculed by feminized politicians. Physical comfort and pleasure, sentimental economics, " technical " education, the line of least resistance, leaning on others and " safety first," are the aims of a feminist Parliament. Government is no longer executive : the chatter of a mothers' meeting has usurped the manly habit of command. Pacifism, a horrid distillation from feminism, represents the feminine approach to the realities of war. Whether championing or denouncing war, a woman's mind, emotion, and sense, fix themselves on the panoplies and horrors of war and not at all on the abstract principle at issue. " Nothing can justify war," a popular belief to-day, is a feminist view. The thought of wounds and physical death, the loss of pleasure, wealth, security, and of ego-centric loves, excludes from the woman's mind those eternal verities for which a man will die.

And what of the sexes—woman's everlasting concern? Feminism kills mutual respect, and finally love, but of self-respect naturalism knows nothing. for to Nature there is no self. Woman is the earthly home of a manly spirit, but homes are becoming brothels in which Mr. and Mrs. Hyde wanton with feminism while Dr. Jekyll stands at the door and knocks.

The language, conversation and habits of feminism. once given an ugly name· by men, are now sanctified by Feminist Bishops.

If this is decadence feminism is the cause, and femirism stands condemned.

NO, by The Lady Muriel Kirkpatrick

Immediately a woman does anything which is at all remarkable a number of prominent men make it an opportunity to point an accusing finger at the female sex.

" Another step nearer decadence," they say, assuming that an increasing number of women in public life means a corresponding decrease in national efficiency.

This condemnation is merely the result of fear. Man sees his centuries old monopoly dwindling, and dreads the day when it may disappear altogether. Each day his barriers grow weaker and in despair he talks of " home and children being sacrificed to feminine love of notoriety."

Because women have entered the political field, the law courts, counting houses and offices once sacred to man, because her feats on the sports field, the race track and in the air have called forth a certain measure of praise, we are at once denounced as being on the way to decadence. Surely our ability to do something more than look after a home and bring up children is in our favour rather than to the contrary. Woman's capabilities are equal to those of men. but are different. She has had neither his training nor his opportunities and in trying to make her influence felt she is derided by the sex whose old monopoly is threatened.

I can well understand the 1890 type of man denouncing us as decadent. He is the pompous individual who opposed our franchise and independence in public life. To accept woman as anything but a mere shadow compared with himself is a violation of every existing canon and principle of his life. But I doubt whether the majority of men regard woman's increasing influence and work as anything but satisfactory. If women doctors can bring fresh minds to surgical problems, if women economists can view matters from a new angle so much the better for the common good. It is a fact that women are achieving great things. In the cinema, the theatre, the newspaper world and in literature as well as art women are showing powers quite equal to those of man.

Till the present century woman has been under the domination of man, and our financial troubles and industrial depression could be traced to man's superb egotism untempered by the unfailing instinct of woman. In the home man and woman play an equal part with generally satisfactory results, yet in national and international matters if woman lends assistance immediately the word " decadence " makes its appearance.

Feminism, far from exercising a decadent influence, is one of the most healthy movements in a war-weary world. Some of the most ardent pacifists are to be found in feminist circles and I believe their power and influence will go far towards outlawing war. If foreign affairs were run conjointly by men and women. I doubt whether world peace would again be jeopardized.

At the present time of national and financial crisis we need the best brains, ideals and thoughts. Whether it be a man or woman who provides them is immaterial. Genius is invaluable irrespective of its owner, and if a woman possess it she should have an equal scope for its use. Each time women who are taking an important part in the world, are termed decadent I am secretly glad. It merely means men have a sneaking fear that a really clever woman will come along and take their job, and this, in turn, spurs them on to greater efforts.

A WOMAN'S INVASION OF A FAMOUS PUBLIC SCHOOL AND HOW MEN ENDURED IT.

BY D. P. H.

'And if I am to speak of womanly virtues . . . let me sum them up in one short admonition; to a woman not to show more weakness than is natural to her sex is a great glory, and not to be talked about for good or for evil among men.'—THUCYDIDES II, *Funeral Speech of Pericles*.

BY 1918 all men of military age were required at the Front and men teachers were often not to be had, so the Headmaster of a famous Public School who was suddenly deprived of a form master, courageously availed himself of my assistance. During my first interview there was a ring on the telephone. After putting his ear to the telephone the Headmaster turned to me and said, 'A master suggests that by certain rearrangements you can be relieved of the Fifth and devote yourself exclusively to the teaching of younger boys. Would you like that?'—'No, thank you,' I replied. 'The Fifth is part of the job and I should like to attempt it.' He smiled and at once telephoned my preference. A time-table was then brought by an ancient official, who handed it to me without a word, struck dumb by the sacrilege. 'The Fifth' was only one Division of that Form I gathered later from its master, who added that its members were fully prepared for a woman teacher to know more than themselves though they resented the idea of her punishing them. His tone revealed a sympathy with their objection which I shared. Masters generally seemed exercised on the problem of punishments and asked my views, to which I gave evasive replies. I had not yet taught in girls' schools; and the fact that I had still to benefit from association with their leading staffs was naturally resented by certain masters. But if I had so benefited I might have adopted methods acquired in a very different environment, and asserted professional rights in a way that neither masters nor boys would have tolerated. That I had taught boys in a Sunday School and run a boys' club impressed the Headmaster who discerned the value of that experience.

The most serious of all my disqualifications was the absence of an academic gown. Oxford had not yet accorded degrees to women, though we kept the same terms as men, shared their lectures and tutors and took identical examinations. When therefore I went out at 7.30 a.m. to take the Fifth in Divinity, my appearance provoked an expression of horror on the face of elderly masters which was disconcerting. On my return I discovered its origin, or part of it. The Fifth Form master, who was on the point of departure, said appealingly, 'Isn't it possible for you to wear a gown?'—'No,' I replied. 'Oxford doesn't permit women to do so.'—'Yes,' he said slowly, 'I forgot. When I was an Undergraduate at Cambridge I took part in a rag against women having degrees. I didn't realise what it meant or why I was doing it. Young men don't think.' Boys in the Fourth, who did not suffer from the inhibitions of elder pupils, later asked me outright, 'Why don't you wear a gown?' and on my replying as previously without comment, they exclaimed, 'What a shame!' which led me to conclude that boys do think.

Despite the dismay engendered by my presence and its short-comings, I was conscious of a double attitude on the part of masters : one that was sympathetic towards my difficulties and would have been more so, if I had invited their aid in the maintenance of discipline, and a contrary attitude after meeting others. The Fifth Form master formed an amusing instance. The boys thought a great deal of him, and to his influence over them in my behalf I was much indebted; but when he actually saw me installed, just before he left the sight overcame him. 'Upon my word,' he exclaimed, 'I wonder how they stand it! I should not have at their age'; but he hastened to add that I had favourably impressed them. Hitherto he had chaffed me about 'my adventure,' whose temerity appealed to him, so long as it was in prospect. Even the sympathetic Headmaster, who was responsible for my admission, was not immune from its effect. After his first visit to the Form he stood transfixed as the boys filed out, and exclaimed after an interval of silence, 'It looks so strange to see you standing there at that desk.' Parents and other visitors used to gaze through a window of the form room and their faces expressed the sorrowful astonishment that was proper to the occasion.

After much helpful information my predecessor had uttered a warning. 'Ruskin,' he said, 'is one of the set books, but they can't stand his socialism, so we've given up reading him. We concentrate on R. L. Stevenson, and you'd better do the same.' My anxiety was surpassed by that of my pupils as they stood conning a chapter of Exodus preparatory to my advent; and their faces are still a vivid recollection, like the contents of their chapter whose hero Moses lent timely aid to the daughters of Midian. I began by appealing for their support in a difficult situation, the necessity of which they understood and which was rendered more difficult by having to follow a brilliant master. Their response was immediate and sustained even when later on I ventured to ridicule their taboo on Ruskin.

'Why do you disapprove ? ' I enquired.

'He talks such rot,' somebody replied.

'How do you know that, if you don't read what he says ? A number of people in this country have done so and are influenced by him. If you want to confute them in the future you must understand their arguments. It's absurd not to read him ; besides, he's on your syllabus and I must follow it.'

'Mr. X did not,' protested another, referring to my predecessor.

'I know, but let's make an experiment. It's always interesting to do that. If you will read what he says, you can give your opinions on his views and we will discuss them.'

They concurred, intrigued by the suggestion and thinking it wiser to humour me. Boys are philosophers, as well as other things, and my conduct of the suggested experiment promised entertainment which was, I hope, fulfilled. Of their expressed opinions I only recollect two, which were so devastating as to further lessen their already low opinion of the author. His condemnation of Englishmen's devotion to games as altogether excessive, was shown to rest on ignorance of those games and how they were played. When his attack veered to Englishwomen, whose vanity and inordinate love of dress he exposed with less sympathy than Mr. Justice McCardie, the boys' faces broke into smiles, and they kept looking up at me, hoping I should do battle for my sex. But beyond smiling at the humour of the situation I refrained, wisely I think, though feminists may condemn me.

The crushing retort to Ruskin's economic views was delivered by a boy who impressed me as a future Bank Director and champion of capitalism. 'Men,' he declared (emphasising the word), ' cannot hold such opinions. I refer particularly to business men who have a living to earn and a career to make. They have heavy responsibilities,' and he paused, implying the lack of such burdens on the shoulders of women and authors. Then came the final shot directed specially for my benefit : ' They have families to maintain ' ; and he sat down amid a profound impression. Commissioned, I fancy, by his thoughtful master to assist me, he was also the custodian of Form rights and traditions and strictly held the balance between us. Firmly he insisted that prep. must not exceed the prescribed portion and as resolutely he secured a good mark for the knowledge of it. I once asked him, ' How do you think we are getting on ? ' alluding to myself and the Form. He paused and cautiously replied, ' Well; so far.' After my first lesson there was a mass assembly of the school, and I asked where it was. He told me ; then after a moment's hesitation, ' Shall I conduct you there ? '—' No, thank you,' I replied, ' but it is kind of you to offer.' He didn't appear relieved as I expected, but drawing a wrong conclusion hastened to inform his departing master that I was about to storm the assembled school alone. It was probable that the contingency of my advent had been foreseen and an inconspicuous foothold designed for me near the entrance, which, conductorless, I was likely to ignore. So I found the two in conclave, and overheard as I opened the door the exclamations of the master. ' Is it possible ? She cannot be going alone. It's extraordinary ; most extraordinary.'—' I have no such intention,' I hastened to assure him, ' nor do I ever go where I am not wanted.' Attendance would have rendered the plight of the Fifth as conspicuous as my own, and my refusal of subsequent temptation must have produced a sense of obligation which was strengthened by the following incident.

A boy who was quarter of an hour late for an early morning class stood penitently in front of the tribune.

' I'm awfully sorry. I apologise.'

' But why are you so late ? '

' I overslept.'

' I do hope you won't do so again.'

The boy stood waiting, and when I made no further comment, he said in tones of friendly warning, ' You ought to punish me.'

There was a moment of tensest silence and of strained attention on the part of listeners.

' I shall not do so this time,' I firmly replied.

Deep reflection descended on the Fifth ; and the word spoken or implied went round that its members were not to oversleep and perform similar acts of negligence ; that prep. was not to be evaded —beyond a point—by those inclined to do so ; and that vagaries and *faux pas* on the part of their teacher were resolutely to be ignored by those who might resent them. More compelling than any chivalrous prompting was the steady support of members of

the Eleven who were custodians of my authority. Not until their
absence for matches did I realise their presence or begin to note
their dominance. That they appreciated the absence of punishment more keenly than the rest is likely ; but I paid them no more
attention than the others and never spoke to them out of Form.
So when I hear condemnation of the worship of sport in our public
schools, which is I admit excessive, I remember that Eleven whose
members played the game according to emergency rules. To take
the Fifth after more strenuous experiences was like entering a
haven, because so much of the burden of government rested on
other shoulders, though I did not cease to strive with their convictions or to administer reproof, on occasion, when I preferred the
oblique method.

In a French Division, I noted a pupil in the back row who was
surreptitiously studying another subject, which I concluded to be
German, his next Form. As my glances produced no effect, I
said, ' I am anxious about So-and-so,' naming the boy in question.
Instantly heads were turned in his direction and somebody asked,
' Why ? '—' His brain,' I replied.—' So are we,' agreed a couple of
wags.—' I fear,' I continued, ' that it cannot stand the strain he
is imposing upon it. It's a feat, I know, but ought he to study
French and German at the same time ? ' The boy closed his
German book amid laughter and consolatory winks from his
friends. That points were scored against me in private is likely,
but I was allowed to make them in public. One boy who later
became captain of the Eleven was an incarnation of good humour
and his cheerful participation in the proceedings was a pleasure
to witness. He enjoyed, so I was told, informing his house master
of our non-punitive regime and the order and harmony which it
entailed. The little Form scholar's devotion to study was repro-
bated and detailed for my benefit, but without malice, as if they
were chaffing a comrade for personal oddities. With few exceptions
the gifts of a large percentage lay fallow, reserved for future employment. The refusal to make use of them was in part instinctive,
the resolve of the team, or of Nature to resist the incitements of
tutorial opponents, and largely the conviction that their studies
had no intrinsic use for life but were the accompaniment to more
important occupations. So despite their reputation for ' thickness,'
I was more impressed by their possession of dormant ability which
could have been used, if they had thought it worth while. But
to ensure that would have involved a revolution in my country-

men's attitude to things of the mind, and boys' minds in particular, which did not exist in 1918.

I was plunged into a routine of whose demands on me and themselves the Fifth and other Forms had a settled conviction. In history I was thankful for the path indicated as I had not yet taught a modern period ; and as our mutual study proceeded I strove in various ways to arouse their interest. The work of Lord Cromer in Egypt induced reference to biographical records which evoked my enthusiasm, though his abolition of the *courbash* left my listeners cold. They could hardly be expected to appreciate an immunity which they did not share. Nor did I disdain the reading aloud of extracts from good historical novels which threw light on the personages of the period. My admiration for a philanthropist who had been nurtured within their walls might have been condoned if I had not implied his pre-eminence over other distinguished *alumni* ; and a charged and resentful silence revealed the extent of my error. As I look back I think they were very tolerant of my feminine reactions to events and persons. A subject of polite contention was their strictly quantitative method of measuring prep. without regard to subject-matter ; though for the designing of maps, in which they excelled, they grudged neither the painter's brush nor the time involved. An Indian boy, whose artistic embellishment impressed me, used to wander about the school precincts and stroll into Form, carrying a volume which he read for pleasure. By acute observation I discerned the poetical nature of its contents though not the poet. So extraordinary a habit was explained and condoned, evidently, by his nationality.

The subject whose study was considered most futile was that of French. I can remember a dashing youth's explanation of this as he left the Form Room, conscious evidently that I was impressed by the poverty of his performance. ' There's no need, you see, for an Englishman to use it. When my father and I were motoring in northern France we asked for everything in English and got it.' Recollecting the feats of our Tommies in that particular I was not surprised, but I tried to counter his argument. He listened politely and departed unconvinced. The boy who told me I ought to punish him had made a fine art of reducing mental exertion to a minimum in subjects that did not interest him. His attempts at French composition had a single merit in that he covered the whole ground. He forged straight ahead, inventing, when necessary, his own idioms and vocabulary. He was rather proud, I fancy, of his first effort for my benefit which could not have been produced without thought; though he had ignored the aids provided by the compiler of his text-book. I gave him O of course; and as he returned to his place with the returned composition in his hand, he ruefully made the sign of O with his fingers to interested companions. As he was going out, I expressed regret at my failure to appreciate his ingenuity and asked him why he was bound to have recourse to it. Could any further effort on my part throw light on his mistakes? At first he looked mystified and slightly alarmed; then he discerned in a flash of intuition the cause of my concern. 'Please don't distress yourself; there's not the slightest need. I don't mind having O in the very least. I always do in French and am fully accustomed to it.' For the moment I was nonplussed by such considerate fatalism. Whether I ever succeeded in impairing it, I cannot exactly remember, though I think he deigned to earn a mark or two, in order to keep me quiet.

Equal futility, I regret to add, was attached to the apparent obligation of undergoing preparation for confirmation. The consequent absence of certain boys led to the revelation, and a comment by myself which struck the Form as ingenuous. 'Ought you to be confirmed if you don't want to be?' There was a chorus of dissent, and a victim exclaimed, 'You're talked to until you consent. It's impossible to get out of it. As it is, we have little enough time for ourselves. It prevents us from doing what we want and we get no return from what we have to give up.'

Doubtless he was a leading malcontent, and silent boys may not have shared his views.

To find suitable subjects for literary composition invoked ingenuity on their part as well as mine; and frequent allusions to the beauties of Nature in a set of essays produced smiles on their faces, when I referred to it. While reading R. L. Stevenson I had ventured to compare the attitude of various writers to natural beauty, with the result that listeners had conspired to pacify me. The Shell were less obliging; and I recollect one youth handing me a paper with a flourish as if conferring a favour. It was a sheet of foolscap little more than half filled. Glancing at its contents, I asked, 'How long did it take you? Ten minutes?'—'About,' was the reply. He bore a well-known name in journalism; and I responded after a moment of hesitation, 'You deserve two marks, I think, for celerity.' His benevolent hauteur was perceptibly lessened. A Fifth Form boy whom his master had designated as a 'beauty' sent up an essay which impressed me. The epithet clearly alluded to character, and was interpreted by me as a designation of conduct, which it was better not to investigate, though his behaviour in Form was exemplary. From a choice of subjects he had selected one that offered a peg for his speculative theories. Doubtless he thought them above my head and may have been justified; but I had not read Greats for nothing; so after expressing appreciation of an effort to which I had accorded high marks, I criticised portions of it after the others had left. The stamp of original authorship was not betrayed by his defence. He thought me impervious to the reasoning on which his unorthodox conclusions were based and appeared disappointed. My final remark must have been irritating. 'That you hold such views now does not surprise me; but I am sure that further experience of life will induce you to alter and modify them in certain respects.' I remember an argument with a clever boy whose mention of an apple dumpling to illustrate his thought struck me as inappropriate. He stoutly maintained the contrary, leaving me uncertain whether he really thought so or had inserted the simile to ascertain my literary taste.

As term neared its close the disinclination for essay writing increased; a symptom which aroused my obstinate resolution. So I invoked the aid of a functionary, a retired butler, who visited forms to make and receive communications of importance and thereby provided a welcome interlude in our studies. On one occasion he handed me the notice of a vacant Headmastership. 'This is no good to me,' I said sotto voce, 'I can't apply for it.' In low discreet tones he replied, 'You'd manage all right, Miss. I'd apply, if I were you.' This token of confidence was distinctly encouraging; and I made him the bearer of missives to recalcitrant pupils. My S.O.S. penetrated even to their houses and must have been deeply resented. I heard indeed a group of my victims exclaiming that somebody or other was 'mad,' and concluded it must be myself. But I got my essays, and by reading aloud Conan Doyle's *Tragedy of the Korosko* when marks were being added instead of accorded, I did much to restore my reputation for sanity. The implied game which ruled our relationship was much enforced; so much mental effort on their part to be rewarded by so much reading aloud on mine. This popular author had been chosen in the first place to beguile a portion of Sunday afternoon when masters assembled their forms in mysterious conclave. Some, I was told, gave lectures on Divinity and enjoined the taking of copious notes; while others

read aloud from Rudyard Kipling, a procedure which I was urged
to adopt. This seemed too great a concession to their interpretation
of my obligation, so I resolved to compromise. 'Before reading
Kipling I shall read another book for twenty minutes that ought to
interest you.' Its author was a vivid portrayer of the Gospels and
their historic setting, but his effect on my audience was soporific.
Leaning back in their desks with folded arms and closed eyes they
might have been the victims of a magician's drowsy spell. Such a
spectacle was not to be endured, though I continued reading for a
while in order to avoid admission of defeat. Next Sunday I adopted
an unexpected tactic and asked the Form Scholar to read aloud Our
Lord's parable of the Pharisee and the Publican. He was one of
their best readers, as acknowledged by the Form when we voted
on their achievements, and always glad to render a service. The
others listened alertly, wondering what I was about to spring upon
them ; but I caught them off their guard by suggesting that detective
stories were an essentially Christian form of literature, as maintained
by Mr. Chesterton in a recent debate at a Writers' Club. When a
pearl necklace was missing, the host and hostess, their distinguished
guests as well as the servants, were presumed to be possible thieves,
so a story of this kind testified like no other to the Christian doctrine
of original sin, which places all men and women on an equal footing ;
and his conclusion led naturally to the psychology of the Publican's
prayer and its contrast to that of the Pharisee. Forgetting each
other in their astonishment they listened with absorbed attention ;
then I resorted to our story book. This was our usual practice.
Next Sunday they were prepared for my reflections and accorded
the more deliberative attention to which I was accustomed : whatever their verdict on my procedure, it banished somnolence.

It was the Shell that I found difficult to manage, where there
was no Eleven silently to uphold my authority. So I fell back on
the primal weapon of woman, the tongue, which served me well
at times but to my own detriment. 'If certain of you,' I said
on one occasion, ' cannot behave like gentlemen, I shall request you
to go ouside, like members of my class in Seven Dials, who cannot
be expected to know any better.' (Seven Dials was not geographically exact, but I liked its sound.) The silence which ensued may
have contained a horrified element of compassion for my admission.
An innovator, according to Danton, should have one motto :
' De l'audace, encore de l'audace, et toujours de l'audace,' and my
crowning act of audacity should have won his approbation. ' You

and others pass judgment on me ; it is natural. But it is also natural that I should pass judgment on you. What really matters is not so much what Z (mentioning the school) thinks of me, but what I think of Z.' They were not at the moment consciously passing judgment ; but their behaviour indicated an estimation of my endurance that I wished to correct. It sank like no previous missile, the enemy being stunned by its mere incredibility. The apprehensions of their housemasters appeared lulled by the report of calm seas in the Fifth ; and thought of the effort involved in framing an indictment and designating offenders, induced me to prefer countering storms single-handed whenever they occurred ; with the result that I recollect no current of ill-will between me and the Form, which might have ruffled smoother waters. One boy in particular, I remember, whose long lanky body could not fit into his desk and whose legs extended in various directions. In an instant when provoked he would gather in his legs, leap to his feet and smite an offender. I heard he had recently smitten a housemaster who ventured to pull his ears while parading round the desks. But he had mental as well as physical reactions and was gratified when I lent him a book on Napoleon, which I had some difficulty in recovering. Napoleon fortunately appealed to other mighty men in the Shell who thought him worthy of study.

Boys in the Fourth were Nature's oasis in a world ruled by ghostly convention. They were new-comers and tradition sat so lightly upon them that they openly welcomed my advent, one or two admitting previous acquaintance with governesses, in order to reassure me. They began their test of my disposition by handing me the cane ; and on finding that my tongue could administer necessary flicks in its stead, they flung back their heads in appreciative laughter. They were easier to manage than many a girls' class of the same age, though they tried to procure the admission of a member who might have outclassed the most refractory girl. One morning they brought in a dog which was specially trained, they said, to behave during Form and inspire their efforts, as I would see, if I allowed him to mount guard beside me. But I was stony hearted and said that much as I appreciated their dog (an attractive mongrel) he would have to wait for his admirers outside the door, where he was soon relegated amid consolatory patting. On account of their tender years I did not hesitate to exact penalties in the form of lines from one or two offenders, who betrayed regret but no shame or loss of personal dignity. One boy, however, penitently pleaded for absolution on account of the 'veniality' of his offence, which I admitted after investigation. Despite my resort to approved methods I was harried by housemasters who seemed to think that this Form ought to provide the victim I had so far refused to offer them. Warnings were conveyed by the usual functionary that discipline must not be relaxed at the end of term; one master complaining that boys were knocking balls against a wall during prep. hours. A later message, addressed personally to myself, bade me report T. at once if he misbehaved himself. The next day T. arrived with a form, which I had to fill in regarding his conduct and prep.; and this procedure was repeated on subsequent days. But T. was thereby induced to make the minimum effort to avert his damnation, though his master, I fear, doubted my veracity.

A red-haired boy uttered such strange and unintelligible sounds when he rose to repeat La Fontaine, that the Form burst out laughing and I exclaimed, 'What are you saying? I cannot understand.'

'Nor can I,' he answered doggedly, amid renewed laughter. 'I've tried to pronounce them and I can't.'

'Don't you believe him,' advised a sceptic.

'He's trying to have you on,' added another.

The red-haired boy folded his arms and surveyed his accusers with the dignity of innocence at bay. 'I've tried my best,' he protested, 'but I can't make the sounds.'

I perceived that he could not approximate to their utterance amid these grinning listeners, so I reproved them for their mirth and delivered judgment, 'S——, I believe you. You may sit down.'

'I thank you,' he said with an expression on his face that impressed me by its eloquence. 'For once,' it implied, 'I have found justice on the earth.'

On leaving the room they would gather around the desk in order to satisfy a curiosity which convention had not yet stifled.

'Do you think women should have the vote?' I was asked on one occasion.

'As citizens I think they have the right—particularly when they perform the duties of citizens.'

'So you are a Suffragette?'

'No' (with emphasis), 'a Suffragist, which is different. To smash windows and pour burning oil down pillar-boxes is not the duty of citizens and I should like them to remain without a vote until they learn better.'

'But it's so lovely to smash a window,' exclaimed a listener. 'Isn't it ? ' and he turned to the others, who re-echoed his sympathy with the delights of Suffragettes.

Recognition of their obligations to put away childish things gave me a handle in managing one or two of them.

'You are expected here,' I said, 'to conform to a system of self-government which is peculiar to our country and the admiration of other lands, not to behave like silly schoolboys.' Such a remark which would have been regarded as the most unadulterated impertinence in other Forms, fell like manna on the Fourth, who were more conscious probably of the obligations of fags than those of self-government. One boy in particular, whose kindled face would have rewarded a worthier orator, went out of his way afterwards to show me the friendly consideration which recognition of his maturity impelled. But the acquisitive instinct of boyhood which he shared with the Form remained unabated. Not in the slums have I come across boys who were so eager to appropriate broken pieces of chalk, pencil ends, discarded nibs, pieces of twine, dismembered and blunt penknives, waste paper and any other litter which they considered general property; and I was not surprised that Form Rooms had to be locked. What refuse I could legitimately accord I did; but their importunity deserved a richer harvest, that of Seven Dials for instance, where they would have put other ragpickers to shame.

The correct salutation for those encountering me in the street had been a subject of dispute; but it was finally decided 'to cap' to a lady, the Headmaster being the only school authority who was thus saluted. The Sixth Form, of course, being outside my domain were not required to recognise my presence, though I must have been too much in evidence for one of them, who exclaimed, 'That woman again,' as I turned a corner. Theatricals and a concert formed excellent entertainments at which womenkind were welcome and delighted guests; but the annual match overshadowed all other festivities, among which it was hardly included. It was rather a supreme ordeal weighted with solemn foreboding, which ripened into sorrow nobly borne. I ventured to consult Forms which did not include members of the Eleven, about the prospects of their play and was informed that the odds against them were heavy indeed. 'But,' said one who wished to lighten the gloom that was engulfing me, 'we must go on hoping for the best. It's the only thing to do.' I concurred, gratified by the implied inclusion in 'we.' He was reading for Sandhurst, and unlike others was apologetic over his French, which did not attain the success he would have liked ; one of those quiet English gentlemen who are considerate and reflective without knowing it. Exemption from study was provided by national service, an obligation which patriots announced with pride ; but a day's haymaking did not command my respect like the enforced absence of members of the Eleven, who were exempt from prep. or resting after their exertions. I ought perhaps to have been more impressed by young men leisurely making their way to the fields, as if for a picnic, with provisions deftly attached to their persons which were carefully attired for the occasion.

As term neared its close there were new arrivals in the Fifth, who were naturally scandalised by a regime into which they had not been gradually initiated. One, a decent, intelligent young fellow, betrayed no sign in public of the consternation he privately expressed at the damage wrought to the prestige of his school. Another, who was a professed man of the world, found accommodation more difficult and startled us one morning by exclaiming in unctuous tones, 'Let us pray.' The Form remained unresponsive, awaiting my reaction and that of each other. When he gave signs of further contumely, I paused and surveyed him with the most eloquent expression at my command. He subsided, not as the effect of my charged silence, which impressed the rest more than it did him, but against the solid wall of their resistance, fortified by the cold regard of the Eleven. He must have found compensation, however in my final obsession, which not only shook the allegiance of the Eleven, but was openly opposed by the Bank Director, whom I had been induced to offend in the following manner. The Headmaster on his final visit to the Form, discarding former benignity, revealed the severity of his office. He looked perturbed, provoked no doubt by rumours of the non-punitive regime ; and his perturbation was conveyed to its originator. When the Form had withdrawn, his practised eye sought the floor and discovered litter ; the sign that all was not well. If only the Fourth could have intervened before his arrival and left a desert behind them ! ' Do you see ? ' he enquired, pointing to torn scraps of paper. 'You should not allow it and must tell them to pick it up.' As he left, the Bank Director came back, ostensibly to fetch something ; and in order to impress that departing figure, I curtly bade him pick it up, as if he were a boy in the Fourth. He looked at me with wonder and reproach ; then complied without a word. He might have recovered from this revelation of a latent school marm if the ordeal of adding the term marks had not induced me to confirm it. The mathematical masters had devised a system of percentages which regaled their leisure but tortured mine ; and without the aid of a kindly master and his wife, whom I shall every gratefully remember, I could not have made the necessary calculations. To display the fruits of my toil to those whom it most concerned, became a fixed resolve when I learned that the last Sunday was my only opportunity. In vain the Fifth assured me it was not customary and that they were entitled to a free afternoon ; I remained convinced that I had the right to summon them if I chose. The retired butler was pressed into their service and urged me to give way to them ; but I announced my expectations. Punctually they appeared at three o'clock, looking restive in their Sunday attire and led by a prominent member of the Eleven, whose face was puckered with anxiety. ' You are not going to keep us, are you ? ' he demanded. ' Only to hear the marks,' I answered. After a minute or two he seated himself, as an example to boys who were standing. I explained that much as I regretted having to keep them, I was performing a manifest duty that would speedily be accomplished. With varying degrees of endurance they resigned themselves to a final act of toleration, which was interrupted by the Bank Director. Flinging caution to the winds, he expressed the outraged sentiment of the Form. ' Suppose we don't want to hear the marks ? ' It was my turn to receive a shock like to that I had inflicted on him. But I quickly recovered and made the obvious retort, ' Suppose I wish to read them ? ' and as nobody could deny the assumption I proceeded to carry it out. They may have feared the miniature Day of Judgment beloved by some schoolmistresses, who like to accord appropriate verdicts ; but having secured my point I trespassed as little as possible on their patience, thanking them at the close for the continuity of their support and wishing them a good time in the coming vac. So they filed out, conscious that they had done more than their duty and that I to a greater extent had exceeded mine. It was my last glimpse of the Fifth, and a moving one. The Headmaster, in a very generous appreciation of my services, said that I had maintained discipline without friction, so I like to imagine that the Form judged me by a previous record, in which prerogative had been laid aside in order to facilitate self-government.

THE DISADVANTAGES OF WOMEN'S RIGHTS

By PRINCESS NIRGIDMA DE TORHOUT

THE equality of man and woman is only natural. In the most primitive life the woman does not seem to have been the servant of the man. What appears to have happened was that since each of them was physically adapted to one form of work rather than another they shared the tasks of life in complete equality. The man no less than the woman was subject to the stern laws of nature (the only laws they recognized), gnawing hunger, stress of weather, fear, and so forth, the woman's only inferiority being in respect of maternity, which unfitted her for any activity for a period of the year. This weakness inherent in her sex had the advantage of stirring the sympathy of the man ; hence the woman's privileges. And from the privileges sprang her dependence. It was only after a long social evolution that the benevolent protector became the master who lays down the law.

Today everywhere in the world woman is shaking off the yoke of this dependence and demanding absolute equality—which will compel her in the end to renounce her privileges. Rights or privileges—she cannot have both.

This situation, in which the woman is regarded as the complete equal of the man, can be studied in Mongolia today. In Mongolia everything dates from Genghis Khan. He it is who framed or approved all the existing laws. He it is, too, who formally described equality before the law by one of the earliest articles in his *Jassak* ; adultery shall be punished by death—in the case of the man no less than in the case of the woman. Side by side with that he granted to the woman the rights of inheritance, of owning property, of bringing up children, or seeking marriage or divorce, of serving in the army. I do not know whether the great Khan was thereby honouring the woman or simply putting her in her rightful place at the man's side. To decide that we should have to know what the position of woman was before Genghis Khan, and that we do not know. I have been told that matriarchate prevailed in the remotest times, but its memory is completely lost, for it is never spoken of in Mongolia. In any case there is nothing modern in the conception of the equality of the sexes. It is completely natural, especially in the case of a man like Genghis Khan, who was by no means religious. For it is primitive religions which have lowered women's status, just as more highly devolved religions were destined to exalt the mother. With us, too, Buddhism has inculcated belief in a duality, two beings in one—a complicated and incomprehensible conception—the woman-woman despised and unclean, and the woman-mother sublime above all things. But this point of view exists only among the clergy. It was an importation from Tibet, completely foreign to the Mongolian mind.

For the ordinary Mongolian unconcerned with dogmas woman is a being just like himself, neither more nor less. So much so, indeed, that the word woman no longer exists in the contemporary language ; the same word, " kun," applies equally to either sex. The Mongolian woman is as free as the Mongolian man. She saddles her horse and goes to visit her relatives and friends ; she receives her guests and calls on whom she will. Before the law she stands on an equality with man, completely responsible for herself. She has no vote, because no one has any vote at all. It is all very nice, but the medal has another side which is only noticed by those who have some experience of other customs. Because she is the comrade of the man the Mongolian woman is an object of no particular regard. She shares all the men's hardest tasks, watches the flocks in rain and snow, loads the beasts, cuts wood. She enjoys no kind of precedence; she rises when a man older than herself comes in and gives him up her place at the fireside or the softest cushions. The only priority we know is that of age. Man and woman share equally the expenses of life, and since the woman is almost always physically the weaker her lot is always the heavier, which explains the precarious health of many Mongolian women. All those forms and formalities—flatteries, deferences, everything that in the West is called the spirit of chivalry—is non-existent. The orphan is protected but not the woman. She has the same rights, and consequently the same duties and the same responsibilities. It is the *lex talionis*, inescapable. And it does not seem to me that it is the woman who gains by the bargain. The woman by her constitution, by her general sentiments and habit of mind, is less fitted than man for the struggle of life. I do not mean that she is fundamentally inferior to man. I am no feminist, but neither am I of those who speak of the " feminist utopia." The woman will in time reach equality with man, but she is still far behind him—I mean the woman who has behind her a long tradition of

indulgence; and the readjustment will not be easy. Will women, moreover, gain by their equality with men ? The woman termed inferior has always exerted wide influence. You need only look at the Chinese woman who, up till the most recent times, was of all women the type most dependent on the goodwill of the man. She had no rights in public life. She had no existence, but she was and still is the absolute mistress in her family and, through its influence, almost sovereign in that public life in which she never shared herself. In China a woman is infinitely respected. A man never contradicts her, agrees with her even when she talks nonsense, carries out her whims. Compare these two women and ask which is the more enviable lot. Is it not better to have fewer legal rights and preserve the privilege of exerting influence, of being respected, flattered, spoiled, of being free from all responsibility ? Or should one prefer the Spartan life of the Mongolian women ? Is the emancipated woman, as the Mongolian has been for the last 600 years, really happy ? . . . But perhaps after all to be happy is not the essential. Perhaps we are unconsciously groping for something else. In any case, if feminists claim their rights to restore to women a happiness and a freedom of which they consider they are cheated, they are taking the wrong road. But if their aim is to open new horizons, aiming at a more spacious and more worthy life, if with their new rights they are ready to accept all the consequences, that I agree is courageous and admirable.

THE CULTURAL BACKGROUND OF THE AMERICAN WOMAN

THE men who crossed the Atlantic and settled what became the United States were firm and confident in their intention to make the culture with which they were familiar dominant in the new land, or, in a few instances, to bring into being a different civilization but one conceived and planned in Europe. Rarely was there any understanding of the impossibility of fulfilling their designs. It was distance and the unescapable demands for new adjustments that gradually forced upon the people the building of a culture that became more and more indigenous.

There is nothing to indicate that women were more conscious than men that their migration would mean breaking away from the *mores* of the Old World, although they may have been more troubled by the prospect of trying to work out their household responsibilities in the untried wilderness. In this clinging to European attitudes and customs, which made the new undertaking an outshoot of European civilization, the first comers differed radically from those who immigrated after the Revolution. With the exception of those coming with no thought from the first of actually settling in America, the later immigrants were attracted to the United States in part that they might break away from Europe and free themselves from its irritating or limiting circumstances. They realized that they were passing from one civilization to another. Indeed, to accomplish this often was their purpose.

The English, the Dutch, the Swedish, the Spanish, and the French colonists expected to plant the culture of the land of their birth in the New World where it would flourish and become a portion of the Old Country in the New. Only the last were able to resist successfully the pressure toward change, but even they were broken off from a living, intimate contact with the historic evolution into which they were born, and were left with the task of perpetuating the cultural slice they carried over, which in time became as unlike the civilization that developed later in the motherland as it was alien at the beginning to the American wilderness.

The yeast that was to leaven American civilization was mixed and vitalized in Europe and transported, without change, to these alien shores. The men and women who brought it here, whether birds of passage possessed by the lure of covetous expectation or by the hankering for adventure, or persons committed from religious, political, or economic motives to life in the wilderness, held tenaciously to the customs, the standards, and the philosophic outlooks upon life to which they had been accustomed on the other side. Change came, but it was unsought and, as a rule, resisted. In spite of their natural effort to hold to the old and familiar, the new environment took command and gradually forced a profound reconstruction of European ways of living. This necessary readjustment in turn led to new thinking, until soon in process along the narrow coast line of North America were the beginnings of a native culture. No part of that European importation was more resistant to the new influences than the practices and the attitudes that established the status of woman. Her position was something that was so taken for granted, such a social axiom, that it was accepted by most men and women as a finality not open to question. This firmly established convention by no means assumed the insignificance of women, for it was recognized that they were indispensable in the new settlements.

Woman was the silent sex, since in man's hands were the means of social prestige and political expression, but this does not mean that her part of the burden was light nor that her contribution was considered unimportant. It was rather that the rôle that was considered proper for her kept her away from the spotlight. A long history lay behind this fact, one so interwoven with the growth of Europe that it is now difficult to disentangle the influences that operated to fix so firmly the social status of woman. Change was bound to come here as in other features of the social experience brought over from Europe, but rather more slowly than in most, because so much had contributed to the establishment of woman's position. Moreover, many of these influences were continuing and were less worked upon by the conditions of the new environment than were other aspects of the imported civilization.

The cultural ferment that was brought over from the Old Country was neither simple nor consistent. It also was a composition into which had poured influences for thousands of years, reaching back even to the pre-European civilization of Asia. To assemble all the deposits that entered into the making of this leaven would require retracing the entire evolution of culture from the birth of civilization to the English settlements in the New World. The impossibility of so exhaustive an analysis must not conceal the fact that wherever one locates the beginning in Europe of any of the causal influences that fixed the position of women in the Old World, these choices are arbitrary, since stretching from them backward are chains of events and systems of thought that brought them into being. Moreover, if it were within one's power to trace woman's history by itself through this vast stretch of time, it also would remain a partial treatment, since the experiences of women were neither independent nor distinct but organically built into the entire life of all the people, irrespective of sex.

The life of men and the life of women cannot be severed as the skilled surgeon can separate one portion of the body from its surrounding tissue. The most that can be done in seeking to trace the various factors that have established the status of women and decided their career is to draw together the most immediate of the influences of European origin and suggest their more remote genesis, in so far as they were continuing sources of contribution affecting the life of women in the civilization of the seventeenth century. Although the task in hand requires that we gather only as much of the deposit accumulated by centuries of human experience as helps us understand the background of American women, our findings are useful in their attempted interpretation, not as they are isolated but as they are related to the entire life of the people who at any time or place contributed to the composite that made up the cultural background of the colonial settlers.

It would be an anachronistic misinterpretation of this fact to go searching through the past in the attempt to establish a conspiracy against the advancement of women. It is, of course, possible to find isolated occurrences that reveal individual or organized efforts to keep women to their allotted position, but to give these much emphasis would be to distort the cultural picture. It is the *mores* rather than persons that are responsible for the retardation of women in those cases where there clearly is discrimination. For the most part, what we find are *mores* and systems of thought, natural products of the time and place, that assign women their responsibilities and, therefore, in the analysis of the modern critic, hamper the self-expression and self-determination of one sex as compared with the other. The resistance met by ambitious and aggressive women who seek freer life is not usually born of any disposition on the part of men to keep women from going forward but rather from the reluctance to accept social changes and to make the adjustments that a new order demands.

It also leads to misunderstanding to regard these clashings between persons as necessarily due to masculine opposition. The feminine protest may be great, or even greater, and the resistance to progress may chiefly come from women. On the other hand, the stubbornness may be masculine rather than feminine. It is because of these facts that nothing could be more futile than to go searching human evolution to find evidence of an ever-present conflict between men and women. The *mores* of the past, as is still true of the *mores* of the present, have given, at least so far as social opportunity is concerned, an advantage to men in comparison with women, but rarely has there been any deliberate, organized effort on the part of men to conspire against women in order to make them socially inferior or to keep them in a state of cultural vassalage.

Another common fallacy in interpreting woman's social status has been to think of it as something definite and consistent, a situation easily described and permitting all women to be lumped together. If this were true, it would be far easier to survey the social background of American women. Instead of being permitted to follow such a wide and well-marked-out pathway one is forced to take into account every conceivable variation, as a consequence of differences due to class, religion, and politics. Even the place of habitation has to be reckoned with. In the modern world, in spite of the closeness of people who possess highly efficient means of transportation and communication, we still find differences between city and country folk. These environmental influences were all the greater before the advent of an efficient science. As an example of this, consider how the early history of Christianity reveals the significance of the Roman highways in the spreading of the new religion. It is accepted first by the cities, and the rural centers, distant from the main arteries of travel, take it over much later than the thickly settled and easily accessible parts of the Empire. Every influence, from whatever quarter, that operates upon the culture of a people may also act upon that special part which interests us—the sphere and status of women.

For our purpose, it is necessary to draw together these conditioning elements as they relate to women's culture. For convenience, these can be classified as the more distant factors coming down from Asiatic and European origin and those more immediately represented in the habits, emotions, and systems of thought possessed by the groups of people that established permanent settlement along the Atlantic coast line.

It will be misleading merely to examine the customs and the thinking of those who came to America as permanent settlers. There are also influences of more distant origin that were acting upon these people and continued to be significant even after they were out of the European environment. The most important of these were the fundamental ideas from which flowed thinking that in no small degree established the status of woman and attempted to perpetuate it. Although these underlying systems of thought deserve to be classified as philosophy, they were for the most part brought into the life of the people through religious teachings. They were not regarded as intellectual ideas but as Christian doctrine, and thus they were enforced as moral requirements by the emotions and the convictions associated with religious faith. This fact was to prove a continuous obstacle to the men and women who sought to improve woman's status. Had these notions been regarded as mere intellectual products reflecting the past and present of intellectual leadership, there would not have arisen such an emotional barrier to woman's advancement, and resistance would have lost the fierceness that came from conceiving the *status quo* of woman's life as something established by moral principles.

The thinking that functioned through Christian dogma is so laden with the contributions of the influential philosophies from early Greek thinking down, that to retrace this evolution in its fullness would require exploring the entire cultural watershed as it gave source to all the tributaries of thought that contribute to the main current. It is this latter flow that concerns us, and we are interested in it more as it enters Christianity than as an evolution of philosophy in its strictest sense. This, however, cannot be handled as if it were something fixed, a consistent system. It also has a history of change. Occasionally it has been interpreted, especially by its critics, as a final dogma without recognition that even when there is a prevailing consistency of doctrine at a definite time and place there are nearly always variations and departures from the main teaching and that always, from time to time, there are differences of emphasis as well as considerable shifting in the authoritative doctrines carried forward by the Church. The attempt to deal with the Christian teaching of any period as a consistency explains the ease with which its critics and its advocates can radically differ while they both appeal to definite facts, historically well-established.

In spite of its originality, Christianity, as it historically expressed itself, took over certain liabilities that came out of the social circumstances of the time and the character and background of those who became followers of the new religion and that influenced its teachings and its organization. One of these elements that had appeared on the stage even before the Christian way of living came to expression was asceticism, and it was doubly rooted, for it gained support from the environment as well as from individual inclination. The word *asceticism* carries two very different suggestions, one stressing the effort through a self-conscious program of life to develop high standards of spiritual experience while the other emphasizes morbid trends such as appear in extreme form in oriental fanaticism. The defenders of Christianity conceive of the ascetic expression that so soon appeared in the new faith as essentially the first while its critics are prone to select illustrations that emphasize the second type.

However wholesome the goals of any form of spiritual discipline, there is always risk, especially in those who are unbalanced through neurotic tendencies, of the effort to keep unspotted from the world taking an unsocial or a psychopathic form. Although it must be recognized that these excesses occur in the development of Christianity, the environmental encouragement that asceticism received was of Jewish origin rather than Eastern,[1] for the type of asceticism which was characteristic of Indian Holy Men was fundamentally incompatible with the Jewish teaching of ceremonial cleanliness, with its insistence upon practical moral conduct.

There was in Palestine, at the time of the birth of Christianity, a significant ascetic group, the Essenes, who illustrated what has been described as the natural religious instinct to withdraw from the world.[2] Granting there will always be controversy as to the significance of this sect at the beginning of Christianity, there is no doubt that they influenced the new faith. Although Philo tells us that this group of Jews were given their name on account of their saintliness, the etymology of the word is doubtful.[3] He describes the Essenes as pacifists who kept away from ordinary life to escape its evils, who looked upon a reverent mind as the only true sacrifice, and regarded love of God, love of virtue, and love of man as true religion. The Essenes lived in colonies and had no private home life.[4] Josephus, however, speaks of one group of Essenes who made a trial of women for three years and married them if the union was fruitful.[5] Eusebius tells us that the Essenes did not marry because they believed that association with women weakened man's character and made his spiritual life difficult. The having of children also hindered fellowship with other men.[6] It has been suggested, however, that his statements express the misogynous opinion of the writer and are therefore misleading.[7]

It is a conservative opinion that Christianity copied many features of the organization of the Essenes and their propagandistic activity,[8] and it has been shrewdly observed that the fact that *The New Testament* is entirely silent regarding them suggests that they may have had no small influence upon Christianity at the start.[9] At least in the teaching of John the Baptist, who ushered in the new faith, we have preachings very similar to those of the Essenes, and we know that the place where the reformer held forth was in the vicinity of a community of the Essenes. Although it seems probable that there were differences in the practices of Essene communities, celibacy was usually a part of their program. It was followed as a means of preserving ceremonial purity, but even so it provided a motive for conceiving woman as a tempter of the flesh, an attitude which later appeared in the teachings of some of the Church Fathers during the formative period of Christianity. It has been suggested that the Essenes were familiar with Greek thinking, especially the doctrine of the Stoics, and that the desire for self-discipline explains their sex policy,[10] but although Stoicism emphasized the need of command over one's passion, this was never interpreted in such a way as to emphasize chastity, much less continence.[11]

Whatever influence the Essenes may have had upon early Christian thinking and behavior, whether little or much, their teaching shows that there was among some of the Jews at the time of Jesus an ascetic trend which frowned upon the sex appeal of women. Even so, it was certainly not related to the Eastern traditions which fixed the subordination of the oriental woman. It is not in the power of the most cautious and discerning of modern scholarship to retrace history so as to charge to the Essenes their contribution, if any, to the tendency of religious philosophy through the first centuries of Christianity to conceive of women as females rather than as persons, but at least it is clear that this unorthodox sect of the Jews illustrated a prejudice brought forth from the experience of men who in their struggle for Holiness had to wrestle with sex impulses difficult to discipline.

Later we find an asceticism, born of this experience and associated with St. Paul, that more significantly contributed to the attitude which regarded woman as inferior to man. Whatever else may have influenced the teaching of St. Paul, it is evident that two notions were back of his preachments. One was the belief in the earlier period of his missionary career that the end of the world was near at hand and that the reign of the Lord, as he conceived it, was to come about in his generation. The other was his strong feeling that women should not by unorthodox conduct become an occasion for scandal and suspicion, thereby hampering the progress of the gospel. His insistence that women should accept subordination in the family and limitation in their religious service was not only in accord with the spirit of the time but also, in the effort to win converts, good judgment.

Much of this instruction to his churches, taken as isolated passages, became powerful ammunition in the hands of those who later, in spite of the complete recasting of civilization, attempted by appealing to this religious doctrine to hold women in a social status even below that given them in the first century, but, alongside these teachings of the apostle, other words of his maintained principles antagonistic to the position he himself held. His insistence upon the intrinsic value of personality was destined, with the passing of time, to become sufficient answer to the argument of those who tried to perpetuate the time-reflecting ideas of the great apostle. The situation was similar to that resulting from Paul's recognition of the slavery that existed in his day. Christianity, as it accepted woman's social inferiority and the slave type of industry, was inconsistent with its essential insistence upon the worth of the human individual, but this discordance was not uncovered until, with the passing of centuries, conventional thought had matured sufficiently to recognize this clashing of contradictory teachings.

The various places in Paul's letters where he writes regarding the need of women's observing the proprieties and avoiding temptations now sound strange to the modern ear, and, without question, they have served through the centuries as a defense of the social and religious discrimination against women, but when they are put back in the setting that called them forth, they seem less harsh. Undoubtedly it was because of the new activities assumed by leading and aggressive women in the churches, their use of the new opportunity provided by a religious faith which gave them practical means of expressing talent, that Paul spoke words of caution. It was less to hold them back than it was to restrain them from going to such lengths as would appear unseemly and react against the reputation of the churches.

In the light of what has happened through the centuries, as we look backward, the apostle's admonitions appear arrogant and loaded with masculine prejudice, but in the light of the responsibilities that burdened the leader whose task it was securely to plant Christianity in the Gentile world, they were evidences of a prudent and constructive ecclesiastical strategy. Mischief came out of them because they were torn from the situation that evoked them, but we doubly wrong the author when we attempt to use them as finalities of Christian policy.

The modern world is nearly two thousand years away from the experiences of the great missionary. His task moreover was to welcome women into a religious fellowship that gave them greater freedom than that which had been familiar to him or to them, while also cautioning them not to bring suspicion of the Christian way of living into the minds of the Gentiles whom they sought to convert, by unnecessarily antagonizing social customs or by starting scandals. This may seem inconsistent in view of Paul's courage as a soldier of Jesus Christ, but it is another illustration of the strange blending of prudence and defiance often found in the reformer and religious leader. As compared to many things, these problems that concerned women doubtless appeared to Paul trivial and timely, to be handled with the regard to the social conventions to be expected of one who, as an ambassador of his faith, could be all things to all men.

Another and more fundamental element in Saint Paul's teaching has been through the centuries an obstacle to the advancement of women. Here again time has abstracted from the words of the writer something quite different from the meaning of these statements of the apostle at the time they were written. His analysis of his struggle to achieve Christian living as a conflict of flesh and spirit was destined not only to encourage morbid asceticism but to debase sex, whether expressed in marriage or illicitly outside. This acted among Christians until the modern era as a continuing shadow over marriage by making it seem a necessary sop to an inherent weakness of human nature, and thus it has encouraged the conception of woman as a female rather than a person. Whatever leaning Saint Paul may have had toward asceticism, his description of his moral conflict was too profound and characteristic to be considered in the narrow way that it was interpreted by later ecclesiastical leaders.

Aside from questions of expediency which led Paul to discourage marriage on account of his expectation during the earlier years of his missionary work that the Kingdom of God would be established in his generation by the second coming of Christ, making it imprudent for the believers to start families unless driven to marriage by sex pressure, there was recognition by him of the uncompromising clashing of the old order with the new in which religion meant complete consecration to a faith that was itself morality.[12] This he dramatized as war between flesh and spirit. This striving of antagonistic impulses became a central theme in his theology but was later forced into narrower terms, thus providing a basis for sex taboo, a low conception of marriage, and an enormous amount of morbid emotional conflict such as Jerome confesses as he writes: "Now, although in my fear of hell I had consigned myself to this prison, where I had no companions but scorpions and wild beasts, I often found myself amid bevies of girls. My face was pale and my frame chilled with fasting; yet my mind was burning with desire, and the fires of lust kept bubbling up before me when my flesh was as good as dead. Helpless, I cast myself at the feet of Jesus, I watered them with my tears, I wiped them with my hair: and then I subdued my rebellious body with weeks of abstinence." [13] A great multitude of earnest, well-meaning people from this time onward, not only during Puritanism but beyond it until the present, have been led by misconstruing St. Paul's words into a wasteful and usually futile emotional conflict which indeed deserves to be called, with distinct sex meaning, the war of the flesh against the spirit.

St. Paul's interest was less in the content of the two modes of life than in the need and joy of the complete dominance of a holy life that would set the believers apart from both the Gentile and the Jew and make them a light to a lost and corrupt generation. No one would have protested more quickly than Paul any disposition to allow the sex impulse to interfere with the enthusiastic commitment to the Christian way of living, but when we consider his teachings as a whole, it is clear that he would be equally aggressive in attacking any other interest, whatever its origin, whether covetousness or ambition or vanity, that had a hampering influence upon the believer's spiritual progress. Paul's flesh and spirit came out of his vivid contrast of his present life in Christ and his earlier career. It was dualism as far as it was a contrast of experience, ending in a complete deliverance which made it possible for him to exclaim: "I am crucified with Christ: nevertheless I live; yet not I, but Christ liveth in me: and the life which I now live in the flesh I live by the faith of the Son of God, who loved me, and gave himself for me." [14] It is the oneness of affection that Paul is attempting to interpret.[15]

There were social conditions in the Roman Empire of which the churches were to be made increasingly conscious that encouraged the narrower and more literal definition of the term "flesh," Paul's symbol for the temporary and the discordant as compared with the eternal and the unity of successful Christian living. As Christianity spread and grappled daily with these social influences in the great urban centers of population, the struggle for holiness assumed more and more the coloring of a sex conflict, leading to an emphasis which naturally idealized chastity and eventually celibacy.[16] Thus the words of Paul drifted away from their original meaning. This came about all the more easily because from the beginning of his gospel Paul himself recognized a distinction between a morality for the perfect follower and a morality for the lower order which nevertheless was spiritually adequate for salvation.[17]

St. Paul certainly made trouble for women of later generations when he went beyond an insistence upon the proprieties and interpolated arguments based upon the inferiority of women, as when, for example, discussing the dressing of the hair of women, he insisted: "In like manner also, that women adorn themselves in modest apparel, with shamefacedness and sobriety; not with braided hair, or gold, or pearls, or costly array." [18]

The New Testament and the Christian literature immediately following it bear testimony, as Harnack remarks,[19] of the important part that women played in the early days of Christianity through their church activities. There can be no doubt that in the circles where the new faith came, new outlook and new momentum were given to many women, a few of whom achieved permanent recognition through the documents that have come down to us. However conservative and cautious St. Paul may have been in his counsel as to church practices and domestic adjustment, there can be no gainsaying the significance of such an outburst as: "There is neither Jew nor Greek, there is neither bond nor free, there is neither male nor female: for ye are all one in Christ Jesus." [20] As an interpreter of his gospel, he provided a fundamental support for the religious equality of men and women.

Paul is also generous in acknowledging the services of women as fellow workers for Christ. In writing to the church at Philippi he declares: "And I entreat thee also, true yokefellow, help those women which laboured with me in the gospel, with Clement also, and *with* other my fellow labourers, whose names *are* in the book of life." [21] Harnack states that Paul saluted fifteen women for their work in the churches, and eighteen men.[22] Surely no stronger tribute appears in the apostle's letters than when he writes: "I commend unto you Phoebe our sister, which is a servant of the church which is at Cenchreae: That ye receive her in the Lord, as becometh saints, and that ye assist her in whatsoever business she hath need of you: for she hath been a succourer of many, and of myself also." [23]

In view of these generous words, it is reasonable to assume that the commands of Paul that women act seemly in public grew out of his feeling that many were tempted to use unwisely the new freedom and the higher religious status that Christianity had brought them. *The New Testament* discloses that the widows in the churches had an ecclesiastical significance, and Paul feels the need also of giving them admonition.[24] In the Eastern churches there early appeared a class of women who, according to Pliny's letter to Trajan, were called deaconesses. He also described an order of female ascetics or *virgines*.[25]

When one passes out of the atmosphere of *The New Testament* into that characteristic of the later ascetic literature as produced by Jerome, Tertullian, Origen, and others, it is apparent that women have lost much of their original promise with the spread and organization of Christianity, and in spite of the increasing rôle played by the doctrine of the Holy Mother. Christianity, as an incentive for daily conduct and a succor to human needs, came close to the life of the believers during the Middle Ages largely through the meaning that Mary, the mother of Jesus, came to have. The virgin mother symbolizes, as Christian theology dominates Europe, the sympathy and humanizing trend of the early believers. Undoubtedly the influence of the pagan cults that gathered about the female divinities intruded, or at least the new took over the functioning that had gathered about the old, but it surely misconstrues what happened to regard the Holy Mother as the successor of this other worship which emphasized reproduction and fertility.

With monotheistic severity, the Jews had successfully resisted the Eastern cults about them, but at the price of remaining a separate people. Christianity had gone forth and conquered, but, as always happens in any wholesale conversion, its success in bringing an alien people under its banner exposed it to the influences of these men and women whom it took into its faith, many of them still pagan at heart, and as a consequence a complex of dogmas and practices developed through the fusion of different and even opposite reactions to life.

There can be no doubt of the need during the Middle Ages of the human appeal brought by the worship of the Virgin Mary, but its significance as an influence lifting the status of the average woman is quite a different matter. When its importance from this angle is tested by raising the question whether women escaped through it from the overshadowing of the ascetic trends of the theology of the period and the ecclesiastical masculine dominance and gained the dignity and independence that might naturally be expected to follow the elevation of Mary, the doctrine of the Virgin Mother appears to have done little to lift the social status of the average woman.[26] It is important in trying to estimate the practical consequences of this part of the doctrine of the Church to remember that Mary was a symbol not of ordinary motherhood, but that instead she was set aside by a miracle that protected her from the debasement associated with the feminine biological rôle which had evoked the pronouncements that now seem so harsh in the writings and teachings of some of the early church leaders. It was easy for the sentiment that gathered about Mary to be actually turned against the functions associated with the child-bearing of the married woman and be made a means of enhancing the virginity of those who denied themselves marriage and parenthood.

The mere fact that women lost status during the period does not demonstrate that they obtained no advantages from this human stress of the mother of Jesus. The Middle Ages, like all complex social situations, were far too variegated for so simple an interpretation. It is fairer to assert that the Mary cult did not prove powerful enough, in so far as it glorified motherhood, to nullify all the other influences that tended to suppress the value of the woman as an independent personality.

One of the strongest of the influences flowing in the opposite direction was the attitude toward women that found expression in the writings of the early church fathers. Gibbon justly summarizes when he writes: "The use of marriage was permitted only to his fallen posterity, as a necessary expedient to continue the human species, and as a restraint, however imperfect, on the natural licentiousness of desire. The hesitation of the orthodox casuists on this interesting subject betrays the perplexity of men unwilling to approve an institution which they were compelled to tolerate." [27]

Marriage was interpreted again and again as an impediment to the spiritual life. Jerome, for example, writes: "If you want to know from how many vexations a virgin is free and by how many a wife is fettered you should read Tertullian 'to a philosophic friend,' and his other treatises on virginity, the blessed Cyprian's noble volume, the writings of Pope Damasus in prose and verse, and the treatises recently written for his sister by our own Ambrose. In these he has poured forth his soul with such a flood of eloquence that he has sought out, set forth, and put in order all that bears on the praise of virgins." [28]

It was, of course, in the sexual side of marriage that the great menace was chiefly found. "The Apostle Paul tells us that when we have intercourse with our wives we cannot pray. If, then, sexual intercourse prevents what is less important—that is, prayer—how much more does it prevent what is more important—that is, the reception of the body of Christ? Peter, too, exhorts us to continence, that our 'prayers be not hindered.'" [29] Marriage cannot be eliminated, but those who accept it must recognize the lower order of their religious life. "The Church, I say, does not condemn wedlock, but subordinates it. Whether you like it or not, marriage is subordinated to virginity and widowhood. Even when marriage continues to fulfil its function, the Church does not condemn it, but only subordinates it; it does not reject it, but only regulates it. It is in your power, if you will, to mount the second step of chastity. Why are you angry if, standing on the third and lowest step, you will not make haste to go up higher?" [30]

Such an emphasis led some church members to serious moral lapses when they had insufficient will to carry out the program publicly subscribed to. "I am ashamed to say it and yet I must; high born ladies who have rejected more high born suitors cohabit with men of the lowest grade and even with slaves. Sometimes in the name of religion and under the cloak of a desire for celibacy they actually desert their husbands in favour of such paramours. You may often see a Helen following her Paris without the smallest dread of Menelaus. Such persons we see and mourn for but we cannot punish, for the multitude of sinners procures tolerance for the sin." [31]

Jerome admits that his exaltation of virginity leads to protest on the part of some, in these words:

"Some one may say, 'Do you dare detract from wedlock, which is a state blessed by God?' I do not detract from wedlock when I set virginity before it. No one compares a bad thing with a good. Wedded women may congratulate themselves that they come next to virgins. 'Be fruitful,' God says, 'and multiply, and replenish the earth.' He who desires to replenish the earth may increase and multiply if he will. But the train to which you belong is not on earth, but in heaven. The command to increase and multiply first finds fulfilment after the expulsion from paradise, after the nakedness and the fig-leaves which speak of sexual passion. Let them marry and be given in marriage who eat their bread in the sweat of their brow; whose land brings forth to them thorns and thistles, and whose crops are choked with briars. My seed produces fruit a hundredfold." [32]

Perhaps none of the Church Fathers was harsher in his interpretation of woman than Tertullian as the following illustrates.

"And do you not know that you are (each) an Eve? The sentence of God on this sex of yours lives in this age: the guilt must of necessity live too. *You* are the devil's gateway: *you* are the unsealer of that (forbidden) tree: *you* are the first deserter of that divine law: *you* are she who persuaded him whom the devil was not valiant enough to attack. *You* destroyed so easily God's image, man. On account of *your* desert—that is, death—even the Son of God had to die. And do you think about adorning yourself over and above your tunics of skins?" [33]

Origen, the most learned of the Christian leaders up to St. Augustine, was driven, in order to free himself from the temptation of woman, to castrate himself. Although this logical way of release brought widespread recoil, he had disciples who sought the same method of escape.

Granting that these passages are significant, it would be unjust to forget that other things were said that were more favorable to the status of woman. Clement of Alexandria may be cited when, for instance, he declares:

"In this perfection it is possible for man and woman equally to share." [34]

Again he speaks of the program women need to follow in order to achieve the good life.

"The wise woman, then, will first choose to persuade her husband to be her associate in what is conducive to happiness. And should that be found impracticable, let her by herself earnestly aim at virtue, gaining her husband's consent in everything, so as never to do anything against his will, with exception of what is reckoned as contributing to virtue and salvation." [35]

Thus he speaks of marriage.

"The marriage, then, that is consummated according to the Word, is sanctified, if the union be under subjection to God, and be conducted 'with a true heart, in full assurance of faith, having hearts sprinkled from an evil conscience, and the body washed with pure water, and holding the confession of hope; for He is faithful that promised.' And the happiness of marriage ought never to be estimated either by wealth or beauty, but by virtue." [36]

The main thought of the leadership seems to flow along the ascetic channel. In the following words Cyprian tries to show the virgins their advantages.

"Hold fast, O virgins! hold fast what you have begun to be; hold fast what you shall be. A great reward awaits you, a great recompense of virtue, the immense advantage of chastity. Do you wish to know what ill the virtue of continence avoids, what good it possesses? 'I will multiply,' says God to the woman, 'thy sorrows and thy groanings; and in sorrow shalt thou bring forth children; and thy desire shall be to thy husband, and he shall rule over thee.' You are free from this sentence. You do not fear the sorrows and the groans of women. You have no fear of child-bearing; nor is your husband lord over you; but your Lord and Head is Christ, after the likeness and in the place of the man; your lot and your condition is equal [to ours]. It is the word of the Lord which says, 'The children of this world beget and are begotten; but they who are counted worthy of that world, and of the resurrection from the dead, neither marry nor are given in marriage: neither shall they die any more: for they are equal to the angels of God, being the children of the resurrection.' That which we shall be, you have already begun to be. You possess already in this world the glory of the resurrection. You pass through the world without the

contagion of the world; in that you continue chaste and virgins, you are equal to the angels of God. Only let your virginity remain and endure substantial and uninjured; and as it
began bravely, let it persevere continuously, and not seek the
ornaments of necklaces nor garments, but of conduct. Let it
look towards God and heaven, and not lower the eyes raised
up aloft to the lust of the flesh and of the world, or set it upon
earthly things." [37]

This extract acknowledges that there were many pitfalls that
rendered the virginity program difficult.

"And since we are seeking the advantage of continency, let us
also avoid everything that is pernicious and hostile to it. And
I will not pass over those things, which while by negligence
they come into use, have made for themselves a usurped licence,
contrary to modest and sober manners. Some are not ashamed
to be present at marriage parties, and in that freedom of lascivi-
ous discourse to mingle in unchaste conversation, to hear what
is not becoming, to say what is not lawful, to expose themselves, to be present in the midst of disgraceful words and
drunken banquets, by which the ardour of lust is kindled, and
the bride is animated to bear, and the bridegroom to dare lewd-
ness. What place is there at weddings for her whose mind is
not towards marriage? or what can there be pleasant or joyous in those engagements for her, where both desires and
wishes are different from her own? What is learnt there—
what is seen? How greatly a virgin falls short of her resolution, when she who had come there modest goes away immodest! Although she may remain a virgin in body and mind,
yet in eyes, in ears, in tongue, she has diminished the virtues
that she possessed." [38]

Not only were there temptations ever present, enticing to a lower
level those who sought to live the superior life, but apparently, if
we can trust Cyprian's observation, some went out of their way to
make themselves trouble.

"But what of those who frequent promiscuous baths; who

prostitute to eyes that are curious to lust, bodies that are dedi-
cated to chastity and modesty? They who disgracefully behold
naked men, and are seen naked by men, do they not themselves afford enticement to vice, do they not solicit and invite
the desires of those present to their own corruption and wrong?
'Let every one,' say you, 'look to the disposition with which he
comes thither: my care is only that of refreshing and washing
my poor body.' That kind of defence does not clear you, nor
does it excuse the crime of lasciviousness and wantonness.
Such a washing defiles; it does not purify nor cleanse the
limbs, but stains them. You behold no one immodestly, but
you yourself are gazed upon immodestly; you do not pollute
your eyes with disgraceful delight, but in delighting others
you yourself are polluted: you make a show of the bathing-
place; the places where you assemble are fouler than a theatre.
There all modesty is put off; together with the clothing of
garments, the honour and modesty of the body is laid aside;
virginity is exposed, to be pointed at and to be handled. And
now, then, consider whether when you are clothed you are
modest among men, when the boldness of nakedness has con-
duced to immodesty." [39]

The teachings of the early Church Fathers must not be torn
out of their environmental context. Although we have to assume
that the Christian writers revealed prejudice in their descriptions
of the social conditions of the Roman Empire in their time, there
is overwhelming evidence that the only fault that we can charge
against them is exaggeration. Rome had conquered more of the
world than it could unify and socialize. The spread of its power
was too rapid for the cultural assimilation necessary for both political and social security, and it became an example of the sociological principle that disintegration always follows a too rapid introduction of new *mores*. Christianity itself added to the forces which
were tending to break down the integrity of the Roman Empire.
It was more than a religion; it was a new civilization in process
and one which in turn assumed, as had the Empire, the burden of

a heterogeneous following incorporated by organization but not thoroughly assimilated.

Low morals, licentious festivities, cruel sports, political corruption, disorganization of family life, vicious slavery, and widespread indifference to the obligations of citizenship, so characteristic of the life of the people in this period, provide the background for the asceticism and the morbid preachment of such men as St. Jerome and Tertullian.

Christianity was quickly shaping itself out of the ruin of one of the greatest of the empires, but it was not only converting, it was itself being transformed by the multitudes that became allied with it. It was soon so changed that one cannot turn from the pages of *The New Testament* to the Christian writings of the third and fourth centuries without feeling strongly that the wholesome faith and abounding love of the Apostolic Era had been superseded by an idealized asceticism.

This new turn was to give direction to the spiritual life of the Middle Ages and to pass down as a background influence upon the thinking and feeling of the early settlers of the United States. It would be untrue to the facts to insist that this notion of asceticism pervaded the life-practices of the common people of the Middle Ages. There is equal evidence of looseness so that one could argue with as good reason that licentiousness was the significant feature of sex morality. What concerns us is the effect upon the status of woman that came from building the ascetic ideal with its suspicion of the sexual impulses of human nature, whether expressed in or out of lawful marriage.[40]

The monastery was the logical result of such thinking. It was, however, more than this, and we shall miss its social value unless we keep in mind that through the centuries of the Middle Ages European society was making the transition from the Roman Empire to modern Europe and that Christianity was furnishing both the motives and the energy of this long social crisis. The monk and the nun were far from being mere products of a prevailing asceticism; they bore testimony to more than the craving for security in a period when for the average man and woman little was to be had.

The whole meaning of the monastic ideal cannot be gathered until we credit it with keeping alive the desire to practice Christianity in philanthropy and other practical undertakings. Although monasticism took over and organized the ascetic ideal, it represented no mere negative reaction of life. Had this not been, its influence would have been consistently against the emergence of woman. In spite of its aggressive suppression of impulses born of the body, leading to a definition of woman which made her the chief spiritual hazard, it also opened an opportunity to individual women to live a larger life than that ordinarily provided by marriage and domestic experience. There are, as one would expect, many illustrations in monasticism of the proneness of human nature, once it starts on a morbid turn, to go to the utmost extreme, as, for example, when it became a solemn duty of a child to dissolve his love for his parent in order that he might build a high type of spiritual life.

In spite of these morbid exaggerations, the ordinary routine of the monk and the nun was closer to the career of the modern social worker than to the type of religious devotee that we should expect the ascetic teaching to produce. The monastic movement was both a recoil from the evils of the time and an attempt to hold firmly to the other-worldness so distinctive of the Christian attitude during the first century. It was also a vocation, and it was in this aspect of monasticism that we find its chief advantage to women. It seems a harsh description of the prevailing social conditions to say that aside from marriage, which carried inherently a social inferiority for most women, there was opened to them as an alternative only the life of prostitution on the one side or that of a nun on the other.

It would be impossible in interpreting the experience of women in the Middle Ages to forget the prostitute. Her occupation may have been an ugly and challenging one, but it was on this account no less significant. Prostitution came over from the social life of the Roman Empire into the Christian era, and whatever else may be said of it, it offered attractions to a multitude of women, otherwise it would not have flourished as it did. It contributed to the current thinking that helped to maintain the inferiority of women, and it was encouraged by the prevailing asceticism, as this antagonized marriage and supported the low estimation of women.[41]

The nun, who from choice turned away from domestic experience, enjoyed social prestige. This undoubtedly was one of the appeals of the convent. It was more than a refuge in the uncertain life of the period or a mere side-stepping of the burden of the conventional housewife. It offered the only out-of-the-family career that carried social respect and provided opportunity for constructive social service. The prevalence of the nunneries attests the attraction of this calling for women and particularly for the ambitious and socially prominent women.

Granting, as one must, that the convents had their share of trouble in attempting to maintain a mode of life superior to that characteristic of the surrounding social environment, it is only partisanship that would forget their contributions to the intellectual, emotional, and moral growth of women. At the head of each nunnery was the abbess, unmarried and usually a member of an important family, exercising authority and administering responsibilities that explain why she has been described as the first professional woman developed in the Christian era. Her powers were such that even heads of royal families were known not to protest when a princess chose the career of abbess in place of marriage.[42]

The attack of the flesh was, of course, an experience that those who had enlisted under the banner of asceticism had to meet within the monastery walls as well as those less spiritually committed who struggled in the outside world.[43] The ideal Christian chastity, that is, celibacy, found its highest expression in the monastery, but it was not confined to this special type of Christian living. Gradually it became a requirement demanded of the clergy. During the eleventh century, the rule which had been formulated as early as the fourth century that those entering the sacred orders should not marry began to be strictly enforced.[44]

As the priesthood increased its elevation above the laity, pressure increased upon its members to abstain from marriage and
other secular undertakings.[45] Granting that this insistence that the
priest commit himself absolutely to his spiritual calling, with none
of·the distractions that come out of domestic obligations, had its
ecclesiastical advantages, this program suggested again that the
ascetic life was the religious ideal and woman, the man's greatest
temptation.[46]

The inconsistencies of the period, as they had to do with Christian teaching, showed forth in the ecclesiastical regulations that
attempted to deal with the practical problems of ethical control.
In the code, as it had to do with monogamic marriage and infidelity, the male was given no special license releasing him from the
moral demands placed upon the woman. On the other hand, we
find regulations that define the sphere of woman, denying her not
only ecclesiastical prerogatives given the man but also shutting
her out of civic activities and making her ineligible to all civil and
public offices.[47] It is, however, the social function and position of
the average woman that concern us most. It would only be slight
exaggeration to dismiss her with the statement that she was consigned the tasks of toil and burden-carrying as housewife and
mother. Of course, as is always true in any such mass description,
there were exceptions, for some women emerged from the general
obscurity and maintained in greater or less degree individuality.

Men also had a hard life during this long transitional period from
the break-up of the Roman Empire to the European migration to
the new land of America. There was, however, a difference, and
this it is that we need to keep in mind as we survey the background
of American civilization. We must distinguish between the social
value of woman's contribution and her social recognition. Women's
activities were so thoroughly restricted to domestic responsibilities
that it is easy to get the impression that she had little social function. This was not true, for her part in the drama of the Middle
Ages was indispensable. It is rather that she had to keep to the
background while man displayed himself.

Masculine ostentatiousness and its prestige cannot be made the measurement of social service. They demonstrate no more than the dominance of masculine *mores*. Men had command of the mediums of self-expression and social distinction. Women had small part in the constant fighting of the period. They were shut out of ecclesiastical organization, aside from the opportunity of the convent, and were denied any considerable influence in the shaping of theology that so largely determined their social position. Men, aside from their control of social distinction, also gained added importance by the fact that there was a disproportion of the sexes due to the continual fighting. Women did not escape the penalties of warfare, but their deaths were fewer than the males', even though occasionally they participated in the battle, at least during times of siege.

The fact that the woman was ordinarily shut out of soldiering had its effect upon her status, just as, even as late as our own century, the most effective argument against giving women full political equality with men was based upon the insistence that they could not discharge the military responsibilities of citizenship. All through the Middle Ages the individual man, however insignificant in other respects, was at least a pawn who had his use in time of battle.

Thus there were many influences that led to the building of the inferiority status of woman so characteristic of the Middle Ages. Feudalism had lessened the woman's property rights. Her legal subordination was well expressed by Glanvill, when he asserted that husband and wife were one person and that person was the husband.[48] The same author also reveals the prevailing attitude toward women's rights of inheritance when he asserts: "If anyone has a son and heir, and besides him a daughter or daughters, *the son succeeds to the whole;* . . . because in general it is true that a woman never takes part in an inheritance with a male, unless a special exception to this exist in some particular city by the custom of that city." [49]

The limitations and disabilities of women as compared with men were registered in the legal system of the period and were carried forward by the English common law which in turn became the basis of our own legal principles, thus providing for a discrimination against women which in the legal field at least has not yet been entirely eliminated in all our states. As compared with the legal status women obtained in the Roman Empire, the general trend in the Middle Ages was toward legal inequality and incapacity. Principles were extracted from the *mores* of the time and hardened into the basic law providing a resistance to change that has obstructed woman's progress until our time.

This was truer in England than on the continent. There, with the passing of time, the feudal disabilities of women were gradually lightened and the doctrine, which was frozen into the English legal system, that husband and wife were one person, became obsolete. These handicaps discriminated against women all the more because of the advance England was making along other lines toward a more democratic, freer life. Feudal family law was dragged forward along with an increasing of constitutional and political liberties. It has been suggested that the explanation of this anomaly was the emphasis placed upon the idea of families as units as aristocracy grew strong, leading to the tendency to ignore women and younger sons.[50]

Women became the legal victims of the disposition of the wealthy to harden family life into a form that would resist social change. Concerning this Sir Frederick Pollock has written: "It might be a topic of curious meditation for the student of comparative jurisprudence to note how well the English land-owning families have striven, though all unconsciously, to produce in our modern society something like the image of an archaic Aryan household." [51]

This development of woman's disabilities appears to have extended from William the Conqueror to Glanvill. The Anglo-Saxons resisted the change, but without success, for as the military tenure of land increased, the powers and rights of women, who could not perform military service, decreased. Since the husband often had to perform feudal services for the *maritagium* of his wife, he was given certain rights in the *maritagium*. This illustrates how feudalism led to the lessening of the property rights of married women and widows.[52]

Chivalry was a bright spot in the drabness that characterized the life of the majority of women during the Middle Ages, especially those who kept to the conventional pathway and committed themselves to the domestic traditions. It was, however, hardly more than a colorful contrast, for it was distinctly aristocratic. It was a game open only to those of privilege and leisure, a way of escape from the ecclesiastical formalism and the feudalistic routine. It did at least challenge the morbid trends of asceticism and the theological conception of woman by its celebration of the erotic impulses of human nature. Distant as it seems, on account of its applaud of illicit love, from primitive Christianity, in its recognition of the independent personality of the woman and its acceptance of an association of men and women that approached an equality fellowship, it was closer to the spirit of early Christianity as that influenced the life of women than was the sentiment of the church of the period. It is easy, nevertheless, to exaggerate the practical consequences of this outburst of love literature and romantic codes of conduct.

The importance of the Renaissance also, as it has to do with the life of women, was rather in its prophecy than in what it immediately brought the average woman. It was a beginning in the building of the modern program, but at first its awakening came only to the favored few and even to them for the most part indirectly. The new civilization was in ferment, and naturally women began to profit from this as well as men. The old order, essentially static, was challenged, and a disorganization, both in church and politics, provided an opportunity for some women to gain for themselves better training for life and greater freedom of activity.

Protestantism and the counter reform of the Roman Catholic Church that came with it also advanced the status of woman, but less, perhaps, than one would have expected. Defiant as Luther was toward ecclesiastical celibacy, his attitude toward women was characteristically medieval. He conceived of marriage as a civil affair to be regulated by the state. It was "a temporal and worldly thing of no concern to the Church." His notion of womanhood was nothing extraordinary, and there was, as a result of his doctrine, no immediate lifting of the status of woman. The Reformation was middle-class in outlook and fundamentally, so far as it had to do with domestic experience, conservative. Woman remained socially inferior to man, and the proprieties defined childbearing and a narrow type of home-keeping as the obligation of her sex. Even in the home the male was dominant and there was little incentive for the woman of talent to seek self-expression in out-of-home activities, and very little opportunity.

Luther is representative of the other reformers. In his attitude toward women, John Knox was more backward than Luther, and, as one would expect, brutal in his preachments regarding the inherent inferiority of the woman and her subordination to man. If the Protestant leaders can be indicted for failure to carry their reforming far enough to permit women to recapture the promises of Christianity at its beginning, they cannot be accused of failure to recognize the social importance of the family. In his insistence upon the value of early education in the child's life, Luther comes nearer to modern thought, although, of course, his emphasis was to our present thinking narrowly religious. The effect of the Reformation upon the evolution of woman's status was something quite different from the pronouncements of the leaders. Luther, Calvin, Zwingli, and Knox were certainly not champions of woman's freedom, but unquestionably their assault on medievalism added considerably to the momentum essentially born of social circumstances that was to lift women to a higher status. In their acceptance of woman's inferiority, they were creatures of their time; as crusaders for greater individualism in their religion, they were contributing to the forces that were to enlarge the life of women and release them from social handicaps.

Protestantism had its economic aspect in addition to its religious significance. It was an expression of the final breakdown of the feudal system and an economic reconstruction that gave greater opportunity to the laboring and to the middle classes. In England, for example, the Reformation brought little transformation in the religious life, but with it came important changes in the political and the economic order that had continued on from the Middle Ages. The new situation made more important the economic contribution of woman's labor. By the sixteenth century in England, women, in addition to their rôle as domestic toilers, contributed to the economic support of the nation as skilled workers, even as persons who had achieved craftsmanship in the industrial arts and, in some instances, had become experienced in managerial responsibilities. Some women had been given partnerships in their husbands' businesses and others, as widows or daughters, had taken over trading enterprises that had been developed by their husbands or their fathers. Public documents of various sorts establish without the possibility of controversy the fact that there were women who were becoming experienced in all sorts of industrial, religious, and even political activities.[53]

Women were engaged as pawn-brokers, money-lenders, stationers, booksellers, contractors, and even ship-owners.[54] They were not only entering trade but were continuing the contribution in industry first started by the primitive woman, a basic social service that in fact has been rendered by ordinary women from the earliest stages of civilization continuously until now. For example, the number of women engaged in the seventeenth century in the woolen industry in England has been estimated from the ratio of three women to one man to the more radical statement of eight women to one man.[55] The silk industry, although not monopolized by women as once was true, was still chiefly a feminine industry, and it is interesting to note that the word "spinster" was originally used for spinner, bearing testimony to the importance of woman's part in the textile industry. Even agriculture, in all its forms, gave employment to women who in strength and skill proved themselves, in spite of the fact that they were commonly paid lower wages, not hampered by their sex in strenuous outdoor labor. Their part had become so important in agriculture that it was realized from the start by the colonization companies that aside from the value of the stabilizing influence of women as wives and mothers, they were greatly needed as workers, if the new settlements were to be made permanent and profitable. The majority of the women who went to the New World did not need to cross the Atlantic to learn the discipline that comes from earning one's living by the sweat of one's brow or to prove themselves capable of entering with their husbands and brothers into the fellowship of toil. Whether they sailed from England, Holland, Spain, Sweden, Portugal, or from France, most of them were prepared, whatever their previous class experience, to share the life of hardship and productive toil that survival in the wilderness required.

Puritanism was another influence that affected the life of women. This expression of the changing religious situation, ascetic in its disposition rather than its practices, and for the most part traditional in its concept of women, through its practical consequences led her forward. Its development in England interests us, since it had a part in the founding of American civilization.

As the feudal system crumbled away, the middle class, especially those in trade or commerce, increased their power. On the whole, this change tended to lift the social status of woman. The wives of the mercantile and craftsman classes had enjoyed a degree of freedom and responsibility throughout the Middle Ages, but the breaking up of feudalism as it occurred in the fifteenth and sixteenth centuries increased this.[56] However one interprets the political efficiency of Queen Elizabeth, there cannot be question of the significance of her position as it influenced the *mores* that fixed the status of women. Her reign stimulated interest in the relation of the sexes and encouraged discussion which in itself was testimony of a changing social situation. Books dealing with the woman question were popular. The same topic was taken over by the drama and there were plays defending and criticizing the new freedom of women. The attacks that were made by various writers on the conduct of women reveal to us that individuals had broken away from the coercive routine sufficiently to bring confusion and to draw the protest of the traditionalists.

These criticisms of women's behavior are directed especially against their attention to fashion and their extravagance. Naturally these outlets of women's interests would be the first chosen, especially by the wives of men in prosperous circumstances. Whatever else might be said of this self-expression, it evidenced an enhancement of the woman as an individual and her attempt to gain prestige by dress and luxuries that would enable her to rival other women and to distinguish herself in her contacts with men. However trivial it now appears as an expression of personality, it announced the advent of a new opportunity that English Puritanism was to give women. The criticism that resisted this self-assertion of luxury-loving women came especially from writers who belonged to the aristocracy and who were opposed to the widening of the prestige of women. There were facts enough to give support to their fault-finding, but the chief motive, whether they recognized it or not in their writing, was their desire to protect the nobility from the encroachments of the commercial class. The ambition of the wives of the merchant princes offered the most vulnerable point for attack.

We are told that even demands for equality of woman with man accompanied the social changes inaugurated by the coming to power of the wealthy middle class in England. These were, of course, few but significant as forecasting a future trend. Examples are the writings of Daniel Tuvil, William Heale, and the unknown author of *Haec-Vir*.[57] In contrast with this sentiment the opposition to the enlarging freedom of women was frank and aggressive, and those hostile to the change denounced the new woman for her vices and extravagance. In spite of this, the evidence seems to be that the attitude of people in general was not unfriendly to the progress women were making.[58] This was not due to a widespread indifference as to whether or not home life was healthy, for, on the contrary, there seems to have been some interest in the idea of strengthening domestic relations by specific instruction in preparation for marriage and for motherhood. This program, as one would expect, was built upon the Bible as its basic text and represented the constructive answer to the criticisms that the luxury-loving, irresponsible woman was getting. It is easy in these times to underestimate the importance of this program for the buttressing of the family, because it seems so clearly static in character. There was no thought of preparing the woman for the freedom of life that she was to gain by sharing in the development of the American civilization on the other side of the Atlantic, but rather the thought was merely to help the middle-class women handle more successfully their household and motherhood responsibilities. It at least stressed the importance of the domestic career of the usual woman.

From another quarter also appears evidence of the changing status of woman. There began to be greater interest in the problem of divorce and a weakening of the conventional acceptance of woman's subordination to man. It is easy to exaggerate this because it stands out in contrast with the bulk of opinion which still defines woman's status in the spirit of the Middle Ages. In the literature that dealt with women and their problems this discussion of the spiritual and material rights of women at least opened up the way for the spread of the idea of their theoretical equality. It gave a slant toward contemporary social problems that enhanced the individuality of the woman and provided a way of escape from the general definition of inequality that had for so long remained an unquestioned assumption of the dominant feeling and thinking.

The trend toward a broader and freer opportunity for women that had so faintly started in the English environment was to gain impetus, without intention and for the most part without protest, as a result of the conditions that had to be met by the immigrants in the New World England could not be carried across the Atlantic. A new world forced a new order. In man's realm, politics, this was destined to appear in the most impressive and dramatic of possible expressions—a collision of the old and the new that made war inescapable. The quieter and less recognized social mutation in woman's sphere, with its ramifications and practical consequences, is beginning to seem, however, in its contrast to the trend of centuries, the most profound and the most revolutionary contribution to the modern world that has as yet come out of human experience in America.

FOOTNOTES

THE CULTURAL BACKGROUND OF THE AMERICAN WOMAN

[1] R. Briffault, *The Mothers,* Vol. III, p. 360.

[2] *The Catholic Encyclopaedia,* Vol. I, p. 771.

[3] *The Jewish Encyclopaedia,* Vol. V, p. 224.

[4] J. Hastings, *A Dictionary of the Bible,* Vol. I, p. 768 (Philo Judaeus, *Quod Omnis Probus Liber*).

[5] Josephus, *De Bello Judaico,* Vol. II, Books 8 and 13.

[6] J. Hastings, *op. cit.,* (Eusebius, *Praeparatio Evangelica*).

[7] *The Jewish Encyclopaedia,* Vol. V, p. 228.

[8] J. Hastings, *op. cit.,* p. 771.

[9] *The Jewish Encyclopaedia,* Vol. V, p. 232.

[10] J. Hastings, *op. cit.,* p. 771.

[11] R. Briffault, *op. cit.,* p. 349.

[12] W. W. Fowler, *The Religious Experience of the Roman People,* p. 466.

[13] St. Jerome, *The Nicene and Post-Nicene Fathers,* Vol. VI, p. 25.

[14] *Galatians,* 2: 20.

[15] F. C. Porter, *The Mind of Christ in Paul,* p. 219.

[16] R. Briffault, *op. cit.,* p. 372.

[17] A. Harnack, *The Mission and Expansion of Christianity in the First Three Centuries,* Vol. I, p. 216.

[18] I *Timothy,* 2: 9.

[19] A. Harnack, *op. cit.,* Vol. II, p. 64.

[20] *Galatians,* 3: 28.

[21] *Philippians,* 4: 3.

[22] A. Harnack, *op. cit.,* Vol. II, p. 67.

[23] *Romans,* 16: 1–2.

[24] See I *Timothy,* Ch. 5.

[25] A. Harnack, *op. cit.,* Vol. II, p. 71.

[26] For a stronger statement see S. D. Schmalhausen and V. F. Calverton, *Woman's Coming of Age* (A Symposium), p. 52.

[27] E. Gibbon, *The Decline and Fall of the Roman Empire,* Vol. I, p. 414.

[28] St. Jerome, *op. cit.,* Vol. VI, p. 31.

[29] *Ibid.*, p. 75.

[30] *Ibid.*, p. 71.

[31] *Ibid.*, p. 260.

[32] *Ibid.*, p. 29.

[33] W. Goodsell, *A History of Marriage and the Family*, p. 170.

[34] *The Writings of Clement of Alexandria*, Vol. II, p. 193.

[35] *Ibid.*, p. 196.

[36] *Ibid.* p. 197.

[37] *The Writings of Cyprian*, Vol. I, pp. 348–349.

[38] *Ibid.*, p. 346.

[39] *Ibid.*, p. 346–347.

[40] W. E. H. Lecky, *History of European Morals*, Vol. II, p. 122.

[41] See *Encyclopaedia of the Social Sciences*, Vol. XII, p. 554; also, Paul LaCroix, *History of Prostitution*, Vol. II, especially Ch. VI.

[42] L. Eckenstein, *Woman Under Monasticism*, p. 152.

[43] G. G. Coulton, *Five Centuries of Religion*, Ch. 28.

[44] *The Encyclopaedia of the Social Sciences*, Vol. III, p. 284.

[45] G. B. Fisher, *History of the Christian Church*, pp. 62 and 101.

[46] *The Encyclopaedia of the Social Sciences*, Vol. III, p. 284.

[47] M. B. Messer, *The Family in the Making*, p. 167.

[48] W. Goodsell, *op. cit.*, p. 227.

[49] *Ibid.*, p. 226.

[50] Buckstaff, F. G. "Married Women's Property in Anglo-Saxon and Anglo-Norman Law," *Annals of the American Academy of Political and Social Science*, 4, 1893–1894, p. 261.

[51] *Ibid.*, p. 262.

[52] *Ibid.*, pp. 256–257.

[53] C. A. and M. R. Beard, *The Rise of American Civilization*, p. 25.

[54] *Ibid.*, p. 26.

[55] *Ibid.*, p. 26.

[56] L. B. Wright, *Middle-Class Culture in Elizabethan England*, p. 202.

[57] *Ibid.*, pp. 506–507.

[58] *Ibid.*, p. 507.

CORRESPONDENCE

Deterrents to Parenthood

To the Editor, Eugenics Review

DEAR SIR,—The information presented—largely statistically—in your pages with regard to the forces that are affecting both the quality and quantity of the births occurring inside civilization is of immense importance and value. But is it not possible to claim that this very natural reliance on figures is not all that should affect our conclusions? Reproduction depends on the exercise of functions upon which there is so much diffidence and suppression that the collection of statistics that are reliable must be—at least in some aspects —extremely difficult. In so much, therefore, that relates to the matters in which we are particularly concerned we are left too much to the revelations made to those who act as father confessors—with a consequent necessity of concealing their knowledge. It is tempting to the generous-minded to attribute an undue value to economic forces. If we can persuade ourselves that an improvement in material conditions will ensure a corresponding advance in the average intelligence it enables us to hope that we shall one day, and that a not very distant one, have what is called an educated people. Now no one ought to minimize the very great importance of economic forces. Indeed, there is no likelihood of any considerable number of advanced people doing that at the present time. The tendency is too much the other way, and that tendency calls for someone to emphasize the other forces that are at work.

Let me put it as it appears to me. The same benevolent enthusiasm that makes the value of economic forces so attractive to us, because they imply that the achievement of social justice will be rewarded by an improvement in the peoples who enjoy it, includes in this social justice the extension to women of every facility for higher education. It not only appeals to a sense of social justice but to a very strong instinctive chivalry. Hence that anyone should question the unalloyed good of this policy of education seems to most generous-minded people as something like a superfluity of naughtiness. Many of these people claim to have scientific minds, and to me that means that they claim to look facts in the face without being blinded by prejudice or sentiment. It is to be feared that this claim is not always borne out by the actions of those who make it. Even if we do see other causes at work beside the economic or recognize that there are some things in the matter besides statistics, we are all tempted to avoid putting them forward since they seem to debit us with an ungenerousness that is contemptible.

Yet what is our demur? Is it the invention of some entirely illusory theory? What we say is that we have noticed that the student habit in women aborts the sexual instinct and consequently removes from the field of reproduction the very best type of mother. That is the emotional and psychological aspect. On the economic side we find that the better off people become, the lower falls their birth rate, so that the prospect in that direction is no more comforting than that seen in the other just mentioned.

These remarks are confined to the effect of emotional and economic causes on the birth rate of the best types. But if by our enquiries we are seeking to find a happier social order, and that is the justification for our policy, can we be said to make for this happiness by ensuring that nearly every marriage of one of the better types of women is a disaster to her husband? Indeed, we may accompany this with an immense improvement in the environment of that husband; but will that outcome of our stressing the importance of economics compensate for a permanently unhappy marriage? Will it compensate the nation for the steady reduction in the intelligence of its members? I have seen these marriages. My opinion is that a dinner of herbs and love therewith is very much better than the stalled ox of improved economic conditions, if along with them is sacrifice and strife.

Of course it can be contended that it is an advantage that we are heading for a population of dull mentality. If we make higher education accessible to all, if all could profit by it then there would be such a demand for the black-coated jobs of society and such an incapacity to supply that demand that we should have a population suffering from such a sense of frustration as to make certain that the new order would not be happier than the old. Thus a prominent medical man never tires of impressing on me the very great importance of securing a sufficiency of mental defect in the people if we are to get the world's work done. It is a disappointing prospect. Society without intelligence or marriage without love. If some way out of the dilemma could be found it would be welcomed by those who, in spite of wishful thinking, have been compelled to recognize disagreeable facts.

S. H. HALFORD.

7 Bruce Grove,
Tottenham, N.17.

CORRESPONDENCE

An Objective View ?

To the Editor, Eugenics Review

SIR,—One wonders if it is generally possible for those who are really concerned about the future of the human race to be capable of objectivity. The frame of mind that is responsible for their interest makes them alas! in too many cases far too wishful readily to face disagreeable facts. They become like the fond parents whose great affection for their children makes them claim, when these fail at school, that the failure is due to the schoolmaster, or to the system that he operates, and not to the inherent incapacity of the pupil. It seems as if the April issue of the *Eugenics Review* manifests such wishful thinking in a more than usually marked degree ; and I find it depressing in spite of having become all too familiar with the attitude it represents during the fifty years in which I have been in the Labour movement. Statements appear about what would have happened to Shakespeare if in his childhood he had been deprived of iodine. These do not seem to mean much, nor does calling the dispute about the relative value of heredity and environment " sterile " amount to anything more than sterile declamation.

The same notes quote from a writer who states that " there is every reason to believe that innate mental capacity is more or less equally distributed in all its phases in all human groups." When I read that amazing claim there came back to my mind a book written by the Director of Education of the South African province of Natal in which the achievements of Negro, Hindu and European children in the state schools were compared. He anticipated that the poor position of the negro child would be explained by wishful thinkers as being due to working in a language not its own and so being unfairly handicapped against the whites. The writer of the book effectually disposed of this very natural argument by pointing out that the Hindu children were under the same disadvantage and yet in some departments excelled the whites.

Indeed, no one has ever attempted to explain why, if all races are inherently equal, the negro, although from the earliest ages in close contact with civilization, has never even borrowed, let alone developed a civilization. That fact alone should effectually destroy extravagant claims made for the equality of all races.

It looks as if the same desire to believe in the possibility of indefinite improvement in human beings accounts for much of the blind clinging to the notion that the only force seriously affecting humanity is the economic. It is asserted that every problem will be solved and mankind made happy, wise, honest and healthy if economic factors are properly organized. Achieve but a fullness of bread and everything else will fall into

its right place! Marx does seem to claim that economic forces are the only things that matter ; yet another famous thinker—Freud—argues that sexual desire is the one that really counts. But another writer of the same language—Goethe—makes a statement that appears to me to be nearer the truth where he says " Lust and Hunger rule the world." I submit that Goethe hits the mark, and that those who require us to believe that only one of these forces is effective are asking us to plan a lop-sided society for future generations. No sensible person would deny the importance of economic forces. Their inclusion in the forefront of our planning for the future is essential. Yet to those who have some grasp of psychological principles it seems quite as important to bring these also into account. We actually take a Pharisaic pride in ignoring them and count it a merit that we decline to face the consequences of processes that are making for an intelligent womanhood incapable psychologically of wifehood and motherhood and economically deterred from both. Are we not, perhaps unintentionally, working for a future in which men will discover that the stalled ox and sacrifice and strife—which the economists are unconsciously preparing for mankind—are no improvement on the dinner of herbs and love therewith ? But, it may be contested, as a consequence of ignoring psychological factors and the resultant elimination of intelligent women from the business of reproduction there will, in the future, be generally none but the dull to deal with and their unintelligence will ensure the capacity for love. That is true, but can anyone think that the future is a happy prospect if it consist, as McDougall suggests, of a vast mass of dull clods governed and led by a very small minority of intelligent persons ? Those who think they have found the truth as it is in Marx and deny the potent force of heredity claim that the system of education they intend in the society of the future will remedy the paucity of inborn mental capacity in the great majority of people. How common this delusion about the effect of education is! The average man or woman thinks, for instance, that children of the rich are all intelligent and are so because their parents' wealth secures them entrance without question to one or other of the great public schools where the training is so effective that they must emerge accomplished scholars with nothing in front of them but an easy walk over at the university. I remarked this recently to the headmaster of one of our greatest public schools. " What nonsense! " he exclaimed. " I have just turned down five boys whom I considered unsuitable. I can't make a silk purse out of a sow's ear." Unfortunately the claim of most social reformers is that we can ; and they are indignant at the " inhuman " frame of mind that says otherwise. The new Education Act abounds in intellectual dishonesty because it truckles to the unproved belief that most children have a limitless capacity for reacting beneficially to a properly-designed system of education.

The attitude of so many of the writers referred to in the April *Review* suggests that too many who address themselves to the matters in which our *Society* is interested are afraid to face facts that are disappointing to their kind hearts. There is a tendency to adopt a belief in the efficacy of improved environment just because that seems to be within our control. Besides, it affords the wishful thinker more room for hope and less fear of the consequences of stimulating the psychological and economic tendencies that are so rapidly impoverishing human stocks. Their attitude may be judged by such assertions as " Let Justice be done though the Heavens fall! " As if justice could be done so.   S. H. HALFORD.
London, N.17.

Trend of National Intelligence

To the Editor, Eugenics Review

SIR,—I was unfortunately prevented from attendance at the very interesting Galton Lecture delivered by Dr. Godfrey Thomson last February. Otherwise I might have drawn attention to what seems to me a very important omission in his treatment of the " Trend of National Intelligence." In a contribution that I made recently to the EUGENICS REVIEW I referred slightly to the psychological factor operative in the process of reproduction and it appears necessary to call attention to the omission of its consideration from Dr. Thomson's paper. I refer to the now undoubted fact that the highly educated woman as a direct consequence of her adoption of the student habit very frequently loses the sexual instinct. But she is just the one who achieves the highly paid post and thus also endows herself with a strong economic bias to celibacy, or, if she does marry, against the bearing of children. But while recognizing this economic factor one must claim that it is the psychological that is really the important one even if the economic intensifies the problem. Let me illustrate and emphasize the matter by quoting a specific instance. I had a friend who was engaged to a girl with whom he was very much in love. She was a young schoolmistress (that type that is such a favourite with American novelists), a perfect blonde and with a good deal of intelligence. She married and the union resulted in a most unhappy situation and after a long endurance was ended by a divorce. Now had the modern very natural desire for the higher education of women not provided the opportunity for it in the case mentioned the girl would have entered some manual or domestic calling where the big salary would not occur and fairly early in life she would have married and passed on her intelligence to her children.

The statement will probably arouse in many minds a profound resentment. Especially will the highly educated woman be provoked, for the associations of sex to which, if she be a well-brought-up person, she will attach many powerful educational prejudices, will make it seem repulsive. She will never have these prejudices corrected by the emergence of desires that would naturally adjust them. It is a strange disappointing situation for civilization to bring us to. It seems ironical that the general desire to give to women all those things that seem most beneficial should be leading to the inevitable impoverishment of the race and in addition should be making marriage difficult in the case of those who are most attractive as wives and very disastrous to those who achieve it. To the husbands it promises a Dead Sea apple.

It seems impossible to suggest any remedy, especially in the present state of popular prejudice, but the difficulty will not be removed by ignoring it.

S. H. HALFORD.

7 Bruce Grove,
N.17.

Her Work

6:30	Nurse Baby
7:15	Dress Shawn, Rusty
7:30	Fix Breakfast
7:45	Breakfast for All
8:00	Husband John to WorK
	Wash Dishes
	Clean Downstairs
	Call Grocer's
9:00	Shawn, Rusty in Yard
	Bathe Baby
	Make Beds
	Clean Upstairs
10:30	Nurse Baby
11:00	Fix Lunch
11:30	Lunch for Shawn, Rusty
12:00	John Home
	Lunch with John
1:00	John to Work
	Naps for Shawn, Rusty
	Wash Dishes
	Nap for Marjorie
2:30	Nurse Baby
2:45	Rouse Shawn, Rusty
3:00	Shawn, Rusty Play
	Gardening Outdoors
	or
	Mending Indoors
5:00	Fruit Juice for Baby
	Fix Supper
5:30	Supper for Shawn, Rusty
6:00	John Home
	Baths for Shawn, Rusty
6:30	Shawn, Rusty in Bed
	Nurse Baby
7:00	Dress for Dinner
7:15	Cocktail with John
7:30	Fix Dinner
8:00	Dinner with John
9:00	Wash Dishes
10:30	Nurse Baby
10:45	Take Shawn, Rusty
	to Bathroom
11:00	Bed

American Woman's Dilemma

She wants a husband and she wants children.
Should she go on working? Full time? Part time?
Will housework bore her?
What will she do when her children are grown?

by Frances Levinson

The friendly young lady in the picture above is Miss Gwenyth Jones, 23, secretary to an investment counselor in New York City. She has clear brown eyes, a shy and pleasant smile, good health, a college education and several young men who think she would make a fine wife. Like most of her contemporaries she cannot sew or cook very well but expects to manage all right when the time comes.

If she had been born a generation ago, she would probably still be living with her parents in the white-stucco house in Lovelock, Nev. where she was born. She would consider marriage quite a complete future, and her one big decision would be the choice of a husband. But being a typical young lady of 1947 she has a good degree and a range of interests that make her situation more complicated. She is just as interested in getting married and having children as she would have been a few decades ago. But housework and child care alone no longer seem interesting enough for a lifetime job.

Her choices after marriage are 1) a full-time career combined with motherhood, and 2) full-time housework. The first is likely to be very hard when her children are young and need her attention, but it will leave her well-rounded in interests and experience when she has reached the free years after 40.

Full-time housework, on the other hand, has compensations when her children are small. But a mother's schedule is so filled with routine tasks that she cannot keep up with her husband's interests. And once her children have grown, a housewife of 40, lacking outside interests or training, is faced with vacant years.

Miss Jones has, however, a third choice. It is to combine part-time work with housekeeping while she is young and to use this experience more fully when her children have left home.

One the following pages LIFE shows how a number of U.S. women are spending their lives—in full-time careers, housework, idleness and part-time occupations. From their experiences Miss Jones of Lovelock and other Miss Joneses of the U.S. may draw lessons for their own futures.

Full-Time Career

Many young girls go right on working at full-time jobs after they get married because they find offices and factories more satisfying than housework and child care. This is a good plan but only if they are very successful and earn enough money to provide their children with secure and well-run homes.

The two women pictured at left have exceptional careers. One runs her own public relations firm, the other is a top-ranking lawyer. Together with their husbands they have family incomes which run well into five figures. Their households are staffed with expertly trained help, so that they can enjoy their non-working hours in leisurely comfort with their children.

But for Mrs. Joseph Gloss (*right*), a factory employee, things are not so simple. She and her husband do not make enought money to hire a servant and have had to board out their 4-year-old son during the week. Recently a sister came to stay and look after the child, but if she leaves, the mother will again have to resign herself to seeing her boy only on weekends.

Housewife: A Nice Husband, Three Fine Children Keep Her Busy 100 Hours a Week

Mrs. John McWeeney of Rye, N.Y. has a big, good-looking husband who works in a nut and bolt company and three children, Shawn, a grave little 4-year-old; John, called "Rusty," almost 2, and baby Mark, 4 months old. She lives in a bright new seven-room house that has a safe backyard for Shawn and Rusty to play in and a number of modern machines to help her with her household chores. She uses a diaper service and she can afford a cleaning woman once a week who does the heavy laundry.

But even under these better than average circumstances Marjorie McWeeney's hours are long and her work demanding. She must keep an eye on her children during their 70 waking hours a week and also watch over them when they are supposed to be in bed but may actually be popping down the stairs to ask for water or an extra goodnight kiss.

The picture at the left shows the household tasks that Marjorie must accomplish every week. She has a crib and four beds to make up each day, totaling 35 complete bed-makings a week. She has hundreds of knives, forks and utensils to wash, food to buy and prepare for a healthy family of five and a whole house to dust and sweep. Every day of the week Marjorie must stick to the minimum schedule of chores listed in the time column.

Actually Marjorie's chores are much lighter than they would have been a few generations ago. She cleans with machinery propelled by electricity, she uses food prepared in canneries, she buys clothes factory-made to fit every member of the family. But her jobs, though relieved of old-time drudgery, have none of the creative satisfactions of home baking, home preserving, home dressmaking. And, because her family unit is small with no aunts or cousins in the household, all the time she saves from housework must go into supervision of her children. Unless she makes special arrangements with a baby-sitter, she has no relief from child care.

Many women in Marjorie's position feel that this is a life of drudgery, that it is not good for Marjorie, a graduate of a junior college, to stay with small children long, continuous hours. Marjorie herself has no desire to work outside. Because as an individual she likes the job that she does, she has no problem right now. Like most busy young housewives, however, she gives little thought to the future—to satisfactory ways of spending the important years after her children have grown up and left home.

Idleness: Millions of Women Find Too Much Leisure Can Be Heavy Burden

The Bureau of Labor Statistics lists 20 million women, nearly half of all adult female Americans, as essentially idle. They do not have children under 18, they are not members of the labor force, they do not work on farms, nor are they aged or infirm. With not nearly enough to do, many of them are bored stiff.

The fact that time hangs heavily on their hands is not entirely their fault. Many are over 40 and belong to a generation which frowned on work for any but poverty-stricken women. Their husbands have worked hard to give them an easeful life. Now that they have it, it is a burden. This is because an untrained woman has difficulty finding satisfying tasks to fill her days. Social work, which once busied many women, is now largely handled by professionals. As a result, many of these "idle" women fall back on numbing rounds of club meetings and card-playing. They read too much low-grade fiction and escape too readily into dream realms of movies and soap operas.

It is this group that has become the butt of the cartoonists and of critical social commentators. Marynia Farnham and Ferdinand Lundberg, in their best-seller, *Modern Woman: The Lost Sex*, complain, "Some unknown percentage of the women classified as housewives are functionally little more than wastrels seething into afternoon movies, tea shops, cocktail lounges, expensive shopping centers."

In this desert of wasted time, a few women, particularly young ones, nevertheless, are discovering that there are more satisfying and useful ways of spending their days.

Part-Time Career

One solution for a bored housewife or an idle woman is the part-time career. It is usually possible for a housewife, once her children are off to school, to find a few hours a week to begin a program of absorbing work. As her children grow independent, she can give more and more time to her outside interests.

Young women who can afford to work without pay can make useful, satisfying careers out of civic and charitable work if they take time to develop professional skills like Mrs. Johnson. Part-time jobs are harder to find and not all are as glamorous as that of the television announcer on the opposite page. But the other women shown here have all found jobs they like.

In some communities play clubs for children and group sitter plans are giving housewives time to spend away from home. Multiple laundries, "washeterias," where women can do their washing pleasantly and quickly by machine, are helping too. Once she has arranged for free hours, it is up to each woman to fill this time with really satisfying efforts. She will find it much easier to make a beginning at this while still in her 20s and 30s.

If she finds none of the jobs in these pictures suited to her individual needs, she might read books for a publisher, do research projects for an author, write scripts for local radio broadcasts. She might prefer to bake cakes at home for community sale.

She might open a bookshop, run a circulating library of art prints for the town museum, design Christmas cards, sell real estate, open a school for women's handwork, become a laboratory assistant in a hospital or work on a town slum-clearange project with other women. She might discover that certain businesses in her locale such as department stores are giving their regular staff two-day weekends and need part-time help to fill in the extra days.

When she finds really satisfying work to do she will discover that she is more interesting to her friends, to her husband and herself.

What the Experts Say: Books, Articles Debate "Woman Question"
by Frances Levinson

Any woman of 1947 trying to plan a way of life for herself does not lack for advice. She can pick up a current magazine, go into the nearest book shop and find a welter of literature scarcely dry from the presses. In these she will discover herself castigated, pitied, praised, worried over and analyzed into scientifically positive but completely contradictory generalizations. She is never described as an individual. She is, instead, always a mythical figure called "the American woman." Within the pages of a single article she is told that she cries less than grandma because increased sex equality has relieved her sense of frustration and at the same time that she drinks almost three times as much as she did a decade ago.

If she has a hardy constitution she can peruse the works of a violent school of critics, who leaped into the fray when Philip Wylie, in *Generation of Vipers*, sounded the cry, "Gentlemen, mom is a jerk." Wylie claimed, "Mom ... is about 25 pounds overweight ... there is not sex appeal enough to budge a hermit 10 paces off a rock ledge. She none the less spends several hundred dollars a year on permanents and transformations, pomades, cleaners, rouges, lipsticks, and the like—and fools nobody except herself ... . She smokes 30 cigarets a day, chews gum and consumes tons of bonbons and petits fours ... . She plays bridge with the stupid voracity of a hammerhead shark ... . On Saturday nights ... [she] is liable to get a little tiddly, which is to say, shot or blind. ... Mom is organization minded ... . Clubs afford mom an infinite opportunity for nosing into other people's business."

Only slightly less acid pens have compiled data on, "The Trouble with Women," "Do American Men Like Women?" (the answer, naturally, is "no"), "Women Have No Manners," "Women Aren't Funny," "Most Women Aren't Gentlemen," "Are Women Drinking Too Much?" replete with references to women's "aggressive and uncontrolled behavior."

When the attacked female feels the need for solace and sympathy she can find that too. She may pick up *Why Women Cry, Woman's Chains,*" Woman, The Scapegoat," and if really bruised she can turn to "Are Wives People?" She may buy a copy of *Modern Woman: The Lost Sex*, by Dr. Marynia Farnham and Ferdinand Lundberg, which depicts in most despairing tones the desolate and utter tragedy of her lot. After reading this Dorothy Parker mused, "There is something curiously flattering in being described by the adjective 'lost'. ... I find myself digging my toe into the sand and simpering, 'Oh

Dr. Farnham and Mr. Lundberg, come on now—you say that to every sex!'"

The impact of all these words has an inevitably disturbing effect on an average woman. Mystery-writer Dorothy Sayers commented in *Vogue*, "Probably no man has ever troubled to imagine how strange his life would appear to himself if it were unrelentingly assessed in terms of his maleness. ... If from school and lecture-room, press and pulpit, he heard the persistent outpouring of a shrill and scolding voice, bidding him remember his biological function. If he were vexed by continual advice on how to add a rough male touch to his typing, how to be learned without losing his masculine appeal, how to combine chemical research with seduction. ... His newspaper would assist him with a 'Men's Corner'. ... If he gave an interview to a reporter ... he would find it recorded in such terms as these: 'Professor Bract, although a distinguished botanist, is not in any way an unmanly man. He has in fact, a wife and seven children'. ... And at dinner parties he would hear the wheedling unctuous predatory female voice demand: 'And why should you trouble your handsome little head about politics?' If, after a few centuries of this kind of treatment, the male was a little self-conscious, a little on the defensive and a little bewildered about what was required of him, I should not blame him. If he traded a little upon his sex, I could forgive him. If he presented the world with a major social problem, I should scarcely be surprised. It would be more surprising if he retained any rag of sanity and self-respect."

Some writers blame society for woman's dilemma; others blame woman herself. But whatever the cause, most of them admit that millions of women today are not particularly happy. And they agree on the following basic facts.

What they agree on

1) The old-style rural home as a center for family life is virtually extinct, and with it has gone the function of women-mothers, women-relatives and girl-daughters as administrators and producers in household activities. The home is a small, single-family unit, which consumes the contents of cans, ready-made clothes, and the energy of electric wall-plugs. Even babies are no longer born within its walls. The writers who do maintain that women must "go back to the home" do not take into account that an entire economic revolution would be necessary to restore the ideal agrarian homesteads.

2) Women have lost their places as educators of the young. Children go to school younger and for longer hours than ever. They receive no training in reading, writing or old-time household skills from the women of their family.

3) Many husbands evince less and less interest in the activities of their wives. One book says, "She is deprived of her husband's companionship during the long hours of the day when he is away from home and often the evening finds him preoccupied and distintersted in the affairs that concern her." A skyrocketing national divorce rate attests to very serious cleavages between husbands and wives.

4) Concurrently women seem obsessed to look and behave like the slim and fashionable manikins they see gliding before them on movie screens, magazine pages and poster

advertisements. Last year U.S. women contributed $650 million to cosmetics industries. "Women feel it necessary," complains one heckler, "not to improve on nature but to disguise it." Fed by Hollywood romances and impressed by the odd siren-housewives who star in soap operas, women dream their way into a life that contrasts unhappily with their own surroundings and prosaic relations with their husbands.

5) Women as displaced persons are unadjusted to their lot. Farnham and Lundberg say, "In the U.S. at the present time there are, despite all the women who work in and out of the home, a greater proportion of aimlessly idle women than at any previous time or other place, not excepting imperial Rome."

The experts who stand ready with solutions for the U.S. woman's dilemma are divided into two classes: the feminists, who believe women are unhappy because they are still tied to the home, and the antifeminists, who believe women are unhappy because they have ventured too far from the home.

The antifeminists state that woman made her big mistake when she began to imitate man and made progress in the out-of-the-home working world. "Every new step she takes toward freedom lands her higher and drier in nowhere." Dr. Helene Deutsch in *The Psychology of Women* insists upon certain psychic qualities of femaleness that must not be denied: "All observations point to the fact that the intellectual woman is masculinized." Another psychiatrist, Dr. Ralph S. Banay, maintains, "Women are restless and dissatisfied because they cannot or will not accept their physical destiny."

Some of the suggestions of these antifeminists include government subsidy for motherhood and prizes for excellence in raising a family. "Even the best mother resents the fact that she is never promoted, ... never gets paid, though her hours are longer than in any men's industry." Some even propose that no spinsters be allowed to teach in schools, that mothers take over all educational posts.

Quite firmly on the other side of the fence are the feminists, who insist, "bearing babies may account for women's slight predisposition to conserve human life, some slight difference in attitude toward society and aptitude for citizenship, or it may not. It is not, at any rate, a very important factor."* They take the view that women have always worked, must work, and if they have lagged behind men in leaving the home and entering the community, it is time they busied themselves and caught up with men in the new fields. The belief is that every adult must feel functional and secure and this state may be achieved just as well by performing necessary tasks outside the home as well as in. "Modern woman is not lost," says a psychiatrist, Lena Levine, who takes issue with her colleague, Dr. Farnham. "She will not be free, however, and will not have the emotional security she seeks until she integrates her emotions with the physical independence she has achieved by her entrance into the industrial and business world."

Elizabeth Hawes, in *Why Women Cry*, recommends a vigorous regimen for the working mother. She visualizes first-rate child-care nurseries, group plans for housecleaning, cooking, baby-watching, and reads a desperation in the young mother's wish to be away from her children. She says, "Of course every woman wants some kind of work outside her home. No woman on God's earth wants to have her entire life swing around a solitary, boring, repetitive business which means exhausting herself washing the same dishes and clothes day in and day out—cooking food for the same people, seldom seeing a living soul other than a tired husband and her own children for more than a very short time." But many a young girl, in her early stages of motherhood, would murmur along with Marjorie McWeeney (pp. 104-107), "O come now, it isn't so bad as all that." Any many a modern woman, seriously interested in her vocation, is realizing that her children for the first five or six years of their lives need more time and loving attention from their own mother than the average woman with a full-time outside job can reasonably provide.

A Moderate Solution

A middle-of-the-road view between feminism and antifeminism is expressed by those who feel woman should concentrate on her home at one stage of her life and on the community at another stage.

A successful mother-and-historian, Margaret Perry Burton, writes, "Still generally unrecognized are the results of the fact that a woman's life today usually falls into discontinuous sections. ... The basic necessity is to prepare herself while living through one stage of her life for the one which is to follow. If it were frankly recognized that the majority of women find their greatest happiness in the successful fulfillment of their role as wife and mother, and that their vocation will probably ... become an avocation during the years when they are bringing up a family, would it not be easier for girls to accept the severe restrictions on their activities which come to the mothers of young children?"* Along these lines it is suggested that modern daughters would find easier adjustment if they learned child psychology, physiology and household engineering along with their necessary sound schooling in scientific method, history, economics and literature. One psychiatrist even recommends a course in mothercraft as compulsory for all schoolgirls. A Vassar alumna turned wife, with tongue only slightly in cheek, suggests a course to build up in women students "Frustration Tolerance" that starts as follows:

"Lesson I: *Resisting Noise* (Elementary) 'Student's regular assignments for the day are to be prepared in a room next to *a*) a crying baby and *b*) a group of 4-year-olds re-enacting the Invasion of Normandy. (If such are not readily available at Vassar, use a drill compressor.) Start student with 15 minutes' exposure, work up to one, two and three hours.'

"Lesson II: *Accepting Interruption*. (Elementary) 'Give student one hour to prepare a bibliography on *Dry Soil Erosion in Dutchess County*. Interrupt her at irregular intervals ... with requests to bandage your finger, to tie a string, to hold baby, to put toddler on toilet ... to answer telephone, to let in gas man, to shut door after gas man.'"

Mrs Burton suggests that the busy young housewife, as well, must eye her future years, "If the young mothers were better trained to understand that they must be constantly building their bridges out into the community, then, instead of being confronted in the 40s with relative unemployment and the loneliness, frustration and suffering which go with it, they would be more ready to use their experience and talents creatively outside the home."

The most confusing part about her dilemma is that every woman finds herself classified with all women. She is considered intuitive, practical, like all of them, good at interior decorating, endowed by nature to select cereal brands on grocery shelves. It may be perfectly right, natural and normal for a man to choose to be a mathematician, musician, beachcomber or circus barker, but such variation is seldom considered for a woman. Mrs. Burton concludes, "People are forever saying that women are thus and so; whereas women are not all thus and so. ... A pattern of life which is entirely satisfying for one kind of woman may be torment for another. ... Women will have to hammer out their own solutions in an infinite variety of patterns fitted to the needs and limitations of their personalities and circumstances."

Whichever way a woman chooses to solve her dilemma, arguments will continue to rage. She must steel herself because sooner or later some man is bound to comment, "a woman hasn't any problems if you keep her pregnant in summer and barefoot in winter."

*The Annals of The American Academy of Political and Social Science

SHOULD MOTHERS WORK?

IRENE M. JOSSELYN, M.D., AND RUTH SCHLEY GOLDMAN

THE belief that it should not be necessary for a mother to work in order to provide bare sustenance for her small children is becoming increasingly a part of our social philosophy. As this conviction has gained support throughout this country, it has found expression not only in the practices of private social agencies but also in provisions of the federal social security legislation which make available financial assistance for mothers who have no other means of providing for their children.

A social philosophy translated into its practical implications means increased taxes and/or increased demands upon the budgets of community chests. All the forces against increased taxation or increased expenditures by private agencies are then mobilized to hamper the fulfilment of the theoretically acceptable social philosophy. The struggle between the desire to aid fatherless children and to lessen the burden their mothers must carry and the demand that expenditures be kept at a minimum results in various attempts to find a satisfactory compromise. At times it is suggested that mothers with one child can work or that mothers who are physically and mentally able should work. In other cases the anger of society or the resentment of the social worker is expressed in the demand that a particular mother work. If the mother has violated social mores, society wishes to punish her. If her rapport with the social worker has been poor, the worker may wish to punish her. The underlying motivations, as well as unwise penuriousness, can be masked by subservience to the demands of economy.

The limits of taxation or of a community-chest budget are dangerous criteria for evaluating the responsibility to be assumed by any community. Funds for preventive measures are too often sacrificed in order to meet the demands for community care of those who, because preventive measures were curtailed, have become either a danger to, or a burden upon, society. Funds supplied to care for destroyed personalities provide only relative safety and a clear conscience for society. Funds utilized for the proper care of children are invested funds paying dividends in terms of the ultimate contributions made by those children when they become adults. It is, after all, an established fact that what the adult becomes is to a large extent dependent upon his childhood. Taxation or private agency expenditures which provide an optimum physical and emotional environment for a child reimburse the community during the entire lifetime of that child.

Certainly, therefore, the mother's decision to seek employment should not depend on the need for financial assistance. It must be based on a full evaluation of the emotional and social needs of herself and her child. To set up criteria for mothers in financial need different from those for mothers with lesser need is, in effect, to defeat the basic purpose of the Aid to Dependent Children Law (its predecessor, Mothers' Pensions), the Children's Charter of the White House Conference in 1909, and the fundamental philosophy of public assistance. Regulations urging the employment of mothers as an alternative to seeking financial assistance for themselves and their children cloak the application policy with duress.

The significance of the philosophy that a mother with small children should not be required to work in order to provide for her children is dependent upon the wisdom of, rather than the economic reasons for, plans to work or not to work. It is dangerous to assume that a necessary corollary to that philosophy is that a mother of small children should not work. There are too many factors involved to make a dogmatic statement or a generalization.

The social worker carries a responsibility to help the mother evaluate the inherent strengths and weaknesses of her relationship with her children and the factors in the cultural and environmental pattern that frame the family's adjustment in the community. He also is responsible for helping the agency and the tax-supporting or contributing groups to recognize the basic rights of mothers to make their decisions regarding employment.

In an attempt to contribute to thinking through the various considerations necessary before determining whether or not a mother should work, the following material was offered at the Illinois Welfare Conference in Peoria, Illinois, on November 8, 1948.

FROM A PSYCHIATRIST'S POINT OF VIEW

When the child is an infant, the mother is the source of his security in the world into which he has entered and which he has practically no tools to master. Physical discomfort is the first anxiety-creating event the small infant experiences. Food and warmth relieve this discomfort. Such comfort theoretically could be given in a nursery and by anyone. It has been observed, however, that impersonal physical care does not give complete comfort. Recent studies of newborn infants indicate that the child does better under the ministrations of a responsive person who fondles the child as well as meets his physical needs. His respiratory and cardiac rhythm are established more quickly. Furthermore, he behaves as a contented, responsive infant rather than as a fussy or vegetable-like piece of protoplasm.[1] From birth the child thrives in a maternal atmosphere. Such atmosphere should be provided in order to facilitate the infant's physical adjustment to the external world. It must be provided either by the mother herself or by an adequate mother-substitute.

This experience with a maternal person has expanding value to the child as he begins to respond to and explore the external world. As the child becomes aware of opportunities, possible dangers, and more and more unknowns in the world about him, he is stimulated but uneasy. This uneasiness is no longer relieved by physical care. If the mother has been the source of relief from his first unhappy experiences, he now turns to her for relief from the anxiety created by his growing awareness. He has become emotionally dependent upon her. Through this dependency he gains a feeling of security. She will offer protection against dangers that may exist and with which he cannot cope. This sense of security makes it possible for him to expand his activities and interests without being overwhelmed by fear. It is important, therefore, that the relief from physical discomfort in the first few weeks of life be associated with people who are consist-

[1] Margaret A. Ribble, *The Rights of Infants* (New York: Columbia University Press, 1943).

ently present, so that he does not have to explore his environment for a source of emotional security but finds it in the same contacts he has known as a source of comfort during his brief life. It is this continuity of gratification that makes possible the most comfortable, and therefore the most constructive, transition from interuterine life, through infancy and childhood, to adulthood with its achievement of a mastery of the external world.

This dependency gratification that is so essential in early infancy gradually loses its importance during the maturation of the child. Its significance is most apparent during the first six years of life. As the child, through social contacts and through school experiences, gains new confidence in his own ability to handle situations that arise and as he transfers some of his emotional ties to his own age group and to other adults, he manifests less need for an intense tie to his parents or parent-substitutes. This shift, however, is possible only when the child is confident of his ability to deal with the demands which the external world places upon him and when he requires only diluted experiences of dependency gratification. Faced with some problem with which he feels completely incapable of dealing, he has again an intense need to turn to someone who will give him the same depth of security that was so essential in his earlier life. He then seeks the security he can consistently find only in parent-figures.

The child's need, therefore, is to have through childhood a source of dependency security and gratification, from which he may draw as he has a need for it and which he may gracefully relinquish as he ceases to have that need. Permission for the latter step is as important as assurance of gratification is in the former. The

parental role is that of giving security when it is needed but of permitting the child to break away as the child feels ready to hazard more self-dependence. The child gains confidence in himself partly through success in handling experiences to which he is exposed. He gains it, also, because of evidence given by parental figures that they have confidence in his growth. Furthermore, the goal of maturity is not easy to attain. If the child must meet, in addition to all the normal stresses of the maturing process, barricades irrationally placed by parents who resist his maturation, the task may prove too great. The child may then give up his attempt to attain emotional adulthood and, accepting defeat, remain a child.

Adults have another function in their role as parents. They are the chief source of the child's concept of adulthood. Standards of behavior and attitudes toward life are not gained primarily through listening to lectures or innuendoes concerning what people as adults should be. Concepts of ideals, morals, and ethics, if gained only through the ears, tend to remain intellectual abstractions and become a part of the emotional structure of the child only after a long struggle. It is not what we know but what we feel that determines the more significant aspect of our behavior in a social world. The child "learns" his code of living most easily through living with people to whom he has a strong emotional tie. What he "learns" is then a part of his personality structure rather than of his intellect alone. Thus the most stable philosophy of life and social living has its roots in the interrelationship between the child and the parent-figures and the experiences the child has with their philosophy.

It is a characteristic of human nature

to dream of a utopia, a utopia in which all our sentimental ideals are translated into valid sentiments. Nowhere is this tendency more apparent than it is in regard to our attitude toward motherhood. Since it appears that children need mothers, there is a wish to believe that all women can fulfil that mission. Such wishful thinking ignores the fact that the mother of a child is also an individual in her own right and therefore has a personality that is a composite picture of all her needs, conflicts, potentialities, and inadequacies. In evaluating a mother-child relationship, it is thus important to approach the mother sympathetically and with understanding in order to determine her potentials in her biologically imposed role as a mother. It is folly to dream that all mother-child relationships will meet the child's needs. It is imperative that in each individual case plans be formulated that guarantee a maximum utilization of what the relationship can offer and a minimum opportunity for the expression of its destructive aspects. Translated into practicalities, this implies that the mother must be expected to meet the dependency needs of her child only to the extent to which she is capable. Demanding more of her will arouse resentment in her that will result in diminished returns to the child. She must also be given an opportunity to fulfil her maternal role with her optimum capacity. If she does not, she will feel frustrated and unhappy and thus, inadvertently, will fail to meet the child's needs because she herself is too preoccupied with her own distress. She must further be assisted to find gratifications outside her role as a mother, so she can relinquish the child as the child feels safer. Otherwise she may unconsciously attempt to arrest the child's development so as to continue to meet her own emotional needs. Finally, she should be given an opportunity and encouragement to find a pattern of life gratifying to herself and acceptable to the community. Otherwise the child may have greater difficulty in developing an attitude toward life and social living that will constructively serve rather than destructively attack the social world.

In order to understand the problems of mothers, we must understand the individual not only as a mother but also as a person beyond the realm of motherhood. The following material by no means elucidates all the factors to be considered. It outlines briefly and inadequately some meanings a child may have to a mother.

While children do, at times, find other parental figures, the mother should not be expected to carry alone the responsibility of giving the child emotional security and support; nor should she ideally be the only contributor to the child's developing sense of his place in the world. The child needs both parents, particularly to furnish the pattern of adult womanhood and manhood. Many mothers must, because of the inadequacy, desertion, or death of the father, carry the major part of the task of parenthood. For her to fulfil her role to the best of her ability under any circumstances, but particularly when she is the only parent, is not by any means a simple undertaking.

Some women do not have the capacity to be mothers under any circumstances and thus have an unfortunate effect upon the emotional development of their children. This fact does not negate the value of mothers. It only indicates that, because of character distortion or of emotional immaturity, certain women are incapable of functioning in a mother-role. Between the extremes of the theoretically ideal mother and the woman incapable of functioning in that role at all there is a wide range of individual differences. Most women who have children have some capacity for maternity. This capacity, however, may be crippled under certain conditions and may be brought to its maximum availability under modified circumstances.

Some women can be maternal within certain limits, beyond which they destroy the rewards of their achievements as mothers. This limit may be defined by time span alone. In such cases the mother can, for a few hours a day, respond warmly to the child, only to become exhausted and then antagonistic to him as the time lengthens beyond her tolerance. The limit may rather be set by the tasks the mother has to complete. Keeping the child clean, cooking three meals a day, hearing "mamma" too often, may be the experiences that exhaust her patience and cause her to abandon her role of mother to give full vent to her own angry tension.

Another woman can give richly to her child if the emotional energy that is depleted in giving to him can be replaced by some gratification of her own needs. A woman, for example, may be frightened by the responsibilities she faces and may wish a support similar to the type for which her child is asking. She may be unable to master her anxiety without the security to be found in a dependent relationship or in a safe world. If her needs are met, she may be more capable of meeting those of her child.

Some women find optimum gratification in their roles as mothers and find other pleasures gratifying but of secondary importance, pleasures to be enjoyed successfully only after the optimum expression of themselves as mothers. Under ideal conditions motherhood is the most important function of a woman but is

not, even then, the sole gratification the woman seeks or should have. Other experiences must be a part of her life. It should also be recognized as axiomatic that, within rather broad limits, the positive value a mother has to her child is qualitative rather than quantiative. It is not solely the time a mother gives to the child that is important. It is the quality of emotional response she gives within the time span that is most significant!

It is because of the multiplicity of facts which play a part in the success or failure a woman experiences in motherhood that it is important to evaluate not only the meaning she has to the child but also the meaning the child has to her. It is often difficult to evaluate the latter. It is also not simple to determine how well she is functioning in her emotional relationship with a child. Some women seem completely absorbed in their children. Such a relationship may on the surface be an excellent one but basically may be destructive to both, more even to the child than to the mother. A mother who finds no gratification in life other than the fulfilment of the maternal role during the infancy of her child will struggle to avoid relinquishing it as the child develops his own potentialities, so that his need for his mother is lessened. In spite of the security such a mother gives to the infant, she will ultimately thwart his growth unless she has developed other outlets for satisfaction, so that she can gradually lessen her hold on the child and still not find herself in a vacuum.

On the other hand, a wholesomely maternal woman may feel cornered by the economic responsibilities of caring for her child. She may consider that the greatest contribution she can make as a mother is to work. Working, and thus caring for her child, comes to symbolize for her all her maternity. Such a point of view is consistent with the belief of our culture that acceptance of financial responsibility and the maintenance of financial independence are the criteria of adequacy as an adult. The mother may then exhaust herself fulfilling her concept of maternity and adulthood, working long hours, and trying to maintain her home as well. In many instances the mother is so exhausted by the physical strain she is under that she is unable to give emotionally to the child, in spite of a primary capacity to do so. The child and the mother suffer in a relationship that actually need not be frustrating. Such a mother could perhaps find her satisfaction in being a mother rather than a provider. She often needs help in redefining her goal so that she can accept financial assistance in order to be free to be a mother.

In certain cases women who seem to be devoting all their time and thought to their children are doing so not because of any strong maternal feeling. They are actually investing emotional energy in their children that should be directed elsewhere. For example, a woman may be a widow with a child to care for. She feels frightened and alone in the world. She has a great need to find security and love somewhere. She turns to her child for emotional gratification and a sense of being loved. She, then, is asking the child to take the place of husband and parent. Her life is centered around the child, not because of the child's need but because of her own. She does not give emotional security to the child but rather creates anxiety in him because of her own anxiety. Furthermore, again, she will be unable to relinquish the child as he seeks to free himself from his infantile dependency relationships. A woman who is attempting to utilize her relationship with her child to meet multiple needs of her

own rather than expressing her own maternal feelings and meeting the needs of the child can perhaps be assisted to find another means of answering her emotional requirements that are beyond those of maternity.

Under certain circumstances mothers are sharply in conflict concerning their feeling toward their children. Many mothers are capable of being fairly adequate mothers if that role is not a matter of twenty-four-hour complete preoccupation with their children. A mother of this type may be ambivalent toward the child. On one hand, she wishes to be a good mother and often shows affection by overindulgence or oversolicitude. At the same time, perhaps without realizing it, she is struggling with real hostility toward, and actual rejection of, the child. This latter aspect of her relationship creates a feeling of uneasiness and guilt, which is then expressed through the overanxiety, overindulgence, and effervescent type of affection that is associated with the so-called "rejecting" mother. It is important, however, to evaluate that terminology. Most mothers who are classified as rejecting mothers are actually ambivalent mothers. They are confused in their relationship with their children. The guilt is not solely the result of the rejection. There is some reason why the rejection causes guilt. One can reject an unsatisfactory acquaintance without guilt. Why is guilt aroused if one's own child is not accepted? A rejecting mother cannot overtly manifest the rejection, in part because of fear of society's condemnation. In most cases the stronger reason is the conflict created by the existence of a real affection for the child. This affection may be relatively immature. It may have many facets aside from maternal feelings. There is, in most cases of so-called "rejection," some positive nucleus in the relationship to the child. This positive element should be preserved. It should again be preserved, however, by diverting the mother into other interests at times or by working through with her the meaning the child has to her. Until such a case can be adequately understood, the answer is neither to have the mother remain at home to hover anxiously over the child nor yet to have her be completely away from home in order to "distract" her and free the child. It is important that the child be given an opportunity to profit by the positive in the mother's relationship and to suffer a minimum of the mother's unwise handling of her rejection and resultant anxiety.

Why does a mother seek employment? She may do so because it is the only real solution she sees to her economic problems. It is not safe to assume, however, that that is her only or her real reason for working. As indicated earlier, some mothers, valuing their sense of adultness and their capacity to meet reality, see working and supporting their children as expressions of their genuine wish to care for their children. On the other hand, they may fear the stigma of "charity" with its implication of inadequacy and condemnation. Thus pride in themselves as adults is threatened. They then will need help in understanding that financial support of the mother when a father is not available to care adequately for the family is not charity but a wise investment upon the part of the state or a private agency in her as a mother. The support serves the function of investing the interest of the people in the potentialities of her children, potentialities which she, above all others, can develop.

Another woman may seek employment in an attempt to free herself from the care of her child. In such incidences a careful evaluation is again indicated. If she cannot bear the role of motherhood and is unable to give to her child except in terms of material benefits, she may be giving as much as she can give by working. On the other hand, through help in understanding herself she may be able to re-evaluate her relationship to her child, so that she can give more than financial support to him.

Women may seek employment because they feel the need to achieve in fields other than their homes. Maternity alone does not completely satisfy them. Social contacts are not available or offer too little satisfaction. These women try to fill in voids in their lives by being occupied outside their homes. Certainly, in some cases of this type the mother returns from employment stimulated and eager for the short period of companionship and emotional relationship with her child. She has just so much to give a child. She can give it intensely in a few hours, whereas spread over an entire day it would soon wear thin. Such mothers are actually better mothers because they do work.

The mother may further feel the need for support from adults. Often fellow-workers, foremen, or employers serve as parent-substitutes for an insecure woman who is frightened by being too much on her own. Her apparent gesture of independence as expressed in working is actually a cover-up for a strong need in herself to be dependent, a need she meets in the interrelationships in the job situation. Until she finds other security, it is preferable that she seek it in the world of employment rather than in the relationship with her child!

Employment may mean an opportunity to express some of her emotional energy in relationships with other people rather than investing all in her child. In working, she may feel she is expressing some of her maternal drives in providing the needs and some luxuries for the child whom she loves above all else. If her work is also interesting, it may give her an opportunity to develop a broader emotional horizon than that encompassing only the needs of her dependent child.

The question to be studied in evaluating the desirability of any mother's working is therefore not that of the number of children she must care for, her physical or mental ability to work, or the availability of employment. The first step in deciding whether or not a mother should work is the evaluation of her potentialities as a mother and of the conditions under which she can give the optimum emotional gratification to the child. She must be relatively happy to be able to express her fullest emotional potential. Therefore, she must not be punished for working or for not working. Furthermore, she must be gaining other gratifications over and above those she gains from being a mother, so that she is able to let her child grow up without her remaining an emotional burden to him. She must also be fulfilling herself as a person, so that her own approach to life will be one which the child visualizes as a happy one to emulate rather than one of bitter resignation. Our goal in assisting mothers should be to foster any plan which helps them to be the most adequate mothers they are capable of being.

Employment for a mother may in many instances be very unwise, placing too great a burden upon her when she already faces responsibilities in her role with her child that taxes her ability to the utmost. On the other hand, it may offer a wise solution to mounting strains in the child-parent relationship. If the mother cannot function adequately because her resentment over daily domesticity smothers her maternal feelings, if her capacity to give to the child must be nurtured by experiences outside the home that are gratifying to her, if she is unable to allow the child to mature because her own emotional needs are met only through her relationships with an immature child, if any situation exists which detracts from her values as a mother, employment may offer a constructive means of dealing with the situation.

Full-time employment may not, on the other hand, be the wisest answer. It is unfortunate that many communities penalize the mother for part-time working by subtracting her earnings from the financial support given to her. In many situations the greatest therapeutic value of a mother's working could be obtained only if she is permitted the reward of moderate luxuries for her work, so that she can contribute material pleasures to herself and her child by working and yet have the assurance that essential needs will be met whether she works or not. Such a utilization of employment would imply a double budget. One would provide bare physical necessities, to be assured by the social agency. The other budget would, in addition, assure simple gratifications, to be provided by the mother's earnings. Until the latter budget is exceeded, the mother's earnings should not affect the contribution made by a social agency.

It should be borne in mind, furthermore, that not employment but social activities outside the home may offer a more constructive solution to the dilemma the individual mother faces. P.T.A.'s, settlement house programs, informal neighborhood activities, or freedom in the evening for social engagements may be the wisest way to meet her needs.

During her time out of the home she should be free of responsibility for her child's immediate needs. Whether the mother works or becomes wholesomely involved in social activities, wise care of the child should be provided. Such provision not only should relieve the mother of anxiety concerning the child but should also assure the community that the type of care provided protects the child, both physically and emotionally. Whether this requirement is met by a nursery or by a "sitter" again requires evaluation of the particular situation.

Employment for a mother with small children should be considered as a tool to be used if it fosters a healthy child-mother relationship and should be discarded if it is a detriment to such an adjustment.

FROM A SOCIAL WORKER'S POINT OF VIEW

The decision to work or not to work is made by mothers with young children in all economic levels of our society. The problems of working mothers are also universal. However, when mothers apply to social agencies for assistance, there is a tendency to set up different criteria for determining the advisability of their seeking employment. Whether a mother with children should work is, at present, one of the most difficult problems with which social workers, particularly in public assistance agencies, are faced.

The approach of social agencies to this problem has varied, depending on the skills of its workers, the pressure of the community and press, and the attitude of the contributor or taxpayer. Thus the mother seeking assistance from a social agency may be encouraged or discouraged from seeking employment. Some agencies, public and private, discourage all mothers with young children from working; others openly encourage their employment, even under duress of rejecting applications for assistance. Some-

where between these extremes is the true position for the agency—the determination of whether the mother should work being based on full evaluation of her needs, her child's, the community's, and, eventually, those of the public welfare.

During the war there was an increase in the number of working mothers due to the attraction of large salaries, the emotional as well as the economic need to compensate for the absence of the normal wage earner, the appeal of the patriotic motive, and the general acceptance by the community of the working mother and her arrangements for her children during the working day. The development of day-care centers and their support by the government, as well as by industry, was an outgrowth of this movement of mothers into employment. Social agencies found it difficult to compete with these outside pressures in helping mothers to make their decision to work on a more fundamental basis. Some social agencies encouraged employment of mothers with children in order to reduce the financial tax or subscription burden, and they continue to do so.

There still is apparently too little regard for the public welfare, and what is ultimately less costly, and too much regard for what is presently less costly in amounts of current public assistance. There has been too little attention given by social agencies and the lay public to determining whether the needs of the mother with children, as well as the public welfare, are better served by the mother's working or by remaining at home. There has been too little recognition that some mothers are better mothers and members of society if they are employed either full or part time and that some children are happier children because their mothers work. There have been too many generalizations about whether mothers should work and not enough evaluation of individual situations.

Much of the confusion regarding agency policy relating to the employment of mothers is due to the inability to state in specific terms which mothers should be encouraged to work and which discouraged from working. The agency cannot, nor should it, issue a directive advising staff which mothers should work and which should not. Directives, unfortunately, are desired by unskilled staff, for they feel protected under this umbrella of rigidity. A detailed directive which leaves little opportunity for the use of judgment and analysis by the social worker is in conflict with the principle of individualization of need. For example, let us consider some directives which an agency might consider releasing regarding policy concerning mothers' working.

Were the directive to state that mothers with one child should work, what if the one child were a sick child and the mother the person best able to care for him?

Were it to state that all mothers living with relatives should work, what if these relatives were bedridden or otherwise physically or emotionally unable to carry responsibility for children?

Were it to read that all mothers should be urged to work if they lived within walking distance of a licensed day nursery, what if the intake policy discriminated against youngsters of the ages specifically being considered or if the hours of the nursery's operation did not synchronize with the mother's workday?

Were the directive to state that all mothers with satisfactory work records prior to the birth of the child should be required to seek employment, what if the mother had been employed in an occupation for which she is now physically disqualified? Perhaps her previous employment required her to stand for long periods, but now she has varicose veins, which require her activity to be sedentary.

Were the directive to state that all mothers who were physically able to work should be encouraged to seek employment, how would the agency meet the problem of the mother who is physically able to keep a job in industry but physically and/or emotionally unable to assume the dual responsibility of maintaining both the job and the home?

One finds, therefore, that it is not possible to measure the advisability of a mother's working by applying a rule related to any one factor, whether it be health, former occupation, availability of relatives, or arrangements for suitable care of the children. At best, social agencies may be able to offer staff some criteria as guides which emphasize the necessity of considering with the mother the emotional, physical, social, and cultural factors affecting her thinking about her decision to work. In the final analysis, the social worker will only be as effective as his ability to evaluate the functioning of the mother-child relationship, the expressed and suppressed motivations of the mother's search for financial security, and the impact of the community and cultural pressures as they affect her decision.

It is recognized that the primary factor to be considered in helping the mother decide whether she should work is the relationship between her and her child. The strengths and/or weaknesses of the relationship are not easily determined. It is recognized that there are many factors which determine the success or failure a woman experiences in motherhood and that each must be evaluated—not only the meaning the mother has to the child but also the meaning the child has to her.

Too often the relationship is evaluated by the manner in which a mother meets the physical needs of the child, by the crisply starched dresses on the little daughter, or the highly polished shoes on the son. However, the love for a child does not express itself in these criteria, or in the physical effort of producing snow-white laundered diapers, or in the picking-up of toys. Such physical tasks can be accomplished by a person other than the mother without any jeopardy to the mother-child relationship, provided they are given with a quality of warmth and a positive emotional response to the child. It is possible for mothers to enjoy happy relationships with their children without meeting the daily responsibilities for their physical care. Many mothers are able to combine the responsibilities of motherhood and employment in such a way that positive values result in the mother-child relationship. Women happy in their responsibilities are able to transfer these feelings to their children.

It is recognized also that even mothers who do not work are not with their children every hour of the child's day. Our society encourages the development of interests outside the home, urges the participation of mothers in clubs, cultural and social. Such outside interests develop happier mothers, and this results in happier children. Society suffers when parents wear blinders and are completely "wrapped up in their children." However, although the number of hours spent by working mothers and those in community activity may be the same, the social worker should be aware that the censure of leaving children during the day is usually reserved for the working mother.

In addition to the evaluation of the mother-child relationship, there are other factors which are important to the social worker as he helps the mother think through her decision to work. The emotional and physical strain of leading "a double life" must be considered. In social agencies we help mothers whose salaries are seldom adequate to pay the cost of a homemaker. Thus, in addition to carrying the full responsibilities as an employee of industry, the mother will have

the physical toil of caring for a household.

The extent of this physical activity must be carefully reviewed. If the housekeeping standards of the mother make her a meticulous cleaner, a finicky cook, a laborious shopper, or a fastidious laundress, her problems in carrying two responsibilities will be different from those of the mother who is satisfied with "a lick and a promise" for the house, so that she can play with her children. The woman who for the first time has a job in industry requiring strenuous physical effort will have a problem in carrying her home responsibilities different from one who has always done heavy manual work.

The emotional strain on married working women, as well as on working mothers, in establishing satisfactory relationships with their employers is real. Often anxieties borne during the day deplete the energy which is needed when the working wife or mother returns home. Even those working wives and mothers who are relieved of the physical chores involved in homemaking are always aware of the emotional tensions of leading "a double life."

Another factor that must be considered is the working mother's feeling about the community's attitude toward her. She may feel defensive because she is working and, rather than risk the censure of neighbors should her children misbehave, curtail their normal activity. She may fear that, by working, she will be thought by the community to be disinterested in her children. Or she may feel that she should work because other mothers in her economic and social sphere work and because she should not be dependent on the taxpayer or private agency subscriber if she is physically able to work.

She may be a member of a cultural

group that considers it indecent for a woman to work outside her home. Or it may be that her cultural pattern accepts, condones, and even encourages the employment of mothers.

In evaluating these factors which relate to the culture and the community, the social worker must appreciate the depth of meaning the pressures of the mores of the group have to the mother. The stamp of approval or disapproval by members of the mother's family, cultural group, and community determines in good measure the mother's decision and adjustment to full- or part-time employment.

It is important for the social worker to understand why the mother is thinking about working. Is it because she is a rejecting mother who wishes to compensate for her feelings by bestowing material goods on her child? Is it because she believes that she will be a happier person if she has an opportunity to do a job she is trained to do? Is it because she would enjoy the response of approval of those around her when she works and also raises a family—enjoy the luxury of such comments as "the brave little woman"? Is she thinking about working solely because of economic need?

It is also necessary to consider why she thinks she should not work. She may be anxious about the arrangements for her children while she is employed. She may be fearful of their adjustment to a substitute mother-person. Will they resent her absence? What will happen if Johnny's nose is running and the nursery teacher thinks he ought to be sent home? What if Tom forgets his glasses and is unable to enter the house to get them? What if Alice gets hurt during the day? What if she or the children take ill and she cannot go to work? Who will pay the bills? What if, after a full day's work, she is too tired to keep her house clean, her chil-

dren's clothes immaculate? What will her relatives, her neighbors, and the children's teachers think of her?

In these considerations it has been presumed that the father is not in the home. If he is a member of the family, the mother's decision must be evaluated with full recognition of the need to maintain and protect the husband-wife and parent-child relationships, as well as the mother-child relationship. One of the most difficult decisions is that to be made by a mother who, through working, in effect takes on the father's role as the wage-earner for the family.

Also to be considered are the effects on the child of the mother's working. Does he feel he is an unloved child, and does the absence of the mother reinforce his feelings of not being wanted? Does he already feel he is "different" because he has no father, and does the absence of the mother add to his anxiety? Does he feel his activity is circumscribed because his mother works? These examples, as well as other problems which arise, may affect his relationship with his working mother. At the other extreme are the problems which would be better handled if his mother worked, particularly when his relationship with her is best described as his being consumed or overpowered by her.

In this discussion I have delayed mentioning the importance of suitable care for the children as it must first be determined whether a mother should work, these factors having to be considered before plans are reviewed for the children's care. Unless plans for suitable care for the children follow the determination that a mother should work because her needs and those of her children are best served, the parent-child relationship enhanced, and the community protected, we defeat the underlying purpose of our assistance programs. Much time could be spent here in discussing criteria for suitable care. For our purpose we might consider that it is that arrangement which, to the mother's satisfaction, protects her relationship with her children and makes it possible for the mother to perform one job at a time, although it may never relieve her of the responsibility of either.

Too often agency policies are stated or interpreted so that the mother is advised to seek work primarily because there appears to be suitable care available for the children. Such an approach violates the principles which this paper supports, that is, that only a careful evaluation of all factors can determine whether a mother should work.

What does it mean to a mother to apply for assistance for herself and her family and to be advised by the application worker to seek employment? She had probably considered going to work before making application but decided against working at present because of problems she saw in her family's situation. She may be emotionally distressed at present because of the recent loss of her husband and is not ready to think about working. The response to the suggestion that she work will depend on her emotional needs and her relationship with her children. If she has feelings about her own inadequacy, symbolized to her by the need to apply for assistance, this response from the agency will make her more anxious. She may feel guilty about having applied and may withdraw her application, although it may not be to the best interests of her family. If she has negative feelings toward her children, this suggestion that she work may make her most hostile to them or more rejecting.

It seems to me that it is possible for the social worker to help the mother make her decision only after the mother's total needs have been determined and that this evaluation is not possible until a good client-worker relationship has been established. Social agencies have a responsibility to meet the needs of the mother first as she sees them. In this instance it is the need for assistance for herself and her children. Then, as the relationship develops, exploration of the advisability of employment may be indicated.

It is questionable whether the intake department of a public assistance agency should explore the possibility of employment with the mother. Staff standards in these departments, as well as the emphasis on the legal requirements for determining eligibility, would not in many instances be conducive to the development of the kind of relationship which would bring about an understanding of the social needs of the mother and her children.

The social worker assigned to the mother must be capable of understanding her real needs. Dr. Josselyn's goals for the social worker are particularly pertinent in this area of service. She states:

The worker must be capable of understanding the needs of the client. He must be able to evaluate the difficulties the client presents and judge whether they are the result of voids in his past experience which can be filled at this late date, or whether the failure of the individual is related to early conflicts that must be resolved before he can accept the gratifications of reality. The caseworker must be able to evaluate the psychological positives and negatives in the environment in terms of the client, and not in terms of a distorted identification with the client. He must thus be able to see what the client needs, not what the worker would need in the same situation. His program must be the result of his understanding of the psychological dynamics involved in the problem and of the resources in reality which will therapeutically fit in with those dynamics.[2]

[2] Irene Josselyn, M.D., "The Caseworker as Therapist," *Journal of Social Casework* (November, 1948), p. 352.

However, it may be that the social worker is not able to establish a helping relationship because of his or her attitudes toward working mothers. These attitudes may have their roots in the social worker's feelings about persons who apply for assistance. He may be hostile to physically able mothers who seek assistance if there are jobs in the community. The worker may herself be a working mother and set the activity standards for other mothers on the basis of what she can accomplish. She may have been reared by a working mother and recall the two long hours each day between her return from school and her mother's return from work, as she sat in the house alone because of the mother's fear of her playing in the street while she was away. The worker may be affected by his recollection of years of financial deprivation when he and his mother lived on a small pension, his mother being "too proud" to go to work. The worker may believe that the Aid to Dependent Children Law is too broad in its philosophy to keep mothers home with their children and that it should apply only to those mothers who are physically unable to support themselves. It is important to the agency to be aware of the attitudes of its staff toward working mothers.

The social worker must look to the agency for a policy which states that mothers should not work because of economic need alone. The agency must stress with the community the necessity for adequate grants and services, so that no mother will work solely because she cannot maintain her children in health and decency on the amount of authorized assistance.

The agency has a further responsibility to equip its workers with the skills and knowledge to understand what basic concepts are involved in helping a mother decide whether she should work. It must keep case loads at a tolerable level, so that workers have the time to be of maximum assistance to the mother. It must make available adequate supervision and good in-service training programs. It must make possible the opportunity for workers to be kept aware of the principles of behavior and personality development. It must work toward breaking down rigid responses of staff which defeat the intent of the social philosophy embodied in agency policy. And, above all, the agency has a responsibility for helping the community understand its goals—the maintenance of effective parent-child relationships which help to create the kind of social climate in which people can live happier and more satisfying lives.

In this area of helping mothers decide whether they should work is the optimum opportunity for the use of casework skills. The determination of which mothers should work and which should not must be determined on an individual-case basis. The only generalization which can be made to the best interests of the public's welfare is that some mothers should work and some should not.

CHICAGO

SOCIAL PSYCHOLOGICAL CORRELATES OF UPWARD SOCIAL MOBILITY AMONG UNMARRIED CAREER WOMEN

EVELYN ELLIS

Cedar Crest College

THE rags to riches success story has long captivated the imagination of the American people. Few other themes have been so glorified or so enduringly popular. But despite its familiarity, the upward climb has been more admired and envied than understood. There has been comparatively little scientific study of the motivations of the mobile person, the methods of achieving mobility, or the effects of status changes upon the individual. Upward social mobility has usually been accepted rather uncritically as a natural and desirable part of a democratic, open-class society, and with reference to the individual, mobility has often been regarded as a coveted prize awarded almost automatically to the able and energetic.

Certain social scientists, however, have suspected that the rags to riches story is not always an entirely happy one for the person who lives it. Some of the social scientific literature regarding vertical mobility has hinted that the experience is often a traumatic one for the individual, growing out of neurotic drives and resulting in further neurotic tendencies. Such a view of mobility is implicit in the writings of Karen Horney,[1] Pitirim Sorokin,[2] and John Dollard.[3]

This paper is a report on an attempt to make an empiric test, with female subjects, of that largely unverified theory. The major underlying hypothesis, suggested particularly by Horney and Sorokin, is that mobility frequently is inspired at least partly by emotional drives generated by unsatisfactory early primary group relations, and that mobility leads to further deterioration of primary group relations with accompanying neurotic symptoms. The early primary group relations would have been characterized by a lack of affection from others and by a series of humiliating experiences which wounded the child's self-esteem.

DESIGN OF THE STUDY

The basic plan of the investigation was to compare a selected group of mobile persons with a comparable group of non-mobile persons in regard to a number of factors thought to be associated with upward social mobility. The groups were kept as homogeneous as possible with respect to such important variables as marital status and occupational status, so that statistically sig-

---

[1] Karen Horney, *The Neurotic Personality of Our Time*, New York: Norton and Co., Inc., 1937, pp. 80–82, 178–179.

[2] Pitirim Sorokin, *Social Mobility*, New York:

Harper and Brothers, 1927, pp. 510, 515, 522–525. Most of Sorokin's hypotheses were expressed in terms of the characteristics of a mobile society. The implication was, however, that the societal characteristics are largely a reflection of the personal characteristics of mobile individuals.

[3] John Dollard, "The Life History in Community Studies," *American Sociological Review*, 3 (1938), p. 735.

nificant differences between the two groups could be assumed to be associated with upward mobility. The sample included sixty outstanding unmarried career women now living in one city, Montgomery, Alabama.

Although there was an interest in overall social mobility, in this study movement was defined in terms of a single dimension— that of occupation, which has been regarded by leading students of social stratification as the most easily determined and probably most valid single index of social status.[4]

Respondents were divided into mobile and non-mobile sub-samples on the basis of a comparison of each respondent's occupational status with the occupational status of her father. Occupational status was reduced to numerical scores suitable for comparisons by a method developed by Cecil C. North and Paul K. Hatt.[5] The method was based on ratings of occupations made by a cross-section of the American population during interviews conducted by the National Opinion Research Center. Persons interviewed were asked to evaluate ninety jobs at all status levels by giving their "own personal opinion" of the "general standing" of each job. Possible ratings were 5 (excellent), 4 (good), 3 (average), 2 (fair), and 1 (poor). Final rating of each job was the average of the individual ratings made by all persons interviewed. The resulting averages were reported on a scale with possible ratings ranging from 20 to 100. A separate scale for each major geographical region of the country also was computed by averaging the ratings of interviewees living in the section.

The North-Hatt method was modified to take into consideration the fact that occupations of both men and women were important in this study, while North and Hatt were concerned only with occupations of men. It was believed that, because of the different social expectations for men and women, ratings of specific jobs would vary somewhat with the sex of the holder.

The North-Hatt ratings for the Southern region were used for men's occupations listed in that study. Final ratings of all women's occupations and of men's occupations not appearing on the North-Hatt scale were the average of individual ratings made by twenty persons, ten sociologists now living in Alabama and ten residents of Montgomery. Occupations for the two sexes were listed on separate sheets, with directions asking the rater's personal opinion of the "general standing" of each job as an occupation for the sex indicated. As in the North-Hatt scale, individual ratings were on a five-point scale and final average ratings had a possible range of 20 to 100.

The sample was comprised of women whose occupations received ratings of 75 or more. Since no refusals were encountered, the group included virtually all unmarried women in the city with such occupations. A mobile person was defined as one whose occupational rating exceeded that of her father's major occupation by more than ten points. A non-mobile person was defined as one whose occupational rating exceeded that of her father's major occupation by ten points or less, or whose rating was lower than that of her father. The sample included 27 mobile women and 33 non-mobile. Occupational ratings of the mobile respondents were an average of 26 points above father's occupational rating, while ratings of non-mobile respondents averaged about 2 points below father's rating.

The research was done through intensive personal interviews, guided by a schedule composed largely of broad open-end questions. Factors studied were based chiefly upon hypotheses found in current social scientific literature. The variables fell into three major categories: (1) presumed causes of upward social mobility, (2) presumed effects of upward social mobility, and (3) steps and methods in achieving high status.

EARLY PRIMARY GROUP RELATIONS

Probably the most complete treatment of the presumed role of deep-seated personality factors in the drive for upward mobility is given by Horney[6] in her discussion of neurotic quests for power, prestige and wealth.

[4] W. Lloyd Warner, Marchia Meeker, and Kenneth Eells, *Social Class in America*, Chicago: Science Research Associates, Inc., 1949, p. 40; and Cecil C. North and Paul K. Hatt, "Jobs and Occupations: A Popular Evaluation," in Logan Wilson and William L. Kolb, *Sociological Analysis*, New York: Harcourt, Brace & Co., 1949, p. 464.

[5] *Ibid.*, pp. 464–474.

[6] Horney, *op. cit.*

The invariable basic cause, she says, is a "lack of genuine warmth and affection" from others during the child's early years. Referring to those in whom the desire for prestige is paramount, Horney says that the underlying motivation is a hostility, usually taking the form of a desire to humiliate others. That desire, she says, is uppermost in "those persons whose own self-esteem has been wounded by humiliation and who have thus become vindictive." Such persons, she asserts, usually have gone through a "series of humiliating experiences in childhood." Horney lists among the possible contributing factors parental preference for other children, unjust reproaches, rejection by parents, jealousy of a parent or of siblings, minority group membership, and being poor but having wealthy relatives.

Accordingly, in attempting to isolate presumed causes of upward social mobility, the major emphasis of the present study is upon early primary group relations. Results indicate that the proportion of respondents having had a series of humiliating experiences during childhood is significantly larger among mobile women than among non-mobile. Larger proportions of mobile women had experienced both rejection by the general community and at least a partial rejection by parents who had showed favoritism toward a sibling or siblings. Marked preference for a sibling or siblings was reported by 56 per cent of the mobile respondents, but by only 27 per cent of the non-mobile. Percentages having experienced relatively complete rejection by the general community were 20 for mobile women and 0 for non-mobile. Both differences are statistically significant at the five per cent level. Critical ratios are 2.32 for parental favoritism and 2.50 for community rejection. Another interesting point is that within the mobile group the women reporting parental or community rejection were more highly mobile than those with neither background factor. Those whose parents had preferred another child had risen an average of 32 points, while those not reporting favoritism had risen an average of 22 points. Despite the smallness of the numbers involved, the difference was statistically significant (C.R.=2.35). Similarly, those reporting community rejection had risen an average of 31 points.

One further specific indication of a lack

of the affection apparently necessary for emotional security in our society was found among mobile women. A significantly larger proportion of mobile respondents rated their attachment to parents during childhood and adolescence as "less than average" (see Table 1).

TABLE 1. SELF-RATING OF DEGREE OF ATTACHMENT TO PARENTS DURING CHILDHOOD AND ADOLESCENCE BY 58* CAREER WOMEN

Self-Rating of Attachment	Percentage of Mobile Women (N=25)	Percentage of Non-Mobile Women (N=33)
More than average**	36	61
Average	28	33
Less than average†	36	6
Total	100	100

* Two respondents were orphaned during childhood or early adolescence.
** C.R.=1.92.
† C.R.=2.24.

CHARACTERISTICS DURING ADULTHOOD

The basic hypothesis regarding characteristics during adulthood is that the mobile woman would continue to have unsatisfactory primary group relations and would exhibit generally neurotic tendencies. The assumption, suggested particularly by Sorokin, was that the mobile person as a result of childhood conditioning is less than normally capable of achieving lasting, satisfactory primary group relations. That incapacity would then be further encouraged by movement through different social class subcultures with conflicting values and customs. Sorokin also suggested that in an attempt to alleviate the resulting loneliness the mobile person might turn to a frantic "hunt for pleasure." [7]

The plan of the study, of course, did not permit determination either of the extent to which the mobile woman's adult characteristics were simply the result of a continuation of personality traits developed in childhood, or of the extent to which the already existing characteristics were further aggravated by upward movement.

In general, the theory that mobile persons are more socially isolated than non-

---

[7] Sorokin, *op. cit.*, pp. 522–525.

TABLE 2. NUMBER OF INTIMATE FRIENDS REPORTED BY 60 CAREER WOMEN

Item	Mobile Women (N=27)	Non-Mobile Women (N=33)
Mean number of intimate friends*	8.9	17.8
Mean number of intimate friends in Montgomery**	5.6	9.4
Mean number of friendships of more than five years duration†	3.2	8.2

* C.R.=3.21.
** C.R.=3.72.
† C.R.=3.50.

mobile is supported by the findings. Significant differences between mobile and non-mobile women are found with respect to number of intimate friends, length of friendships, and conflict with parents during adulthood (see Tables 2 and 3).

Sorokin's theory that the mobile person may turn to a mad "hunt for pleasure" in an attempt to overcome loneliness also received some support. A statistically significant difference (C.R.=2.26) was found in the proportions of mobile and non-mobile women who named as their major leisure-time activities drinking and going to parties and night clubs. Percentages were 22 for mobile respondents, and 3 for non-mobile.

Another hypothesis regarding attempts to alleviate loneliness was that a disproportionately large number of mobile women acquire pets as outlets for affection. A highly significant group difference in the ownership of pets was found (C.R.=3.05). Percentages

TABLE 3. INCIDENCE OF SERIOUS CONFLICT WITH PARENTS IN FOUR AREAS OF BEHAVIOR REPORTED BY 58* CAREER WOMEN

Area of Behavior	Percentage Reporting Conflict	
	Mobile Women (N=25)	Non-Mobile Women (N=33)
Religion	16	3
Politics	20	12
Respondent's Career**	40	18
Respondent's Personal Conduct†	40	12

* Two respondents were orphaned during childhood or early adolescence.
** C.R.=1.82.
† C.R.=2.47.

were 40 for mobile women, and 15 for non-mobile.

In an attempt to find at least crude indications of neurotic tendencies, each respondent was asked for a description of any of her own health problems, and for a self-rating of happiness during adulthood. The assumption was, of course, that the neurotic tends to be less happy than the well-adjusted person and is thus more likely to have psychosomatic and similar ailments.

A significantly larger proportion of mobile women did have relatively severe psychosomatic symptoms of the types generally regarded as emotionally based. Percentages were 32 for mobile women, and 9 for non-mobile (C.R.=2.10). No one in the non-mobile group had more than one type of psychosomatic illness, while in the mobile group half of those with such complaints had more than one type of disorder.

Self-ratings of happiness during adulthood did not show statistically significant differences between the mobile and non-mobile groups. It perhaps is noteworthy, however, that the answers of both groups had a more or less normal distribution rather than the heavy majority of "very happy" replies frequently found in happiness ratings.[8] Self-ratings given by respondents in this study appear in Table 4.

One interesting question was the extent to which respondents' careers were actually major ends or only second-choice substitutes for marriage. Answers to two questions offered some evidence that successful careers were major ends for mobile women more often than for non-mobile. A significantly larger proportion of mobile women indicated a desire to continue working in the event of their marriage, and, among those previously married and now widowed or divorced, a significantly larger proportion of mobile women actually did continue working during marriage. Percentages of respondents wishing to continue careers if married were 52 for mobile, and 27 for non-mobile

[8] For example, two well-known marriage prediction studies report that more than 50 per cent of the wives in the samples rated their marriages as unusually happy. See Ernest W. Burgess and Leonard S. Cottrell, Jr., *Predicting Success or Failure in Marriage*, New York: Prentice-Hall, Inc., 1939, p. 39; and Lewis Terman, *Psychological Factors in Marital Happiness*, New York: McGraw-Hill Book Co., Inc., 1938, p. 203.

(C.R.=2.00). Of those previously married, 75 per cent of the mobile and 8 per cent of the non-mobile worked during marriage (C.R.=3.10).

TABLE 4. SELF-RATINGS OF HAPPINESS DURING ADULTHOOD BY 58* CAREER WOMEN

Rating	Percentage of Mobile Women** (N=25)	Percentage of Non-Mobile Women (N=33)
Very happy	16	33.3
Happy	48	30.2
Average	20	30.3
Unhappy	12	6.1
Very unhappy	4	0.0
Total	100	100.0

* Two respondents said they were unable to answer the question.
** Differences between mobile and non-mobile groups were not statistically significant.

METHODS OF ACHIEVING HIGH STATUS

The study included questions dealing with four major hypotheses regarding steps and methods in achieving high occupational status. Two of the hypotheses, formulated especially by Warner and his associates, are that advanced education[9] and geographical mobility[10] are factors facilitating upward mobility. Geographical movement is said to be helpful because it makes determination of a person's background more difficult and the prejudicial effect of former status, therefore, becomes less definitive. The other hypotheses are that the mobile person requires a longer time period than the non-mobile to reach a high-status position, and that, with the "maturing" of the American economy, the professions have offered a better road to mobility than has business.

Statistically significant differences were not found regarding any of these hypotheses. Mobile and non-mobile groups are almost identical with respect to mean age at reaching present high status, and in proportions in business and professional occupations.

Average educational level is the same for

mobile and non-mobile sub-samples. The mean number of years in college is 3.7 for each group. Attempts to measure the influence of education in the rise of mobile women, however, should be based partly upon comparison of the respondent's education with parents' education. In this study the mobile women were unable to give sufficiently exact information about parents' schooling to permit such a comparison. Other available information about parents, particularly occupational status, hints that the educational attainment of the mobile women was considerably higher than that of their parents. It seems very probable that advanced education is one of the important factors facilitating upward mobility.

While no specific question regarding geographical mobility yielded statistically significant group differences, there are numerous small differences, without exception pointing in the direction of more geographical movement among mobile women. Although the evidence is inconclusive, it seems doubtful that chance alone would result in so many small differences in the same direction, and it appears probable that the occupationally mobile women do tend to be somewhat more geographically mobile (see Table 5).

TABLE 5. STATISTICS REGARDING GEOGRAPHICAL MOVEMENTS OF 60 CAREER WOMEN

Item	Mobile Women (N=27)	Non-Mobile Women (N=33)
Per cent born in Alabama or an adjacent state	66.7	78.8
Mean number of years residence in Montgomery	10.8	14.8
Mean number of jobs held in Montgomery	1.7	2.1
Mean number of cities worked in	3.5	2.7
Mean number of states worked in	2.4	1.8
Mean number of cities lived in before working	2.0	1.6
Mean number of states lived in before working	1.7	1.2
Per cent having worked outside the United States	22.2	9.9

Differences between mobile and non-mobile groups are not statistically significant.

[9] W. Lloyd Warner and Paul S. Lunt, *The Social Life of a Modern Community,* New Haven: Yale University Press, 1941, p. 119.
[10] *Ibid.,* p. 436.

SUMMARY AND CONCLUSIONS

The evidence is consistent with the theory that upward social mobility is likely to be an outgrowth of basically neurotic drives resulting from unsatisfactory early primary group relations, and that mobility leads to a continuation of superficial, impermanent primary group relations and other overt manifestations of emotional maladjustment.

A comparison of mobile and non-mobile career women reveals that significantly larger proportions of mobile individuals had experienced both rejection by parents and by the over-all community during childhood. The mobile women continued to be more socially isolated than the non-mobile during adulthood. A further indication of the relative maladjustment of the mobile women was the significantly greater incidence of psychosomatic ailments.

The group differences, however, are not as marked as those suggested in the original hypotheses. It appears that in regard to upward social mobility, as with most other complex social phenomena, no single explanation is entirely adequate. But since the presumed indicators of maladjustment in general have the greater incidence in the more highly mobile half of the mobile subsample, it is possible that larger differences in the anticipated directions are somewhat obscured by the inclusion of cases of only moderate mobility. A more crucial test of the hypotheses probably would be furnished by a more extensive study of very highly mobile persons.

My Great-Grandmothers Were Happy

PRISCILLA ROBERTSON

THERE HAVE BEEN TIMES AND PLACES in which it was fun to be good, and others in which it was more fun to be bad. American society today teeters on the balance, where we often find traditions and opportunities which help us live lives as full as any in past history, yet at the same time we sometimes find ourselves saying (occasionally in earnest, often only in wistful jokes) that the best way to have a really good time is to break some of the rules. Is this a heritage from our distant past, or only from the 1920's? I have recently had a chance to find out a good deal about my ancestresses for six generations back, and have come to the conclusion that for them it was fun to be good; they lived at a time and place where such a life was possible. It was only as conditions changed, toward the end of the nineteenth century, that women's sphere narrowed down rather suddenly so that there were a good two generations that were either left partially idle or had to fight for the right to use their abilities freely.

If people want to break the rules, the trouble is not necessarily with the people; it may be with the rules. Tom Sawyer is a wonderful example of a boy who had fun being bad. Most of the restrictions which he ran into no longer exist. Today schools and homes are adapted to boys' interests, so the chances of having fun as a good boy are much greater. A hundred years earlier, say in 1740, Tom Sawyer might not have been allowed to get away with his pranks at all, and then he could not have had fun either as a good boy or as a bad boy. I am using the words *good* and *bad* for the moment as the authorities concerned would have looked on the matter. Tom's aunt called him a bad boy, however worthy and normal a modern psychologist would judge him.

○ PRISCILLA ROBERTSON is the author of *Revolutions of 1848: A Social History*. The material for this article comes from a privately published volume which she wrote for her family, *Lewis Farm: A New England Saga*.

185

Very much the same sort of thing is true about women and their place in life, though the idea of goodness in women has so often been narrowed down to one particular form of goodness that the broad problem is harder to see. There have been ages when bad women had, or seemed to have, more fun than good women, and other ages when hardly any women led exhilarating lives. There have been still other times when women acting from the highest moral motives have been punished for being unladylike. In recent times, various processes which cramped women's life came to a peak in my mother's generation—freedom was actually greater both before and after that period. Having just been through a severe struggle, women are now used to the excitement of battle and perhaps a little tired of it. They have forgotten, and may be unwilling to believe, that there have also been periods in history when women have lived full, rich lives while doing exactly what they were supposed to do. In fact, there are signs that another such period is coming now, a period when women can enjoy their status without fighting for it or having to justify it. These thoughts came as a surprise to me after I had a chance to brood over the kind of happiness my great-grandmothers enjoyed—their lives were unified, their responsibilities serious ones, and gaiety was no stranger to them.

The women I am talking about lived in a Massachusetts village during the eighteenth and nineteenth centuries. They were in no way distinguished or unusual. In fact, their very ordinariness reveals a basic American pattern of equality and independence—a pattern which indicates that we have in times past offered women more of a place in the world than we realize.

A good life should offer affection, appreciation and a secure social position—and women used to enjoy these things. It should also offer responsibility, a chance for imagination and adventure. Some people say the trouble with women today is that in demanding these latter advantages they have deprived themselves of the former. What I have come to believe about my New England family, however, is that both sexes received both sets of privileges. As a matter of fact, if there was a slight edge, it was on the girls' side, for as wealth and leisure increased, the girls began to get good educations at a time when the boys still could not be spared from farm work. But this education was regarded as an investment for the whole family, certainly not as a form of conspicuous waste. The girls often became teachers and were certainly supposed to be better mothers for it.

Beyond this, whatever life offered of hard work, family affection, religious consolation, community responsibility and adventure was open equally to the women and to the men. In their simple sort of life, no one's influence reached beyond the town in which he lived. The men were farmers first and may have been blacksmiths or saddlers on the side. The first sign of division or discrimination between the sexes came a generation after the new industrial system had drawn men away from work at home into places where women did not go. Only then did women begin to suffer the slightly contemptuous treatment of being left out, even if it was called sparing them pain and trouble.

Of course I realize that the persons who made the great public decisions during the time of which I write—the judges, theologians and great merchants—were men. This may have involved a theoretical injustice, but it was certainly one which did not rankle in the hearts of my great-grandmothers. It is a very different thing for the social structure to put one man in twenty in a position of wide power ahead of his wife, and to pull three men out of four away from their homes. One of my ancestors, Henry Plimpton, sat in the legislature in 1853, but I doubt if his wife, Susanna, felt his opportunities for public service were greater in the State House than her own had been in organizing a new church and public library for her community.

Let me take a sample out of each generation to indicate how life changed for the women of this probably typical family.

The earliest one for whom a distinct picture of personality remains is Deborah Fisher (1739-1828). When she was a girl in Dedham, the passion of her life was to go to school, but no school was provided for girls then. She had to learn to read by asking questions and by studying alone, except for one winter when her father and some other men hired a teacher for a few girls. This accomplishment set her somewhat apart from her own generation—she became quite noted as the girl who could read, and used to be called on to comfort the sick by reading the Bible to them. But what sets her apart from *our* generation is her impressive list of household accomplishments. The year before she was married she raised a crop of flax, prepared it for spinning, and spun and wove sheets, pillowcases and ticking for mattresses and feather beds. At the same time, she raised sheep, prepared the wool and spun and wove her own bed blankets. Nor could life have become much easier for her after she married John Lewis in 1758, for the couple raised six children on the land and labor of their farm at Walpole, Massachusetts.

As is true for most people, it was her old age that showed the true texture of Deborah's character. After she broke her hip at the age of sixty, she could never walk again except by pushing a chair in front of her. Up to that time she had ridden horseback to church with a grandchild behind her. Yet for almost thirty years longer she maintained her cheerfulness and usefulness. Her great-grandchildren could remember her at nearly ninety, sitting at her spinning wheel with her close white cap and clean checked apron. She still made thread for their sheets and towels, and mended the huge piles of clothes that were brought her from the clotheshorse, saying, "A stitch in time saves nine." Every evening she read her Bible, her "spiritual food"; and as long as she lived, the whole family loved to gather in her room to hear her stories or consult her about important decisions, "for she was aimiable and wise, and a referee in matters requiring wisdom and experience." A serene old age like this is no longer the easy outgrowth of a normal life. We might call this one test of a well-balanced society. Yet also by a more modern test, that of success, Deborah came through with colors flying; for her ideas, especially about education for girls, worked through the family clearly for at least four generations, and indirectly, of course, are still operating.

A very different set of problems confronted Ruth Allen (1768-1863) in the generation after Deborah's. Deborah's problem was to get an education; Ruth, on the other hand, was plunged into a pioneering situation and had to learn to live and make a living in it. As a marriage gift, her father, a Walpole carpenter, gave her a tract of land in Marlborough, New Hampshire, land which he probably acquired as a grant to Revolutionary veterans. In October of 1787, Ruth's fiancé, a young saddler named David Wilkinson, went up to get the land ready for his bride. He picked out a site for a house, cut the woods and burned them, built a log house, dug a well and sowed rye in the clearing. He and Ruth were married in the spring and set out for the new homestead with all their worldly goods on two horses. She carried a feather bed, linen and crockery on hers, while David loaded his with leather and tools for his trade. When they reached the log hut they found the rye as high as the roof, and at first they had to sleep in the loft at night, pulling the ladder up after them for fear of wolves.

It was not an easy thing to adjust to such an environment, and indeed, poor Ruth was so homesick that when her first baby was four weeks old she took her on her saddle and rode all the way back to her father's house, a distance of 125 miles. The tale says she reached home on the second night—which even for an unencumbered man would break most records. At home, apparently, no one either reproached her or urged her to return—these New Englanders had extraordinary respect for individuality—and probably because of that treatment, the time arrived when, as the record put it, "she could go back content."

"Content" for Ruth, nevertheless, always involved frequent visits to her first home; and she managed to make these profitable as well as pleasant by bringing down produce to sell. At first she sold woolen yarn and knitted socks, carried down like her babies on the saddle horse. On some of these trips she had the company of an old colored man, who immortalized himself in the family saga by remarking that he never knew before that white women had to go into the bushes. Later, when the road was built, she made her journeys in a large market wagon in which she carried eggs and butter. Her grandchildren used to enjoy their lively grandmother, and a trip in the old market wagon represented the high spot in their childhood. They also loved to listen to her jokes and stories, her favorite one being of how one night as a young girl she had entertained three young men at once without letting any of them know of the others' presence in the house. So we have a picture of another gay and entertaining old lady; even when she began to stumble she passed it off with the remark that she was still "spry." "She could fall down as quick as ever she could."

In the generation after this, life clearly became a little bit easier for women. There was a definite connection between the invention of baking soda, matches and "tin kitchens" (which stood up in front of the fireplace to roast meat) and the origin of women's clubs.

Nevertheless, as life became a bit more leisurely in the early 1800's, it also became more refined—and this meant a certain decline in spontaneity as well as rudeness, the beginnings of Victorian prudery. Instead of laughing heartily when the deacon, rising to pray in church, lost the narrow front piece of his pantaloons, the serious new generation would pretend not to notice. The temperance movement, too, began to gain headway, and there was a revival of the save-or-be-damned school of religious orthodoxy.

Still, the new life had new opportunities, and Susanna Gay (1796-1864) showed how they could be exploited as they came along. She married Henry Plimpton, a blacksmith's apprentice who bought a "water privilege" and started a small foundry. Susanna found herself called upon to run a general store in one wing of her house to accommodate the men who worked in the mill, and soon afterward she took charge of the books of the "Ladies' Literary and Moral Society" and thus, in effect, supplied the neighborhood with a public library.

The aim of this first women's organization in Walpole was to "promote a rational sociability" among the ladies of the church. To do this they met once a month at some member's house, and while one of their number read aloud from *Sermons to Young Women* or Hannah More's discourses on female education, the rest braided straw to be sold to hat factories. With the money thus earned they bought more books. So for the first time, women had practice in working together, in running an organization and handling the money they earned. This was a real innovation in the community, being different from anything the men had in their town meetings or militia practice—it was the beginning of the voluntary associations which handle so much of the sociability and so many of the good works in America today.

In 1828, Susanna and some other souls in Walpole, outraged at the drift toward Unitarianism in the established church, decided to secede and form a more orthodox congregation. This was not so easy as it sounds, for the church was still part of the township and supported by taxation. In town meetings feelings grew bitter, and it was many years before any of the seceders could hope to win political office in town. Perhaps this was the reason why twenty women and only three men signed the first organization roll of the new church. (This is an interesting contrast to the South, where two generations later my husband's grandmother, a preacher's wife, felt it was neither necessary nor proper for women to organize anything, even a missionary circle.)

Susanna Plimpton was in the thick of all the work for the new church. She opened her home for Saturday prayer meetings and year after year was elected a directress of the new "Maternal Association." Gifted, capable, sociable, Susanna was the sort of person to whom her neighbors turned in any crisis. When she died, people somehow had the feeling that if she had not married so young she might have turned into a great intellectual figure. I do not believe she felt that way about herself. To be sure, she gave her daughters the best education then to be found and was undoubtedly pleased that one of them turned into a brave and successful missionary. At the same time, her letters show as much concern that the girls should wear sunbonnets to keep off freckles as that they should learn correct spelling. To me she seems more modern, combining interest in family and community, than many of the women who followed her in the latter part of the century.

For the girls who were born in the 1820's, the sweep toward Victorianism made life still more rarefied. No longer were they expected to play ball with the boys, or slide, or ride bareback after the cows, though they still did some of the milking. This was the first generation that did not have to learn to spin and weave—a heavy burden lifted; but at the same time, as part of the more earnest concern with religion, dancing went out for young people; and no more pranks, such as stuffing the pulpit Bible with a stack of playing cards, were played in church.

Nevertheless, there was still scope for energetic young women to use their abilities. Five girls were growing up at the Lewis farm at this time, and their great-grandmother Deborah was there to encourage their love of learning. The Lewises persuaded their neighbors to build a little schoolhouse nearby, with some parents giving labor and others giving materials. The children were trained meticulously in spelling and arithmetic, but their teacher also made them give reasons for what they knew. She introduced algebra, philosophy and astronomy, with a model of the solar system and a globe at her side. When Priscilla Lewis (1820-1889) went on from this school to Wheaton Academy, she was much surprised to find no equipment except blackboards, and hardly any books.

As the girls outgrew the neighborhood schools, they were sent away to the seminaries that were springing up all over New England. The very fact that they could be spared from home for a year or two at a time shows that women's work was getting lighter. The boys either could not be spared from the farm or were given vocational education for a trade, except for the few who went to Harvard to prepare for the ministry. So the women had a better liberal education on the whole than the men, a fact that is very evident from their letters. The girls had no chance to get lazy under this system, but their energies were not so completely taken up with the elemental struggle of food and clothing.

As the boys went to work at their trades, the girls too were able to find employment. Priscilla and all her sisters taught school before they were married, and thus represented the first generation for whom a paid job outside the home was freely available.

Marriage, however, still brought such formidable responsibilities for housekeeping that no one could have thought of continuing her job afterwards. Priscilla Lewis became engaged to Calvin Plimpton at the age of sixteen. Her younger sister remembered the courtship as follows: "The first time I suspected any devotion was when he offered me five cents to milk Priscilla's cows so she could go walking with him—then there was a picnic or something in Dedham and Calvin hired a team uptown. A remark there I remember by some prominent man, 'Calvin had a little the slickest team and a little the slickest girl in the crowd.'" During the interval of four years before they were married, Priscilla taught school and Calvin worked in his father's iron foundry and built an eight-room house for his bride.

Priscilla's life offered few conflicts, but increased leisure and refinement appear to have made new problems for her younger sister, Lizzie. Lizzie felt that life in the East was stagnant and that Walpole offered her neither culture nor adventure, so she toyed with the idea of going West. The Board of Education for the West, she says, offered "to find young ladies a home, pay their fare out, furnish part of their outfit and give a salary from seventy-five to three hundred dols. a year." Lizzie ended the letter outlining these plans plaintively, "I have no desire to be a burden to anyone. I hope I shall be wanted somewhere." This was a plea that would be echoed by energetic girls for the next three generations. Lizzie herself, however, never got West. Instead she went to Mount Holyoke, and soon thereafter married.

By the time my grandmother Idella Plimpton (1848-1941) was growing up, the changes in domestic work were coming faster and faster. Idella's father bought silks and muslins in Boston for making dresses, and the help of a seamstress was needed for making the elaborate modes of the day. Meanwhile the boys were beginning to buy their suits and overcoats in Boston. When his children were small, Calvin Plimpton used to go to a shoestore and bring out a huge box of assorted shoes, telling his nine young ones to pick out and keep whatever they could make fit. The family still grew a good share of food on their farm, but to vary the diet they had oysters by the barrel, raisins and figs by the basket, delicacies which Calvin would bring home from his business trips into the city. During this period too, the butcher wagon started coming around, making fresh meat available in seasons when no killings took place on the farm. These simplifications gave more free time for education (which now included the boys as well as the girls), travel, and those jobs outside the home which were still the expected occupation of a young girl before marriage.

At the age of fourteen, my grandmother lost her father; and her mother, Priscilla Lewis Plimpton, was left with a family in which her oldest boy was only twelve and the youngest, two. People told her she ought to sell her farm, but she believed that living there was good for the family and bravely put her twelve-year-old in charge of its operations. Meanwhile she kept up the family tradition of good education: her daughters went to seminaries which were soon to become colleges, while for the first time some of the boys went to college, and one son to medical school.

As for my grandmother, it happened that she was the first American college girl to spend her junior year abroad, for she was invited to go along with two of her Mount Holyoke teachers and another girl. In a way, this trip to Europe represented the flowering of the theory of education which the Lewises had been following for five generations. From the days when a desire for reading stirred in the heart of Deborah Fisher, every generation saw greater opportunity for its girls and rose to the occasion by giving it to them. Nowadays we are likely to think of 1870 as a time of formal manners, chaperons and great constriction for women. Nothing could be further from the truth about Idella's trip abroad. She moved with perfect spontaneity among young men and young women, never lacking a male escort, apparently never turning down a chance for strenuous fun such as walking over the Alps or through the dust of Vesuvius. During the winter, the Mount Holyoke party and three young American clergymen took an apartment together in Rome; and in a way they were freer than they might be today, for in the 1950's a mixed household of young unmarried persons might arouse suspicions which were warded off in those days by their perfect innocence. On the single occasion when Idella took some liberty with a young man which went beyond her teachers' idea of propriety (its exact nature unhappily shrouded behind an allusion in a letter), she was neither disciplined nor reproached but left to decide how she felt about it for herself. She probably felt pretty good; at least we have the young man's fervent assertion that he would commit the same indiscretion any time the future gave him an opportunity and his hope that she felt the same way. It is hard to see how anybody in any generation could have had more fun and friendship, or more freedom to learn about life.

Like her mother, my grandmother taught school until she was married and then devoted herself to bringing up her family. After that job was over, she was more or less retired to a position in which she was cherished and respected. Like her ancestress Deborah Lewis, she lived to be ninety, and also like her she was lame for the last thirty years of her life. I have no way of knowing whether she was as happy during those years, but certainly she was not nearly so much in the thick of family life and work. Deborah could help make important decisions for her family; but by 1920, so many of the questions that occupied the men of the family were in areas outside anything that Idella had ever encountered that often even whom to invite to dinner was not her decision.

The generation that was really put in a false position was that of my mother, Helen Kendall (1879-1913). She was sent to college, but not allowed to teach as she would have liked to do. Perhaps the men who kept her from it were right, for the women who did teach in that generation often did not marry. The world had time to waste now, and the men seemed to want women to be the ones to waste it. Some of them, like my mother, tried to keep busy with women's clubs and missionary study groups, and if she had lived longer I am sure she would have found more to do—but the point is that she had to look for it. The letters that passed to and from her Mount Holyoke classmates in the years following their graduation searched again and again the question of whether they were really justifying their education. For the first time a full job with full responsibilities was not pressed upon a girl. Other women in that period threw themselves into the fight for women's rights. They fought devotedly for this right, that their work should not be trivial—but in becoming serious, it somehow became forced. Very few women in that generation could sink back into any accepted role and feel natural.

This was why—when the 1920's came along—being good seemed less worthwhile than it had for generations. In a good society, virtue is quite literally its own reward; and by the same token, vice hardly needs inflicted punishment because it brings its own pain. When virtue goes stale, when its ordinary or expected rewards become too meager, then the hunt for fun—or fulfillment—becomes a matter of going after other rewards. A good deal of the fiction of the world, from *Tom Sawyer* to *Faust,* shows people in this predicament.

Many things about our present society make our vices still precious to us. Nevertheless, it is eighty years since there has been as good a chance for men and women to live in the world as partners. It is not only that women won the right to go into parts of the world where men went, so that they now can think, talk and act in the same terms as their husbands, even if they do not work at the same type of job all their lives. Men are learning too—learning that they can, and in fact need to, help run their households; and the forty-hour week gives them a real chance to do so. The sort of work the world now requires is different from that of the days when Deborah Lewis wove her blankets and John Lewis made tallow candles on the same farm, but the mutual support and interest the two sexes can give each other are once more very similar. A few people, including some psychiatrists, still need to be convinced that women are not unsexed by being citizens, or men by taking active roles in their homes with their children. These two orientations have equal importance. Enough of a revolution has been accomplished, however, so that a person like me feels, in some ways, closer kinship with women three or four generations back than with the last two —even though we have every day to thank the mothers, aunts and grandmothers who tried to lay out new paths in which we can move today as happily as *their* mothers and grandmothers.

The Passage Through College

Mervin B. Freedman

This paper is an account of the major events or adjustments characteristic of each of the important stages of a college career in one institution, i.e., entrance, freshman, sophomore, junior, and senior years, graduation. It is based on information derived from interviews with students, discussions with teaching faculty and administrative officers, and general observations of the College "in action."

The Entering Freshman

The 400 odd freshmen who enter each year are seventeen or eighteen years of age, chiefly upper-middle or upper-class in background. They have good academic records, and most have chosen the College with the expectation that it will be very demanding scholastically. Their knowledge of the institution varies somewhat with their backgrounds. About half of the freshmen come from private schools which prepare for Eastern liberal arts residential colleges. Such students are likely to have considerable prior acquaintance with the College. Possibly they have visited it, have a relative who is an alumna or friends already among the students. We shall call these students Group A. The majority of the remaining students, Group B, are public school girls, a shade below Group A in social status. They are likely to have a fair amount of knowledge of the College although not so much as Group A. Group C consists of students for whom the College is a very new experience. This group is rather heterogeneous, containing girls from foreign countries and areas which do not ordinarily furnish students to the larger Eastern women's colleges, a small number of students from lower middle-class origins who have been given scholarships, and some students from minority group families with limited educational backgrounds.

As one would expect, there tend to be different reactions or adjustments to the College characteristic of each of these groups. To understand these, some familiarity with the general functioning of the College is necessary. In describing the College we shall concentrate on institutional goals and procedures on the one hand and student culture on the other.

Institutional Goals and Procedures

By institutional goals and procedures is meant the major formal influences to which students are subjected through conferences with members of the administration and teaching faculty, lectures and assignments, and official writings and publications of the College. The major goal of the College is simple enough—the development of liberally educated individuals. Although a liberal education is not easily defined, there is general agreement as to the kinds of traits possessed by the liberally educated person, e.g., knowledge of our cultural heritage, disciplined intelligence, responsible citizenship, curiosity, sense of reality, independence of judgment, interest in other cultures. As for the procedures by which the College attempts to attain its major goal, examination of the general curriculum seems to yield the most significant information. Study of the curriculum reveals first of all that the College is a "traditional" educational institution, not a "progressive" school.

"Traditional," in this context, does not mean inflexible, conservative, and the like; it means simply that adherence to certain formal curriculum requirements constitutes an important part of the academic program. This is in contrast with those educational programs in which such formal requirements are likely to be regarded as secondary to the needs of individual students. Thus, students must take a science and a language; in order to guard against over-specialization, they may not take more than a certain number of hours in their major field, and so on. Such regulations are by no means hard and fast; often they may be altered or waived, but by and large they serve as guideposts outlining the educational path for the student. These general academic requirements have administrative counterparts in regulations designed for the supervision of the student's social and recreational life. Students are not completely free to come and go as they please or to spend their time entirely as they see fit. For example, there are rules specifying the time by which students must return to their dormitories and the number of weekends permitted away from the campus. Upperclassmen are expected generally to behave more responsibly and to require less supervision, however, and consequently they are subjected to fewer social regulations.

The Student Culture

We believe that a distinguishable student culture exists, one superordinate to the differences among students mentioned earlier or to be discussed later in this paper. The student body as an entity may be thought to possess characteristic qualities of personality, ways of interacting socially, types of values and beliefs, and the like, which are passed on from one "generation" of students to another and which like any culture provide a basic context in which individual learning takes place. We contend, in fact, that this culture is the prime educational force at work in the College, for, as we shall see, assimilation into the student society is the foremost concern of most new students. Suffice it to say now that in our opinion the scholastic and academic aims and processes of the College are in large measure transmitted to incoming students or mediated for them by the predominant student culture.

Although leadership in the student culture is likely to be provided by those students who are **Group A** on entrance, the general student climate is not one of snobbishness or exclusion. On the contrary the weight of the student or peer group culture is markedly in the direction of friendliness, acceptance, leveling of difference, and general ease of relationship. Participation in all activities on campus is open to almost every girl regardless of social background, race, or religion. All that is required for acceptance by fellow students is that one act pretty much like the rest—be cordial and friendly. Not that class or caste differences or distinctions of other kinds are completely obliterated. They appear on occasion in subtle ways, but as compared to American society at large, such distinctions are greatly minimized.

These qualities of agreeableness and cooperativeness are directed toward the faculty and administration as well as toward other students. Most students are dutiful, hard-working, and generally accepting of the College status quo and of the demands made upon them. Few girls, even those "snowed under" with academic work or subject to pressure of some other kind, are critical of the College structure or its procedures. When queried during interviews about the functioning of the College or about changes which might seem to be indicated on the basis of their own experiences, very few students believed that important changes should be made. Almost all felt that the way of life and the opportunities offered were nearly perfect. Where things were not going well, must students blamed themselves rather than the College structure, faculty, or administration.

Most students are interested, even enthusiastic, about at least some of their courses and academic achievements, particularly after they have chosen a major area and may pursue their own interests somewhat more freely. Many are attracted and excited by the rewards of intellectual activity as epitomized by certain faculty members. The student body in general can hardly be described as indifferent to academic work or as unaffected by it. However, except for a minority, the fundamental philosophy of the College and its academic and intellectual aims do not enter primarily into the formation of the central values and habits of life of the student body. Instead, for most students, educational experiences are assimilated to a central core of values and dispositions which is relatively independent of the more formal academic influences.

Marriage at graduation or within a few years thereafter is anticipated by almost all students; the percentage who state that they are not likely to marry, or who are quite uncertain about it, is negligible. Strong commitment to an activity or career other than that of housewife is rare. Many students, perhaps a third, are interested in graduate schooling and in careers, for example, teaching. Few, however, plan to continue with a career if it should conflict with family needs. Some report that they plan to forego careers when children are small and then resume them when children no longer require intensive care. As compared to previous periods, however, e.g., the "feminist era," few students are interested in the pursuit of demanding careers, such as law or medicine, regardless of personal cost or social pressure. Similarly, one finds few instances of people like Edna St. Vincent Millay, individuals completely committed to their art by the time of adolescence and resistive to any attempts to "tamper" with it. Of course, strong interest in intellectual activities, careers, and forms of artistic expression is by no means lacking. The important fact is that such interests tend to be secondary in the lives of most students. The life goals of the students are, therefore, primarily to be wives and mothers, useful and intelligent members of communities. They wish to work, and often at some profession, but only when this does not interfere too much with family activities.

If the peer culture is relatively autonomous with respect to faculty, it is also relatively free from direct influence by the students' families. There are few instances of home-sickness, even among freshmen, and the daily lives of most students seem little affected by thoughts of home or family. Moreover, influence from other extra-College sources, including young men, is not great. Of course, the values and expectations regarding their future wives which prevail among the young men whom the student knows must be considered. The important fact is, however, that these are interpreted for her and often pressed upon her by her own female peer culture.

Our observations on the role of young men in the lives of the students seem to run counter to what appears to be a rather universal campus "myth," namely, that most of the time not spent in academic pursuits is spent by students discussing dates, male friends, and week-end activities involving men. Our observation about the importance of early marriage as a life goal would appear to point in this direction. It must be kept in mind, however, that for a majority of students this interest in men, despite appearances, is really quite limited. Thus, most dating and concern with men is based less on interest in the men involved than on desire to maintain prestige among fellow students by doing what is expected. Since successful participation in student culture calls for some dating and interest in men, students engage in such activities, often in fairly routine fashion. Student society frowns upon "too much" dating or interest in men, a degree of interest that might interfere with adequate academic work and campus friendships. It is interesting to observe that sophomores and juniors commonly report that they dated more as freshmen, that somehow at the time it seemed "expected of them" but that now they "can relax" and not feel obligated to go out with men, when they really do not wish to. Interest in men is revived among upperclassmen, particularly in seniors as graduation and an end to the security of student days approach.

The influence of the student culture would not be so great or pervasive were it not characteristic of American society in general, of adolescence in particular, that status and security depend in large measure upon relationships with one's peers. The student culture provides order and comfort. It instructs in how to behave in various social situations, in what to think about all manner of issues, in how to deal with common problems and troublesome external influences. It even offers instruction in how to keep the faculty at a distance, how to bring pressure that will insure that the faculty behaves in expected and therefore manageable ways. It permits pleasant association with faculty members but discourages genuine relationships of a kind that might challenge the basic values of students. Although many students say that they would like greater opportunity to associate with the faculty, what they often have in mind is aid in the solution of practical problems rather than relationship on an adult basis.

Whereas for most of the students involved the peer culture provides merely a convenient and comfortable means for dealing with a fairly complex social situation and valuable preparation for the social world that they will enter after graduation, for others it is necessary to the maintenance of stability of personality. There are students who have been unable to develop internal agencies of control, who consequently have depended for a long time upon the direction of their peers. Separation from the peer group would put them under a very severe strain. This is a source of that rigid adherence to peer values which we sometimes see in individual students and is also a factor making for resistance to change in the culture itself.

The Freshman Year

Entrance. Most freshmen arrive enveloped by an air of eager expectancy. Those who are familiar with the College may be relaxed, those with little first hand knowledge of it may feel some trepidation about what will happen, but by and large most freshmen arrive anticipating new and different experience and ready and willing to meet it. Getting into the College represents a real accomplishment for most of them; they are proud to be members of the College community and are eager to live up to the honor of having been admitted.

The prime concern of most entering freshmen, although often not a matter of explicit or conscious knowledge, is with acceptance by their fellow students. Not that entering freshmen are unconcerned about educational or intellectual matters. These constitute, in fact, their greatest conscious anxiety. When queried concerning the areas in which they anticipated their chief problems and difficulties, in thinking ahead to college life, most freshmen reply with some expression of uncertainty about intellectual competition with other students, the difficulty of the courses, and the like. Such considerations are real and important, but in our view they are, for the majority of students, secondary to often less conscious but more pressing social concerns.

In considering the earliest adjustments to the college we may focus on the differential adjustments of the three groups of entering students described earlier. Of the largest, Group A, no great academic adjustments are required. They have been well prepared both in terms of course content and in work habits for the demands that will be made upon them. To be sure, the courses they take as freshmen are likely to be more difficult than any in preparatory school, and greater individual responsibility in planning work is expected, but by and large important academic readjustments are not necessary. Similarly, these students are not likely to be faced by novel or truly pressing demands of social adjustment. The student culture tends to be in many ways a continuation of the kind of social life with which these students are already accustomed. Moreover, students of this group are likely to have friends and acquaintances in the College.

So it is that college entrance makes few demands upon these students in the sense of requiring major changes in their established ways of perceiving or doing things. Or at least it may be said that the way is open for this kind of "status quo" adjustment to the new environment of the College. Of course, all students of this group need not and do not choose this path of least resistance; but it is our impression that most do, perhaps because inertia and resistance to change are strong forces in most people. If one important function of a college is to induce students to re-examine their established ways and accepted habits of thought, it appears that the difficulties in the way of carrying out this function with the present group of students are great.

The initial situation is different for the second group of students, Group B, those who are similar to Group A in social or geographic background but who are graduates of public schools. Most of these students do not enter the College with the basic knowledge or habits of work that permit a relatively easy transition to the academic life of the College. Their secondary education has usually been neither so good nor so thorough. Some of the most able of the students in this group can effect the necessary academic readjustments with a minimum of effort, but for the majority the initial academic impact of the College is very great. For a good part of the freshman year many of these students are under great pressure; they work long hours, often get poor grades, and feel generally incompetent intellectually and academically.

Such involvement with academic problems tends to obscure the social adjustment of this group, which is for them a more subtle process. There are no clearly defined social distinctions analogous to the educational differences between this group and the previous one. Prior to entrance the members of this group are likely to be concerned about the social fate awaiting them. They wonder if they will be liked and if they possess the requisite qualities of personality and attractiveness to enable them to enter into the general social scheme of things. Above all they do not wish to be excluded by their peers or to be "out of things." Although these concerns loom large, they are not likely to be so explicit or clear as the matter of academic adjustment. This is so because qualities like social ease and poise facilitate the desired social adjustment; and in order to maintain these qualities at as high a level as possible, one is likely to play down concern or anxieties of this nature, to hide them from others or even to deny them to oneself, when this is necessary for the maintenance of self-esteem.

The initial social impact of the College on these students is a gratifying one. They are happy to find the student culture so friendly and agreeable, and they are pleased to learn that entrance into the prevalent student society makes few demands upon them for change of accepted thoughts or ways. By behaving pretty much as they always have or by modifying their behavior only slightly, they can get on well socially. So almost without giving these matters "a second thought" this group of students is absorbed into the main stream of student culture. They are happy to relax and let this happen, to find that their social fears are so easily allayed. Thus, while attention is centered on academic adjustments, these students implicitly and quietly slip into the student society which is to play so large a role in molding the values they will live by.

Things are different again for the third and smallest group of entering students described earlier, Group C, the one containing the more atypical students. The educational adjustments of the students in this group are similar to those of the second group in that they find themselves to be not quite prepared for the academic demands made upon them and consequently find the academic going rather rough at first. They differ from the second group, however, in that social adjustment is also a demanding process. These students, like those in the previous group, enter with considerable concern about how they will be received by other students, and they are similarly gratified to discover the agreeableness, the openness, the friendliness of the prevalent student society. Unlike the previous group, however, they are sufficiently different from the major peer culture in social background, habit, and custom so that they cannot subtly adjust to it almost automatically or unthinkingly. Some greater effort is required. Not that participation in the general student society is in any way barred to this group: most of these students who so desire can enter into it, depending, of course, to some extent upon their qualities of general attractiveness. For these students adjustment to the student culture is much more a matter of explicit or conscious decision. They do not enter into it as a matter of course, like the first group, or unconsciously through subtle adjustments, like the second. Standing somewhat apart from the student culture to begin with, these students must make some explicit decisions concerning the degree to which they wish to participate in it and the methods by which they wish to do so. They are thereby forced to consider alternative modes of behavior and alternative values.

The Remainder of the Freshman Year. Within a short time, several weeks or months after entrance, most students have settled into a relatively characteristic student role; that is to say, certain patterns of student behavior and attitude may be identified (they may be thought of as subcultures within the predominating student culture), and most students may be characterized quite early in their college careers as exhibiting one or another of these patterns. These educational patterns, which bear some systematic relationships to the groups of entering students described above, will be discussed in detail in Dr. Brown's paper. Here we shall concentrate on over-all characteristics of the student or general College community at various stages, ignoring for the time being variations from one type of student to another.

The freshman year determines the basic orientation to the College and goes a long way toward either establishing or reaffirming certain enduring habits and values of life. For the great majority of students it is a happy year. Almost all adjust successfully to the peer society and find appropriate companionship, at least one or several students, if not many, with whom they can share thoughts and feelings, in whom they can find support. Those who are not quite prepared on arrival for the high level of work expected of them may have a difficult time academically, but social satisfactions often offset this strain. Within a short time freshmen are caught up in the relatively self-sufficient student culture; family ties are attenuated, extra-College pressures are minimal, real faculty influence is yet to come.

There is, however, a small group of students whose general adjustment to the College runs rather counter to the predominant student culture. These are the students who are already faculty-oriented or, better possibly, "adult-oriented." They are interested in establishing personal relationships with members of the faculty. Often the attempt is to reconstitute some family or parental situation with the faculty member, to establish, for example, a mother-daughter or father-daughter kind of relationship. These students, often, are very promising. Since they are not encapsulated within the student culture, the possibility exists of "reaching" them intellectually and hence of coming closer to attaining the goals of the College. The "trick" in achieving this end is for the faculty member to place the emotional force of the relationship behind striving for academic or intellectual goals. The student learns, in short, that the road to adult or faculty approval and to mature adult relationship is real scholarship.

One other small group of students should be considered here, because it comprises many of those who withdraw from the College in the freshman or sophomore year, particularly in the freshman year. This group of students is not cooperative, dutiful, agreeable, and the like. Rather these students tend to be assertive, somewhat rebellious toward authority, unconventional; in short, quite the opposite of the majority of students. They tend to be resentful of college regulations or prescriptions, social or academic, and so they find adjustment to the College community very trying, if not impossible. When such students leave the College, it is often to attend other schools which they think will place less restraint upon them. It is interesting to note that these students, who are rebellious toward authority and unusually independent, tend to seek out one another

266

and to find support thereby for their rather deviant attitudes or behavior.

The phenomenon of withdrawal from college before graduation merits some attention as a problem in its own right, since the percentage of students who withdraw from liberal arts colleges has risen in recent years. What seems to be reflected in this increase in withdrawals is a conception of a college or of a college education as some sort of marketable product, as something one purchases essentially, as something one can obtain at one institution just as readily as at another. Thus, a student considers it quite in the scheme of things to "shop around" from one college to another. Prior to World War II, however, entrance into a college probably implied much greater commitment to it. It is interesting to note that in England, if a student leaves a university, it is assumed that he has done so because of academic failure. There is seldom any other reason.

The Sophomore Year

By the sophomore year the basic processes of adjustment to the college which were started in the freshman year have reduced many if not most of the marked differences among freshmen. The predominant student culture and the subcultures within it now stand out clearly; pre- and extra-College influences and forces seem to shrink even more into the background. So it is that the importance of the quality of secondary schooling now becomes a negligible factor. By sophomore year those students who were handicapped in the beginning by deficiencies of secondary schooling have had opportunity to overcome them, and the level of a student's work is now pretty much a function of her intrinsic ability, interest, and motivation. As we have observed earlier, many sophomores display less interest in young men. Those students who were interested in men chiefly because of external social pressure no longer yield so readily to this pressure. The chief energies of most students are now concentrated on the campus, in academic work and in associations with fellow students.

The sophomore year is the one in which a major field of concentration must be selected, and by the second semester of the year most students have made a choice. Often, of course, the choice of major is one based on real awareness and evaluation of the potentialities involved and the meanings of such a choice in one's general life plan; and thus, it represents a real commitment to a field or discipline. Sometimes choice of a major is a function of deep unconscious motivational forces in the personality which tend unduly to influence the contemporary scene or more purely educational considerations. In a large number of cases, choice is based not so much upon either one of these factors as upon conditions relatively peripheral to the student and her real needs for growth and development, for example, reasons of convenience or expediency. As one would expect, there are certain majors which are more "fashionable" than others, which have more prestige value among students. On occasion students select a major field or turn away from one because of feelings of liking or dislike, often temporary, for students or faculty in that field. But perhaps most common of all is choice of an area of concentration which is calculated not to upset one, to allow one to go along with a minimum of change in fundamental values or beliefs. It is not surprising that expressions of dissatisfaction with choice of major in college are common among alumnae. When asked if they would choose another major were they again to be students, from a third to more than a half of the alumnae in various samples say that they would do so.

Academically things are likely to go rather smoothly in the sophomore year. Where there were handicaps of inadequate secondary schooling, they have often been overcome, and those students who have been lacking in direction tend to become better oriented. On the whole sophomores are industrious and enthusiastic about academic work. They enjoy most of their classes and look forward to being upperclassmen, anticipating that they will have the privilege of greater freedom in choice of courses and in work performance. Evidences of what has been called "sophomore slump" are rare. Rather it appears that the inertia or disorganization implied by this term are more likely to occur in the second semester of the freshman year.

If academic industry and enthusiasm are common among sophomores, they are, as we have observed, also characteristic of the student culture at large. It might be said, then, that in these respects students are sharing in both the explicit goals of the College and in the general value system of student society. The influence of the student culture is, however, rather a leveling or moderating one from the point of view of scholastic motivation and aims. On the one hand, it pulls in the direction of serious scholarship for those students whose academic motivations are dubious. Often a student learns the excitement and enjoyment of intellectual pursuit from another student before she does so from any particular book or class. On the other hand the student culture may soften or blunt strong intellectual or career drive. For example, students who enter college with the aim of achieving high artistic or intellectual goals often find themselves tempted to "relax and take things easier." Often such ambitiousness is associated with factors like the desire to rise socially in the world, and students learn that they can do this merely by being pleasant, nice, agreeable. In fact being "too outstanding" might interfere with one's acceptance by certain groups. Or again it may be suggested by one student to another that some great or noble aim may be merely a "cover-up" for certain unfortunate personal characteristics, such as competitiveness with men.

In summary, the lives of sophomores are centered in the College community, in the enjoyment of friendships and associations with fellow students and in academic work which is highly demanding of their time and effort but which nevertheless provides much satisfaction. Before going on to the junior year, we should comment on a number of students who are rather exceptions to the general type of sophomore. These are students who are interested in men in a serious way, and whose interests are therefore not centered primarily or almost solely in the College community.

These students are of two rather different kinds. The first kind seems to be primarily socially oriented. They do not share in the explicit aims of the College or in the predominant student culture. They have come to college to make a good marriage or to acquire a smattering of a liberal education for its usefulness in social situations, and they are quite resistive to real intellectual development. This group of students finds the academic demands of the College very onerous, and many are likely to withdraw at the end of the sophomore year. Two years is sufficient for most of these students to get what they think they want out of college. This group plus the rebellious type referred to earlier who remain beyond the freshman year comprise most of the withdrawals during the sophomore year.

The second kind of student with strong interest in men is quite different, because this interest is not accompanied by a paucity of academic or intellectual interests. Rather these students tend to be superior scholars. They are girls who are engaged to be married or are seriously involved with men but who do not feel any need to sacrifice their own individuality or intellectual, professional, or career aims in the process. Thus, these students tend to have rather clear notions concerning the place of their current educational interests or esthetic or intellectual pursuits in their future lives. One gets the impression that in these cases the interest in men is a meaningful expression, that it is not, as it is with many students in the former group, some kind of defense against intellectual development. In not every case is a deep interest in men indicative of an educational loss.

The Junior Year

The junior year may be thought of as the year of maximum solidarity in the College community both educationally and socially. Many of the more deviant kinds of students have withdrawn. Those who remain comprise a student body held together by such strong bonds as shared experiences and common values. The forces of socialization within the student culture have in a sense achieved their maximum effect in the junior year, and it is the juniors who seem to be the chief heirs and transmitters of student culture. They are the torchbearers in this process, the individuals who serve as the chief models upon which lower classmen will pattern themselves. Seniors, to be sure, are the acknowledged campus leaders in the sense of filling the highest offices of student government and the like, but they already have one foot outside the College, and, as compared to juniors, they are moving away from the center of student culture.

In some ways the junior year contains elements which make of it a unique social experience, one not likely to be repeated again in the lives of most students. It is unlikely that a student will find herself at some future date in a society which offers so great an opportunity for differentiation of role and function and at the same time such a high degree of order and security. The junior class exhibits this great social solidarity despite the fact that sub-groups within the junior culture display a considerable degree of variation. There are groups of juniors who may be identified by their common interest in political affairs, there are a few Bohemians and esthetes, there are the girls whose lives are centered on more purely intellectual activities, and so on. Yet the bonds of cohesiveness are such that these differences may be tolerated without detracting from the unity and identity of the class as a whole.

Educationally the junior year is likely to be the most satisfying. There is the gratification of being an upperclassman, of having required courses out of the way, of being able to take elective courses in one's chosen field of concentration. Intellectually or academically, the juniors may be thought of as the group most identified with the College, with both its explicit and implicit values. The juniors participate most in the general College culture which exists over and beyond the student culture. Thus, it is likely that the differences in values and general outlook between seniors and freshmen reported on later by Dr. Webster already exist among juniors. As observed earlier these changes are a compromise between the explicit goals of the College and its faculty and the defenses of the student culture against too radical an encroachment upon their habits and mores; but nevertheless, as compared to freshmen, the juniors have been "liberated" in the direction of the aims of a liberal education. In short, juniors, more than any other class share in the general value system of the faculty and administration. Not that seniors do not share in this, but, as we shall see, the imminence of graduation and future changes complicates their participation in this aspect of the life of the College.

Juniors have a fairly stable sense of identity as liberal arts students and as members of the College community. For most students this is somehow a broader, a more differentiated or complex identity than the one possessed as a freshman. Consequently such an identity usually represents an advance on the road to self-development. There is some danger, of course, that this identity may be too satisfying, that too many students will wish to return to it in the face of the difficulties and anxieties of subsequent periods of life. From this point of view one may think of the "perennial junior" rather than the "perennial sophomore." Such a person would not have grown beyond the secure, stable, and satisfying identity of her junior year and would like to return to it.

The Senior Year

The senior year is climaxed by graduation and highlighted by the imminence of the "after-life," as it is called by some of the students. No longer is the student's life largely circumscribed by the College, and no longer is her major task that of adjusting to the College community. The processes of the past three years must suddenly be reversed, as it were. We have seen that the first three years are characterized by increased adjustment, increased solidarity within the College structure, this process reaching its apex in the junior year. Now suddenly a student must respond to very different pressures, ones external to the College community. Many students are on the verge of losing their chief emotional support, the friendship of fellow students. Many are likely soon to find themselves in environments emphasizing values and a general orientation to life quite different from their own. Despite these new and pressing concerns, however, there is really no let-up in current demands. However much seniors may be oriented to the larger community, they must deal with the pressures, academic and social, of the College. Small wonder then that seniors often feel tense, frustrated, confused.

One way of looking at the situation of the senior is to consider that as a freshman she entered with a fairly stable and integrated notion of what she was and where she belonged, with some real sense of identity based on her place in the family and home community. Certain religious, social, and political convictions were accepted almost as given in the nature of things. The process of education brought about changes in this identity, as the student shared more in the general values and outlook of the College community, as she took on the identity of a liberal arts student. These changes could occur fairly smoothly, without a great deal of anxiety and difficulty, however, because the weight of the College environment supported them. The changes did not place a student in a situation of actual or potential confusion or conflict, at least not to a marked degree. The situation of the senior, however, is different. She has lost the identity with which she entered college and fears that her new one, that of the student and liberally educated woman, will not be adequate to the demands of the "after-life." As we have elsewhere (27) put it, "Many seniors are in a situation of having thrown off traditional values without having fully established others of their own, of having loosened long-standing inner controls at a time when new experiences have to be integrated, of having rejected old identities at the very time when important decisions have to be made. We should not be surprised, then, if they tend to be rebellious rather than autonomous, dominating rather than self-assured, cynical rather than realistic, hungry for sensations rather than able to enjoy them in a relaxed way."

Since an essential element of the senior experience is preoccupation with one's future role and identity, let us examine some of the possibilities open to seniors after graduation and the ways in which the College experience is related to them. The most common expectation is that students will marry and thus have as their prime identity that of wife and mother. Usually this concept of wife and mother or housewife is broadened by notions of contributing to the community, i.e., to the Red

271

Cross, the League of Women Voters, and the like. Now how is one's college experience related to this future goal? The College, of course, does not prepare a student for being a wife and mother in the same way that it may prepare her for certain professional careers, such as teaching or law. Rather, the relationship is somewhat less close, the reasoning being somewhat as follows. A liberal education, regardless of field of concentration, enables one to function more creatively and efficiently, to live more fully, no matter what one's specific life situation. The emphasis is not so much on doing something then as on being something, a person who can think rationally and logically, who can appreciate and understand another person, another culture, a book, play, political discussion, and so on. The aim of a liberal education is to produce a free person, one who is liberated from prejudice and blind adherence to convention and tradition, free to apply herself as reason and morality seem to dictate.

In effect, though, a stumbling block often arises in the transition from the role of liberally educated student to that of the liberally educated member of society at large. Particularly in the senior year, the translation from the one to the other may well become quite obscure. The reason for this appears to be the absence in our society of a real place for the liberally educated individual who is not identified with some accomplishment or activity. The emphasis in our society is, in short, on doing, not being; and unfortunately, the doing involved in being a wife and mother often brings little recognition, no matter how demanding the tasks involved, no matter how creative the participation.

Many seniors, then, experience a sense of conflict between what they have been educated for and what awaits them. They seldom can define this conflict for themselves or elaborate its details; but it is present nevertheless, and it often contributes considerably to the perturbations and doubts of the senior year. One has but to question a number of college alumnae on the subject of what meaning their college education has had in their lives in order to realize the extent of this feeling, for often from the housewives among them comes a kind of half-hearted response to the effect that their education has enabled them to appreciate a play more fully, to understand a newspaper editorial better, or to participate more effectively in an intellectual conversation. Implicit in their replies is often a note of apology. Somehow they feel that they have let their college down and have not lived up to what has been expected of its graduates. They seem to feel that accomplishments within the home and family are hardly worthy of mention.

So it is that many seniors, when considering marriage, find that their intellectual and academic pursuits and accomplishments lose much of their luster. Marriage and commitment to a certain discipline or body of knowledge are often seen as mutually incompatible, and to the extent that marriage is seriously considered, a senior is likely to question the value or relevance to her future life of her current intellectual activities. Unfortunately, this conflict is likely to be strongest for the more serious students, since those not strongly committed to a discipline can more readily abandon it. Indeed, anticipation of this type of conflict is a major reason why many students avoid any serious commitments throughout their college careers.

In this area, it should be noted that students with professional ambitions often fare better. As we have pointed out earlier, most of these students plan to marry and to forego their careers or at least interrupt them in accord with family needs. These students, however, are not faced by what seems to be the all or none conception of marriage of the foregoing group of students. Rather, marriage is more an activity in which they voluntarily choose to participate and is not one which determines their entire sense of identity. They are not wives and mothers solely but are also actual or potential teachers, scientists, business or professional women, and the like. What appears to be evident in this group of students is a measure of success in combining career and marriage in their anticipations. Indeed, one may well wonder if a more equal admixture of professional and liberal schooling may not at the present time, given the current status of the housewife in our society, be more effective in "liberating" women than is the current liberal arts philosophy with its secondary emphasis on professional training. One might argue, in short, that an important contribution to the "freeing" of a woman would be to give her the feeling she could do something of importance, if she wished to, besides being a housewife. Voluntary choice of a housewife's career would then make of it less a secondary avocation into which one "sank" out of lack of ability or inertia.

The foregoing leads directly into the general meaning, or meanings, of marriage for seniors. In keeping with the general tenor of the times, most students marry fairly young. Many are engaged by graduation and marry shortly thereafter. The majority of the remaining students work at something, usually something well below the level of their ability, or else they attend school for one or a few years, marking time, as it were, until "the right man" comes along. For many students, of course, marriage is the natural outcome of a meaningful relationship. They know the man well and are ready for the demands of married life. For many, however, early marriage represents in essence an attempt at solution of seemingly insurmountable problems. Thus, many seniors rush into marriage, hardly knowing the man involved, as a way of resolving the dilemmas thrust upon them by graduation. It often seems to be an inviting resolution of difficulty to a student unaccustomed to choice who must now make many choices, to a student facing the prospect of working at something which has but little intrinsic meaning for her, or to a student who feels somehow abandoned in the face of loss of the emotional support of her classmates.

It seems that the most characteristic feature of the senior year is the sense of uncertainty, of strain, of confusion in the face of the need to make choices or decisions. Unfortunately, in many cases, seniors have had little practice in making meaningful decisions. They come to college as fresh-

273

men almost automatically, as another step in an orderly life progression. They enter a college community which, led by the predominant student culture, is well calculated to protect students from uncertainty and strain, from experiences of failure and defeat, from the need for making difficult decisions. (As we have seen, often even the very important matter of choice of major rests upon peripheral factors and does not deeply involve students).

One would hope, of course, that seniors would rise to the demands of the occasion; that faced by the loss of the protective environment of the College and by the need to deal with complex issues of life in society at large, they would carry out the examination of their position, the "soul-searching" necessary to the charting of their future courses. Many do so, of course. Militating against this process, however, is the general pressure of other forces during senior year. It is, after all, only one academic year of some nine months duration, and during this brief time a senior is subject to much academic pressure. She may recognize some of the issues involved and desire to do something about them but still be blocked from doing so by lack of time and energy. Under such circumstances one would hope that at the least a process could be begun in the senior year which would be carried over into the "after-life" and continued there. From this point of view postponement of major decisions for a time after graduation through such means as additional schooling or working is preferable to an attempt at premature solution, for example, a marriage for which the student is really not prepared. The former provides opportunity for further growth, while the latter may place one in a situation that makes further development difficult if not impossible.

The difficulties faced by seniors would seem to argue for some sort of college environment which does not shield students from experience with complexity, difficulty, even failure, and from the necessity for making meaningful decisions. This might mean an attempt to "challenge" the predominant student culture in some way so that most students can not get along well simply by being what "they have always been." Probably the earlier in a student's career that this can be done the better. It may be that many students, when they achieve the intellectual heights desired for them in the senior year, find that there is not time enough to exercise these functions adequately; and as we have seen, for many, intellectual growth stops with the senior year.

Women, Husbands, and History

COUNTLESS commencement speakers are rising these days on countless platforms all over the world to tell thousands of helpless young captives how important they are—as citizens in a free society, as educated, rational, privileged participants in a great historic crisis. But for my part I want merely to tell you young ladies that I think there is much you can do about that crisis in the humble role of housewife—which, statistically, is what most of you are going to be whether you like the idea or not just now—and you'll like it!

To explain what I mean I must ask you to step a long way back and recall with me that over vast periods of history and over most of the globe the view has prevailed that man is no more than a unit in the social calculus. Tribal life—the way of life pursued by man for by far the longest period of his history, of which there are many remnants today in Africa—knows no individuals, only groups with disciplines and group sanctions. But then at a certain point in time and place there took place the most momentous revolution yet achieved by mankind—a revolution compared with which such achievements as the discovery of fire or the invention of the wheel seem modest. In the origins of our Western civilization, among two small peoples of the eastern Mediterranean, the Greeks and the Jews, the great Copernican revolution of politics began: the discovery that the state exists for man, not man for the state, and that the individual human personality, spirit, soul—call it what you will—contains within itself the meaning and measure of existence and carries as a result the full range of responsibility and choice.

Once the Greek vision of reason and the Jewish concept of moral choice had sent man forth onto the stage of history in

From an address at the Smith College Commencement, Northampton, Massachusetts, June 6, 1955.

182

this new guise of self-determination and responsibility, clearly only one form of society would provide a framework for the new energies and capacities that could now be released. That form of society is the free society upon which the peoples of the West have been engaged for the last two thousand years, with disasters and setbacks, with triumphs and tragedies, with long sweeps of history's pendulum between the extreme of freedom and tyranny, of individualism and collectivism, of rationalism and spiritualism.

The peoples of the West are still struggling with the problems of a free society and, just now, are in dire trouble. For to create a free society is at all times a precarious and audacious experiment. Its bedrock is the concept of man as an end in himself, as the ultimate reason for the whole apparatus of government, and the institutions of free society fulfill their task only in so far as this primary position of the free citizen— the *homo liber et legalis*—is not lost to sight. But violent pressures are constantly battering away at this concept, reducing man once again to subordinate status, limiting his range of choice, abrogating his responsibility, and returning him to his primitive status of anonymity in the social group. And it is to these pressures in their contemporary forms that I want to call your attention because I think you can be more helpful in identifying, isolating, and combating these pressures, this virus, than you girls perhaps today realize.

As you have learned here at Smith, science, among other things, arose out of the disintegration of feudal society and the rebirth of individualism in the Reformation and the Renaissance. As the individual mind was released from medieval bondage, as reason again became the test of faiths, the processes of free inquiry opened vast new fields of knowledge and human endeavor. There followed an almost explosive expansion of mental horizons. Science, born of freedom, and technology, born of science, grew by leaps and bounds into a giant of power and complexity. Certainly the material well-being of Western man was advanced with a speed and to an extent never before seen on earth. And there were great spiritual advances.

183

But, as always, history's pendulum swung too far, this time toward the extreme of social fragmentation, of individualism, of abstract intellectualism. And it seems to me that the very process which, in the name of individual liberty, disintegrated the old order—this very process has developed into a powerful drive toward the precise opposite of individualism, namely totalitarian collectivism.

Let me put it this way! Individualism promoted technological advances, technology promoted increased specialization, and specialization promoted an ever-closer economic interdependence between specialties. The more intense the specialization, the more complete the interdependence of the specialties—and this necessity of interdependence constitutes a powerful economic drive toward that extreme of a machine state in which individual freedom is wholly submerged.

As the old order disintegrated into this confederation of narrow specialties, each pulling in the direction of *its particular* interest, the individual person tended to become absorbed—literally—by *his particular* function in society. Having sacrificed wholeness of mind and breadth of outlook to the demands of their specialities, individuals no longer responded to social stimuli as total human beings: rather they reacted in partial ways as members of an economic class, or industry, or profession whose concern was with some limited self-interest.

Thus this typical Western man—or typical Western husband!—operates well in the realm of means, as the Romans did before him. But outside his specialty, in the realm of ends, he is apt to operate poorly or not at all. And this neglect of the cultivation of more mature values can only mean that his life, and the life of the society he determines, will lack valid purpose, however busy and even profitable it may be.

And here's where you come in: to restore valid, meaningful purpose to life in your home; to beware of instinctive group reaction to the forces which play upon you and yours; to watch for and arrest the constant gravitational pulls to which we are all exposed, your workaday husband especially, in our specialized, fragmented society that tends to widen the breach between reason and emotion, between means and ends.

And let me also remind you that you will live, most of you, in an environment in which "facts," the data of the senses, are

184

glorified, and value judgments are assigned inferior status as mere "matters of opinion." It is an environment in which art is often regarded as an adornment of civilization rather than a vital element of it, while philosophy is not only neglected but deemed faintly disreputable, because "it never gets you anywhere." Even religion, you will find, commands a lot of earnest allegiance that is more verbal than real, more formal than felt.

You may be hitched to one of these creatures we call "Western man," and I think part of your job is to keep him Western, to keep him truly purposeful, to keep him whole. In short— while I have had very little experience as a wife or mother—I think one of the biggest jobs for many of you will be to frustrate the crushing and corrupting effects of specialization, to integrate means and ends, to develop that balanced tension of mind and spirit which can be properly called "integrity."

This assignment for you, as wives and mothers, has great advantages. In the first place, it is home work—you can do it in the living room with a baby in your lap, or in the kitchen with a can opener in your hands. If you're really clever, maybe you can even practice your saving arts on that unsuspecting man while he's watching television. And, secondly, it is important work worthy of you, whoever you are, or your education, whatever it is—even Smith College—because we will defeat totalitarian, authoritarian ideas only by better ideas; we will frustrate the evils of vocational specialization only by the virtues of intellectual generalities. Since Western rationalism and Eastern spiritualism met in Athens and that mighty creative fire broke out, collectivism in various forms has collided with individualism time and again. This twentieth-century collision, this "crisis" we are forever talking about, will be won at last not on the battlefield but in the head and heart.

If the Colosseum at Rome is, as some say, the symbol of Roman failure to integrate mind and spirit, or means and ends, the hydrogen bomb, we might say, is the symbol of our own very similar self-betrayal. And one may hope that Hiroshima, like Rome's bloody arena, may be remembered at some distant day as a scene symbolizing a new beginning for mankind.

So you see, I have some rather large notions about you young ladies and what you have to do to rescue us wretched slaves of specialization and group thinking from further shrink-

185

age and contraction of mind and spirit. But you will have to be alert or you may get caught yourself—even in the kitchen or the nursery—by the steady pressures with which you will be surrounded.

And now that I have dared to suggest what you should do about your husbands and friends, I am, recklessly, going to even make some suggestions about your children as well.

In the last fifty years, so much of our thinking has been in terms of institutional reform—reform of the economic system, social security, the use and misuse of government, international co-operation, etc. All this thinking has been necessary and salutary, but somewhere along the line the men and women whose personalities and potentialities will largely determine the spirit of such institutions have been lost to sight. Worse than that, we have even evolved theories that the paramount aim of education and character formation is to produce citizens who are "well adjusted" to their institutional environment, citizens who can fit painlessly into the social pattern.

While I am not in favor of maladjustment, I view this cultivation of neutrality, this breeding of mental neuters, this hostility to eccentricity and controversy, with grave misgiving. One looks back with dismay at the possibility of a Shakespeare perfectly adjusted to bourgeois life in Stratford, a Wesley contentedly administering a county parish, George Washington going to London to receive a barony from George III, or Abraham Lincoln prospering in Springfield with nary a concern for the preservation of the crumbling Union.

But in this decisive century it seems to me that we need not just "well-adjusted," "well-balanced" personalities, not just better groupers and conformers (to casually coin a couple of fine words) but more idiosyncratic, unpredictable characters (that rugged frontier word "ornery" occurs to me); people who take open eyes and open minds out with them into the society which they will share and help to transform.

But before any of you gallant girls swear any mighty oaths about fighting the shriveling corruptions and conformations of mind and spirit, before you adopt any rebellious resolutions for the future, make no mistake about it—it is much easier to get yourself and yours adjusted and to accept the conditioning

186

which so many social pressures will bring to bear upon you. After all tribal conformity and archaic dictatorship could not have lasted so long if they did not accord comfortably with basic human needs and desires. The modern dictators are reviving a very ancient and encrusted way of life. Hitler discovered this. The Fascists knew it. The Communists are busy brainwashing all over Asia. And what they are washing out is precisely independence of judgment and the moral courage with which to back such judgments. And there are, alas!, some leaders in our country who certainly have a brainwashing glint in their eye when they meet with an unfamiliar idea.

Now, as I have said, women, especially educated women such as you, have a unique opportunity to influence us, man and boy, and to play a direct part in the unfolding drama of our free society. But I am told that nowadays the young wife or mother is short of time for the subtle arts, that things are not what they used to be; that once immersed in the very pressing and particular problems of domesticity many women feel frustrated and far apart from the great issues and stirring debates for which their education has given them understanding and relish. Once they read Baudelaire. Now it is the *Consumers' Guide*. Once they wrote poetry. Now it's the laundry list. Once they discussed art and philosophy until late in the night. Now they are so tired they fall asleep as soon as the dishes are finished. There is, often, a sense of contraction, of closing horizons and lost opportunities. They had hoped to play their part in the crisis of the age. But what they do is wash the diapers.

Now, I hope I have not painted too depressing a view of your future, for the fact is that Western marriage and motherhood are yet another instance of the emergence of individual freedom in our Western society. Their basis is the recognition in women as well as men of the primacy of personality and individuality. I have just returned from Africa where the illiteracy of the mothers is an obstacle to child education and advancement and where polygamy and female labor is still the dominant system. The common sight on the road is an African striding along swinging his stick or his spear, while a few feet behind comes the wife with a load of firewood on her head, a baby on her back and dragging a couple more children by the hand.

187

The point is that whether we talk of Africa, Islam, or Asia, women "never had it so good" as you do. And in spite of the difficulties of domesticity you have a way to participate actively in the crisis in addition to keeping yourself and those about you straight on the difference between means and ends, mind and spirit, reason and emotion—not to mention keeping your man straight on the differences between Botticelli and Chianti.

In brief if one of the chief needs in these restless times is for a new quality of mind and heart, who is nearer to the care of this need, the cultivation of this quality, than parents, especially mothers, who educate and form the new generation?

So, add to all of your concerns for Western man, your very special responsibility for Western children. In a family based upon mutual respect, tolerance, and understanding affection, the new generation of children—the citizens of tomorrow—stand their best chance of growing up to recognize the fundamental principle of free society—the uniqueness and value and wholeness of each individual human being. For this recognition requires discipline and training. The first instinct of all our untutored egos is to smash and grab, to treat the boy next door as a means not an end when you pinch his air rifle, or deny the uniqueness of your small sister's personality when you punch her in the stomach and snatch her lollipop.

Perhaps this is merely to say that the basis of any tolerable society—from the small society of the family up to the great society of the State—depends upon its members learning to love. By that I do not mean sentimentality or possessive emotion. I mean the steady recognition of others' uniqueness and a sustained intention to seek their good. In this, freedom and charity go hand in hand and they both have to be learned. Where better than in the home? And by whom better than the parents, especially the mother?

In short, far from the vocation of marriage and motherhood leading you away from the great issues of our day, it brings you back to their very center and places upon you an infinitely deeper and more intimate responsibility than that borne by the majority of those who hit the headlines and make the news and live in such a turmoil of great issues that they end by being totally unable to distinguish which issues are really great.

188

Yet you may say that these functions of the home could have been as well fulfilled without your years of study, performed perhaps better by instinct and untroubled by those hints of broader horizons and more immortal longings which it is the purpose of a college education to instill.

Well, there are two things to say to that. The first, of course, is that in modern America the home is not the boundary of a woman's life. There are outside activities aplenty. But even more important is the fact, surely, that what you have learned here can fit you as nothing else can for the primary task of making homes and whole human beings in whom the rational values of freedom, tolerance, charity, and free inquiry can take root. You have learned discrimination. You have the tolerance which comes from the realization of man's infinite variety. Because you have learned from history the pathos and mutability of human affairs, you have a sense of pity. From literature you have learned the abiding values of the human heart and the discipline and sacrifice from which those values will flower in your own hearts and in the life of your families.

There can be no waste of any education that gives you these things. But you can waste them, or you can use them. I hope you'll use them. I hope you'll not be content to wring your hands, feed your family, and just echo all the group, the tribal ritual refrain. I hope you'll keep everlastingly at the job of seeing life steady and seeing it whole. And you can help others —husbands, children, friends—to do so too. You may, indeed you must, help to integrate a world that has been falling into bloody pieces. History's pendulum has swung dangerously far away from the individual, and you may, indeed you must, help to restore it to the vital center of its arc.

Long ago at the origins of our way of life it was written of a valiant woman in the Book of Proverbs:

Strength and beauty are her clothing; and she shall laugh in the latter day. She hath opened her mouth to wisdom and the law of clemency is on her tongue; she hath looked well to the paths of her house and hath not eaten her bread idle. Her children rose up and called her blessed; her husband and he praised her.

I could wish you no better vocation than that. I could wish a free society no better hope for the future. And I could wish you no greater riches and rewards.

189

The Found Generation

DAVID RIESMAN

IT IS NOT EASY TO SAY WHEN ONE GENERATION ends and another begins (as Karl Mannheim noted in his essay on "The Problem of the Generations"), for people are not produced in batches, as are pancakes, but are born continuously. And it is only in certain countries and in certain epochs that historical events, as unconsciously transmitted through parents to their children, lead to a generational gap rather than a smooth and silent succession—a gap across which the young cannot easily talk to the old who grew up in a different world. Obviously, moreover, even the most drastic changes fail to break the continuity in every family, and there will always be members of any current generation who resemble their ancestors more than they resemble their peers.

Still, we have certain conventions, as illustrated in silver weddings, twenty-fifth reunions—and twenty-fifth anniversaries of magazines, colleges and corporations; these make sure that people with a normal life span will have some occasions for an intellectual sabbatical or day of reflection. What for others, however, is a sabbatical occasion is for me, as a social scientist, a regular preoccupation with discontinuities in attitudes and values, both between "my" generation and its predecessors and successors. I have become a reader of college class-reports, which permit the comparison at least of college "generations" with their rapid turnover, as well as make it possible to follow shifts in the attitudes and career patterns of the same generation at five-year or ten-year intervals.

○ Author of *The Lonely Crowd* and *Faces in the Crowd*, DAVID RIESMAN is a member of the sociology department and director of the Center for the Study of Leisure at the University of Chicago, and a member of the Editorial Board of THE AMERICAN SCHOLAR. His most recent book, *Constraint and Variety in American Education*, will be published this fall.
This article is developed from an address presented to the Harvard Class of 1931 Symposium in Cambridge, June 11, 1956. It is based on research under way at the Center for the Study of Leisure at the University of Chicago (supported by a grant from the Behavioral Sciences Division of the Ford Foundation), and especially on memoranda prepared by Robin Jackson, research associate of the Center.

To be sure, there are flaws in such a procedure, among them the fact that the regional and social-class base of a college does not remain constant: one might find great changes which said more about the "career" of the college—for instance, its loss of religious tone, or its wider geographic base—than about changes in the values of comparable individuals. We know, moreover, that not everyone responds to the appeals of the class secretary to get his report in; and if he does, he may respond in a very perfunctory way with little more data than "name, rank, and serial number"; the nonrespondents are very likely the less successful, but they may also include those who despise old-grad nostalgia and ceremonies.

If I put aside such misgivings, I can find a certain coherence of values uniting those who were graduated from the major Ivy League colleges between, say, 1920 and 1946. (I shall touch later upon certain differences.) Thus, in the Yale 1946 report, *Decade of Decision*, which has just appeared, one gets an impression of men who remember the Great Depression, who attended college in a wartime era of transition, and whose impetus and drive reflect these origins.[1] In contrast with this, however, it is at least arguable that the men just graduating, whose parents experienced the Depression but who were themselves growing up as the economy improved— men, moreover, many of whose parents, rigidly raised, shifted to a more permissive child-rearing—that these men would belong to a different psychological generation from any comparably large body of previous college graduates. While as a teacher I have had some impression that this may be the case, I have hesitated to trust my impression, since I know I am getting older while my students are not, and that I may not be free of old-grad nostalgia myself.

Thus, I was delighted when recently given the opportunity to study 183 *Time*-commissioned interviews of seniors in last year's graduating class—interviews asking the student respondent what he expected his life to be like in fifteen years, i.e., 1970.[2] Perhaps

[1] I owe to Professor Richard D. Schwartz of the Yale department of sociology, a member of this class and an author of its report, helpful comments concerning the nonrespondents. I am also indebted to my colleague Reuel Denney for discussion of Dartmouth class reports.

[2] *Time* wrote a letter to the deans of twenty colleges, including Harvard, Princeton, Notre Dame, Williams, Dartmouth, Georgia Tech, the Universities of Houston, Michigan and Wisconsin. They were asked to find a student, preferably a graduate student, who

since so much of that life seemed to be concerned with hunting and fishing, golf, boating and puttering, *Time* turned the interviews over to our Center for the Study of Leisure at the University of Chicago. Our first reaction to the material—I speak here for myself and for Robin Jackson, who independently studied the interviews—was that it was too unreliable to take seriously. Nevertheless, a picture of the Class of 1955 emerged which was congruent with other data—a picture which contrasts sharply, I believe, with what would have been obtained from seniors in the same colleges twenty-five years ago.

Twenty-five years ago, of course, the Great Depression had been under way for two years, forcing many who were graduated then to drop plans for further training, others to take refuge in graduate school against the uninviting job-market. But it was not only the Depression that made students of the Class of 1931 feel uncertain about the future (in contrast to the relative certainty felt by college graduates today); it was ambition also. Many of us wanted to make our mark, and were not sure how high we would get. Our class had no floor under it, and by and large did not want a ceiling—indeed, in our generation a number of wellborn men whose floor seemed all too solid chose, in many different ways, to test their ability to live without a floor: they beachcombed (although not so drastically as George Orwell in *Down and Out in Paris and London*); or they became anthropologists, labor organizers or cold-water-flat artists and poets; and a number became that bright combination of adventure and responsibility, the foreign correspondent. Such men often wanted to lose the self they had inherited and, romantically, to create a new one out of whole cloth.

---

would do ten interviews, and sent an illustrative interview with a Princeton senior. Regrettably, we do not know how the respondents (or, for that matter, the interviewers) were selected. In what they did, they followed a variety of forms or no form; thus, at Ohio State the interviewees tended to respond in terms of what the planet would be like in fifteen years (mostly science-fiction extrapolations) rather than of what they would be like. So, too, the interviews vary from long and searching ones at Stanford or Columbia to perfunctory paraphrase at some of the schools. There is a like difference between those colleges where the respondents appear to be talking "for the record," rather piously, and those where the discourse, or the report of it, seems more spontaneous. In each case, the interviewees declared themselves, after the interview was over, willing to let their names be used. I am greatly indebted to the promotion department of *Time* for making this material available.

Most aspirations pursued by our class, and by classes of the same era at Princeton, Yale, Dartmouth and other colleges concerning which I have scraps of evidence, were more conventional: to make much money, to rise high in the government, to become a doctor, lawyer, merchant or chief. Since the first jobs we got were often makeshifts or didn't appear to lead anywhere, we changed jobs frequently. In a rough estimate, I would say that at least 40 per cent of us in the Class of 1931 have actually changed occupations at least once, not counting war service. There are, naturally, a great many exceptions: men who went into medicine were captured in all but a few cases by the severe system of rehazing and resocializing the student in the medical apprenticeship (but we should recognize that a man who has shifted from internal medicine and private practice to epidemiology and the Public Health Service has actually made a drastic shift of self-definition); men who went into their fathers' businesses and stayed there; men who are teaching school or practicing law or architecture without infidelity to their first love.

One reason so many of us shifted jobs was that we didn't know ourselves very well, and we knew the world even less well. As Charles McArthur of the Harvard Psychological Clinic has observed, many of the upper-middle-class boys at Harvard in the late 1930's did not know what they wanted to become but only where they wanted to land—up. The route had to be surveyed as they proceeded. Upper-class boys, in contrast, knew what they were expected to become—lawyers, bankers, trustees—but may have tired later of that inherited role and switched into something closer to their repressed desires.[3] In line with these findings, a number of us became critical of our values as we went along. I recall two friends who left Wall Street, where they were doing nicely, one to run a mattress factory for the unemployed, and the other to develop a ranch in the West and get into local politics. Quite apart from depression and taxes—though as part of the same world that brought the latter as a homeopathic remedy for the former—some of our generation

[3] Charles McArthur and Lucia Beth Stevens, "The Validation of Expressed Interests as Compared with Inventoried Interests: A Fourteen-year Follow-up," *The Journal of Applied Psychology*, XXXIX (1955), 184-189.

concluded that money isn't everything. I remember in college snorting a bit sarcastically at those of my classmates who said that they were going to make a million before they were forty and then retire and "live." But the astonishing thing is how many did something not so dissimilar: they left a profitable job in New York—the mecca for so many then at Harvard and other New England colleges—to find "the good life" in some other work and some other part of the forest. We shall see in contrast to this that hardly any of the Class of 1955 would ever want to live in New York in order to make a million, or in any other big city. "No life in the ulcer belt for me," as one of them says, explaining why: although he plans to enter advertising, he will stay away from New York despite his realization that most big firms have their head offices there.

The same uncertainties that led to changes in occupation and aspiration also seem to me to have been a factor, along with the obvious economic hazard, in the relatively late marriages of so many of our generation. Many of us were searchers, not sure of the type of family life we wanted. Many did not want to be tied down. Nor would it have occurred to us to have our wives support us through graduate school, as is so common today among the young. And, indeed, if we think of the Class of 1931 at Radcliffe or Smith, Bryn Mawr or Skidmore,[4] we realize that these young women were often ambitious, too: they wanted careers, and not simply an intermittent series of low-level jobs that would help support four or five children and the suburban life the children "deserved." Those of us who did marry before or soon after graduation were often the well-to-do boys who seemed clearly headed down the ancestral occupational paths; and not a few changed wives as well as jobs—perhaps marrying the Mary Monahans that the George Apley family tradition had first forbidden.

World War II served some in these uncommitted groups as a punch bowl serves at a cocktail party—as a switching point allowing the formation of new affiliations. Coming after ten years of doubt or underemployment, it permitted us to discover the potentialities we were often unaware of, to find new confidence and see new parts of the country. It served, of course, for many non-

4 I am indebted to Mrs. Doris B. Shartle for the Skidmore twenty-fifth anniversary report.

college men in the same way, and California—the great American suburb, which many saw for the first time during the War—still gains light industry and population as a result. Others, obviously, were affected in other ways: some became better at what they already were—notably so, the doctors, who beefed if the War wasn't arranged for their postgraduate benefit; or, sadly, still others were cut off or, though still living, remained lost. Coming back from the War into an expanding economy (so different from some of the post-World War I economies) we were able to confirm experiences which had only been potential; age might, with equal prosperity, have brought much of this, but the War speeded up things and gave us, I think, more differentiated fates.

Going over our class reports, that recount this at five-year intervals, I have detected a tendency to emphasize increasingly the non-vocational aspects of our lives: the family and hobbies and, markedly, the fabulous array of philanthropic and civic activities into which we have been drawn. It is hard to think of a disease or a civic bane that one of us hasn't "taken" and become a vice-president of! Many of us have, we report, moved to the suburbs for the benefit of the children, or even become exurbanites for the sake of a better family life. Still, we bring these things up because we have done well enough vocationally to "afford" these concessions to the rest of life. Were we without drive, men without readiness to sacrifice the nonwork sides of life, we would not seek the high and demanding posts in business, government and the arts which so many of our class and neighboring classes do hold in far above average trajectories of energetic mobility (even taking account of our inheritances of opportunity). In reading the reports, moreover, I get the impression that our class, though it may no longer have as many Frank Merriwell ambitions, is by no means ready to retire, even if it could financially afford it. (Some of the Class of 1955 talk in the *Time* interviews of the retirement plans in the companies they are going to enter). Our class still has wants which are unfulfilled, not for things—which it owns in a measure to gladden *New Yorker* advertisers of gifts for the man who has everything—but rather for meaning and purpose. George Weller defined us, in his novel of Harvard, as coming to college "not to eat, not for love, but only gliding" (an observation Emerson once made of snakes in Concord); we have done a lot of gliding but, unlike snakes, we want to understand what we have endured.

If, then, in this perspective upon ourselves (a perspective which may be too "projective"), we look at the *Time* interviews, we are struck by the knowingness of the present college generation: they come to college to eat, to love (and often to get married), but certainly not to glide. Although they enter a far more prosperous and secure world in economic terms, they appear in more of a hurry—not from a driving ambition which, as we shall see, not many have, but because they have already made up their minds as to exactly who they are and exactly where they want to go on the superhighway of their chosen corporation or profession.

Each knows, understandably enough, the branch of military service he is entering. (At Michigan, for example, the students speak of the "deal" they have in the guided missiles branch of the Army or the personnel section of the Marines or a reserve branch.) No one voices objection to service on political grounds or as a pacifist; and only two complain of the interruption to their careers; a great many see the period of military service as a kind of postgraduate training, helpful to their careers. In any case, such service is a fact of life to be casually accepted and gotten over with. War as a possible interference is scarcely contemplated by these rather optimistic men, and not anticipated by any but a few—largely Catholics for whom world communism is more of an omnipresent menace than it is for most of the respondents. Nor is there anything opaque for the majority about their careers: they know the type of professional office or large corporation they want; and most who are going into business (which includes many who have majored in engineering or chemistry and are going to business school after that) prefer the salaried life of the large corporation. As one Princeton senior says:

Let's face it, I'll be on salary, not making capital gains, even at 36. . . . Why struggle on my own, when I can enjoy the big psychological income of being a member of a big outfit?

And he points out that he doesn't have the brass his father had to be a lone wolf—a comparison a number of them make, in almost every case with detached admiration for the old man's toughness, but with hardly any despondency for not living up to him as a model.

As another young man says, speaking of the large corporation in general:

They try to do what's best for you and best for them—if they see you'd do better in one department than in another, they transfer you. . . . There's no back-stabbing and politics like there is in a small firm. Your worth is recognized.

The notion that the company might also recognize negative worth, failure, just doesn't come up; it is the company's role to develop and train, never to threaten or fire. This, indeed, is part of the benevolent world these men foresee and will perhaps help create as a self-confirming prophecy. As one of them remarks:

I've always believed that if you are honest and sincere and can convince other people that you are, you'll get ahead, and I don't think I'll find out that I am wrong when I get out in the business world.

This is an understandable outlook, especially in view of the experience these men have had of being courted by large corporations. One Michigan senior tells the interviewer:

One nice thing about it is you don't really have to go out looking for a job—they come around looking for you!

In Stephen Potter's handbook of gamesmanship, he has a ploy to floor any generalizer, namely, "What of the South?"—a question you can ask in any country, for whether in Italy or France, China or the United States, the South is always another country, sometimes another colony. So it is that in these interviews, some of the Southerners, including Texans, seem more eager for the big money, and more willing even to desert the big corporation and the suburb in its pursuit. One senior at Georgia Tech tells the interviewer:

Fifteen years from now—well, I'm pretty ambitious and I think that I'll be with a progressive company at Burlington. Maybe I'll be a division director making—say—$25,000 a year.

This is a modest aim enough, in all reality, but large in comparison with the others who expect to be making $15,000 or $18,000 at most to support the four children and the two cars, the club dues and church contributions, the vacations in Europe and Bermuda, and the small boat on the lake. He continues:

And I'll probably be working in the Southeastern states since the trend is definitely toward the elimination of the Eastern mills. But South and Central America are going to move up as textile areas . . . if I do get overseas I think I would enjoy it.

Another Georgia Tech student wants both to write a big novel about the Civil War—he says he thinks there's still a big market for all the magnolia stuff—and to make a lot of money on his father's Mississippi Delta farm. A Texas boy at Princeton is going into the oil and gas business with his father. To this group I should add a Notre Dame boy from Pittsburgh who expects to make big money practicing law, in part because he can count on the influence of his father, a probate judge; and another Catholic, son of an oil and gas producer, a Harvard senior, who says, "Christ, I'd live in Nome, Alaska, if there was money there."

These are the exceptions, however, the immoderates, who want neither the fringe benefit nor the fringe suburb. Their idiosyncracy is evident in the fact that they say more about their careers and less about their prospective wives and families than most. Rather than looking to a large corporation to advance them if they deserve it, they want to find a situation to which *they* make a difference—a situation small enough for them to make an impact on it. They want a ladder, not an escalator.

Most of them, however, as I've indicated, think of themselves as too mature—and perhaps of the economy as too mature as well— to be that interested in self-advancement. The career they want is to find the good life, for which their corporation or profession serves as the good provider. These men already know they won't be president—they wouldn't want the job with its unpredictable demands, its presumptive big city locale, its disruption of family and recreational life. This is all the more striking since it is my impression that the interviewers tried to get "representative men," who were often big men on campus (a strategy which seems to have totally failed at Harvard, where the respondents—some of them prospective doctors—include neither the intellectual nor the social elite who would, I suspect, have avoided or kidded the whole "deal").[5]

This relative subordination of career ambition goes together with the fact that for most of the respondents the girl they are to marry is already picked out in fact or fancy, and the style of life the family will lead is foreshadowed with equal clarity. Some sound rather psychological about it (like a Harvard man, already engaged, who declares: "Well, it's supposed to be psychologically bad for the middle child if you have three, so I suppose we'll have four"). Others are as uncomplex as the Michigan engineering student who says that he and his girl have "talked some about a family, and we're agreed that we'd like a pretty fair-sized one—maybe four or five kids. We're both fairly easygoing and a lot of noise wouldn't bother us."

One Princeton senior is so very explicit that I first thought he must be pulling the interviewer's leg, but that was because I happened to read his interview first and didn't realize that it only highlighted a norm. He is going into law, and he declares:

I'll belong to all the associations you can think of—Elks, V.F.W.'s, Boy Scouts and Boys' Clubs, Y.M.C.A., American Legion, etc. It will keep me away from home a lot. But my wife [a purely hypothetical wife, remember] won't mind. She'll be vivacious and easy with people. And

5 At the University of Denver, the interviewer got a more Bohemian and unconventional range of respondents. They include an actor, aggressively individualistic, who says he's willing to live in "a room which is yours and nobody else's"; a man who wants to produce plays (but not live in New York); a self-proclaimed Taft Republican, who's going into nuclear engineering because that's the future; and a girl who wants to become a missionary. Oberlin also presents a contrast, with one man who wants to be a foreign correspondent; another who plans to become an agronomist for missions to underdeveloped lands; one wants to be a philosopher; and several are going into psychology (one of whom aims at becoming a dean of students). In general, the Oberlin seniors are quite outspokenly idealistic and prepared to accept modest incomes.

Nevertheless, taking the interviews as a whole, it seems probable that many of the more interesting students were either left out or sounded more "normal" in their interviews than they might under less stilted conditions. But three women got into this jumbled sample: the comments of one form a curious obbligato to the image the men have of the kind of wife they want. She is a Wisconsin senior who says that she's afraid of "that nice little pattern that everyone wants to fit into; the cheery little marriage and the husband working to get ahead in his job, the wife being a clubwoman and helping her husband to advance. . . . Beating the pattern is the hardest thing of all, and I'm not much for fighting. It would be a lot easier just to go off to Africa or somewhere and live there. . . . It isn't that I want to be an odd-ball. I like odd-balls but I wouldn't want to be one."

she will belong to everything in sight too—especially the League of Women Voters. I won't marry her until I'm twenty-eight, and so when I'm thirty-six we will have only two of the four children I hope for eventually. We'll be living in an upper-middle-class home costing about $20,000 by then, in a suburban fringe. . . . We'll have two Fords or Chevvies when I'm thirty-six, so we can both keep up the busy schedule we'll have. But in addition to this public social life, we'll have private friends who don't even live around Toledo—friends with whom we can be completely natural and relaxed. That's where Princeton friends will be very important.

To members of an older generation, this may sound like a young man on the make who wants contacts. But that is only a small part of it: the civic-minded life, the gregarious life, is at once felt as an obligation, seen as professionally useful, and anticipated as a pleasure and an end in itself. The wife is an indispensable auxiliary to this life which, even if it is a very outgoing, two-car life, is still centered in the backyard bosom of the family. This is an element in the resentment which appears again and again in the interviews toward the (almost purely hypothetical) career girl. One Harvard man says about the sort of girl he wants to marry:

She shouldn't be submissive, she can be independent on little things, but the big decisions will have to go my way . . . the marriage must be the most important thing that ever happened to her.

Another says what many feel:

My wife can work if she wants when we are first married, but she shouldn't work when we have children.

At the same time, they don't want a stay-at-home wife; they want a presentable date who, as we have seen, will be active in community affairs; she must be college-bred, she must understand her husband and know how to bring up children. There are contradictions lurking here; as one Harvard man says:

I want someone who would stay home and take care of the children, but on the other hand I want someone who can stimulate me intellectually, and I don't know if those things are compatible . . . if a woman goes to Radcliffe and takes up economics, she isn't learning how to bring up children.

In order to see what kind of mother their girl will make, a number of men say they will take a hard look at the girl's mother, to see what kind of a model mother she is—a rather awesome theme for those of us in the Class of 1931 who have eligible daughters and hopelessly impractical wives.

One Princeton senior is more graphic than most about all this. He says:

Life will not be a burden for me at thirty-five [How old and tired he makes that august age sound!] because I will be securely anchored in my family. My main emotional ties will center in my wife and family—remember, I hope for five children. Yes, I can describe my wife [again, quite a hypothetical person]. She will be the Grace Kelly, camel's-hair-coat type. Feet on the ground, and not an empty shell or a fake. Although an Ivy League type, she will also be centered in the home, a housewife. Perhaps at forty-five, with the children grown up, she will go in for hospital work and so on. . . . And improving herself culturally and thus bringing a deeper sense of culture into our home will be one of her main interests in fifteen years.

And then he concludes: ". . . in fifteen years I look forward to a constant level of happiness."

It is this vision of life on a plateau that perhaps most distinguishes the Class of 1955 from that of 1931. We who were graduated twenty-five years ago found our way by trial and error—and I emphasize the error as well as the trial—to many of the values and styles of life the Class of 1955 already begins with. We were, as I've suggested, more immature in many ways, and by the same token we expected to change and to be changed by our work and our experiences. The Class of 1955, judging by these interviews and forgetting their unreliability, would appear to expect to go on successfully adapting as they've already done, but not to change in any fundamental way, save that the family will take the place of the fraternity. The girls in question, however, may find it harder to stay on the plateau—or if they're *that* good, they may not want these boys;[6] after all, Grace Kelly has had a career and has married a prince.

6 In 1954, *Mademoiselle* magazine sent out questionnaires to women undergraduates at a number of colleges, and also to a few graduates. I had an opportunity to examine these, and the picture they present is not different from that presented by the men: they, too, want the well-rounded life, suburban and family-centered (but, like the men in the *Time*

But there is very little evidence in the interviews that the respondents have had to struggle for anything they want—or have wanted anything that would cost them a struggle. Some of the things they have surrendered are surely baubles. Thus, I have the impression that hardly anybody seeks swank or social distinction, and this seems not merely an artifact of the interview but an expression of the prevailing democratic ethos. A number who themselves went to prep school say they will send their children to public school. The suburb they aim for is regarded as the scenic backdrop for the happy family, not the locale of mobility as in *Point of No Return*. As I have implied, they have very few dreams, these young men; they dream of neither conventional prestige and social éclat nor, in general, of unconventional accomplishments. A fortune which can be passed on to children would be one sort of accomplishment, but very few of these seniors look for even modest capital accumulation; the capital is, as it were, society's, built into the schools and suburban developments and Blue Cross plans and corporate reserves. A floor is under these men, a low ceiling over them (analogous to the ranch-type houses in which they will live, in contrast to the high-ceilinged Victorian home), and these provide a narrow and "constant level of happiness." As one Harvard senior declares, explaining why he had dropped his plan to enter the strenuousness of a medical career: "I think contentment is the main thing."

Do they see the political future as a possible interference with having all utilities "laid on," as the British would say? They were all asked about the political future—a boring topic for most of them. I am sure few know or care who is our Ambassador to France, and, save for a few Catholic nationalists already referred to, they expect peace within the country and with the Soviet powers. Their political views are decent and, in a nonpolitical sense, liberal; the Southerners are generally opposed to segregation, and are optimistic that it will cease to be a problem as the older generation dies

---

interviews, near enough to a big city for cultural advantages—it isn't clear who will populate the city), and fear ambition in themselves and their prospective spouses. Russell Lynes, in "What Has Succeeded Success?" (*Mademoiselle*, September, 1954), discusses these interviews perceptively, pointing out how demanding and strenuous the goals of well-roundedness and contentment can become, and what effort it takes to be "cool."

out. They like Ike; and in a certain complacency, a fondness for golf (which many in our generation thought an old man's game) and the outdoors, they are like Ike. For most of them, save for a few who are going into law and want to dabble in politics, the national and international political scene holds neither fear nor fascination.[7]

This doesn't mean they aren't civic-minded; they are very much so. Whereas quite a few of our generation moved to the suburbs, at least allegedly on the children's account, while resenting the life of a commuter, the Class of 1955 has an emotional attachment to the suburb and sees it as far more than a spawning bed. As one Michigan student says:

I'm definitely interested in community activities. More than anything, I'd like to work with the youth of the community, especially in athletics. . . . When I say I'm interested in community activities, that doesn't mean politics. I'm not interested in politics whatsoever, and I never will be! I hate to say anything against politicians, but they just waste too much time. . . . I want to live my own life, not a public life.

The suburb appears to be an extension of private life: its P.T.A.'s, its Little League baseball, and in some cases its general cultural level—these the Class of 1955 wants to take on as its proper responsibilities. This goes for religion, too; as one civic-minded Cal Tech senior says:

I think that I will be going to church. . . . It is good for a whole family to do things together; more or less builds unity.

Indeed, it would perhaps be as correct to say that private life is the domestic intensification of the suburb, as we can see in the remarks of a Harvard senior:

I'd like six kids. I don't know why I say that—it just seems like a minimum production goal. I like kids and I've done a lot of work with them. . . . I like group life and family life and I want to have a home filled with inner richness. Nothing is as human as a child.

[7] One Harvard man of top academic standing, who is going into law, says: "I suppose as I become more allied with the business world and with business associates I'll tend to shed my Democratic preferences." This is not said cynically or bitterly, but as part of an image of a relaxed, suburban future.

A world populated by the men who appear in these interviews, and by the girls they almost without exception have in mind—the bachelor's freedom is a vanishing theme—would be a decent world; nobody in it would blow up or blow it up. If we ourselves manage to live the next fifteen years in such a world, we may count our bland blessings, though some of us of 1931 may not regret that we lived for our first fifteen years after graduation in a world of passion and turmoil which many of us experienced as such, whether it touched us closely or at one remove.

Afterthought: When I presented the foregoing observations to the Class of 1931 and to their wives and college-age children, I set going something of a cross-generational argument in which the "younger generation" felt a need to explain their apparent security-proneness and members of my own generation to berate them for it; to berate them even for not revolting against us—and then to berate ourselves for being so mild and nice as not to produce revolt. Indeed, as I have indicated, the Class of 1955 is at peace with its parents in so far as the *Time* interviews shed light on the matter. They may regard their fathers as tougher men than they (perhaps we are not as tough as we appear), but they do not regard them as Philistines to be overcome by fight or flight, but rather as helpful and even exemplary older siblings. On the other hand, judging from our discussions in Cambridge, parents worry that life has been made too easy for their children, that they do not crave eminence or seek excellence, that they are almost too well rounded. In this particular sequence of the generations, as so often in the history of this country, the self-made person finds that—at least in the absence of powerful Puritan traditions—he cannot reproduce his kind.

But it is, of course, much too early to predict to what degree the Class of 1955, with all its considerable realism, will succeed in finding the good life so many now look forward to. Perhaps unjustifiably extrapolating from the interviews, they appear to have encountered few moral and psychological hardships; school and college have been for many an extension of the nest rather than a traumatic initiation outside its protections. Military service still lies ahead of most of them, and after that the suburb with (as William

Whyte of *Fortune* has indicated in many articles[8]) its subtle pressures for smooth performance in personal relations. Moreover, the job may not turn out as promised, either in terms of what it will buy or of what strains in family life it may involve. Just as many of us in the Class of 1931 could not tell what we were like until war experience revealed us to ourselves, so obviously we cannot know in advance what demands will be made on our children or how in the light of their experience they will interpret them. Conceivably, they will have to face an existence which at forty-five, with the children grown and flown, the job ceilinged and routine, the hobbies long since explored, will bring a quiet crisis of meaning—somewhat like that of some members of an older generation who cannot, being work-driven, face retiring at sixty-five or seventy. But such a notion is probably ethnocentric to our generation, as it stares into the opaqueness of another age-culture; and I guess our curiosity will have to wait until the Class of 1955 tells us, in more artistic and dramatic ways than through brief interviews, what it feels like to belong, by birth rather than individual effort, to an economy (though it be a war economy) of abundance.

[8] I have learned much from his forthcoming book, *The Organization Man*, describing the junior executive life on and off the job; see, also, his *Fortune* article on "The Class of '49," June, 1949, the argument of which is largely congruent with my own. Whyte (in correspondence) observes one interesting difference between the Class of 1949 and that of 1955, namely that the former chose the big corporation reluctantly, out of a Depression-bred insecurity, and fearing for their individuality, whereas the Class of 1955 does not, for the most part, feel the need to make a choice.

Family Structure and Sex Role Learning by Children:
A Further Analysis of Helen Koch's Data

Orville G. Brim, Jr., *Russell Sage Foundation*

Traits Assignable to Male (Instrumental) or Female (Expressive) Roles

Trait name	Pertains primarily to instrumental (I) or expressive (E) role	Trait is congruent (+) or incongruent (−) characteristic of role
1. Tenacity	I	+
2. Aggressiveness	I	+
3. Curiosity	I	+
4. Ambition	I	+
5. Planfulness	I	+
6. Dawdling and procrastinating	I	−
7. Responsibleness	I	+
8. Originality	I	+
9. Competitiveness	I	+
10. Wavering in decision	I	−
11. Self-confidence	I	+
12. Anger	E	−
13. Quarrelsomeness	E	−
14. Revengefulness	E	−
15. Teasing	E	−
16. Extrapunitiveness	E	−
17. Insistence on rights	E	−
18. Exhibitionism	E	−
19. Uncooperativeness with group	E	−
20. Affectionateness	E	+
21. Obedience	E	+
22. Upset by defeat	E	−
23. Responds to sympathy and approval from adults	E	+
24. Jealousy	E	−
25. Speedy recovery from emotional disturbance	E	+
26. Cheerfulness	E	+
27. Kindness	E	+
28. Friendliness to adults	E	+
29. Friendliness to children	E	+
30. Negativism	E	−
31. Tattling	E	−

An Impolite Interview

In this dialogue, the subjects grind by like boxcars on a two-mile freight. Never do so many intellectual items seem to be handled so quickly—it would be fatal if the cargo were fragile, or the mind of the reader. Done with elegance, such an interview might be appropriate to a President. As done by Paul Krassner and myself it reads, if one may shift the metaphor, like a blow-by-blow of two strong club fighters going sixteen rounds in a gym. Here is the schedule of our rounds: Pacifism, the FBI, the sexual revolution, birth control, literary style, totalitarianism, the new revolutionary, the aesthetics of bombing, masturbation, heterosexual sex, adolescent sex, sexual selection, homosexual sex, the sex of the upper class, and Negro sex. What a fight! Considerately, the last round is devoted to mysticism.

Q. When you and I first talked about the possibility of doing an impolite interview, we kind of put it off because you said: "I find that when I discuss ideas, it spills the tension I need to write." Which seems like a very Freudian explanation. Does it still apply?

A. It does. Sure it does. I think putting out half-worked ideas in an interview is like premature ejaculation.

Q. Then why bother?

A. I got tired of saying no to you.

Q. That's all?

A. I'm beginning to get a little pessimistic about the number of ideas I never write up. Perhaps the public is better off with premature ejaculation than no intellectual sex at all. I'm just thinking of the public, not myself.

Q. All right, this is a question which I'm asking in the context of the cold war and the possibility of a hot war: Isn't there a basic dichotomy between creative artists who express themselves in their work—there's a definite excitement in their life—as opposed to the average person whose days are filled with boredom—in the factory, in the office—and who can almost find a sort of pleasure in identifying nationalistically with international tensions? And so the people who are happy in their own creative outlets are the ones who write poems about peace . . .

A. First time I've heard you talking like a totalitarian. Very few artists I know are happy. The kind of artist who writes a poem about peace is the kind of guy I flee.

There's something pompous about people who join peace movements, SANE, and so forth. They're the radical equivalent of working for the FBI. You see, nobody can criticize you. You're doing God's work, you're clean. How can anyone object to anybody who works for SANE, or is for banning the bomb?

Q. You're not questioning their motives, are you?

A. I *am* questioning their motives. I think there's something doubtful about these people. I don't trust them. I think they're totalitarian in spirit. Now of course I'm certainly not saying they're Communist, and they most obviously are not Fascists, but there are new kinds of totalitarians. A most numerous number since World War II.

I think, for example, most of the medical profession is totalitarian by now. At least those who push antibiotics are totalitarian. I think the FBI is totalitarian. I think pacifists are totalitarian. I think *Time* magazine is a Leviathan of the totalitarian. There's a totalitarian *Geist,* a spirit, which takes many forms, has many manifestations. People on your own side are just as likely to be totalitarian as people on the other side.

Q. Yes, but totalitarian to me implies force—

A. A dull, moral, abstract force. There is just such a force in the campaign for "Ban the bomb." It's too safe. That's the thing I don't like about it. You don't *lose* anything by belonging to a committee to ban the bomb. Who's going to hurt you? Is the FBI going to stick you in jail?

Q. There are certain employers who frown upon it—

A. Which employers? I think many good people are beginning to get a little complacent. The sort of good people who are militant and imaginative and active and brave, and want a world they're willing to fight for; if there were a revolution they would carry a gun; if there were an underground they would fight a guerrilla war. But there is no real action for them, and so they end up in what I think are essentially passive campaigns like "Ban the bomb."

I'm against sit-down strikes. I'm against people sitting down in Trafalgar Square, and cops having to carry them off. I think if you're not ready to fight the police, you mustn't sit down and let them carry you off. You must recognize that you're not ready to fight to the very end for your principles. I was carried off in a chair not so long ago and I'm not proud of it.

Q. Well, extending this to its logical conclusion, then, would you say that Mahatma Gandhi was a totalitarian?

A. I think so. He was a fine man, a great man, etc., etc., but many totalitarians are fine men. Sigmund Freud, for example.

For all we know—I don't know anything about Albert Schweitzer—Schweitzer might be totalitarian. How do you know? He seems too safe. The kind of people who seem to love Schweitzer are the sort who take a pill if their breasts hurt. Anybody who wants a quick solution for a permanent problem is a lowgrade totalitarian.

Q. At the risk of making you seem totalitarian, what would you substitute for sit-down strikes and other passive forms of protest?

A. Sketch the outline of a large argument. What I don't like about the "Ban the bomb" program, for example, is that it is precisely the sort of political program which can enlist hundreds of thousands, and then millions of people. Half or two-thirds or even three-quarters of the world could belong to such an organization, and yet you could still have an atomic war. I'm not saying the "Ban the bomb" program would *cause* an atomic war, but there's absolutely no proof it would prevent it. If you have people who are evil enough to lust for an atomic war, they are even more likely to force that war if there looks to be a real danger that they will never have a war.

Our best hope for no atomic war is that the complexities of political life at the summit remain complex. One has to assume such men as Kennedy and Khrushchev are *half-way* decent, are not *necessarily* going to blow up the world, that indeed if everything else is equal they would just as soon *not* blow up the world. So I say create complexities, let art deepen sophistication, let complexities be demonstrated to our leaders, let us try to make *them* more complex. That is a manly activity. It offers more hope for saving the world than a gaggle of pacifists and vegetarians. The "Ban the bomb" program is not manly. It is militant but it is not manly. So it is in danger of becoming totalitarian.

Q. Joe Heller told me that he admires you for—and may join you next time—just standing in City Hall Park and not taking shelter during the Civil Defense drill. Why is this any more manly than other activities?

A. I didn't stand there because I was a pacifist, but because I wanted to help demonstrate a complexity. It's a physical impossibility to save the people of New York in the event of atomic attack. Anyone who chooses to live in New York is doomed in such a case. That doesn't mean one should not live in New York, but I think it does mean one should know the possible price. Air raid drills delude people into believing that they're safe in New York. That's what I object to, rounding up the psyches of New Yorkers and giving them mass close order drill to the sound of an air raid siren. It's piggish. It makes cowardly pigs of people.

Q. You once referred in passing to the FBI as a religious movement; would you elaborate on that?

A. I think a lot of people need the FBI for their sanity. That is to say, in order to be profoundly religious, to become a saint, for example, one must dare insanity, but if one wishes instead to flee from insanity, then one method is to join an organized religion. The FBI is an organized religion.

The FBI blots out everything which could bring dread into the average mediocrity's life. Like a weak lover who rushes to immolate himself for love, since that is easier than to fight a long war for love, the mediocrity offers the FBI his complete conformity. He gives up his personal possibilities. He believes he is living for the sake of others. The trouble is that the others are just as mediocre as he is. Such people not only use themselves up, their own lives, but if there *is* a God, they use *Him* up.

Naturally these lovers of the FBI can't even think of the possibility that they've wasted themselves. Instead they believe rabidly in that force which agrees with them, that force which is rabidly for mediocrity. The only absolute organization in America, the FBI. At bottom, I mean profoundly at bottom, the FBI has nothing to do with Communism, it has nothing to do with catching criminals, it has nothing to do with the Mafia, the syndicate, it has nothing to do with trustbusting, it has nothing to do with interstate commerce, it has nothing to do with anything but serving as a church for the mediocre. A high church for the true mediocre.

Q. In terms of the mass media being a force to which one subjects oneself more voluntarily than to the FBI, isn't it possible that the mass media which you call totalitarian are a reflection rather than a cause of this condition in society?

A. A reflection of what people want? No, I don't think so. That's like saying that the United States Army was a reflection of what the soldiers wanted.

Q. But they were drafted—

A. And you're not drafted—your eye is not *drafted* when you turn on that TV set? To assume that people are getting what they want through the mass media also assumes that the men and women who direct the mass media know something about the people. But they don't know anything about the people. That's why I gave you the example of the Army. The Private exists in a world which is hermetically alienated from the larger aims of the Generals who are planning the higher strategy of the war. I mean part of the tragedy of modern war (or what used to be modern war) is that you could have a noble war which was utterly ignoble at its basic level because the people who directed the war couldn't reach the common man who was carrying the gun. As for example, Franklin Delano Roosevelt and the average infantryman.

And the reason they can't is because there *is* such a thing as classes, finally. And the upper classes don't understand the lower classes, they're incapable of it. Every little detail of their upbringing turns them away from the possibility of such understanding.

The mass media is made up of a group of people who are looking for money and for power. The reason is not because they have any moral sense, any inner sense of a goal, of an ideal that's worth fighting for, dying for, if one is brave enough. No, the reason they want power is because power is the only thing which will relieve the profound illness which has seized them. Which has seized all of us. The illness of the twentieth century. There isn't psychic room for all of us. Malthus's law has moved from the excessive procreation of bodies to the excessive mediocritization of psyches. The deaths don't occur on the battlefield any longer, or through malnutrition; they occur within the brain, within the psyche itself.

Q. There's a certain indirect irony there. I'm under the impression that you have almost a Catholic attitude toward birth control.

A. I do. In a funny way I do. But I've come a long way to get there. After all, if my generation of writers represents anything, if there's anything we've fought for, it's for a sexual revolution.

We've gotten things printed here that twenty years ago would've seemed impossible for a century or forever. I can name them. Not only *Lady Chatterley's Lover* and *Tropic of Cancer,* but little things like "The Time of Her Time"; extraordinary works like *Naked Lunch.*

We've won this war, or at least we're in the act of winning it. You might say that the church and the reactionaries are in long retreat on sex.

It's altogether their fault, as far as that goes. They flirted with sex. They used sex in order to make money or gain power. It was the Church, after all, who dominated Hollywood. They thought they could tolerate sex up to a point in Hollywood, because there was obviously a fast buck if you used sex in the movies, and they didn't want to alienate the producers of movies. So the Church compromised its principles.

What happened was that they set something going they couldn't stop. And then people came along who were sincere about sex, and idealistic, naive no doubt like a good many of us, innocent sexual totalitarians, we felt sex is good, sex has to be defended, sex has to be fought for, sex has to be liberated. We were looking for a good war. So we liberated sex.

The liberation goes on now. It's going to keep going on. But the liberation's gotten into the hands of a lot of people who aren't necessarily first-rate. A crew of sexual bullies may be taking over the world. Sexual epigones. Corporation executives who dabble.

The fact of the matter is that the prime responsibility of a woman probably is to be on earth long enough to find the best mate possible for herself, and conceive children who will improve the species.

If you get too far away from that, if people start using themselves as flesh laboratories, if they start looking for pills which prevent conception, then what they're doing, what really at bottom they're doing, is acting like the sort of people who take out a new automobile and put sand in the crank case in order to see if the sound that the motor gives off is a new sound.

Q. You're forcing me to the point of personalizing this. Do you use contraception? Do you put sand in your crank case?

A. I hate contraception.

Q. I'm not asking you what your attitude toward it is.

A. It's none of your business. Let me just say I try to practice what I preach. I *try* to.

Q. Then you believe in unplanned parenthood?

A. There's nothing I abhor more than planned parenthood. Planned parenthood is an abomination. I'd rather have those fucking Communists over here. Will you print fucking?

Q. You said it, didn't you? Just tell me if you want it spelled with two g's or a c-k.

A. Those fucking Communists.

Q. You want a 'g' on the end of it, or just an apostrophe?

A. No, I want a 'g' on the end of it.

Q. In "The Time of Her Time," the protagonist calls his penis The Avenger. Doesn't this imply a certain hostility toward women?

A. Of course it does. Is that news?

Q. All right, why is the narrator of your story—or why are you—hostile toward women?

A. If you're assuming there was an identification with the character, I can only say I *enjoyed* him. He was not altogether different from me. But he certainly wasn't me. I thought The Avenger was a good term to use. I think people walk around with terms like that in their unconscious mind. There're a great many men who think of their cock as The Avenger.

But O'Shaugnessy happened to be enormously civilized. So he was able to open his unconscious and find the word, find the concept, and use it, humorously, to himself.

Q. If there was any hostility beneath the humor, would you say it was justified?

A. I would guess that most men who understand women at all feel hostility toward them. At their worst, women are low sloppy beasts.

Q. Do you find that men and women have reacted differently to "The Time of Her Time"?

A. I've found that most women like "The Time of Her Time" for some reason. Men tend to get touchy about it. They feel—is Mailer saying this is the way he makes love? Is he this good or is he this bad? Is he a phony? Is he advertising himself? Does he make love better than me? To which I say they're asses.

Q. *Oh, so you're hostile toward men!*

A. I'm hostile to men, I'm hostile to women, I'm hostile to cats, to poor cockroaches, I'm afraid of horses. You know.

Q. *Several months ago I mentioned, in order to make a very definite point, a Cuban prostitute—this was the first prostitute I'd ever gone to, and I had been asking her all these questions about the Revolution—and she stopped later in the middle of fellatio to ask me if I was a Communist.*

A. You were in Cuba at the time?

Q. *Yes. And she was anti-Castro.*

A. Because he was cleaning them out of the whorehouses?

Q. *Well, there were no more tourists coming to Cuba, and it was ruining their business. Anyway, I described this incident in the* Realist, *and was accused of exhibitionism by some friends of mine. And I'm secure enough in my life that I had no need to boast about this; but it was a funny, significant thing which I wanted to share with the readers.*

A. Oh, I remember that, I remember reading your piece now. I was a little shocked by it.

Q. *You're kidding.*

A. No, I was shocked. I wasn't profoundly shocked. It threw me slightly. I had a feeling, "That's not good writing." And the next thought was, "Mailer, you're getting old." And the next thought was, "If you're not really getting old, but there is something indeed bad about this writing, what is it that's bad about it?"

Q. *And?*

A. A whore practicing fellatio looks up and says, "Are you a Communist?"—that's what the modern world is all about in a way. Saying it head-on like that probably gave the atmosphere honesty. But, in some funny way, it didn't belong. I don't want to start talking like a literary buff, because I dislike most literary language, Hemingway's perhaps most of all (it was so arch), but still in a way a good writer is like a pitcher, and a reader is happy when he feels like a good batter facing a good pitcher. When the ball comes in, he gets that lift.

But writing it the way you did, Krassner, you were in

effect hitting fungoes. You were making the reader field it, which is less agreeable than batting. If the reader had been able to guess that this was what was going on with the whore—I don't know how you could have done it; that would have been the art of it—to phrase the language in such a way that the reader thinks, "Oh, Jesus, she's sucking his cock, and she asks him if he's a Communist." If it had happened that way, it might have been overpowering. What a montage.

Maybe it was the use of "fellatio," maybe you just should have said, "I was having my cock sucked and she said, 'Are you a Communist?'" If you're getting into the brutality of it, get into the brutality of it. Throw a beanball. Don't use the Latinism. Maybe it was the Latinism that threw me. All I know is that there was something bad about it, the effect was *shock*.

Q. So you were shocked by a euphemism . . .

A. Shock is like banging your head or taking a dull fall; your wits are deadened.

Q. That's what I wanted to do in the writing, because that's what happened to me in the act.

A. Then you're not interested in art, you're interested in therapy. That's the trouble—there are too many people writing nowadays who give no art to the world, but draw in therapy to themselves.

Q. No, not in my case. It didn't change me one way or the other, writing it. I just wanted to put it into the consciousness of the reader. That's not therapy for me.

A. Well, then you should've said, "She was sucking my cock." I mean that's my professional opinion.

Q. It wasn't in Roget's Thesaurus. . . . Would you agree that you have an essentially biological approach to history?

A. I think I do, but I could never talk about it. I don't know enough history.

Q. To narrow it down to the present, if you were a future historian of sex, how would you look upon the Kennedy administration?

A. I'd say there's more acceptance of sexuality in America today than there was before he came in. Whether that's good or bad, I don't know. It may be a promiscuous acceptance of sexuality.

Q. Are you saying it's because of . . . ?

A. Because of Kennedy—*absolutely*. I mean, just think of going to a party given by Eisenhower as opposed to a party thrown by Kennedy. Do you have to wonder at which party you'd have a better time?

The average man daydreams about his leader. He thinks of being invited to his leader's home. If he thinks of being invited to Eisenhower's home, he thinks of how proper he's going to be. If he thinks of going to the Kennedys for a party, he thinks of having a dance with Jackie. Things liven up.

Why do you think people loved Hitler in Germany? Because they all secretly wished to get hysterical and *stomp* on things and scream and shout and rip things up and *kill*— tear people apart. Hitler pretended to offer them that. In some subtle way, he communicated it. That's why they wanted him. That's why he was good for Germany—they wanted such horror. Of course, by the end he didn't tear people apart, he gassed them.

If America gets as sick as Germany was before Hitler came in, we'll have our Hitler. One way or another, we'll have our Hitler.

But the point is, you see, the political fight right now is not to deal with the ends of the disease, but the means right here and now. To try to foil the sickness and root it out rather than calculate political programs for the future. One can have fascism come in any form at all, through the church, through sex, through social welfare, through state conservatism, through organized medicine, the FBI, the Pentagon. Fascism is not a way of life but a murderous mode of deadening reality by smothering it with lies.*

Every time one sees a bad television show, one is watching the nation get ready for the day when a Hitler will come. Not because the ideology of the show is Fascistic; on the contrary its manifest ideology is invariably liberal, but the show still prepares Fascism because it is meretricious art and so sickens people a little further. Whenever people get collectively sick, the remedy becomes progressively more violent and hideous. An insidious, insipid sickness demands a violent far-reaching purgative.

Q. When I interviewed Jean Shepherd he made the point —sarcastically—how come it's always the Bad Guys who become leaders?

A. Lenin wasn't a Bad Guy. Trotsky wasn't a Bad Guy. I don't think Napoleon was such a Bad Guy. I don't think

---

* See Appendix A.

Alexander the Great was such a Bad Guy. Bad Guys become leaders in a bad time.

One can conceive of a man who's half-good and half-bad who comes to power in a time of great crisis and great change, a time when awful things are going on. He's going to reflect some of the awfulness of his time. He may become awful himself, which is a tragedy.

A man like Danton begins as a great man, and deteriorates. Castro may end badly, but that will be a tragedy. No one's ever going to tell me he wasn't a great man when he started.

Q. Then you're saying it's bad times which result in bad leaders.

A. Well, if a time is bad enough, a good man can't possibly succeed. In a bad time, the desires of the multitude are bad, they're low, they're ugly, they're greedy, they're cowardly, they're piggish, shitty.

Q. Let's get into this, then. How do you sap the energy of bad leaders who are caught up in their own bad time?

A. In a bad time, a leader is responsible to his own services of propaganda. He doesn't control them. In a modern state, the forces of propaganda control leaders as well as citizens, because the forces of propaganda are more complex than the leader. In a bad time, the war to be fought is in the mass media.

If anyone is a leftist, or a radical, if a man becomes an anarchist, a hipster, some kind of proto-Communist, a rebel, a wild reactionary, I don't care what—if he's somebody who's got a sense that the world is wrong and he's more-or-less right, that there are certain lives he feels are true and good and worth something, worth more than the oppressive compromises he sees before him every day, then he feels that the world has got to be changed or it is going to sink into one disaster or another. He may even feel as I do that we are on the edge of being plague-ridden forever.

Well, if he feels all these things, the thing to do, if he wants political action, is not to look for organizations which he can join, nor to look for long walks he can go on with other picketeers, although that's obviously far better than joining passive organizations, but rather it is to devote his life to working subtly, silently, steelfully, against the state.

And there's one best way he can do that. He can *join* the mass media. He can bore from within. He shouldn't look to form a sect or a cell—he should do it alone. The moment he starts to form sects and cells, he's beginning to create dissension and counter-espionage agents.

The history of revolutionary movements is that they form cells, then they defeat themselves. The worst and most paranoid kind of secret police—those split personalities who are half secret policemen and half revolutionaries (I'm talking of psychological types rather than of literal police agents)— enter these organizations and begin to manufacture them over again from within.

It's better to work alone, trusting no one, just working, working, working not to sabotage so much as to shift and to turn and to confuse the mass media and hold the mirror to its guilt, keep the light in its eye, never, never, never oneself beginning to believe that the legitimate work one is doing in the mass media has some prior value to it; always knowing that the work no matter how well intended is likely to be subtly hideous work. The mass media does diabolically subtle things to the morale and life of the people who do their work; few of us are strong enough to live alone in enemy territory. But it's work which must be done.

So long as the mass media are controlled completely by one's enemies, the living tender sensuous and sensual life of all of us is in danger. And the way to fight back is not to look to start a group or a cell or to write a program, but instead it is to look for a job in the heart of the enemy.

Q. In The Naked and the Dead, *there was a theme about the futility of violence on a grand scale; and yet, in "The White Negro," there's almost a justification of violence, at least on a personal level. How do you reconcile this apparent inconsistency?*

A. The ideas I had about violence changed 180 degrees over those years. Beneath the ideology in *The Naked and The Dead* was an obsession with violence. The characters for whom I had the most secret admiration, like Croft, were violent people.

Ideologically, intellectually, I did disapprove of violence, though I didn't at the time of "The White Negro."

But what I still disapprove of is *inhuman* violence— violence which is on a large scale and abstract. I disapprove of bombing a city. I disapprove of the kind of man who will derive aesthetic satisfaction from the fact that an Ethiopian village looks like a red rose at the moment the bombs are exploding. I won't disapprove of the act of perception which witnesses that; I think that act of perception is—I'm going to use the word again—noble.

What I'm getting at is: a native village is bombed, and the bombs happen to be beautiful when they land; in fact it would be odd if all that sudden destruction did not liberate some beauty. The form a bomb takes in its explosion may be in part a picture of the potentialities it destroyed. So let us accept the idea that the bomb is beautiful.

If so, any liberal who decries the act of bombing is to-talitarian if he doesn't admit as well that the bombs were indeed beautiful.

Because the moment we tell something that's untrue, it does not matter how pure our motives may be—the moment we start mothering mankind and decide that one truth is good for them to hear and another is not so good, because while *we* can understand, those poor ignorant unfortunates cannot—then what are we doing, we're depriving the minds of others of knowledge which may be essential.

Think of a young pilot who comes along later, some young pilot who goes out on a mission and isn't prepared for the fact that a bombing might be beautiful; he could conceivably be an idealist, there were some in the war against Fascism. If the pilot is totally unprepared he might never get over the fact that he was particularly thrilled by the beauty of that bomb.

But if our culture had been large enough to say that Ciano's son-in-law not only found that bomb beautiful, but that indeed this act of perception was *not* what was wrong; the evil was to think that this beauty was worth the lot of living helpless people who were wiped out broadside. Obviously, whenever there's destruction, there's going to be beauty implicit in it.

Q. Aren't you implying that this beauty is an absolute? Which, beauty is never . . .

A. Well, you don't know. How do you know beauty is not an absolute? Listen, you guys on the *Realist*—I read you because I think you represent a point of view, and you carry that point of view very, very far, you're true to that point of view—but I think you're getting a touch sloppy because you get no opposition whatsoever from your own people; you'll get your head taken off at its base some day by a reactionary. He'll go right through you, because there are so many things you haven't thought out.

One of them is: How do you know beauty isn't absolute?

Q. Recently I referred in the Realist *to Sonny Nunez, a dead prizefighter, and Sherri Finkbone, a pregnant woman, and I suggested that if she really wanted to get a legal abortion, she should just sign up for a boxing match—to point out the irony that it's legal to kill a man in the ring, but it's illegal to remove a fetus from a woman. Would you like to attack that comparison?*

A. Ah, yes. Atrocious. I think that's taking a cheap advantage. In one case a man is killed who is able to defend himself. In the other, an embryo who may have voyaged through eternity to be born again is snuffed out because of his mother's cultural propensity for socially accepted drugs like the limb-killer thalidomide.

Q. Both incidents took place in Arizona, and I just felt it was a dramatic way—

A. If somebody takes a handful of shit and throws it against the wall at a party, that's dramatic, but it's distasteful. Your example is distasteful. You were appealing to the low emotions in your readers. You have a terrible responsibility in the *Realist,* because *your* readers have low emotions too. Just because nobody could find the sort of stuff that's printed in the *Realist* except in the *Realist,* there is a danger that the people who read the sheet are going to begin to think there's something superior about them, just from the sheer fact they're reading the *Realist.*

Q. Do you think you're something of a puritan when it comes to masturbation?

A. I think masturbation is bad.

Q. In relation to heterosexual fulfillment?

A. In relation to everything—orgasm, heterosexuality, to style, to stance, to be able to fight the good fight. I think masturbation cripples people. It doesn't cripple them altogether, but it turns them askew, it sets up a bad and often enduring tension. I mean has anyone ever studied the correlation between cigarette smoking and masturbation? Anybody who spends his adolescence masturbating, generally enters his young manhood with no sense of being a man. The answer—I don't know what the answer is—sex for adolescents may be the answer, it may not. I really don't know.

Q. But can't one kid start young with heterosexual relations and yet develop all the wrong kinds of attitudes—while another kid will go through his adolescence masturbating and yet see the humor of it, see the absurdity of it, know it's temporary?

A. I wouldn't dream of laying down a law with no variation. But let me say it another way. At the time I was growing up, there was much more sexual repression than there is today. One knew sex was good and everything was in the way of it. And so one did think of it as one of the wars to fight, if not *the* war to fight—the war for greater sexual liberty.

Masturbation was one expression of that deprivation. No adolescent would ever masturbate, presumably, if he could have sex with a girl. A lot of adolescents masturbate because they don't want to take part in homosexuality.

Q. There are certain societies where masturbation—

A. All I'm talking about is the one society I *know.* I'll be damned if I'm going to be led around with a ring in my nose by anthropologists. I mean the few I've known personally have always struck me as slightly absurd. They're like eccentrics in a comic English novel. I won't take any anthropologists as a god. I'm sure they don't know A-hole from appetite about "certain societies."

But we were talking about masturbation as the result of sexual repression. I don't see any reason to defend it. If you have more sexual liberty, why the hell still defend masturbation?

One has to keep coming back to one notion: How do you make life? How do you *not* make life? You have to assume, just as a working stance, that life is probably good—if it isn't good, then our existence is such an absurdity that *any* action immediately becomes absurd—but if you assume that life is good, then you have to assume that those things which keep life from happening—which tend to make life more complex without becoming more useful, more stimulating—are bad.

Anything that tends to make a man a machine without giving him the power to increase the real life in himself is bad.

Q. Is it possible that you have a totalitarian attitude against masturbation?

A. I wouldn't say all people who masturbate are evil, probably I would even say that some of the best people in the world masturbate. But I am saying it's a miserable activity.

Q. Well, we're getting right back now to this notion of absolutes. You know—to somebody, masturbation can be a thing of beauty—

A. To what end? To what end? Who is going to benefit from it?

Q. It's a better end than the beauty of a bombing.

A. Masturbation is bombing. It's bombing oneself.

Q. I see nothing wrong if the only person hurt from masturbation is the one who practices it. But it can also benefit —look, Stekel wrote a book on autoeroticism, and one of the points he made was that at least it saved some people who might otherwise go out and commit rape. He was talking about extremes, but—

A. It's better to commit rape than masturbate. Maybe, maybe. The whole thing becomes very difficult.

Q. But rape involves somebody else. The minute you—

A. Just talking about it on the basis of violence: one is violence toward oneself; one is violence toward others. And you don't recognize—let's follow your argument and be speculative for a moment—if everyone becomes violent toward themselves, then past a certain point the entire race commits suicide. But if everyone becomes violent toward everyone else, you would probably have one wounded hero-monster left.

Q. And he'd have to masturbate.

A. That's true . . . But—you use that to point out how tragic was my solution, which is that he wins and still has to masturbate. I reply that at least it was more valuable than masturbating in the first place. Besides he might have no desire to masturbate. He might lie down and send his thoughts back to the root of his being.

Q. I think there's a basic flaw in your argument. Why are you assuming that masturbation is violence unto oneself? Why is it not pleasure unto oneself? And I'm not defending masturbation—well, I'm defending masturbation, yes, as a substitute if and when—

A. All right, look. When you make love, whatever is good in you or bad in you, goes out into someone else. I mean this literally. I'm not interested in the biochemistry of it, the electromagnetism of it, nor in how the psychic waves are passed back and forth, and what psychic waves are. All I know is that when one makes love, one changes a woman slightly and a woman changes you slightly.

Q. Certain circumstances can change one for the worse.

A. But at least you have gone through a process which is part of life.

One can be better for the experience, or worse. But one has experience to absorb, to think about, one has literally to digest the new spirit which has entered the flesh. The body has been galvanized for an experience of flesh, a declaration of the flesh.

If one has the courage to think about every aspect of the act—I don't mean think mechanically about it, but if one is able to brood over the act, to dwell on it—then one is *changed* by the act. Even if one has been *jangled* by the act. Because in the act of restoring one's harmony, one has to encounter all the reasons one was jangled.

So finally one has had an experience which is nourishing. Nourishing because one's able to *feel* one's way into more difficult or more precious insights as a result of it. One's able to live a tougher, more heroic life if one can digest and absorb the experience.

But, if one masturbates, all that happens is, everything that's beautiful and good in one, goes up the hand, goes into the air, is *lost*. Now what the hell is there to *absorb?* One hasn't tested himself. You see, in a way, the heterosexual act lays questions to rest, and makes one able to build upon a few answers. Whereas if one masturbates, the ability to contemplate one's experience is disturbed. Instead, fantasies of power take over and disturb all sleep.

If one has, for example, the image of a beautiful sexy babe in masturbation, one still doesn't know whether one can make love to her in the flesh. All you know is that you can violate her in your *brain*. Well, a lot of good that is.

But if one has fought the good fight or the evil fight and ended with the beautiful sexy dame, then if the experience is good, your life is changed by it; if the experience is not good, one's life is also changed by it, in a less happy way. But at least one knows something of what happened. One has something real to build on.

The ultimate direction of masturbation always has to be insanity.

Q. But you're not man enough to take the other position, which is sex for the young. Except for petting, what else is there between those two alternatives?

A. I'd say, between masturbation and sex for the young, I prefer sex for the young. Of course. But I think there may be still a third alternative: At the time I grew up, sex had enormous fascination for everyone, but it had no dignity, it had no place. It was not a value. It had nothing to do with procreation, it had to do with the bathroom—it was burning, it was feverish, it was dirty, cute, giggly.

The thought of waiting for sex never occurred—when I was young my parents did not speak about sex, and no one else I knew ever discussed the possibility of holding onto one's sex as the single most important thing one has. To keep one's sex until one got what one deserved for it—that was never suggested to me when I was young.

The possibilities were to go out and have sex with a girl, have homosexual sex, or masturbate. Those were the choices. The fourth alternative—chastity, if you will—was ridiculous and absurd. It's probably more absurd today. If you talked to kids of chastity today, they would not stop laughing, I'm certain.

But the fact of the matter is, if you get marvelous sex when you're young, all right; but if you're not ready to make a baby with that marvelous sex, then you may also be putting something down the drain forever, which is the ability that you had to make a baby; the most marvelous thing that was in you may have been shot into a diaphragm, or wasted on a pill. One might be losing one's future.

The point is that, so long as one has a determinedly atheistic and rational approach to life, then the only thing that makes sense is the most comprehensive promiscuous sex you can find.

Q. Well, since I do have an essentially atheistic and more-or-less rational approach to life, I think I can speak with at least my individual authority. As a matter of fact, the more rational I become, the more selective—

A. You know, "selective" is a word that sounds like a refugee from a group therapy session.

Q. I've never been in any kind of therapy—

A. No, I know, but there's a *plague* coming out of all these centers—they go around *infecting* all of us. The words sit in one's vocabulary like bedbugs under glass.

Q. But I can't think of a better word. "Selective" is a word that means what I want to communicate to you.

A. *Selective.* It's arrogant—how do you know who's doing the selecting? I mean you're a modest man with a good sense of yourself, but suddenly it comes to sex and you're selective. Like you won't pick *this* girl; you'll pick *that* one . . .

Q. Exactly. It's arrogant, but—

A. Yeah, yeah, yeah—but the fact that one girl wants you and the other girl *doesn't*—I mean, that has nothing to do with it?

Q. Well, they have a right to be selective, too.

A. Then it's mutually selective. Which means you fall in together or go in together. Now, those are better words than "selective." They have more to do with the body and much less to do with the machine. Electronic machines *select*.

Q. Well, what I'm saying is you make a choice. A human choice. It has nothing to do with a machine . . . I'll tell you what's bugging me—it's your mystical approach. You'll use an expression like "You may be sending the best baby that's in you out into your hand"—but even when you're having intercourse, how many unused spermatozoa will there be in one ejaculation of semen?

A. Look, America is dominated by a bunch of half-maniacal scientists, men who don't know anything about the act of creation. If science comes along and says there are one million spermatozoa in a discharge, you reason on that basis. That may not be a real basis.

We just don't know what the *real* is. We just don't know. Of the million spermatozoa, there may be only two or three with any real chance of reaching the ovum; the others are there like a supporting army, or if we're talking of planned parenthood, as a body of the electorate. These sperm go out with no sense at all of being real spermatozoa. They may appear to be real spermatozoa under the microscope, but after all, a man from Mars who's looking at us through a telescope might think that Communist bureaucrats and FBI men look exactly the same.

Q. Well, they are.

A. Krassner's jab piles up more points. The point is that the scientists don't know what's going on. That meeting of the ovum and the sperm is too mysterious for the laboratory. Even the electron microscope can't measure the striations of passion in a spermatozoon. Or the force of its will.

But we can trust our emotion. Our emotions are a better guide to what goes on in these matters than scientists.

Q. But in the act of pleasure—go back to your instincts, as you say—in the act of sex, you're not thinking in terms of procreation, you're thinking in terms of pleasure.

A. You are when you're young. As you get older, you begin to grow more and more obsessed with procreation. You begin to feel used up. Another part of oneself is fast diminishing. There isn't that much of oneself left. I'm not talking now in any crude sense of how much semen is left in the barrel. I'm saying that one's very *being* is being used up.

Every man has a different point where he gets close to his being. Sooner or later everything that stands between him and his being—what the psychoanalysts call defenses—is used up, because men have to work through their lives; just being a man they have to stand up in all the situations where a woman can lie down. Just on the simplest level . . . where a woman can cry, a man has to stand. And for that reason, men are often used more completely than women. They have more rights and more powers, and also they are used more.

Sooner or later, every man comes close to his being and realizes that even though he's using the act, the act is using him too. He becomes, as you say, more selective. The reason he becomes more selective is that you can get killed, you literally *can* fuck your head off, you can lose your brains, you can wreck your body, you can use yourself up badly, eternally—I know a little bit of what I'm talking about.

I think one of the reasons that homosexuals go through such agony when they're around 40 or 50 is that their lives had nothing to do with procreation. They realize with great horror that all that wonderful sex they had in the past is gone—where is it now? They've used up their being.

Q. Is it possible that you're—pardon the expression— projecting your own attitude onto homosexuals?

A. You can see it in their literature, you can see it in the way they get drunk, you can see it in the sadness, the gentleness, that comes over a middle-aged homosexual. They could've been horribly malicious in the past—bitchy, cruel, nasty—but they become very, very compassionate. There comes a point where they lose their arrogance; they're sorry for themselves and compassionate for others. Not one-half their lives are behind them, but nine-tenths.

Q. Isn't it something of a paradox that your philosophy embraces both a belief in a personal God on one hand and a kind of existential nihilism on the other hand?

A. I've never said seriously that I'm an existential nihilist. I think I've said it facetiously. I am guilty of having said I'm a constitutional nihilist, which is another matter. I believe all legal structures are bad, but they've got to be dissolved with art. I certainly wouldn't want to do away with all the laws overnight.

The authorities, the oppressors, have had power for so many centuries, and particularly have had such vicious and complete power for the last fifty years, that if you did away with all the laws tomorrow, mankind would flounder in *Angst*. Nobody could think their way through to deal with a world in which there were no laws.

We've got hung up upon law the way a drug addict depends on his heroin.

Q. There's a certain irony in this thing about laws. Do you think that if you weren't a famous writer—if one weren't a famous writer and one had stabbed one's wife, would one have gotten a sentence which you escaped?

A. I have no desire to comment on that. It's a private part of my life. I don't want to talk about it. I'll just say this. As far as sentencing goes I think it would have made little difference, legally. If I had been an anonymous man, the result, for altogether different social reasons, would have been about the same.

Q. How can you say that incident I just referred to is "a private part" of your life when you seem to refer to it yourself in Deaths for The Ladies—*in a poem called "Rainy Afternoon with the Wife," you have the lines:*

> So long
> as
> you
> use
> a knife,
> there's
> some
> love
> left.

A. One can talk about anything in art. I wasn't trying to reveal my private life in that poem. I was trying to crystallize a paradox.

Q. Do you think that creativity—art in general—is an effective force in society, or is it in the end, you know, a sop to the individual artist's ego, and maybe entertainment for—

A. Art is a force. Maybe it's the last force to stand against urban renewal, mental hygiene, the wave of the waveless future.

Q. In his book, Nobody Knows My Name, *James Baldwin —referring to your essay, "The White Negro"—complained*

about "the myth of the sexuality of Negroes which Norman
Mailer, like so many others, refuses to give up." Are you still
denying it's a myth?

A. Negroes are closer to sex than we are. By that I don't
mean that every Negro's a great stud, that every Negro
woman is capable of giving great sex, that those black people just got rhythm.

I'm willing to bet that if you pushed Jimmy hard enough,
he'd finally admit that he thought that the Negroes had more
to do with sexuality than the white—but whether he really
believes that or not, Baldwin's buried point is that I shouldn't
talk this way because it's bad for the Negro people, it's going
to slow them up, going to hurt them; talk about Negro sexuality hurts their progress because it makes the white man
nervous and unhappy and miserable.

But the white man is nervous and unhappy and miserable
anyway. It's not I who think the Negro has such profound
sexuality, it's the average white man all through the country.
Why deny their insight? Why do you think they react so
violently in the South to having their little girls and boys go
to school with Negro kids if it isn't that they're afraid of
sexuality in the Negro?

That's the real problem. What's the use of avoiding it?

Q. Are you saying that, whether it's a myth or not, in
effect—

A. First of all, I don't believe it's a myth at all, for any
number of reasons. I think that *any* submerged class is going
to be more accustomed to sexuality than a leisure class. A
leisure class may be more *preoccupied* with sexuality; but a
submerged class is going to be more drenched in it.

You see, the upper classes are obsessed with sex, but they
contain very little of it themselves. They use up much too
much sex in their manipulations of power. In effect, they exchange sex for power. So they restrict themselves in their
sexuality—whereas the submerged classes have to take their
desires for power and plow them back into sex.

So, to begin with, there's just that much more sexual
vitality at the bottom than there is at the top. Second of all,
the Negroes come from Africa, which is more or less a
tropical land. Now I don't care to hear how many variations
there are in Africa, how complex is its geography, how there's
not only jungle but pasture land, mountains, snow, and so
forth—everybody knows that. Finally, Africa is, at bottom,
the Congo. Now tropical people are usually more sexual. It's

easier to cohabit, it's easier to stay alive. If there's more time, more leisure, more warmth, more—we'll use one of those machine words—more support-from-the-environment than there is in a Northern country, then sex will tend to be more luxuriant.

Northern countries try to build civilizations and tropical countries seek to proliferate *being*.

Besides the Negro has been all but forbidden any sort of intellectual occupation here for a couple of centuries. So he has had to learn other ways of comprehending modern life. There are two ways one can get along in the world. One can get along by studying books, or one can get along by knowing a great deal about one's fellow man, and one's fellow man's woman.

Sexuality is the armature of Negro life. Without sexuality they would've perished. The Jews stayed alive by having a culture to which they could refer, in which, more or less, they could believe. The Negroes stayed alive by having sexuality which could nourish them, keep them warm.

You know, I don't think "The White Negro" is not vulnerable; I think it can be attacked from every angle—there's hardly a paragraph that can't be attacked. I would love to see some first-rate assaults in detail upon it. Occasionally I'd like to be forced to say, "This argument is more incisive than mine."

I honestly don't believe I mind an attack on "The White Negro," but I think an attack at a low level is dim. Jimmy knows enough to know that "The White Negro" is not going to be dismissed. When he stands there and in effect says, "I as a Negro know damn well that Norman Mailer doesn't know what he's talking about when he talks about Negroes" —well, he's being totalitarian. Even Jimmy Baldwin can be totalitarian.

Q. Would you say that your conception of life is mystical as opposed to rationalistic?

A. I would assume mystics don't feel mystical. It's comfortable to them. When the savage was paddling his canoe, and a breeze entered his nose from the East, the savage said to himself, "The God of the East Wind is stirring"—he *felt* that god stirring. He could picture that god in his mind.

Now, for all we know, that god may well have existed. We don't know that he didn't exist any more than we know that beauty is not absolute.

The savage didn't say to himself, "I'm a mystic who is

now thinking that the God of the East Wind is stirring. Therefore I'm engaged in a mystical transaction." He was just having a simple, animal experience.

Any mystic who's worth a damn is animal. You can't trust a mystic who gets there on drugs. I had mystical experiences on drugs, and great was my horror when I discovered I couldn't have them without the drugs.

What it meant to me was that the experiences were there to be had, but that I wasn't sufficiently animal to have them, not without having a chemical produced by a machine to break down the machine in me.

But I don't like to call myself a mystic. On the other hand, I certainly wouldn't classify myself as a rationalist. I'm not altogether unhappy living in some no-man's-land between the two.

Q. Okay, final question: You beat me two out of three times in thumb-wrestling matches; would you care to expound briefly on Zen in the art of thumb-wrestling?

A. They are the same.

Acknowledgments

Beyer, Clara Mortenson. "What Is Equality?" *Nation* 116 (1923): 116. Reprinted from "The Nation" magazine. Copyright the Nation Company, L.P.

Ford, Henry. "Are Women's Clubs 'Used' by Bolshevists?" *Dearborn Independent* (March 15, 1924): 2, 12.

Bertram, Anthony. "The Unfemale Feminine." *The Saturday Review* (Dec. 20, 1924): 628–29.

Johnson, Guion Griffis. "Feminism and the Economic Independence of Woman." *Journal of Social Forces* 3 (1925): 612–16.

Rynd, Reginald F. "The Collapse of Feminism." *English Review* (April 1926): 537–42.

Armstrong, Anne W. "Seven Deadly Sins of Woman in Business." *Harpers* (August 1926): 295–303. Copyright 1926 by *Harper's Magazine*. All rights reserved. Reprinted from the August issue by special permission.

Johnson, Ethel M. "The Problem of Women in Industry." *American Federalists* 33 (1926): 974–77.

Macy, John. "Equality of Woman with Man: A Myth—A Challenge to Feminism." *Harpers* (Nov. 1926): 705–13. Copyright 1926 by *Harper's Magazine*. All rights reserved. Reprinted from the November issue by special permission.

Ferrero, Gina Lombroso. "Feminism Destructive of Woman's Happiness." *Current History* 25 (1927): 486–92.

Mure, Iona. "Second Thoughts on Feminism." *Outlook* (Feb. 26, 1927): 208–209.

"Feminism and Jane Smith." *Harpers* (June 1927): 1–10. Copyright 1927 by *Harper's Magazine*. All rights reserved. Reprinted from the June issue by special permission.

Ludovici, Anthony M. "The Enfranchisement of the Girl of Twenty-one." *English Review* (June 1927): 651–56.

Bondfield, Margaret G. "Public Opinion—Women in Industry." *American Federalists* 34 (1927): 836–38.

Collins, Joseph. "Woman's Morality in Transition." *Current History* 27 (1927): 33–40.

Ludovici, Anthony M. "Woman's Encroachment on Man's Domain." *Current History* 27 (1927): 21–25.

McMenamin, Hugh L. "Evils of Woman's Revolt Against the Old Standards." *Current History* 27 (1927): 30–32.

Cole, John Leonard. "Fanatical Females." *Homiletic Review* 94 (1927): 434–38.

Carey, Henry R. "This Two-Headed Monster—The Family." *Harpers* (Jan. 1928):
162–71. Copyright 1928 by *Harper's Magazine*. All rights reserved. Reprinted
from the January issue by special permission.

Black, Ruby A. "Common Problems of Professional Women." *Equal Rights* (Aug. 4, 1928):
206–208.

Hudnut, Ruth Allison. "Sex Inferiority." *Social Forces* 7 (1928): 112–15. Reprinted
from *Social Forces*. Copyright The University of North Carolina Press.

"Chivalry and Labor Laws." *Nation* 127 (1928): 648. Reprinted from "The Nation"
magazine. Copyright the Nation Company, L.P.

Lawrence, D.H. "Cocksure Women and Hensure Men." In *Sex Literature and
Censorship*, edited by Harry T. Moore (New York: Twayne Publishers, 1929):
47–50. Reprinted with the permission of Lawrence Pollinger Ltd.

Saunders, Eleanor B. "Emotional Handicaps of the Professional Woman." *Mental
Hygiene* 13 (1929): 45–61.

Peet, Creighton. "What More Do Women Want?" *Outlook and Independent*
(Aug. 5, 1931): 433–34.

Wells, Marjorie. "Are Ten Too Many?" *North American Review* (March 1929): 262–68.

Nock, Albert Jay. "A Word to Women." *Atlantic Monthly* (Nov. 1931): 545–54.
Reprinted with the permission of the Atlantic Monthly Company.

Acworth, Bernard and Muriel Kirkpatrick. "Is Feminism Decadent?" *The Saturday
Review* (Nov. 28, 1931): 683.

D.P.H. "A Woman's Invasion of a Famous Public School and How Men Endured It."
Cornhill 73, n.s. (Oct. 1932): 400–13.

de Torhout, Nirgidma. "The Disadvantages of Women's Rights." *Spectator*
(Aug. 2, 1935): 183–84.

Groves, Ernest R. "The Cultural Background of the American Woman." In *The
American Woman: The Feminine Side of a Masculine Civilization* (New York:
Emerson Books, Inc., 1942): 5–38, 425–26.

Halford, S.H. "Deterrents to Parenthood." *The Eugenics Review* 34 (1943): 141–42.

Halford, S.H. "An Objective View?" *The Eugenics Review* 37 (1945): 138–39.

Halford, S.H. "Trend of National Intelligence." *The Eugenics Review* 38 (1946): 104–105.

Levinson, Frances. Transcript of "American Woman's Dilemma." *Life Magazine*
(June 16, 1947): 101–102, 105, 109–10, 114. Reprinted with the permission
of Time Inc.

Josselyn, Irene M. and Ruth Schley Goldman. "Should Mothers Work?" *Social Service
Review* 23 (1949): 74–87. Reprinted with the permission of the University of
Chicago Press. Copyright 1949.

Ellis, Evelyn "Social Psychological Correlates of Upward Social Mobility Among
Unmarried Career Women." *American Sociological Review* 17 (1952): 558–63.
Reprinted with the permission of the American Sociological Association.

Robertson, Priscilla. "My Great-Grandmothers Were Happy." *American Scholar* 23
(1954): 185–96. Reprinted with the permission of *American Scholar*.

Freedman, Mervin B. "The Passage Through College." *Journal of Social Issues* 12
(1956): 13–28. Reprinted with the permission of The Society for the

Psychological Study of Social Issues.

Stevenson, Adlai E. "Women, Husbands and History." In *What I Think* (New York: Harper and Brothers, 1956): 182–89. Reprinted with the permission of HarperCollins Publishers.

Riesman, David. "The Found Generation." *American Scholar* 25 (1956): 421–36. Reprinted with the permission of *American Scholar*.

Brim, Orville G., Jr. "Table of Traits Assigned to Male and Female." *Sociometry* 21 (1958): 7. Reprinted with the permission of the American Sociological Association.

Mailer, Norman. "A Rousing Club Fight." In *The Presidential Papers* (New York: G.P. Putnam's Sons, 1963): 125–48. Reprinted with the permission of the Scott Meredith Literary Agency.